THE STRUGGLE FOR GREECE

1941–1949

T0385118

C.M. WOODHOUSE

The Struggle for Greece
1941–1949

with a new Introduction by
RICHARD CLOGG

Hurst & Company, London

First published in the United Kingdom in 1976 by Hart-Davis, MacGibbon Ltd

Republished in 2002 in the original impression by

C. Hurst & Co. (Publishers) Ltd.,
41 Great Russell Street, London, WC1B 3PL

© Executors of C.M. Woodhouse, 1976

Introduction © Richard Clogg, 2002

This paperback edition, 2018

All rights reserved.
Printed in the United Kingdom

The right of C. M. Woodhouse to be identified as the author of this publication
is asserted by him in accordance with the Copyright, Designs and Patents Act,
1988.

A Cataloguing-in-Publication data record for this book
is available from the British Library.

ISBN: 978-1-78738-026-4

www.hurstpublishers.com

Acknowledgements

Most of the sources on which I have relied are to be found in the Gennadeion Library in Athens, the British Library (Reference Division) in London, or the Burrows Library at King's College, University of London. The newspapers quoted are mostly to be found in the British Newspaper Library at Colindale. I am grateful to their respective Librarians for their help in making them available to me.

Other documentary sources were in my own possession. I have deposited them in the Burrows Library at King's College.

I am indebted to Mr Constantine Lambrias for providing me with a copy of the document cited as 'Vlandas's MS'; and to Mr Richard Clogg and Mrs Domna Dontas for verifying certain facts for me in documents held in the Public Record Office in London and the Greek State Archives in Athens respectively.

C.M.W.

Contents

Illustrations

Introduction

by Richard Clogg

IN THE SUMMER of 1944, as the liberation of Greece appeared imminent, Colonel C.M. Woodhouse, the commander of the Allied Military Mission to the Greek Resistance, was brought out of Greece for consultations with, among others, the Prime Minister, Winston Churchill, and the Foreign Secretary, Anthony Eden. In connection with his visit to London, Lord Selborne, who as Minister for Economic Warfare had overall responsibility for the Special Operations Executive which had sent Woodhouse into Greece, wrote on 8 August to Eden. In emphasising the brilliance of Woodhouse's academic record, Selborne credited him with scholarships to Winchester and New College, a double first in classics and the Ireland, Craven and Hertford scholarships at Oxford (in fact he had won the Gaisford Prize and not the Ireland Scholarship). His academic record at Oxford had been so brilliant, Selborne maintained, that it had not been equalled by F.E. Smith (later Earl of Birkenhead) or by Sir John (later Viscount) Simon. The few who had matched it, as Selborne somewhat infelicitously put it, had become 'either lunatics or schoolmasters': 'When, therefore, one finds such an academic record combined with the gifts of a man of affairs and of action, one has found something very unusual.'[1]

Christopher Montague Woodhouse, generally known as Monty, or in wartime Greece as Chris, was born on 11 May 1917, the second son of the 3rd Baron Terrington. On graduation from Oxford in the summer of 1939 he had seemed destined to pursue an academic career. Indeed, on graduating he left for Italy and Greece to prepare for the All Souls fellowship examination and arrived in Greece on 24 August, barely a week before the outbreak of war on 3 September. He was delighted to discover that 'living people still spoke Plato's language',[2] but in contrast to not a few of those nurtured from an early age on the classics (he had been introduced to Euripides at the age of eleven) he was not affronted by the fact that the modern inhabitants of Athens bore no very clear resemblance to the worthies of the age of Pericles. On the contrary he was intrigued and fascinated by the modern country. It was while walking through the Plaka, the jumble of streets at the foot of the Acropolis, that he heard on the radio of the outbreak of war, through an open window, 'the thin, plaintive voice of Chamberlain lamenting the collapse of his illusions and mine'.

He returned home to enlist in the Royal Artillery, a choice determined by his excellence in mathematics. In the course of his training he encountered 'a dynamic, tubby little major called Keble, whose eyes almost popped out of his head with lust for killing'. This was the legendary C.M. 'Bolo' Keble who was later to serve as chief of staff to Lord Glenconner, the head of SOE's Middle Eastern headquarters in Cairo. Greece entered the war on 28 October 1940 after the dictator General Ioannis Metaxas had rejected a humiliating Italian ultimatum. Churchill, anxious to shore up resistance to the Nazis in south-eastern Europe and conscious of the need to honour commitments made to small countries prepared to stand up to the Axis, offered limited military support. Woodhouse was an obvious choice to join, as an intelligence officer, the British Military Mission to the Greek Army, headed by Major-General T.G. Heywood. But Britain was able to offer little in the way of concrete assistance to the Greeks, who had already repulsed the attempted Italian invasion by the time the Military Mission arrived in Greece. Woodhouse occasionally interpreted at staff conferences, 'which were all quite fruitless'. The remainder of his time was spent 'in still more futile occupations: charting Italian wireless-traffic, translating communiqués, sticking pins in maps'.

Metaxas declined the British offer of ground troops for fear of provoking Hitler into coming to the aid of his ally Mussolini, whose forces were hard-pressed by the Greeks on the Albanian front. Following the dictator's death at the end of January, his successor did agree to accept a British, mainly Commonwealth, Expeditionary Force. The German invasion on 6 April was over almost before it began. During a campaign which lasted barely three weeks, Woodhouse acquired an inkling of the will to resist that was so firmly embedded in the Greeks. He found a much reduced platoon of Australians attempting to hold the pass of Thermopylae. An old peasant in the capote or shaggy cloak of the shepherd and bearing an ancient Mannlicher which had belonged to his grandfather, asked if he could join the Australians, an offer which was accepted. 'Leonidas', Woodhouse wrote, 'would have recognized a kindred spirit.'

He was evacuated, along with much of the Expeditionary Force, to Crete, which British military planners hoped to hold as a kind of unsinkable aircraft-carrier from which it might prove possible to bomb the Romanian oilfields upon which the Germans were heavily reliant. But such hopes were dispelled when the island fell, in a close-fought battle, to German airborne attack. On the day that the attack began, 20 May, Woodhouse was breakfasting with General Bernard Freyberg, the New Zealander commanding the island's defences. On looking up, Woodhouse was surprised to see the brilliant blue sky awash with gliders and parachutists. Freyberg carried on eating his breakfast, remarking only 'Well, they're on time.' For Freyberg was privy to *Ultra* intercept intelligence, of which, inexplicably, he failed to make full use. Woodhouse was witness to the chaos and demoralisation of the evacuation of the island at the end of May. On arriving in Cairo, he once again encountered Keble, 'now more bloodthirsty than ever'.

In the late summer of 1941 Woodhouse was appointed to the staff of the training school established near Haifa by the Special Operations Executive (SOE), the clandestine organisation that had been charged, in Churchill's now almost hackneyed phrase, with 'setting Europe ablaze', through the encouragement and supply of resistance in occupied Europe. Woodhouse, along with Paddy Leigh Fermor and Nick Hammond, the latter one of a number of classicists and archaeologists to be inducted into SOE, was posted to the section responsible for training Greeks who were to be infiltrated back into their homeland. Disappointed by the poor quality of those sent for training, Woodhouse formed the opinion that 'resistance in the Balkans would be misdirected and negligible unless Allied officers from outside were there to give it shape'.

During the winter of 1941–2, Woodhouse spent what was clearly a somewhat dispiriting six months on behalf of SOE on the island of Crete, which served as a kind of apprenticeship for the two years that he was to spend on the mainland. Here, while assisting in the evacuation of Commonwealth troops left behind in June 1941, in gathering intelligence and in assessing the prospects for resistance, he learned 'to live clandestinely, to feed on snails, mountain grass and ground acorns …' On being evacuated from Crete he once again returned to SOE's Mount Carmel school as an instructor.

In September 1942 he responded enthusiastically to a suggestion by David Stirling that he join the Special Air Service but, on visiting SOE's Middle East Headquarters in Cairo to negotiate his release from the organisation, he was asked whether he would be prepared to be parachuted into Greece the following week, which entailed a crash course in parachuting, and accepted. This mission arose from an urgent request from the military authorities in the Middle East to SOE to cut the railway line between Thessaloniki and Athens. This was considered an important source of supplies for Rommel's Afrika Korps, which earlier in the summer had come close to capturing Egypt and which continued to threaten this key British position in the Middle East.

The twelve-strong party, code-named 'Harling', was rapidly assembled under the command of Brigadier E. C. W. 'Eddie' Myers, the only parachute-trained professional sapper officer available in the Middle East. After its mission had been accomplished it was intended to withdraw all the members save Woodhouse and Lieutenant Themistocles (Themi) Marinos, the only Greek member of the team, who, together with two wireless operators, were to stay behind to liaise with the Greek resistance. One of the still unresolved puzzles associated with the mission was its lack of any comprehensive briefing either about the political

complexities of the resistance and, in particular, about the existence of the
National Liberation Front (EAM) which, following its foundation in September
1941, had rapidly emerged as the largest and best organised resistance group,
and of its military arm, the National People's Liberation Army (ELAS), or of
the critical role played in the establishment and control of both organisations
by the Communist Party of Greece (KKE). This was despite the fact that SOE's
Cairo headquarters was relatively well-informed about these organisations
and their political orientation. Only when he had been in Greece for several
weeks did Woodhouse learn about EAM, ELAS and the KKE. This makes
nonsense of the claim sometimes advanced that Woodhouse had been sent
into Greece with the express intention of destroying EAM as a political force.[3]

At first, much trust was placed in Napoleon Zervas and his (non-communist)
National Republican Greek League (EDES) forces for the conduct of the
proposed operation, but there was uncertainty as to Zervas's whereabouts.
After a confused landing, Myers deputed Woodhouse to make contact with
Zervas in his home territory of Epirus. This Woodhouse did after a prodigious
feat of high-speed walking, sometimes for fifteen hours at a stretch across the
rugged mountains of Rumeli. With the indispensable co-operation of units of
ELAS, under the command of its *kapetanios* or politico-military leader Ares
Veloukhiotis, and of EDES, under the command of Zervas, the Harling team
was able to bring down the Gorgopotamos railway viaduct on 25 November
1942, disrupting rail traffic between northern and southern Greece for six
weeks. This was one of the most spectacular acts of resistance in occupied
Europe even it was too late to affect the outcome of the second battle of El
Alamein in North Africa. Such was the success of the operation that the military
authorities developed a new enthusiasm for the potential of guerrilla warfare
in Greece and ordered the entire party, and not merely Woodhouse, Marinos
and the two wireless operators as had been originally planned, to remain in
Greece to work with the resistance. Not all of the Harling party were enamoured
with the news.

The Gorgopotamos operation was one of the very few occasions during
the occupation when ELAS and EDES co-operated fully in operational matters.
As a consequence Myers and Woodhouse soon found themselves entangled
in the complex politics of the resistance. In January 1943 the singularly un-
Greek-looking Woodhouse was infiltrated into Athens in an attempt to learn
more of these complexities. Here he came into contact with one of SOE's
key collaborators, Lieutenant-Commander Charalambos Koutsogiannopoulos
who, under the code name of 'Prometheus II', had operated one of the wireless
transmitters left behind in Greece by SOE in the chaos of the evacuation in
April 1941 and had played an essential role in the preliminaries to the despatch

of the Harling party. He also met Yannis Peltekis who was subsequently to become one of SOE's most valuable Greek collaborators. However, he was unable to come into contact with a group known as the Six Colonels, of whom SOE Cairo had high and unwarranted expectations that they might act as the nucleus of a resistance group obedient to the Greek government-in-exile, soon to move from London to Cairo, and to King George II of the Hellenes, who was likewise in exile. Much more important, Woodhouse was able to meet with five members of the Central Committee of EAM—four of them, significantly, communists. He found that the communists were much more security-conscious than members of the non-communist resistance.

Woodhouse returned from Athens to the mountains to find that the manically efficient Colonel Keble was building up the British presence in Greece at a rapid pace. He and Myers were the only two members of the mission privy to the fact that the series of sabotage operations, code-named 'Animals', unleashed in late June and early July 1943 was part of a deception plan designed, successfully, to persuade Hitler that the British were planning to invade Greece rather than Sicily. One of these operations was the destruction of the Asopos viaduct, to the north of the Gorgopotamos viaduct, in some ways a more spectacular operation than even the Gorgopotamos operation had been. Woodhouse, who spoke excellent Greek, was very much involved with the negotiations in the summer of 1943 of the National Bands agreement which led to the creation of a Joint Guerrilla General Headquarters, whose purpose, never achieved, was to co-ordinate resistance activity in Greece with the strategic plans of the British military authorities in the Middle East.

Shortly after the establishment of the Joint Guerrilla General Headquarters, Myers was to accompany a delegation of resistance leaders, drawn from the major resistance groups, which was flown out from a secret airstrip in the Greek mountains for consultations in the Middle East. This visit of the guerrilla delegation to Cairo afforded a unique opportunity to try to bridge the gap that had opened up between the resistance forces on the ground in Greece and the Greek government-in-exile and King George II. But the visit was very badly handled by the British diplomatic and military authorities in Cairo, and the delegation returned to Greece in mid-September in high dudgeon, convinced that the British were determined to restore the unpopular King to his throne, by force if necessary. During their absence, in the wake of the Italian surrender on 9 September, Woodhouse had negotiated an armistice with a substantial section of the Italian forces stationed in Greece.

Myers was barred from returning to Greece at the behest of the Foreign Office, which believed him to be over-inclined to make concessions to EAM/ELAS, and held him responsible, erroneously, for the widespread demand from within occupied Greece for a referendum on the future of the monarchy before the King would be allowed to return to his throne. Woodhouse had warned him in vain not to leave the mountains of Greece, and his fears were confirmed by events. Woodhouse, a full colonel at the age of twenty-six, was appointed on 17 October 1943 to succeed Myers as commander of what, with the arrival of a small American presence, became the Allied Military Mission to the Greek Resistance. The second US officer to be seconded to the Mission as Woodhouse's deputy by the Office of Strategic Services (OSS), the American counterpart of SOE, was Major Jerry Wines, with whom Woodhouse, scarcely more than half Wines's age, got on particularly well.

Although, on the ground in Greece, Woodhouse had good relations with the Americans attached to his Mission, and particularly with Wines, OSS analysts in Cairo were critical of British policy and of what they deemed to be the subservience of Wines to Woodhouse. One of these analysts, Moses Hadas, in civilian life a classical scholar at Columbia University, thought Wines 'a political illiterate with no knowledge of Greek or Greeks, who seems to have followed Col. Woodhouse about, flattered by the consideration shown him and uncritically echoing and giving wider currency to all Woodhouse's attitudes.' Hadas was obsessed with the notion that British policy in wartime Greece was much influenced by the personal financial interests of those involved in its making. He reported back to Washington that 'the charge of having economic interests in Greece, which they might be suspected of trying to protect or which might at least affect their political convictions' had been laid against a number of British officials and, more particularly, Woodhouse. He described the commander of the Allied Military Mission as 'an extremely young, affable, athletic, handsome, polished Oxonian, whose genuine charm is irresistible' and whose Greek was 'fluent to the point of volubility'. His family was thought to possess large interests in Greece: 'One cannot take exception to Woodhouse's views because his Toryism is congenital and he is not sufficiently mature to have evolved a different attitude.' When I showed this letter, which I had come across in the very rich but disorganised archive of the OSS in Washington, to Woodhouse, he pointed out that this Toryism can scarcely have been congenital as his grandfather, the first Lord Terrington, had been a Liberal peer. In a subsequent memorandum Hadas dropped his previous qualification and flatly stated that Woodhouse had 'considerable financial interests' in Greece. Needless to say, Woodhouse had no financial interest in the political outcome in Greece. As Hadas would have it, Woodhouse's critics claimed that while he was 'perfectly sincere, cultivated and competent', he was not capable of 'appreciating Greek problems in their totality'.[4]

Woodhouse's political skills were to be tested to the full by the outbreak of outright civil war within the resistance, shortly after the return to the mountains of the disgruntled and disillusioned guerrilla delegation. EAM/ELAS, convinced that the liberation of Greece was imminent, sought to eliminate its main rival, the much smaller EDES, claiming that Zervas had made a compromising agreement with the Germans. The position of the Mission became very difficult; relations with ELAS were, Woodhouse subsequently wrote, as cold as the winter in the mountains. In February 1944 he was able to negotiate a truce between the warring groups in what was known as the Plaka agreement, but Churchill, who always had a particular interest in Greece, had by the summer of 1944 become almost obsessed with preventing a communist take-over in the country. He and Anthony Eden, his foreign secretary, advocated the breaking off of relations with EAM/ELAS and the withdrawal of members of the Allied Mission.

Woodhouse took the view that such a breach with EAM/ELAS would play into the hands of the communists who controlled both organisations. When, therefore, he was brought back to London in July 1944 for consultations he took the opportunity of a characteristically eccentric lunch with Churchill to argue that his officers should remain in post. Finding difficulty in getting Churchill to concentrate on Greek issues, Woodhouse decided to try a direct appeal to Churchill's emotions: 'I said that if we followed the course he intended, I doubted if many of my mission would escape from Greece alive. Churchill brooded on this for a moment, and then put his hand on my shoulder. "Yes, my boy", he said: "I quite understand."' That was the last that Woodhouse was to hear of the proposal to break with EAM and withdraw the members of his Mission.

By the time Woodhouse returned to Greece in September 1944, the liberation of the country was near. On 18 October George Papandreou's government of national unity returned to Greece amid scenes of frenzied enthusiasm, accompanied by a small British force commanded by General Ronald Scobie. Woodhouse was rapidly to be disillusioned by the condescending attitude adopted by the British military authorities towards the resistance forces and by their unwillingness to take advice from those such as himself who knew the situation in Greece from the inside. Scobie, under the terms of the Caserta agreement, had been given overall command of all resistance forces in Greece, yet when a victory parade through the city of Athens was organised, no room could be found for the guerrillas. Scobie's ADC offered Woodhouse a seat in one of the cars that accompanied the parade, but when Woodhouse replied that he would prefer to be placed with the guerrilla leaders, the uncomprehending ADC asked 'What has it got to do with them?'. He declined the offer, just as he turned down appointment as political adviser on Scobie's staff, being unwilling to accept a privileged position while his Greek and British subordinates 'were being disbanded and relegated to insignificant positions'. Instead he moved north to witness the last shots being fired at the retreating Germans as they fled across the border on 1 November 1944.

Nothing so much illustrates the mental gulf that existed between SOE operatives and the regular army officers in Scobie's entourage than the reaction to a party organised by SOE for some of those Greeks who, more often than not at the risk of their own lives, had been of such help to the Mission during the occupation. By an unfortunate chance it was held in a house uncomfortably close to Scobie's own residence. At midnight Scobie decreed that the party should break up. This was an unconscionably early hour for an event of this kind to terminate in Greece, and some stalwarts continued partying until 3 a.m. or even later. Such *lèse-majesté* resulted in the SOE officer who had organised the party being forthwith removed from Athens. Woodhouse records that the brigadier responsible for passing on Scobie's edict that the party should end was the same one who came up with the bright idea of organising a football match between ELAS and EDES teams as a means of defusing the mounting political tension in Athens.

Woodhouse was away from Athens when these tensions erupted in the *Dekemvriana*, the fighting in the capital between units of ELAS and the exiguous forces at the disposal of the Papandreou government, backed up by the British troops under Scobie's command. Woodhouse did, however, witness at first hand the attack by ELAS on Zervas's forces in Epirus which resulted in their evacuation to Corfu. At the end of December 1944 Woodhouse was ordered to return to Cairo. Some months later he was to return to Greece to join the staff of the British Embassy in Athens. By this time he had married Davina, the widow of the 5th Earl of Erne who had been killed during the war. In 1946 Woodhouse was to serve as one of the three secretaries-general of the Allied Mission for Observing the Greek Elections (AMFOGE). This had been established to monitor the elections that had been promised as part of the Varkiza agreement of February 1945, which had formally concluded the hostilities that broke out in Athens in December 1944. These elections took place in March 1946. In May he was demobilized and his formal connection with Greek affairs was at an end.[5]

Over the next fifty years, however, until his death in 2001, Woodhouse was to write, in the interstices of a busy public life, numerous books on the Byzantine and modern history of Greece. The first of these, published in 1948, was *The Apple of Discord: a survey of recent Greek politics in their international setting*. This profound but somewhat austere analysis made only marginal reference to his own comprehensive immersion in Greek affairs during such a critical period in the country's history. It should be supplemented with his delightful, and now difficult to find, collection of twelve short stories with resistance themes, *One Omen*, likewise published in 1948. None of the characters in this collection, Woodhouse wrote, was 'wholly fictitious, nor are the episodes which they describe wholly imaginary'.

In the 1970s and 1980s Woodhouse revisited the history of the 1940s in Greece in a series of articles (listed in the bibliography appended to this introduction) and in a major book, *The Struggle for Greece 1941–1949*, which is reprinted here. This appeared in 1976, just two years after the collapse of the Colonels' dictatorship which misruled Greece between 1967 and 1974, a dictatorship of which Woodhouse was an early, persistent and effective critic and about which he wrote an authoritative study.[6] It was entirely characteristic of the man that he should have agreed with alacrity to a request to travel to Athens to testify for the defence at the trial of a prominent communist who in 1971 had been arrested after returning clandestinely to Greece. This was Dimitrios (Mitsos) Partsalidis, who for a time had been been secretary-general of EAM, an organisation with which Woodhouse had frequently been seriously at odds. *The Struggle for Greece* appeared just as interest in the period of the resistance and civil war was at its height in Greece. Untrammelled debate on this period had been impossible during the period of the Colonels' dictatorship, and discussion of left-wing perspectives on the period had been restricted also in the pre-Colonels era. The book was immediately recognised as a major contribution to the historiography of the period.

In addition to *The Apple of Discord*, written during the period of the civil war that wracked Greece between 1946 and 1949 and reflecting some of the apprehensions of the early period of the Cold War, and to *The Struggle for Greece*, written during and immediately after the Colonels' dictatorship which had, albeit inadvertently, contributed to the beginnings of a reconciliation between right and left in Greece, Woodhouse also wrote a third major analysis of the period of the resistance, which remains unpublished.[7] This was the detailed history of the Allied Military Mission, which he wrote at the war's end, and which has recently been declassified along with the other papers relating to the activities of the Special Operations Executive in occupied Greece. This extremely valuable document would certainly merit publication and it is to be hoped that before long someone will undertake this task. Meanwhile it is worth quoting from the preface to this brilliant description of the work of the Mission.

In it Woodhouse explained his reasons for writing the work. Although primarily the story of the Allied Military Mission, it was also 'the story of hundreds of others who helped and sympathised in our work'. To some extent it was also 'the story of the individual guerrillas and the ordinary people who suffered under the German occupation'. 'All these people, including ourselves, have come by way of a common experience to see the affairs of Greece from a common point of view. We argue and disagree and quarrel: our differences persist unmodified: our common point of view can never be identified with the individual point of view of any one of us. But any group of individuals, however diverse, acquires a sort of collective mentality from long association in unusual experiences, especially in hardship and danger. Ares Veloukhiotis and [Napoleon] Zervas are easier men for us to talk to than the respectable Greeks of the Middle East: we talk the same language, even when we use it to disagree. What is unfortunate is that it is so hard for anyone outside the group to penetrate its mentality: to share or even understand it.'

Woodhouse saw his history of the Allied Military Mission as an attempt to break down the great barrier that had grown up between those who had experienced the hardships of the occupation and the outside world and in the hope of overcoming the defensive attitude of all the protagonists in the resistance. He was writing to defend the belief that 'we achieved something, against a solid body of opinion which ranges from patronising indifference to fury and contempt. ... If we were guerrillas, we are now regarded as brigands and cut-throats: if we were Greek officers, we are now regarded as fools who ought to have known better: if we were British or American officers, we are now regarded as irresponsible schoolboys playing Red Indians at other people's expense: if we were politicians, we are regarded as dishonest adventurers, whose best hope now is to be coldly ignored.'

While 'terrible things were done and terrible mistakes were made', nonetheless the protagonists, 'despite all our divergences of character, society and nationality', believed that there was 'something to be said on our side'. In particular Woodhouse sought to reflect the experiences of 'the men of the nineteen-forties', who had experienced in Greece 'things which no-one outside Greece could comprehend'. After the liberation these had been displaced by the generation of the nineteen-thirties, a category in which he included the communists.

He gave a graphic picture of Greece during the first half of the 1940s, a picture that is scarcely recognisable after the passage of some sixty years. 'Those wild mountains which cover most of Greece contain no cultivated social life, no picturesque natives, no disciplined society, no interesting ruins except the work of the Germans, nothing but desolation and poverty. They hardly live in the twentieth century: nothing in their material life has changed for two thousand years except the invention of glass, and that not universally. There are almost no motor-roads. The mule tracks reduce travel to about 25 miles in a hard summer's day: sometimes less than 5 in a hard winter's day. [...] To the Athenian it is a foreign country. [...] In the heart of Greece, life has hardly left the Dark Ages. [...] The same seed which flowered in the primaeval desolation of the mountain also flowered in the only part of Greece that has yet reached the twentieth century: in Athens and to a lesser extent in Salonika and Patras. Something quite foreign to the life of the drawing-rooms and the coffee-shops was going on in these towns. It was not the life of the wealthy and cultivated, so many of whom found it hardly more difficult to entertain the British in 1945 than the Germans in 1944, or the Italians in 1943, or the British in 1941. It was the life of the hunted agent and the condemned saboteur, who found a bond with the life of the guerrilla and the franc-tireur in their common exposure to loneliness and discomfort and danger. The underground cells and secret houses of Athens had both a mystical and physical link with the mountain hiding-places. They had a common objective, a common devotion: and the courier who went to and fro between them carried not only the letter but the spirit. But around them were the idleness and indifference of the drawing-room and the coffee-shop, and between them was the vast, dreary void of the German occupation, accepted and unchallenged by the complacent attentiste.'

Nothing, Woodhouse wrote, mattered so much in the story of the resistance as the mountains of Greece. 'The rolling downs of Olympus, the precipitous ravines of Agrapha, the orchards of Pelion, the staggering crags of Smolikas, the long, thin ridge of Taygetos, the pine forests of Giona, are almost individual characters in the story, their roles perpetually changed by snow and sun and rain. Without them no guerrilla movement could have been born. If they were not rendered impassable by snow in winter: if they were traversed by motor-roads instead of goat-tracks: if their villages could have been subjected to the permanent establishment of German and Italian garrisons: then the enemy could have extinguished our first spark at will. We cursed the snow and we cursed the goat-tracks. But we owed our lives to them. [...] Thanks to the nature of these mountains, we could travel at will, without precautions, many days at a time in a single direction, throughout great tracts of Greece which the Germans could only occasionally penetrate (and never hold) even with the most strongly organised expeditions. By crossing the main lines of communication at night, we rendered the whole mainland of Greece accessible.'

The landscape of Greece was matched by the people who inhabited its rugged and remote fastnesses. 'They were rough and simple. They were unspeakably poor. Their women were beasts of burden. Their children had never learnt to play. They were largely illiterate. They had little conception of the world beyond their village, still less of the world beyond Greece. They had a traditional craving for a remote Eldorado called America (difficult to dissociate from the British officers whom they first met, owing to the language problem). A few in almost every village had been to America, but a *nostalgie de la boue* had brought them back: and with them they had brought back some of America's wealth, but almost none of America's spirit. The few who had travelled were given credit, usually wrongly, for worldly knowledge: but they earned it, if at all, only by contrast with their compatriots, to whom the inhabitants of the next village but one were classed with the Russian, the Frenchman, the Hottentot, as "foreigners". (I have been asked by these villagers whether the Austrians were the same as the Australians: and why the invasion of Sicily required the use of ships.) They were natural suckers for the clever demagogue and his baited propaganda. They had the vices and virtues of all poverty: the generosity that can deny nothing to the destitute stranger: the avarice that will rob him of everything within its grasp when he turns out to be rich. (When the Italians lorded it over them, the Greeks hated and tricked and fought them: but within twenty-four hours of their surrender, the Greeks received them with pity and kindness. Only towards the Germans, who had denied the laws of God and man, could they deny the laws of their noblest Olympian, Zeus Xenios, the god of hospitality.) The daily current of their lives was the arduous monotony of just being able to keep alive. During the occupation, none could forget this struggle for a moment. Some succumbed, some turned to the A[llied] M[ilitary] M[ission], some to the Red Cross, some to the black market, some joined the security battalions of the Quisling government, some joined the guerrillas, some fled to the Middle East: all had to devote their principal energies to find a way to keep alive. Their standard of living, their culture, their social outlook, were those of the wilds of Scotland in the seventeenth century. No government had ever given them a thought (except that Metaxas passed a law forbidding them to keep goats, which to many of them was their only livelihood: and even for that they could not see the reason, logical though it was). On this people and on this country the guerrilla movement was imposed.'

The movement was imposed from without, 'by leaders from a more enlightened society'. This fact gave rise to a 'social and mental gulf far wider than exists between, say, the most experienced general and the most uneducated private in the British Army'. 'It was a difference of degree so vast that it almost amounted to a difference in kind. No British officer could persuade his men to believe the cant and lies which guerrilla leaders put into the heads of their followers nor could he hold their devotion, as was so often the case in ELAS, with the mesmeric fixity of mere terror. The Greek leader was more unscrupulous and crafty: the Greek peasant more uneducated and superstitious.' This gulf between the leadership of the guerrilla movement and the peasantry was almost enough to make Woodhouse 'despair of the possibility of democratic government within this generation'.

Resistance leaders did not always abuse their power: 'a part of the upper component of the guerrilla movement consisted of the enlightened conservative middle-class, the regular officers, the professional men, the civil service, the university students, the whole stratum of society from which progressive intelligence and controlled idealism could most easily be expected.' Such men constituted the backbone of 'the moderate organisations'. However, like so many Greeks, they possessed 'brains but little judgement' and thus 'allowed themselves to be regimented and represented by the glibbest speaker who presented himself: this was always a trained Communist.' As a consequence 'all that was best in Greece allowed all that was worst to be its mouthpiece.' By the time these progressive elements came to appreciate the reality underlying the façade of democracy within EAM/ELAS it was too late. 'Some had sworn their lives away to ELAS: some had endangered their families, who were equally at the mercy of the Germans and the Communists: some were simply too terrified by what they knew of communist ruthlessness to declare their feelings.' The hope that such elements might exercise a moderating influence within EAM/ELAS had proved to be a vain one. Woodhouse cited the case of one of these moderates, a schoolteacher from Metsovo: 'a gentle and intelligent socialist' whose devotion to England was such that he had abandoned Orthodoxy for Anglicanism [the mechanics of such a conversion in wartime Greece could scarcely have been easy]. In 1944 his house was burnt down by the Germans, on the grounds that he was the local president of EAM: in 1945 he was imprisoned by the Greek government, on the grounds that he was the local president of EAM.'

It was these moderates who were to ensure that the resistance movement 'did some social good instead of inflicting unmitigated harm'. As a consequence life in the mountains gradually moved into the twentieth century. 'For the first time, adequate communications were established, by telephone, wireless and courier. [...] For the first time an attempt was made in theory to emancipate the women: to give them the vote, to end their use as beasts of burden. But in practice it broke down, because when the guerrillas were fighting each other in the snow-covered mountains, where no mule could go, the only means of transport was still the backs of women. For the first time something in the nature of public services began to work in the mountains. Previously the individual got along as best he could on his own resources. Now flour-mills and sawmills, cobblers' shops and bakeries and tailors, transport and communications, began to work in an organised fashion for a common purpose. Law courts and schools also worked feverishly, though with objects far different from the ideals which they ought to fulfil: indeed, almost solely as a political weapon. Life of a sort (often a barbarous, rough and ready sort, but full of an immense vitality) had at last reached the mountains.'

Allied liaison officers had no easy task in dealing with 'raw, this incredibly raw' material, for nothing in their previous experience could have prepared them for it. In the circumstances the success which most of them made of their role seemed 'almost miraculous'. Indeed it seemed that they must have possessed some common quality in addition to 'the courage and loyalty which go without saying'. Yet, on reflection, Woodhouse could see nothing which they all shared 'except the affection and admiration' which he felt for all of them. 'No commanding officer could have had his task made easier. It was superfluous to command them in the sense of ordering them to attack: all that was needed was to say where and when.'

While a sense of humour was indispensable, other qualities were less important—'least of all the scholar's and the archaeologist's previous knowledge of a country and a language superficially the same as Greece to-day, fundamentally so different [this was of course the knowledge that Woodhouse brought with him to Greece]. [...] Such people had to start by unlearning everything they thought they knew about the country and the people and the language. Then, having caught up with their colleagues, they had to learn some entirely new facts of psychology. If they wanted to understand the inner workings of the Greek language, and thereby the inner workings of the Greek mind, they had to accustom themselves to the delicate nuances of words such as *philotimo* and *aphormi* and *parexigisis*.' This was often achieved most successfully by those with no previous knowledge of the language. 'They had to understand that the most delicate misunderstanding (*parexigisis*) could be an irremediable blow to self-respect (*philotimo*). This could give the victim a handle (*aphormi*) for bitter resentment: a handle which was at the same time rather satisfying, by reason of the moral obligation towards the injured party under which it placed the offender. The Greek language of emotion and psychology is full of words whose contents cannot be fully and accurately rendered into English. Only long experience brings an intuitive understanding of them.'

Some never acquired such an understanding. On briefing officers newly arrived in Greece, Woodhouse would tell them that when they had been in Greece for forty-eight hours they would think that they had all the answers: 'When they had been there a year they would begin to be able at least to state the problems.' This rule-of-thumb applied to everyone except journalists, who never managed to get beyond the first stage, for they had too little time to learn the hard way. 'The hard way is the only way, and it calls for a penetrating study of the people, the country, the customs and the language. An Englishman is qualified to answer Greek problems when he can not only translate Greek words, but explain their connotation. Their connotation is far more significant than their denotation.'

He ended what he termed his 'philological excursus' by describing two states of mind whose significance lay in the fact 'that one is common to practically all Greeks, and the other almost totally lacking'. 'The first is *sympatheia*, which superficially explains itself: the second is *mnisikakia*, which means the remembrance of past grudges. Sympathy in Greece is the most valued quality in human relations: it is the touchstone by which every stranger is tested before he is accepted. But the word does not mean quite the same as in English. In English, if I say I find so-and-so sympathetic, I am saying something about his feelings towards me. In Greek, as in other languages, I should be saying something about my feelings towards him. Given this attitude towards personal relations, it is not surprising that the Greeks are totally incapable of remembrance of past grudges. The leaders of EAM-ELAS, who violently attacked me for two years and fought against British troops in December 1944, see no incongruity in entertaining me at home now. They hold us as bitterly to blame for the events of that winter as we hold them. But they would happily meet and talk with us on equal terms: and they would not understand it if we would not with them. The approach to a Greek is through the heart, not through the head.' Such was the 'sermonising on the nature of the Greeks', as Woodhouse himself put it, with which he introduced his magisterial history of the Allied Military Mission in occupied Greece.

In the preface to this history he paid tribute to the courage and loyalty of the members of his mission and spoke of the affection and admiration which he felt for all of them. His own loyalty to them was manifested when, in the 1980s, controversy arose over the wartime activities in the Balkans of Kurt Waldheim, at that time President of Austria and formerly Secretary-General of the United Nations. This prompted Woodhouse in an article in *Encounter* to examine the question of Waldheim's connection with the case of Captain 'Bunny' Warren, who was executed in Thessaloniki in the early summer of 1944 by the Sicherheitsdienst (SD), the Nazi Party's security service.[8]

Captain D. A. La Touche 'Bunny' Warren was born in Brisbane and educated at Geelong Grammar School.[9] In England on the outbreak of the war in 1939, he enlisted in the Royal Northumberland Fusiliers. Volunteering for service in SOE, he joined the British Military Mission in August 1943, and in early 1944 was charged with the evacuation of a group of some twenty Russian and Polish soldiers who had escaped from labour camps near Athens. The group set out in a caique from the Gulf of Corinth for Italy in March but beyond Cephalonia the engine failed and the caique was blown back towards the island, where it was intercepted by a German coastal patrol. The group was sent for interrogation to Thessaloniki, the headquarters of the German Army Group E. Woodhouse learned of the disaster from one of the Russians who had managed to escape and meet up with resistance forces in the mountains.

Lieutenant Waldheim, serving at that time as an intelligence officer at Army

Group E Headquarters at Arsakli outside Thessaloniki, was involved in processing the interrogation reports relating to Warren, though seemingly not in the actual interrogation. Waldheim's reference in a surviving report to 'sabotage operations' conducted by Warren brought Warren within the scope of Hitler's notorious *Kommandobefehl* or Commando Order of 18 October 1942 which provided for the handing over of forces engaged in sabotage operations to the SD for *Sonderbehandlung* or 'special treatment'.

Although Woodhouse had no time for Waldheim and his equivocations, he was scathing about what he termed the extravaganza of the Channel Four television programme 'Waldheim: a commission of inquiry', an attempt, presided over by five judges of different nationality, to determine whether there was a case for Waldheim to answer in connection with allegation of complicity in war crimes. Woodhouse denounced what he termed the 'fallacy of regarding Waldheim as if he should have been in the dock at Nuremberg alongside the major criminals'. Likewise he was dismissive of the report undertaken by the Ministry of Defence into his possible involvement of the execution of British commandos captured in the course of raids on the Aegean islands.[10]

It is difficult to conceive of circumstances arising in the future in which a non-Greek would ever play such a critical role in Greek affairs as C.M. Woodhouse did between 1942 and 1944. Not only did he help to shape the history of Greece at one of the most critical junctures in its independent history, but he also made a major contribution to the historiography of the country. If there is now a greater understanding outside Greece of the historical forces that have helped to shape Greece in modern times, this in no small measure is due to his voluminous writings on its modern history. Greeks are given to dividing the world into philhellenes and mishellenes, into friends of Greece and enemies of Greece. One might further divide philhellenes into fair-weather friends of Greece and those who stand by the country in the bad as well as the good times. Monty Woodhouse was certainly no fair-weather friend of Greece. In both good times and bad he had the interests of the country and of its people very much at heart.

Ας είναι ελαφρό το χώμα που τον σκεπάζει.

St Antony's College, Oxford
December 2001

Notes

1. Selborne to Eden, 8 August 1944, Selborne Papers, Public Record Office.

2. Unless otherwise indicated quotations are taken from C.M. Woodhouse's autobiography *Something ventured* (London, 1982).

3. See, e.g, Constantine Tsoucalas, *The Greek Tragedy* (Harmondsworth 1969), 61.

4. National Archives and Records Service, Washington, Office of Strategic Services Records, RG 226 Entry 1, Box 15, 24.

5. Details of Woodhouse's distinguished post-war career, as of his time in occupied Greece, can be found in his entertaining and wryly self-depreciating autobiography *Something Ventured* (London 1982). See also the obituaries in *The Independent*, 26 February 2001 (by Lars Baerentzen); *the Guardian*, 20 February 2001 (by Richard Clogg); *The Times*, 15 February 2001; and *The Daily Telegraph*, 15 February 2001.

6. *The rise and fall of the Greek Colonels* (London 1985).

7. Three important contemporary documents by Woodhouse, 'Recent crisis in Free Greece' (dated 19 October 1943); 'Situation in Greece – Jan to May, '44'; 'Report on final phase of Allied Military Mission in Greece, Sept.' 44 – Jan '45' are reprinted in Lars Baerentzen, ed., *British reports on Greece 1943–44 by J.M. Stevens, C.M. Woodhouse and D.J. Wallace* (Copenhagen 1982).

8. 'The case of Captain Warren: Waldheim, TV, and a case to answer', *Encounter*, LXXI (3) September-October 1988, 27–31.

9. 'Bunny' Warren, together with others attached to the British (Allied) Military Mission to the Greek Resistance, including Brigadier Eddie Myers, its first commander, figures as a character in Louis de Bernière's novel *Captain Corelli's Mandolin*. Apparently unaware that Warren was Australian, de Bernière caricatures him as an upper-class English buffoon, dressed in the tasselled cap and *fustanella* or kilt of an evzone, speaking ancient Greek (which de Bernières renders as Chaucerian English) and lacing his English with Biggles-type expressions such as 'spiffing', 'simply ripping' and 'absolutely ghastly'. More seriously, he has Warren murdered by 'the Communists' and not, as happened in reality, by the *Sicherheitsdienst*.

10. Ministry of Defence, *Review of the results of investigations carried out by the Ministry of Defence in 1986 into the fate of British servicemen captured in Greece and the Greek Islands between October 1943 and October 1944 and the involvement, if any, of the then Lieutenant Waldheim*, London 1989.

Select Bibliograpy of C.M. Woodhouse's writings on Greece in the 1940s

The apple of discord: a study of recent Greek politics in their international setting (London n.d. [1948]); reprinted, with a new introduction, 1985).

Prolegomena to a study of resistance (in *The Nineteenth Century and After*, Vol. CXLIV (1948) 269–76; Vol. CXLV (1949) 86–93.

The Greek resistance, 1942–44 (in *European Resistance Movements, 1939–1945*, Oxford, 1960, 374–90) the proceedings of the International Conference on the History of the Resistance Movements, Liège-Brussels-Breendonk, September 1958). See also *Proceedings of a Conference on Britain and European Resistance, 1939–1945, organised by St Antony's College, Oxford*, 10–16 December 1962 (Oxford, 1963)

Early British contacts with the Greek resistance in 1942 (in *Balkan Studies*, Vol. LXII, 1971, 347–63).

Summer 1943: the crucial months (in Phyllis Auty and Richard Clogg, eds, *British policy towards wartime resistance in Yugoslavia and Greece*, London 1975, 117–46).

The struggle for Greece, 1941–1949 (London 1976)

Turning points in the Greek resistance (in *Byzantine and Modern Greek Studies*, Vol. VI, 1980, 169–78).

The National Liberation Front and the British connection (in John O. Iatrides, ed., *Greece in the 1940s: a nation in crisis*, Hanover, NH, 1981, 81–101).

Something ventured (London 1982)

The circumstances of the German withdrawal from Greece in 1944 (in *Balkan Studies*, Vol. XXIII, 1982, 225–36).

The Aliakmon Line: an Anglo-Greek misunderstanding in 1941 (in *Balkan Studies*, Vol. LXXVI, 1985, 159–93).

The case of Captain Warren: Waldheim, TV, and a case to answer (in *Encounter*, Vol. LXXI, No. 3, September-October 1988, 27–31).

The consequences in Greece of the Italian capitulation (in *I Ellada kai o polemos sta Valkania, 1940–41, Diethnes Synedrio* [Greece and the war in the Balkans, 1940–41, International Conference], Thessaloniki 1992, 213–18).

Abbreviations

AAA	*Agòn–Anórthosis–Anexartisía* = Struggle–Restoration–Independence
AMAG	American Mission for Aid to Greece
AMFOGE	Allied Mission for Observing Greek Elections
AMM	Allied Military Mission
ASO	*Antifasistikì Stratiotikì Orgánosis* = Antifascist Organisation of the Army
AVNOJ	*Antifašističko Veće Narodnog Oslobodjenja Jugoslavije* = Antifascist National Liberation Council of Yugoslavia
BLO	British Liaison Officer
BMM	British Military Mission
Cominform	Communist Information Bureau
Comintern	(Third) Communist International
CP	Communist Party
CPSU	Communist Party of the Soviet Union
EA	*Ethnikì Allilengýi* = National Mutual Aid
EAM	*Ethnikòn Apelevtherotikòn Métopon* = National Liberation Front
ECA	Economic Co-operation Administration
EDA	*Eniaía Dimokratikì Aristerà* = United Democratic Left
EDES	*Ethnikòs Dimokratikòs Ellinikòs Sýndesmos* = National Democratic (Republican) Greek League
EEAM	*Ethnikòn Ergatikòn Apelevtherotikòn Métopon* = National Workers' Liberation Front
EKKA	*Ethnikì Kaì Koinonikì Apelevthérosis* = National and Social Liberation
ELAN	*Ethnikòn Laikòn Apelevtherotikòn Navtikòn* = National Popular Liberation Navy
ELAS	*Ethnikòs Laikòs Apelevtherotikòs Stratòs* = National Popular Liberation Army
ELD	*Énosis Laikìs Dimokratías* = Union of Popular Democracy
EOK	*Ethnikì Orgánosis Kritòn* = National Organisation of Cretans

EP	*Ethnikì Politophylakì* = National Civil Guard
EPON	*Ethnikì Panelladikì Orgánosis Neolaías* = National All-Greek Organisation of Youth
ERGAS	*Ergatikòs Antifasistikòs Sýndesmos* = Workers' Antifascist League
ERP	European Recovery Programme
GSEE	*Genikì Synomospondía Ellínon Ergatòn* = General Confederation of Greek Workers
IDEA	*Ieròs Desmòs Ellínon Axiomatikòn* = Sacred Bond of Greek Officers
ILO	International Labour Organisation
IMRO	Internal Macedonian Revolutionary Organisation
JUSMAPG	Joint United States Military Advisory and Planning Group
KGAKAMT	*Klimákion Genikoù Arkhigeíou Kentrikìs kaì Anatolikìs Makedonías kaì Thrákis* = Echelon of General Headquarters for Central and Eastern Macedonia and Thrace
KGANE	*Klimákion Genikoù Arkhigeíou Notíou Elládos* = Echelon of General Headquarters for Southern Greece
KKE	*Kommounistikòn Kómma Elládos* = Communist Party of Greece
KOA	*Kommounistikì Orgánosis Attikìs* = Communist Organisation of Attica
KOAM	*Kommounistikì Orgánosis Aigaíou Makedonías* = Communist Organisation of Aegean Macedonia
LOK	*Lókhoi Oreinòn Katadroméon* = Companies of Mountain Rangers (Commandos)
MAD	*Monádes Aposmasmáton Dióxeos* = Units of Pursuit Detachments
MAY	*Monádes Asphaleías Ypaíthrou* = Units for the Defence of the Countryside
ML	Military Liaison
NOF	(See SNOF)
OENO	*Omospondía Ellinikòn Navtikòn Organóseon* = Federation of Greek Seamen's Organisations
OPLA	*Omádes Prostasías Laikoù Agónos* = Units for the Protection of the People's Struggle
OSS	Office of Strategic Services
PAO	*Panellinikì Apelevtherotikì Orgánosis* = Panhellenic Liberation Organisation (formerly YVE)
PEEA	*Politikì Epitropì Ethnikìs Apelevtheróseos* = Political Committee of National Liberation

Plenum	Full meeting of Central Committee (of CP)
Politburo	Political Bureau (of CP)
PWE	Political Warfare Executive
SIS	Secret Intelligence Service
SKE	*Sosialistikòn Kómma Elládos* = Socialist Party of Greece
SNOF	*Slavomakedonski Narodnoosloboditelniot Front* = Slavo-Macedonian National Liberation Front (later re-organised as NOF)
SOE	Special Operations Executive
UNRRA	United Nations Relief and Rehabilitation Administration
UNSCOB	United Nations Special Committee on the Balkans
YVE	*Yperaspistaì Voreíou Elládos* = Defenders of Northern Greece (later re-named PAO)

PART ONE

The First Round

South-eastern Europe

I

Prelude to Revolution
1918–1941

THE GREEKS commonly distinguish 'three rounds' in the Communists' struggle for power, though the Communists themselves nowadays abjure the phrase. It is better to distinguish three climaxes in a continuous process. The Greek Communist Party (KKE) has been trying to win power ever since it was founded in 1918 (originally as the Socialist Workers' Party of Greece) and it has certainly not ceased to do so today. What distinguished the 'three rounds', however, was that they were attempts to seize power by force of arms. The 'first round' is somewhat vaguely defined: its climax came in 1943–4, during the German occupation of Greece, when the mountain provinces were virtually in a state of civil war. The 'second round' was the attempt to seize control of Athens, as well as the rest of Greece, in December 1944, shortly after the end of the German occupation. The 'third round' was what is generally known as the Civil War, from 1946 to 1949.

What was the object of the KKE in these three confrontations with the rest of Greece? To seize power, of course: but to what end? Their antagonists have no doubt of the answer. It was, they said, to dismember and destroy the Greek state, and to subject its remnants to the tyranny of the Soviet Union. Leaving aside the repeated denials of the Communists themselves, it is impossible to accept so simple an account at its face value. Both during and after the German occupation, thousands of Greeks who certainly had no such object in view followed the leadership of the KKE. Some were hoodwinked and some were afraid, but by 1946 at least, few were unaware of the politics of their leaders. Other explanations must be sought.

One of the best exponents of the positive aspirations of Greek Communism was a guerrilla leader who called himself Aris Veloukhiotis. The name means 'the god of war from Veloukhi' – the highest peak in the central Pindus range, known to the ancient Greeks as Tymphristos. His real name was Athanasios Klaras. He was a trained agriculturist, born in Lamia, who had become a Communist in the 1920s. After several years in prison or in exile, he had been released in 1939 by the Metaxas

Government on signing a 'declaration' renouncing Communism, which
he did apparently on instructions from the leadership of the KKE. During
the German occupation he showed a genius for guerrilla warfare, though
he fought other Greeks more often than the Germans. He also proved an
eloquent propagandist, able to express himself persuasively in simple
terms to Greek audiences who were at once naïve and subtle in their
understanding. A characteristic speech of his was recorded from notes
taken at the time in his native town of Lamia, on 22 October 1944, a few
days after the Germans had left.[1]

He began, as always, with a historical exposition, describing how the
famous and happy land of Greece fell into slavery. He told his audience
how Fallmerayer, the nineteenth-century German historian, said that they
were not true Greeks but half Slavs: 'but we have proved our Hellenism'.
They had fought the Turkish occupation both passively and in arms. The
poet Rhigas Pheraios had inspired them, but 'the Reaction' killed him.
When they had liberated themselves through the *Philiki Etairía* (the
Friendly Society), 'the Reaction' stepped in again to impose on them the
tyranny of Count John Capodistria. He had begun the destruction of the
country, 'and another Johnny, Metaxas, put the lid on it'. A Bavarian
king and then the dynasty of Glücksburg came and went, but 'the
Reaction' thought only 'how to exploit, to torment, to suck the people
dry'. A Republic followed, but it brought no change, so they brought
back the King and imposed Metaxas on us. When the war came the
reactionaries intended to surrender after firing two or three shots: 'we
have documents to prove it'. Only the people fought in Albania. When a
new slavery was imposed on us, a new *Philiki Etairía* came into being –
EAM (the National Liberation Front). But 'the Reaction' conspired
against it, calling us looters, cattle-thieves and brigands. 'Yes, we
slaughtered, and we are ready to slaughter again!'

But something new had happened: 'for the first time the villages
learned what power was'. When the reactionaries saw the growing power
of EAM, they changed their tune and began to form their own guerrilla
bands. EAM claimed no monopoly of the struggle and called on them to
unite. But they were afraid of popular rule (*laokratía*). They had betrayed
the allies in 1941: 'they shitted on Thermopylae and our three hundred'.
When the British parachutists came back, it was not to the reactionaries
but to Aris in Giona. We went with them and blew up the Gorgopotamos
bridge. General Wilson praised us. Now the British are here before your
eyes. We shall go on with them, fighting the Germans, but the reactionaries will not. They say we are Communists. 'Is that accusation a
matter of shame?' The Communists are not now 'marching towards Com-

munism'. That will come one day, but it is 'not for now'. All that the KKE (Communist Party of Greece) wants is 'a democratic solution for the Greek problem'. We have nothing against the Church, only against Capitalism. It is Capitalism, not Communism, that breaks up the family and annihilates national frontiers in quest of profits. 'Where then is their patriotism?' They have tried to deceive the people, but the people saw us and understood us. Our sole object is to help the people to live better: the reactionaries are 'the organisers of civil war'.

We shall not give up our arms, Aris concluded, until we have popular rule (*laokratía*) as well as national liberation. That is what our national government has promised us. Soon we shall have elections, but first a plebiscite on the constitution. The plebiscite will be the first blow in condemnation of the King. Why are we so against him? First, he is not a Greek. Second, he came back to the throne by a faked plebiscite (in 1935). Thirdly, he broke his oath, trampled on the constitution and imposed the dictatorship of the fifth-columnist, Metaxas. Next, he allowed incompetent and treacherous generals and ministers to betray us. Finally, instead of staying to sacrifice himself (like another Codrus, the legendary king of Athens), he deserted us. 'No throne is needed, but *dimokratía* (a republic or a democracy) for the progress of Greece.' Our only ambition is to be the servants of the people. If the people is not allowed to vote freely, and its vote is not respected, 'then I promise you that we shall take to the mountains again'. His final cry was: 'Long live our sovereign people!' So ends the record of Aris's words, taken down on the spot by a journalist who identified himself only by his initials, O.P., and published in the EAM newspaper *Roumeli* on 23 October 1944.[2]

The attraction of Aris's style of argument was that, although new, it sounded patriotic and not revolutionary. It appealed to his audience's sense of history, to their loyalty to their allies, to their pride in being Greeks. It did not ignore delicate subjects on which Communists were open to suspicion, such as their attitudes to religion and the family, to the constitutional monarchy and the northern frontiers; but it set them in an original and striking context. Communism as Aris set it before them was a distant ideal rather than a revolutionary threat. It was a kind of Fabian socialism that he seemed to preach, to be built up from the grassroots in the mountain villages. A phrase which he often used was that the Greek people must be 'master in its own house'. Another was that Greece must never again be anybody's *chiflik* – the Turkish word for feudal property. In this way he linked external independence with internal autonomy. Against both he set up the hazy image of the Reaction (*antídrasis*), both at home and abroad.

He never needed to identify 'The Reaction' with precise names. 'They' were the enemy whom all recognised in their heart of hearts. The object to which he devoted his life was to overthrow 'them' and put 'the people' in their place; and all his audience could identify themselves with the people. In the misery of poverty, oppression and destruction, coupled with the hope of liberation and a new era, Aris's propaganda was mesmerically persuasive: all the more so for being delivered in a conversational, almost dreamy monotone, without flamboyance or gestures; by a short, powerful figure in plain khaki, draped with bandoliers; his sharp, waxen, black-bearded face under a black Cossack-style cap, gazing into the distance, from time to time smiling sardonically; always radiating self-confidence and power.

Aris was not a typical Greek Communist: but then who was? He was abler and more brutal than most, and unwaveringly consistent. For this he was denounced by the Central Committee of the KKE, and finally took his own life in despair in June 1945. The only other leading Communist who had something of his magnetism, and who inherited his mantle in 1946, was Markos Vaphiadis, military Commander-in-Chief of the 'third round'. Though more emotional and mercurial in temperament, he had much in common with Aris: the same consistency, the same selfless dedication to the cause, the same personal magnetism, the same ability to talk simply and effectively to the common people. Unlike Aris, his origins were not middle-class but extremely humble; and he was born, like many leading Greeks of all classes, in Asia Minor, before the enforced exchange of populations under the Treaty of Lausanne in 1923. In some ways these were the most passionately patriotic of all Greeks, but they also had the complexes of a displaced minority. Nothing would have seemed more paradoxical to Markos than the accusation of trying to destroy Greece.

The same was true of all the Greek Communists, even if in the eyes of their fellow-countrymen their actions belied their motives. They wanted, by their own account, to destroy a social system, not a country or even a state. They saw it as necessary to smash the mould, and even to be brutal and unscrupulous in doing so, but only in order to re-mould it nearer to their heart's desire. All would have repudiated the charge of being antinational or anti-patriotic. But, unfortunately, for the most part, they were weak and mediocre men, whose skill lay only in conspiracy and rigid discipline. With few exceptions, of whom Aris and Markos were the most remarkable, they lacked imagination, spontaneity and the common touch. A small minority showed imagination and originality, even eccentricity: intellectuals like D. Glynos and G. Kordatos, and the lone millionaire I. Petsopoulos, who was finally expelled from the party in 1946. But the rank and file were dominated by *apparatchiks*. Their devotion was to an abstraction called the 'party line', which was painfully difficult to identify and changed with alarming suddenness. So obtuse and stubborn was their dedication to it that, whenever it changed, those who adhered to the old line had to be denounced as traitors by those who had discovered the new. There was therefore an extraordinarily rapid turnover in the party leadership. The perpetual shifts in the party line were embarrassing to faithful Communists and ridiculous to their opponents. The line was of course ultimately, but very remotely, laid down by the Communist Party of the Soviet Union. Throughout the period with which this book is concerned, that meant in effect by the Secretary-General of the CPSU, Stalin, for whom the central object of policy was to consolidate the power of the Soviet Union and himself. Being ill-informed about the southern Balkan states, and only intermittently interested in them, he left the precise formulation of that broad policy to the Third Communist International (Comintern), which in turn delegated it to the Balkan Communist Federation in Sofia.* Since the Communist Parties of Greece, Yugoslavia and Bulgaria had all affiliated to the Comintern in the early 1920s, they were theoretically obliged to carry out its directives. But being composed of Greeks, Yugoslavs and Bulgars, they often found it difficult to reconcile Soviet doctrine with national prejudices.

From the 1890s the three nationalities had been locked in violent conflict over Macedonia. That historic land of inextricably mixed population is the key to much of the bitter history of Balkan politics, from which Communism was no more exempt than other parties. Macedonia had been nothing but a name since the Roman conquest. Its boundaries were vague, and it was disputed whether there was such a thing as a Macedonian people or a Macedonian language. At least seventeen mass-movements of population across Macedonia had been recorded by 1925, and sixty-four different ethnographic maps were in existence in 1951, all compiled to support different national claims.[3] The area had been arbitrarily divided between Greece, Yugoslavia (then only Serbia) and Bulgaria as a result of the Balkan Wars of 1912–13; and on the whole the Greeks had done best out of the partition. They had a clear policy – to hellenise Macedonia.

Ever since 1821, the Greeks had assumed that all Macedonia would eventually be Greek, although in a united Macedonia the Greeks would barely have predominated numerically.[4]

Macedonia was partitioned in 1913 simply along the lines where the

* The Balkan Communist Federation was active only till 1930, and the Comintern was dissolved by Stalin in 1943. Subsequently Balkan policy was co-ordinated by a section of the CPSU under the Bulgarian leader Dimitrov and the Ukrainian Manuilsky (Djilas, p. 26).

rival armies met; and so it has remained ever since. None of the three countries concerned could be satisfied. The Bulgarians looked regretfully back to the abortive Treaty of San Stefano of 1878, by which Russia had sought to give Bulgaria almost the whole of Macedonia and an outlet to the Aegean Sea. They took advantage of the First World War to make a temporary expansion into Greek Macedonia, but under the peace treaties they were compelled not only to give up most of the annexed territories but also to accept a large measure of repatriation of Bulgarian nationals from Greece. The Yugoslavs, like the Bulgarians, craved possession of Salonika. In their eyes, the Greeks were usurpers of 'Aegean Macedonia' and the Macedonians were just 'southern Serbs'. Between the wars both Yugoslavs and Bulgarians made some progress, especially when the Greeks were weakened and demoralised by a further catastrophic war against Turkey (1920–2). A free zone in Salonika was granted to Yugoslavia in 1923; and the Slavophone minority in Greek Macedonia were briefly recognised as Bulgarians in 1924–5. But the Greeks soon found that every concession to one of their Slav neighbours was sure to antagonise the other. The safest policy was quietly and unostentatiously to consolidate the *status quo*.

An instrument for that purpose was to be found in the Greek refugees who streamed into the country after the defeat of the Anatolian expedition in 1922. By the spring of 1923 there were three-quarters of a million Anatolian refugees in Greece, mainly concentrated in and around Athens and Salonika; by 1928 the official census recorded nearly a million and a quarter – about one-fifth of the whole population. A high proportion of them were settled in Macedonia as part of the Government's deliberate policy of hellenisation. When Greek Macedonia was first annexed in 1913, only forty-two per cent of its population was Greek, and only seventeen per cent of the neighbouring province of Western Thrace.[5] These figures had risen to almost eighty-five per cent in Macedonia by 1926, and over sixty-two per cent in Thrace by 1924. The subsequent trend has also been upwards. By the 1960s the Slavophone population was recorded at less than two and a half per cent, though it must be remembered that these are official figures and that cautious villagers have always been inclined to record themselves as belonging to the prevailing ethnic group of the day.[6] Moreover, as a result of the Balkan Wars Greece had gained the largest slice of traditional Macedonia: over fifty per cent by area, compared with thirty-eight per cent in Yugoslavia and ten per cent in Bulgaria.[7] It was clearly in Greece's interest between the wars to seek no change.

In all three countries most people naturally looked on Macedonia in purely nationalist terms. Either they denied that there was a Macedonian nationality or they regarded it as a subordinate part of their own. To pure Marxists, however, the problem appeared in a different light. Nationalism must give place to class-consciousness. All the peoples of the Balkans would then see that they had a common interest in overthrowing their reactionary oppressors, and national frontiers would become irrelevant. But if a reconstructed Macedonia were to have its own administrative boundaries, in what way would they differ from national frontiers? How would the whole jig-saw be reassembled, and who would gain or lose what parts of it? Such questions could not be avoided even by doctrinaire Marxists, especially as most of their followers were still nationalists at heart.

The attitude of the Macedonian people themselves is hard to assess. Rival nationalist forces claimed their loyalty: the Internal Macedonian Revolutionary Organisation (IMRO), and the Bulgarian-controlled Supreme Committee.* Their feeling of 'being Macedonian' was of recent growth and has been called 'fraudulent'; but it was certainly there.[8] Greek, Bulgarian and Yugoslav propagandists have each tended to argue that their own Macedonians were contented and patriotic. Probably this was nearest to the truth in Bulgaria and furthest from it in pre-war Yugoslavia. In Greece, where normally the Government recognised only the existence of 'Slavophone Greeks', they perhaps felt subject to discrimination rather than oppression. They were allowed education in their own language but not separate representation in parliament; and under the Metaxas dictatorship (1936–41) they were forced into assimilation. Of the ethnic minorities in Macedonia, their national consciousness was less strong than that of the Turks, but stronger than that of the much smaller groups of Albanians and Koutso-Vlakhs.

The issue of Macedonia therefore presented serious problems for the Balkan Communist Parties, particularly the KKE: it was indeed their Achilles' heel. In times of crisis Balkan Communists have an odd habit of reflecting the aims of their own national governments, while abhorring them ideologically. This weakness was fostered by Soviet policy, which inclined to offer Macedonia as a prize in its entirety to whichever of the Balkan Communist Parties was currently in favour. Usually this was the Bulgarian CP, especially between the wars; occasionally it was the Yugoslav CP, especially during the German occupation; but it was never the KKE. In loyalty to the party line, therefore, the Greek Communists were repeatedly obliged to acquiesce in a policy of surrendering a Greek province to foreign rule, whether as part of an autonomous Macedonia or as

---

* Followers of the Supreme Committee were known as *komitadjis*, a term later applied by the Greeks to all Macedonian nationalists.

a province of Bulgaria or Yugoslavia. Firmly though they might repudiate it, it was hard to shake off the label of national treason.

Throughout its history the KKE has been haunted by this issue. The Communists disguised or evaded it whenever they could. Their first Party Congress in 1918 advocated a Balkan Federation, with no explicit reference to Macedonia. In 1920, at the second World Congress of the Comintern to which they affiliated on that occasion, they accepted a policy denouncing nationalism. A year later, at the third Balkan Conference in Moscow, they were ominously directed to resist 'petty-bourgeois, chauvinist superstitions'. It was not until 1922 that they were pressed by the Bulgarian CP, currently Moscow's favourite, to support an independent Macedonia; and in the aftermath of the collapse in Anatolia, they actually did so. But these pressures also produced convulsions in the party, as well as discrediting them with the public. Some Greek Marxists, including Petsopoulos, the proprietor of their newspaper *Rizospastis* (the Radical), broke with the party over its subservience to the Comintern. At the first General Election in which it took part, in 1920, the KKE polled 100,000 of the votes (but won no seats); at the second in 1923, its poll dropped to 20,000 votes. The vote for the Communists in 1920 was highest in Macedonia, and it included discontented minorities of all kinds: Jews, Turks and gipsies as well as Slavophones.[9] By an interesting coincidence, in the same year, at the only genuinely free elections ever held in pre-war Yugoslavia, Macedonia was one of the two areas (with Montenegro) where the Yugoslav CP was most successful; and there too it was a protest vote, directed against Serbian domination.[10]

But no equivocation over Macedonia was allowed by the Comintern. In 1923 the KKE was forced to accept 'self-determination for minorities', and the Yugoslav Communists were forced to recognise Macedonia as a distinct nation with a right to secede, though they still contrived to do so somewhat ambiguously.[11] The Balkan Communist Federation required a still more explicit acceptance by the KKE in 1924 of 'a united and autonomous Macedonia'. At the fifth World Congress of the Comintern in Moscow (June 1924) Manuilsky sharply rebuked both the Greek and Yugoslav Communists for their recalcitrance. Both in fact regarded the policy dictated from Moscow as equivalent to an enlargement of Bulgaria at their expense. There had been a brief period of understanding between the Bulgarian Supreme Committee and IMRO during the same summer of 1924, in favour of a truly independent Macedonia within a Balkan Federation; but it soon broke down, and Bulgaria's real ambitions ceased to be in doubt. The KKE was nevertheless compelled to adopt the policy of independence for Macedonia and Thrace at its third (Extraordinary) Congress in November–December 1924. Representatives of the Comintern and the Balkan Communist Federation were present to ensure that there was no backsliding. On 14 December *Rizospastis* duly published a manifesto declaring that 'we are struggling for the union of the three parts of Macedonia and Thrace and for their exclusive, independent existence as a single state'.

That Congress marked a turning-point in the history of the KKE. The old-fashioned Socialists, who had founded the party, were finished; the process of 'bolshevisation' was begun; and the Moscow-trained professionals known as the 'Koutvies' started to arrive in Greece.* A clandestine, illegal apparatus was organised in anticipation of legal repression by the Greek Government. The first such repression began in 1925 under the dictatorship of General Pangalos and reached its climax, after a brief intermission, in 1929. During the same period violent feuds broke out within the KKE, reflecting the struggle in Moscow between the followers of Stalin and Trotsky. For a time the Macedonian issue was pushed into the background. In 1926–7 it was scarcely mentioned, except when a Communist intellectual, Kordatos, was so bold as to denounce the idea of Macedonian autonomy in *Rizospastis* on 25 February 1927. Circumstances had made such boldness easier for the time being, since IMRO was tending to become an instrument of Italian policy in the Balkans; and this was anathema to Greeks of all political views. In the changing circumstances, at the General Election of 1926 the KKE won forty-two thousand votes and ten seats in Parliament.

The first ten Communist deputies were a peculiarly unrepresentative group. Apart from two from Thessaly, all came from Macedonia, and two were Jews from Salonika. They thus came from the periphery of Greece, both geographically and sociologically. None came from what was called 'Old Greece', and most of them had not been born Greek subjects. They were men accustomed to think of themselves as members of an oppressed minority of one kind or another. Perhaps this accounts for their choice of an ideology which looked abroad for its inspiration. It is a well-established fact that in eastern Europe between the wars, the Communist vote was chiefly significant in areas where there was a substantial minority problem, particularly if the minorities were Slavs or had other special reasons for looking towards Russia for support.[12] But to see the matter in true perspective, it is also necessary to remember that the total membership of the KKE was only about two thousand: they were a minority of the minorities. At the same time (with the exception of Costa Theos, the trade-union organiser) the party deputies were all anti-Stalinists in the

* From the Russian initials KUTV (the Communist University of Eastern Peoples).

great conflict of the hour; and this was their downfall. In 1928 the Stalinists in the KKE attacked their own deputies for deviating from the party line over Macedonia. At the next General Election, in August 1928, the KKE polled only fourteen thousand votes and lost all its seats. A severe internal struggle ended three years later with the complete victory of the Stalinists.

What was going on inside the KKE was a closed book to the Greek public. Communists lived and functioned in a world apart from the familiar political parties. Paradoxically, one thing that set them apart was that they were nearer than any others in Greece to the Western conception of a political party. They had a programme, a structure and a discipline. Other parties were simply temporary coalitions around a few leading personalities, held together only so long as a particular issue was dominant. If such a party survived its leader at all, it was often because the leadership passed to a close relative: Elevtherios Venizelos was succeeded by his son Sophocles in the Liberal Party; Panaghis Tsaldaris by his nephew Constantine as leader of the Populists. Otherwise new personalities formed new permutations.

The KKE was and still is different. Not only its name but its character and structure have survived intact for more than half a century. Being the most Westernised in style of all the Greek political parties, it has tended to attract men and women from outside the central stream of Greek life. It was not so much that those attracted to Communism were non-Greek, though some of them were: the Slavophones of Macedonia, the Jews of Salonika, or the Chams (Albanian Moslems) of Epirus. Nor did they lack what is called a 'Greek conscience' (elliniki syneidisis), though it was probably a less dominant factor in their make-up than in that of other Greeks. They might be separated from the generality of Hellenism in various ways: geographical, linguistic, ethnic, but above all psychological. They were Greeks from areas which had come late or not at all into the nineteenth-century kingdom; Greeks who had felt the impact of foreign industrialised societies, like seamen or tobacco-workers; or of Western styles of life, like students or returned immigrants. In this respect the activists must be sharply distinguished from the rank and file as well as from the common voter. In Greece, as elsewhere in the Balkans, when the Communist vote was high it came mainly from peasants and agricultural workers, just as in other parties. But it has been calculated that among the activists, some two-fifths were industrial workers, one-quarter from the urban middle-class, and only one-third peasants.[13] Above all, the activists were Greeks whose reactions were cerebral rather than visceral. They thought rather than felt about society and politics.

Such tendencies were naturally more marked in the more recently acquired territories than in Old Greece. Macedonia was a special case, though by no means a homogeneous one, because there were divisions not only between Greeks and Slavophones and other minorities, but also between indigenous Greeks and Anatolian refugees. The latter had characteristics which were to become politically important. Compared with other Greeks they were on the whole more sophisticated, cosmopolitan, urbanised, literate and skilled. They gave to Greece not only the Communist Zakhariadis but the shipping magnate Onassis, and the poet Sepheris and other writers. Their arrival promoted industrial development, which in turn facilitated Communist infiltration among organised labour. Agriculture, banking and maritime trade also owed a stimulus to them, with consequences both beneficial and the reverse. In the 1920s their political sympathies were predominantly Liberal: they strongly supported Venizelos, and had little regard for the monarchy. Later they became disillusioned with Venizelos, especially after he signed the Ankara Convention with Turkey in 1930. Their voting habits then moved steadily leftwards. The correlation between Communist strength and the refugee vote can be seen in simple statistics: of the first ten KKE deputies, eight were from Macedonia; and of the five constituencies in which refugees formed the majority of the electorate, four were in Macedonia.[14] On a much reduced scale, similar trends could be detected among the new Greeks of some other recently acquired territories, such as Epirus and Crete. They felt and were different.

The dominant figure of the KKE in its formative period was Nikos Zakhariadis, a Moscow-trained 'koutvie'. He was installed as Secretary-General in December 1931 on the orders of the Comintern, and soon gained the reputation of being a tough and ruthless leader: he even came to be addressed as *Arkhigòs* — the Greek equivalent of *Duce* or *Führer*. In fact he was by no means a strong man. There seemed to be something of an aggressive complex of inferiority about him, perhaps because he too had been born in Asia Minor and come to Greece as a refugee. Though well educated, and once a teacher by profession, his intellectual level was low. Many incidents in later years showed his inability to make up his mind, or even to interpret the party line coherently and express it in plain Greek. In appearance he was unimpressive — he might have been any Balkan bureaucrat — though he tried to act and speak in an incisive and vigorous manner. If his face seemed mask-like, it was perhaps the best concealment of the limited mind behind it. A certain aura later surrounded him because of the years he spent in German concentration camps (1941–5), yet to hard-core Communists there was something

suspicious about merely having survived in the circumstances. He led the
party for the greater part of twenty years from failure to failure.

The second man in the KKE during most of the same period was George
Siantos, Zakhariadis's deputy and rival. Ruthless and ambitious though he
was, Siantos had a simple bonhomie and good humour. He was a tobacco-
worker, like many other Communists, but he seemed to have no bitterness about his hard life. His comparative amiability was no doubt one of
the reasons why Zakhariadis denounced him later (May 1950) as a traitor
who had sold out to the British and American imperialists at least as early
as 1943, if not before the Second World War.[15] Siantos was a member of
the old discredited leadership which Zakhariadis replaced in 1931. He
then escaped to Moscow, and he and Zakhariadis were only intermittently
together again until Siantos's death in 1947. Zakhariadis controlled the
KKE from 1931 to 1941 and from 1945 to 1956; Siantos from 1941 to
1945. But together or apart, the tension between them was never relaxed.

It was fortunate for the new leadership that in the 1930s Macedonia
was no longer a critical problem in the Balkans. Other issues successively
took priority. One was the need for economic and social reforms, on
which it was decided to focus pressure from December 1931. The
primacy of 'everyday problems' was stressed at the first Panhelladic
Organisational Conference in 1932 and by the Second Plenum (or full
meeting) of the Central Committee in 1934. Among its organisational
preparations for the new line, the party had formed its own trade-union
confederation in 1929. At the same time the importance of forming a
'united front' was stressed as the approach of war seemed inevitable, with
the Japanese invasion of Manchuria in 1932 and the accession to power of
Hitler in 1933. The theme of protecting the Soviet fatherland by 'turning
the imperialist war into a civil war' had been adopted as early as 1929,
though with little effect because the prospect still seemed remote to most
Greeks. But in the 1930s the Balkan governments themselves began forming a defensive coalition (with the exception of Bulgaria, whose irre-
dentist claims to Macedonia could not be accommodated). Calls for a
'united front' against foreign aggression therefore struck a more har-
monious note.

A new *Rizospastis* was launched to promote the new party line. The
themes of 'everyday problems' and a 'united front' had two advantages for
the KKE. First, they were relatively respectable, which enabled the party
to gain votes. In the General Election of 1932 their 'united front' won
58,000 of the votes and ten seats; in 1933 and 1935, although they
won no seats, they first held their vote almost steady and then advanced
it to 90,000 votes; and in 1936 they won fifteen seats, despite a

recession in their vote to only 73,000. Not only were they now a substantial party in Parliament; they actually held the balance between the major groups of parties – the Populists and their allies with 143 seats, and the Liberals and their allies with 141. In the second place, the KKE was able unostentatiously to retreat from its dangerous position over Macedonia. The change came with a suddenness which would have surprised public opinion if it had paid the slightest attention to the KKE. In 1934 Zevgos, a member of the Central Committee, had written that 'the KKE maintains with all its force the right of the populations of Macedonia and Thrace to dispose of themselves, even to the point of separation to form a distinct state'.[16] But in April 1935 the Third Plenum of the Central Committee substituted 'equality of minorities' for Macedonian autonomy, and this formulation was confirmed by the Sixth Party Congress at the end of the year. Macedonia had mercifully almost ceased to be an issue. It did not re-emerge until the German occupation.

In 1936 another issue came to hand with the establishment of the dictatorship of the 'Fourth of August' under General Metaxas, to which was closely related the question of the King and the constitution. The monarchy had had a chequered history since 1917, when Constantine I was deposed. He had been succeeded by his younger son Alexander, then restored himself in 1920, then finally deposed again in 1922 and succeeded by his elder son George II. In 1924 the monarchy was replaced by a Republic, which lasted (though interrupted by several military *coups d'état*) until 1935. George II was then restored, and did his best to govern constitutionally, though handicapped by the deadlock in Parliament which followed the General Election of January 1936. The problem was aggravated by the deaths in rapid succession of many of the country's most experienced statesmen, including the current Prime Minister. Thus in April 1936 General Metaxas, who was already Deputy Prime Minister, succeeded to office; but he led a party of only six deputies, and he was notoriously contemptuous of parliamentary government. The Communists, who held the balance in Parliament, entered into secret discussions with both the Populists and the Liberals on the possibility of forming a coalition to take over the Government. Then they too showed their contempt for parliamentary conventions by publicising the discussions. Their preparations for a forcible seizure of power were scarcely disguised. In May they caused a strike and riots in Salonika, which led to the declaration of a state of emergency. Zakhariadis warned his colleagues of a 'violent struggle' to come, and *Rizospastis* published a series of inflammatory articles. At the end of July the KKE proclaimed a general strike to take place on 5 August. It was an unmistakable challenge.

Metaxas persuaded the King to grant him emergency powers on 4 August. Parliament had already adjourned in April, and its successor did not meet again until 1946. For four and a half years, until his death in 1941, Metaxas governed by decree. Through his ingenious Minister of the Interior, Maniadakis, he handled the KKE with great skill. Its leading members were arrested without delay: Siantos, who had returned from Moscow, in August; Zakhariadis in September; and many others then or afterwards. Maniadakis later instituted the system of 'declarations' (*dilóseis*), which enabled Communists to obtain their release by signed renunciations of the KKE. Some forty-five thousand such 'declarations' were obtained, many of them of course insincere. Maniadakis used those so released, as well as others, to penetrate and divide the party mechanism, and even to create a rival Communist faction under his own control. By 1940 there were no less than three distinct bodies claiming to be the Central Committee of the party, and savagely denouncing each other.[17] Although Siantos escaped from gaol in 1937, he was re-arrested in 1939; and Zakhariadis was in prison throughout. The KKE was in total disarray.

Between the Fourth of August in 1936 and the outbreak of war in 1939, the KKE was incapable of serious activity. It plotted a coup in Crete during 1938, which failed pitifully. The only significance of this attempt was that a leading part was played by the Cretan General Mandakas, who was not himself a Communist, though he had a Communist brother-in-law; and as a result he later became closely associated with the KKE. Another leading participant in Crete was the young Communist, Markos Vaphiadis, who was to prove himself a more accomplished revolutionary ten years later. After that feeble effort, the party sank into confused apathy, which was only momentarily dissipated by the Nazi–Soviet Pact and the outbreak of war in the late summer of 1939. Like other Communist Parties, the KKE was at a loss how to react. A directive from the Comintern, of which two different versions reached the party, increased the confusion. One group, survivors from the old leadership, interpreted the directive as indicating collaboration with the German and Italian dictatorships, because Hitler was now Stalin's ally. Siantos, who was temporarily free, and Zakhariadis, from his prison cell, took the opposite view that they must support Metaxas, because he was standing up to Mussolini.

Even greater confusion was caused by the Italian invasion of Greece in October 1940. The reactions of Communists inside and outside gaol make painful and absurd reading. Zakhariadis fumbled desperately for the correct line in a series of three letters from captivity.[18] On 31 October he wrote that it was the duty of the KKE to support Metaxas against the national enemy. A few months later the party denounced this first letter as a forgery, but in 1945 Zakhariadis admitted that it was genuine and allowed it to be re-published in *Rizospastis*. In his second letter, however, dated 26 November, he repudiated the line of the first and denounced the war as purely imperialist. This line was also supported by the old party leadership, which was still at liberty. Finally Zakhariadis wrote a third letter on 17 January 1941, which was regarded as definitive and was re-published in July 1942. In this he explained the motives for his first letter (thus acknowledging its authenticity); he attacked Metaxas; he called for a separate peace, with Soviet mediation; and by implication he accepted the right of self-determination and secession for Macedonia.

The production of these bewildering directives was overtaken by events. Early successes of the Greek army in southern Albania (which the Greeks claimed as northern Epirus) led to the capture of towns containing a substantial Greek population, such as Korytsa and Argyrokastro, which were mistakenly expected to be annexed to Greece after the war. Then the Greek and Italian armies reached a deadlock. German forces were already moving into the Balkans in anticipation – though the reason was not yet clearly understood – of an attack on the Soviet Union. The British Government sought to send a small expeditionary force to help the Greeks hold a front in Macedonia, but Metaxas declined it on the grounds that it would be provocative and too small to be effective. On 29 January 1941, however, he died, leaving a constitutional vacuum; and Alexander Koryzis, whom the King appointed in his place, allowed the British force to come. On 21 April the Germans attacked both Yugoslavia and Greece. All resistance was quickly swept aside. Athens was occupied on 27 April, and the defence of Crete ended by the beginning of June. Greece and Yugoslavia were under enemy occupation for the next four years.

Although the occupation found the Communists in disarray, luck and discipline enabled them to make a speedy recovery. At the beginning, the Soviet Union was still bound by treaty to Nazi Germany, and therefore briefly severed diplomatic relations with the Greek Government in exile. For some weeks the correct stance for the KKE to take was in serious doubt. On 18 March, when the Germans were already moving unopposed into Bulgaria, the KKE had advised the Greeks to follow the example of 'the heroic fraternal people of Bulgaria'.[19] A few weeks later there were actually hints of possible collaboration between the KKE and the Germans in forming a government under the occupation.[20] Meanwhile large areas of Macedonia and Thrace passed under the administrative control of Bulgaria, and were treated as if annexed permanently. The Bulgarians similarly occupied Yugoslav Macedonia, where on the whole their presence was at first not unwelcome. When the Germans invaded Russia on 22 June, the complex of Balkan relationships was again convulsed. The Bulgarians continued to assume that they would be able to retain their gains at the expense of Greece and Yugoslavia whatever the outcome of the war; but in December 1941 Stalin communicated a document to Eden in Moscow which recommended that Greece should be 're-established with its pre-war frontiers'.[21] Whether the Greek Communists knew this or not, they were understandably in some uncertainty about the future development of the Macedonian question.

In terms of organisation, however, the KKE was not altogether unready for the years of resistance. Its leaders had lived underground since Metaxas seized power, having prepared an illegal apparatus years before. Many escaped from prison in the confused days before German control was complete. The Germans themselves, by a strange miscalculation, released twenty-six prisoners from the gaol on Acronauplia at the request of the Bulgarian authorities, who said that they were Bulgarian nationalists oppressed by the Greeks. All were in fact Communists, and they included Andreas Tzimas and a leading Slavo-Macedonian known in Greek as Lazaros Zisiadis and in Bulgarian as Terpovski.[22] The latter, although almost unknown in Greece, was later described as the 'effective leader' of the Communists in Macedonia.[23] Siantos, who escaped for the second time in September 1941, was elected temporary Secretary-General in the following January. Others who were at liberty included Costa Theos, the trade-union leader; Klaras, who was to create the first armed units of ELAS under the pseudonym of Aris Veloukhiotis; Giphtodimopoulos, an able journalist who also distinguished himself as a guerrilla leader under the pseudonym of Karagiorgis; and a shadowy handful of *apparatchiks* — Ioannidis, Partsalidis, Zevgos, Petros Roussos and his wife Khrysa Khatzivasiliou — who dominated the Central Committee in Athens.

In retrospect what is conspicuous about the KKE during the German occupation is the absence of an outstanding leader with the personality and charisma of Tito. In 1941, it is true, Tito himself showed few signs of becoming the great national leader of later years. He was a devoted Stalinist, like Zakhariadis. He had acquiesced in the Soviet policy of the autonomy of Macedonia. He owed his appointment as Secretary-General of the Yugoslav CP to the fact that he alone survived the purges of the 1930s in Moscow; and that fact was itself held to be suspicious. His relations with the Greek Communists were never particularly friendly. When he returned to Yugoslavia in 1940, he travelled by way of Istanbul and

Salonika, no doubt with the help of local Communists. If the KKE helped him at that time, they had reason to regret it later. Zakhariadis spoke with venomous hatred of Tito in 1950, alleging that he had deliberately betrayed Greek interests from the first. Tito in fact had regarded the Greeks with indifference. He was interested in power; and gradually, almost unconsciously, he had learned that Yugoslav nationalism was a better vehicle for power than doctrinaire Stalinism.

Zakhariadis's attitude to Tito was inspired by jealousy. He felt that only the accident of being in captivity throughout the war had deprived him of the chance to play a similar or greater role in Greece. Certainly he was mistaken: neither in ability nor in character was he a potential Tito; nor was any other Greek. Aris Veloukhiotis had the drive and ambition, but he was temperamentally erratic. Markos Vaphiadis was too junior for the role under the German occupation, and in the 'third round' his luck failed him. There were the makings of a leader in Karagiorgis (Giphto-dimopoulos), who was morally and physically courageous as well as politically intelligent, ruthless and persuasive. He imposed his personality on several British officers during the occupation; and he conducted the single most successful battle of the civil war in 1949. His tongue and pen were eloquent, smooth and bitter; his devotion to Communist ideology was as strong as his sense of Greek patriotism. But his social origins in the upper middle class were unmistakable. Such a man could not be the Greek Tito, nor the unchallenged leader of a movement of workers and peasants.

The weakness of the KKE, well exemplified in the personality o Karagiorgis, was that it had little appeal to the proletariat. There was no class-war in Greece for the party to exploit. Its leaders were drawn mainly from the urban middle classes. Their followers were simply a cross-section of the entire population, just like those of any other party. The party had a certain appeal to aggrieved minorities and under-employed intellectuals. Other sections of the population, such as women and the young, were attracted by promises of social reform; but women and youth are not specifically social classes. Peasants, who wanted land, were not favourably impressed by the prospect of agricultural collectivisa-tion. Industrial workers were too disorganised to be effectively mobilised. Some fifteen hundred trade unions, mostly small and local, had existed mainly as bargaining units under the patronage of the state. Only the tobacco-workers and the seamen were well organised. Communism appealed to the tobacco-workers perhaps chiefly because so many of them were refugees. It appealed to the seamen chiefly in foreign waters: those in Greek waters were just as likely to be monarchists. In general, the devotion of the Greek people to their family and their Church made them poor material for ideological recruitment.

The gap between the doctrinaire leaders and the toiling masses was wide and deep. It could have been bridged only by a man who, like Tito, came from the people but had risen morally and intellectually above them. There was no such man in Greece. But if they had no Tito, they had perhaps a Djilas, which could have been nearly as important in the long run. An intellectual Communist who becomes disillusioned first with Stalinism, and then even with Titoism or national Communism, is a significant phenomenon in the party. It is not possible to equate Andreas Tzimas, the Slavo-Macedonian from Samarina known also as Evmaios or Vasilis Samariniotis, precisely with Milovan Djilas, because the history of the KKE did not run its full course on the same lines as the Yugoslav CP. But he was certainly the ablest and clearest thinker in the party. Tall and gaunt, pale and bespectacled, his hair already white from suffering in gaol by the age of thirty, with his acute thinking expressed in a quiet, nasal voice and in elegantly faultless Greek (which he spoke bilingually with Macedonian), he greatly impressed all those who encountered him, particularly those who had most frequent occasion to be in dispute with him.

Such was the raw material of revolution in 1941. The KKE was tough, disciplined, secretive, hardened by harsh experience. Its rank and file were for the most part not the sinister conspirators of popular mythology, but patriotic and high-minded men and women, inspired by a vague ideal of a new and better Greece. They had criminals among them, just as they had *dilosíes*, or men who had signed 'declarations' renouncing Communism under Metaxas; but both were admitted on sufferance, as an opportunity to redeem themselves. They were genuinely seeking both a social and a national liberation. They had little idea of the magnitude of the obstacles confronting them, of which the enemy occupation was perhaps the least. Much more serious were the backwardness and conservatism (which they called 'reaction') of their own people; the unresolved problems of nationalism and relations with their northern neighbours; and above all, the weakness and division of their own leadership. Police action, accidents of war and ideological controversy had all taken their toll. The ruthless egocentricity of Stalin, who knew little and cared less about the internal problems of Balkan Communism, was the greatest obstacle of all. What is remarkable is that the KKE so nearly achieved so much, failing only by the narrowest of margins to seize power on three occasions. Siantos, Tzimas, Aris Veloukhiotis, Markos Vaphiadis, Karagiorgis, and even Zakhariadis, were not negligible men.

2

Resistance and Reaction
May 1941–July 1943

RESISTANCE BEGAN spontaneously; or rather, it never ceased. The first overt act of defiance was the removal of the Nazi flag from the Acropolis on the last night of May 1941 by two young men, one of whom (Manolis Glezos) later joined the KKE. Secret organisations soon came into existence. The Communists founded National Mutual Aid (EA) in May and the National Workers' Liberation Front (EEAM) in July. A Socialist trade-union leader who joined EEAM described the Communist control over it as absolute.[1] On 27 September 1941 the National Liberation Front (EAM) was founded by the Communists, and its initials were seen on leaflets circulating in October. Its twenty-five-strong Central Committee purported to represent as many parties and organisations. Although EAM was not at first admitted to be a creation of the KKE, most politicians in Athens regarded it with suspicion. Panaghiotis Kanellopoulos, an antagonist of the Metaxas dictatorship, rebuffed an approach by two representatives of EAM at the end of 1941 because they would not identify themselves.[2] George Papandreou, the leading Liberal of the post-Venizelos generation, also treated EAM with caution. So did George Kartalis, a former Populist Minister who had turned Republican.

Republican leaders of the older generation, like the politicians Sophoulis and Kaphandaris and the senior generals, Pangalos and Gonatas, also kept aloof from EAM. But their hostility to the King was implacable. Not only the Communists but all the leading activists in Athens were anti-monarchist. So was the most eminent leader in exile, General Plastiras, who was living in unoccupied France. When Gonatas and Zervas founded the National Republican Greek League (EDES) on 9 September 1941, they made Plastiras its titular leader and included in its charter a phrase opposing the return of the King except after 'a free expression of the will of the Greek people'.[3] Soon afterwards Gonatas sent a letter through Tsouderos, the Prime Minister in exile, to the British Government claiming (though without specific authority) that all the political leaders in Athens regarded the King as deprived of his throne.[4] A more authoritative statement was signed on 31 March 1942 by most of the political leaders in Athens (including Constantine Tsaldaris, leader of the right-wing Populist

Party) declaring that the King must await the result of a plebiscite before returning. Kanellopoulos estimated that the royalists amounted to no more than two per cent of the population, as against sixty per cent Liberals and thirty per cent in the Popular Front.[5]

Much discussion took place in Athens in 1941–2 of the possibilities of armed resistance, but it was always dominated by the constitutional question because it was taken for granted that sooner or later the Germans were bound to be defeated. All the officers who seriously considered taking to the mountains – Grigoriadis, Bakirdzis, Psaros, Saraphis, Zervas – were Republicans. So were the intellectuals on the fringe of politics – Angelopoulos, Svolos, Costa Tsatsos. Looming in detachment over all was the powerful figure of Damaskinos, whom the Germans themselves had appointed Archbishop of Athens because his predecessor refused to swear in their puppet government. A German report described him as 'an extremely cunning politician and diplomat', determined to 'keep in with all parties and always be on the winning side'.[6] The same could have been said of many men much less honourable than himself. There were daily exchanges of conspiratorial ideas, but all lacked the guidance they sought. Some, like Svolos, Grigoriadis, Saraphis and Bakirdzis, eventually gravitated towards EAM, hoping that they could neutralise its Communist influence. Others became its bitter antagonists and openly fought the Communists. But in the winter of 1941–2 all were at a loss how to react. Two groups remained aloof: the KKE, once more confident and sure of its ground; and the royalist officers, headed by General Papagos, the Chief of the General Staff in the Albanian war. Both seemed to await authoritative instructions from abroad.

The question of instructions from abroad cannot be separated from that of the influence of Greece's foreign allies. When the Occupation began, the only ally was Britain, under whose protection the King and Government were established in exile. The Soviet Union and the USA became allies only in June and December 1941 respectively, and their influence on Greek affairs was not great until 1944. The US Government was well informed during 1942–3, but made little attempt to influence British policy.[7] Lincoln MacVeagh, who had been American Ambassador in Athens before the war and resumed the post in Cairo towards the end of 1943 (with additional responsibility for Yugoslavia), was the most experienced diplomatist in Greek affairs. His aim was that the United States should play a more active role, by which he meant one helpful both to the Greeks and the British (whom he often referred to with real affection as 'our cousins'). But the State Department deprecated what its officials called his 'adventurism'. Their chief contribution to allied policy was to express regular dissent from the British Government's attachment to the King; but they in turn were overruled by President Roosevelt. His patrician instincts inclined him to support Churchill's royalist sympathies; and both were strongly reinforced by Field-Marshal Smuts, who formed a warm attachment to the Greek Royal Family. The guidance sent to the officer corps in Athens from its Western Allies bore the stamp of passive conservatism.

Whether the KKE received instructions from Moscow at the same time can only be a matter of speculation. A fragment of negative evidence is that when Bakirdzis (who was close to EAM though not a member of the KKE) left Athens in the summer of 1942, he said that his intention was to make contact with Moscow.[8] The Soviet Government's policy, however, was indifferent to Greece and ill-informed about the Balkans during most of the Occupation. The Greek Government in exile, on the other hand, had at least some contacts with its friends in the occupied country: both by wireless to Athens and Salonika (although to an uncomfortable extent under British control) and occasionally by special emissaries. The first such emissary was a junior naval officer who landed on the coast of Attica on 7 November 1941; but his mission did not envisage armed activity, and was in any case abortive.[9] No further emissary appears to have been sent until August 1942. In the meantime a more energetic but unofficial emissary, Komninos Pyromaglou, arrived in Greece on behalf of Plastiras. He was largely responsible for basing an organisation for active resistance on the political framework of EDES. Similarly the first of the Greek Communists to initiate armed activity were acting without the encouragement of the Central Committee of the KKE, let alone of Moscow. Thus resistance began without instruction or co-ordination; but it began.

German soldiers had expected to be welcome in Greece – at any rate more welcome than the Italians or Bulgarians. The allocation of areas of occupation was decided by expediency. The Germans occupied Western Macedonia as far as the River Strymon (including Salonika) and the area of Thrace bordering Turkey. The area between was assigned to the Bulgarians, who administered it as sovereign territory, and in June 1942 even offered Bulgarian nationality to all its inhabitants; though at the same time they expelled more than half the Greek population. The Germans also occupied the Aegean islands nearest to the Turkish coast and the three western provinces of Crete. The rest of Greece and the islands (including the eastern province of Crete) were assigned to the Italians, except that Athens was jointly occupied. It was, in the words of the German Special Plenipotentiary in Athens, 'a complicated condominium of the Axis powers', which could only work on the assumption of passive acquiescence on the part of the Greeks.[10] To reduce the need for Axis troops, local auxiliaries were recruited from among the minorities: the Albanian-speaking Chams in Epirus, and the Slavophones and Rumanian-speaking Vlakhs in Macedonia. The experiment failed, and was abandoned within a few months. No further recruitment was attempted until the Greek Security Battalions were formed in 1943.

German records indicate that the first acts of subversion, and consequent reprisals, took place in villages of Macedonia in September and October 1941. They were primarily directed against Greek police, and possibly provoked by Moscow-trained Bulgarian Communists.[11] Even these were probably not the first acts of violence. Yugoslav partisans claimed to have been in action as early as July; and the records of the British Special Operations Executive (SOE) contain a report of guerrillas in Mount Olympus during the late summer of 1941, though no armed clash is recorded.[12] Passive resistance in Athens reached the stage of open defiance on 28 October, the anniversary of Greece's entry into the war, when Professor Tsatsos delivered a patriotic speech at the University, and the initials of EAM were seen in letters of fire on Mount Hymettus. These gestures were followed in the New Year by a student demonstration on Independence Day, 25 March, and a series of strikes directed against the conscription of workers in the early summer of 1942.

The emergence of armed bands in the mountains was spontaneous, though many of them initially had some affiliation with EAM. On 16 February 1942 the Central Committee of the KKE proclaimed that EAM was 'taking up arms'. The formation of ELAS, its armed force, was announced on 10 April, and its initials were first seen in print during May. Meanwhile a rash of small bands proliferated: Major Kostopoulos, a republican and at first an adherent of EAM, took the field in Thessaly in February; an unspecified band was reported in the Geraneia hills, between Corinth and Megara, in April; another in the Peloponnese in May.[13] There were also less serious figures in the field, particularly in the area of the southern Pindus known as Roumeli or Sterea Ellas: Socrates Ghekas, who styled himself Athos Roumeliotis, gravitated in and out of ELAS by turns; another, Karalivanos, was a professional brigand with less than half a dozen men.

Although the Communists refrained from announcing the formation of ELAS until they were ready, its early results were not spectacular. The main problem was to recruit officers, a deficiency admitted by Tzimas, who was in charge of recruitment in Athens.[14] It was later boasted, quite truthfully, that 'the KKE formed ELAS', but at the time this fact was concealed, to avert suspicion.[15] A resolution of the Panhelladic Conference in December 1942 claimed only that the KKE had joined with 'a few other parties and popular organisations' in founding EAM.[16] In July 1943 Tzimas denied a claim made by the Bishop of Kozani, the first senior cleric in the organisation, that the KKE 'formed the basis of EAM'.[17] Such denials were in accordance with a general policy, which had also been imposed by the Comintern on the Yugoslav Partisans. Even in 1944 Dimitrov told Djilas not to let it be known prematurely that 'our movement was entirely Communist in character'.[18] Some Partisan leaders refused to conform with the policy, and criticised the Greek Communists for accepting it.[19] The KKE reasoned that only so could they hope for the support of the officer corps, but in fact few were deceived. Saraphis, Psaros and Zervas all refused to join ELAS. Among the few senior officers who were sympathetic was General Grigoriadis, whose son was one of the first regular officers to join. Neither the republican General Mandakas nor the 'red Colonel' Bakirdzis joined in the early days. The latter was even considered in 1942 for the post of Commander-in-Chief of a nationalist force, including Psaros and Zervas under him; but this plan too proved abortive.[20]

In early 1942, therefore, the effort in the mountains was slight. It continued so in most parts of Greece until the end of the year. Although EAM formed embryonic bands in Epirus, Thessaly and Macedonia, there is no record of operations by them until December.[21] But further south a change came about through the initiative of a few determined men. On 12 May, setting out from Lamia, Aris Veloukhiotis took the field in Roumeli. It is doubtful how far he had the support of the KKE: one source says that he and Kapetan Orestis (Moundrikhas) took the field without even consulting the party; another says that he was sent only to reconnoitre the possibility of forming bands; all agree that he was under suspicion by the KKE because he had signed a 'declaration' under Metaxas renouncing Communism, although he did so at the instigation of Zakhariadis.[22] Of his determination there could be no doubt.

The same was true of Dr Stylianos Khoutas, who left his home in Amphilokhia, on the other side of the Pindus range, on 12 June to form an armed band in Valtos. A few weeks later he put himself under the command of Zervas, who left Athens on 23 July with four companions, and took to the hills in Tzoumerka (Epirus). On 1 August Major Tsigantes arrived secretly in Greece by submarine with a triple mission: to contact political leaders, to organise resistance, and to sabotage the Corinth Canal. The pace of action then began to accelerate. Aris's first clash with the Italians took place on 9 September. On the last night of the same month a party of eight British parachutists landed in Roumeli, with Colonel

E. C. W. Myers in command, to be followed by four more a month later. Meanwhile on 11 October Zervas signed an agreement on local co-operation with the EAM of Arta;[23] and on 23 October he fought his first action against the Italians.

Resistance was now reaching serious dimensions, though somewhat later in Greece than in other parts of the Balkans. In Yugoslavia it had been in progress for over a year, and so had the feud between the nationalist Mihailović and the Communist Tito, which was to be reflected in Greece. Partisan emissaries were active in Albania and Yugoslav Macedonia. The northern Greeks were bound to react to these initiatives as well as to the enemy occupation. An organisation called the Defenders of Northern Greece (YVE)* was formed to combat Communist and non-Communist enemies alike. In September 1942 occurred the first serious rising against the Bulgarians in eastern Macedonia. The enemy began to take hostages, executing them in reprisal for acts of sabotage. In Athens the first executions were reported in March 1942, and there were more in the summer. Some German commanders recognised the futility of the policy, but it still continued. Particularly severe reprisals were inflicted after the combined forces of Zervas, Aris and the British parachutists destroyed the Gorgopotamos railway viaduct on 25 November 1942. Operation Harling, as it was called, was the most important single success of the Resistance, and the only one in which ELAS co-operated with other guerrillas under a single command.

The purpose of the Gorgopotamos operation was to support the advance of the Eighth Army in North Africa, which began at El Alamein on the night of 23–24 October. Although it came a month late for that purpose, and caused less disruption to the German supply-line than had been hoped, it had important consequences. In the military context, it showed for the first time in occupied Europe that guerrillas, with the support of allied officers, could carry out a major tactical operation co-ordinated with allied strategic plans. It stimulated ambitious plans for developing Resistance, primarily in Greece but also elsewhere. There was equally a great stimulus to Greek morale. But in the historical context there was an even more important consequence. The Gorgopotamos operation contributed to preventing a Communist monopoly of the Resistance, but also to creating the conditions of civil war. Without the prestige of the operation and the support of the British officers who came to organise it, Zervas would not have been able to withstand the campaign of threats and violence launched against him by ELAS from Christmas 1942 onwards. If he had succumbed, no other nationalist senior officer would have dared to

* Later known as PAO—the Panhellenic Liberation Organisation.

take the field; or any that did so would have had to join ELAS. By the summer of 1943, EAM would have had a monopoly of the Resistance movement, and by the day of liberation they would have had total control of Greece. It would then have been as impossible to dislodge them as it was to dislodge their comrades in Yugoslavia.

These consequences could not have been foreseen at the time. When the Gorgopotamos operation took place, it was difficult to draw distinctions between the armed bands in the mountains. Their leaders were indeed separated by political motives: Aris Veloukhiotis was a Communist, though probably sincere in abhorring dictatorship of any colour; Zervas was a republican, probably much less disinclined to dictatorship. There were virtually no royalist officers in the field. Most of the leaders of ELAS were men of the people, known as *kapetánios*. But in the early stages a few respectable, though elderly, senior officers of republican sympathies were attracted to ELAS, particularly in Epirus, which was also Zervas's main recruiting ground. So were some priests, notably the Bishop of Kozani, and later the Bishop of Elis. But distinctions which might be drawn among the leaders did not apply to the rank and file, whose motives were generally simpler: patriotism, despair, a sense of humiliation, an awareness that the guerrilla's life was preferable to starvation in the occupied towns, or simply a lack of any other way of life.

Those who directed the Resistance — Communist, nationalist, republican, British — simply consolidated in their different ways a movement which originated spontaneously. The British, in particular, so far as their presence was a factor in the course of events, were late on the scene. Apart from escaped prisoners and others left behind by the accident of war, the British were not much in evidence in the early days of the Resistance. Their first organised efforts were concentrated in Crete, where British officers were infiltrated from July 1941 onwards. They were in contact with local leaders on the island, such as Emmanuel Bandouvas and Petrakogiorgis, and also with the left-wing General Mandakas. But the original purpose was not armed resistance: it was firstly to evacuate escaped prisoners, and secondly to collect intelligence. Guerrilla activities did not at first seem possible in Crete, partly because of the small size of the island and partly because so many young Cretans had been left behind in mainland Greece with the Cretan Division. When operations became practicable, which was not until 1943, the Communists played little part.* The leading role was taken by EOK (the National Organisation of Cretans).

* It was, however, in Crete that I first encountered the KKE, in January 1942, in the person of a cousin of Bandouvas.

On the mainland the early British contacts were also mainly for intelligence. The first agents to be infiltrated were soon rounded up, in one case with grave results. A British officer who landed by submarine in March 1942 carried a list of names, including that of Kanellopoulos. The officer was caught with his papers on landing, and Kanellopoulos was obliged to flee for his life. In April he arrived in Cairo by way of Turkey. He was appointed Deputy Prime Minister in the Greek Government, which left him behind in Cairo when it moved its seat to London. Benefiting from his own experience in Athens, he joined in forming an Anglo-Greek Action Committee to supervise clandestine operations in Greece. It was this Committee which authorised Tsigantes's mission in August 1942. It enjoyed the approval of the British Foreign Office, but functioned only until March 1943, when Kanellopoulos was compelled to resign after a mutiny in the Greek forces of the Middle East. Even while the Anglo-Greek Committee functioned, it had only a limited oversight of operations. For reasons of secrecy, the Greek Government, alone among the governments of occupied countries, was almost entirely excluded from operations on its own soil.

Kanellopoulos later referred with justifiable bitterness to the 'inconceivably uncoordinated activities' of the British secret services.[24] The most important of these organisations were the Secret Intelligence Service (SIS) and the Special Operations Executive (SOE), which operated separately in Greece and were responsible to different Ministries. The Greek Government at first relied chiefly on the SIS as a channel of communication. Through that channel, for example, Kanellopoulos was in touch with a group of six Colonels in Athens, led by the future General Spiliotopoulos, and also with the organisation in Salonika known as the Defenders of Northern Greece (YVE) under Colonel Argyropoulos. Both groups were loyal to the King and Government. SOE, on the other hand, was mainly in touch with republican groups, including the KKE. Subversive operations in Greece came under SOE only at the end of 1941, but by early 1942 it was in touch both with EAM and with a group of republican officers headed by Bakirdzis, who operated a clandestine wireless link under the code-name of Prometheus. Bakirdzis left Greece in August 1942, and was succeeded as Prometheus II by a naval captain, Koutsogiannopoulos. Both were in touch with Psaros, Saraphis, Zervas and other officers who were considering how to take the field.

It seems strange that the earliest contacts of SOE in occupied Greece were with ex-regular officers rather than with EAM. Hugh Dalton, the Socialist Minister for Economic Warfare, who was originally responsible for SOE in Churchill's cabinet, defined his aims in quite other terms:[25]

What some of us had in mind was not a military job at all. It concerned Trade Unions and Socialists in enemy and enemy-occupied
territories, the creation of Fifth Columns, of explosions, chaos and
revolution. Some said that hitherto the Foreign Office had prevented all action in this field.

These preconceptions would seem to point directly to co-operation with
EAM. Dalton added that he was 'very action-minded'; and although he
dismissed apprehensions that he was trying to run a foreign policy of his
own, he took an individual line in the Cabinet. Yet SOE, the instrument
of his policy, was slow to make constructive use of EAM.[26] The explanation is not to be found in the fact that Dalton was replaced at the Ministry
of Economic Warfare by the Conservative, Lord Selborne, in February
1942; for the character of SOE's contacts in Greece had been determined
before the Occupation began, and was unaltered during the following
year. When the first British parachutists landed in Greece at the end
of September 1942, EAM and ELAS were still unknown names to them,
although SOE was already well informed about EAM and was in a position
to learn more from Kanellopoulos and Bakirdzis, who had recently
arrived in the Middle East from Athens. For whatever reason, British
sights were already set on republican officers rather than Communists or
monarchists. Such officers were readily available (because excluded from
active service under Metaxas) and were perhaps thought not to be so
dangerous politically as the Communists. This was reasonable; but there
was also a failure to appreciate the power of the KKE. Dalton had reason
to be surprised, in retrospect, at the kind of men whom his agents brought
first into the field. Colonel Napoleon Zervas was the most singular
example.

Zervas, one of the founders of EDES, was the first well-known officer
to form a band in the mountains. He had been urged to do so for many
months by SOE through Prometheus, and had received some twenty-four
thousand gold sovereigns, but he remained reluctant to move. His reputation before the Gorgopotamos operation did not stand high. He was a
revolutionary republican and a professional gambler; he had been forced
to leave the regular Army after being involved in more than one coup
d'état; and his selection as a Resistance leader, though vindicated by
events, was one of the more puzzling decisions of SOE. The final pressure
put on him to leave Athens was a threat to expose him to the Germans.
This distasteful story was withheld from the first British liaison officers
sent to him in the mountains. His rivals, Psaros and Saraphis, were more
respectable and even more hesitant. Psaros would not enter the field

until March 1943, when the prospect of forming an independent band
had almost vanished. Saraphis made a tour of the mountains of Thessaly,
his native territory, during the summer of 1942; but although he met
guerrilla leaders, including Kostopoulos, and heard of others such as Aris
and Zervas, he could not bring himself to the point of decision.[27] In
November he too refused an invitation to join EAM. With Papandreou
and Grigoriadis, he formed instead a separate organisation called AAA
(Struggle–Restoration–Independence).

Like Psaros, but unlike Zervas, Saraphis did not understand guerrilla
warfare. He wanted regular formations, conventionally equipped and controlled by well-trained staffs. As a professional soldier, he had the pride
and stiffness as well as the fine qualities of his kind. He had also an intense
but narrow patriotism, which forbade him to become what he saw as an
'agent of the British', especially since few of the British officers in Greece
were professionals like himself. He was still a republican, unwilling to
serve even nominally under the King. When he learned of Tsigantes's
mission to Greece, at first he declined a meeting, thinking that Tsigantes
must have abandoned his republican principles. Tsigantes was in fact trying to create an all-party committee in Athens, to control the Resistance
movement in association with Kanellopoulos's Anglo-Greek Committee
in Cairo. He had some success with men like the Archbishop, Papandreou
and even Svolos; but diehard republicans like Sophoulis and Gonatas
insisted as the price of co-operation that the monarchy should be submitted to a plebiscite.

Despite his reservations, Saraphis eventually agreed to see Tsigantes,
and was persuaded by him to take the field in Thessaly, where Kostopoulos
and others were willing to serve under him. His principal motive seems
to have been fear that the Communists would monopolise the Resistance.
This argument was also pressed on him by the ex-dictator, General
Pangalos; but Pangalos's conclusion was that it was preferable to have no
Resistance at all, and to that end he also advised Zervas to dissolve his
forces at the same time.[28] In January 1943 Saraphis at last set out for the
mountains. Shortly afterwards, Tsigantes was trapped and killed by the
Italian secret police; and Prometheus II was captured less than three
weeks after Tsigantes's death. These grave events disturbed the British in
the mountains, who were seeking simultaneously to establish direct contact in Athens with Tsigantes, with Prometheus II, with the six Colonels,
and with the Central Committee of EAM. The six Colonels proved to
have very limited notions of guerrilla warfare or resistance of any kind.
There remained the leaders of EAM, particularly Siantos and Tzimas, as
the only organisation in Athens with whom contact was worth establish-

ing. From these contacts in January 1943 also dates the first understanding by the British authorities of the nature and purposes of the KKE.

It was at about the same time that the Communist leaders conceived the possibility of monopolising the Resistance and so gaining control of Greece as the day of liberation approached. This was probably discussed at the party's Panhelladic Conference, which was held in Thessaly in December 1942; and it was followed immediately by Aris's first abortive move against Zervas. The close connection between EAM and the KKE was now becoming unmistakable to British observers. Myers recorded a suspicion of the connection at the beginning of 1943.[29] Not long afterwards, at a meeting in Athens on 2 February 1943 – the day on which Prometheus II was captured, and while the death of Tsigantes was fresh in everybody's memory – a member of the Central Committee of EAM referred contemptuously to the 'lack of conspiratorial experience' of the British agents, and added the revealing words: 'We, on the other hand, have all been outlaws (paránomoi) for years'.[30] These words, which could only refer to Communists, were accepted by four out of the five Greeks present – Siantos, Tzimas, Ioannidis and Petros Roussos – the exception being the Socialist Tsirimokos, who demurred. Realising in consequence that they were now dealing primarily with the KKE, the British were reinforced in their view that it was important to bring the leadership out into the mountains, where alone the Resistance could be effectively controlled.

It has sometimes been suggested that the later trouble in Greece was due to the failure of SOE and its agents to appreciate from the first that they were confronted with the Greek Communist Party. The original texts show how far this is true. When the first British parachutists landed in mainland Greece on the last night of September 1942, they knew nothing of EAM or ELAS and there had been no mention of the KKE in their briefing.[31] The first reference to EAM was in a telegram from SOE in Cairo to Myers in Greece, dated 21 December 1942, asking if he had any contact with a Greek organisation of that name.[32] By then Myers was in fact familiar with EAM, but his wireless was not in working order till January. On 24 January 1943 he sent an indirect reply in a long telegram to Cairo. He stated that Zervas 'wishes free plebiscite end of war and I believe would accept whatever results but am certain would fight enforced return King or establishment Communism'.[33] He added that Zervas and himself both feared 'free plebiscite may be frustrated by EAM'. He went on: 'EAM represent many parties but controlling party extremely left-wing with headquarters Athens radiating strict control civil groups throughout country.' He emphasised that only if the British Government

gave proof of its determination to suppress any attempt at a *coup d'état* by
EAM 'any time whatever cost', and to ensure a free plebiscite at the end
of the war, could a civil war ('otherwise certain later') be avoided.

Myers's message was acknowledged in a telegram from Cairo dated
29 January. It stated that the matter of a plebiscite was being discussed
with the Anglo-Greek Committee with a view to making recommendations to the British and Greek Governments.[34] It further asked whether
Myers feared EAM would frustrate a plebiscite 'for fear of Royalist success
or in order to forestall non-Communist followers of Plastiras'. Myers
replied on 3 February that only the Royalists believed in a Royalist
success, and the sole fear of EAM was of non-Communist Republicans.[35]
He had not yet explicitly identified the leaders of EAM as Communists,
but on 24 February he sent a telegram reporting that the 'chief member'
of the Central Committee encountered in Athens (meaning Siantos) was
'avowedly Communist', though he looked upon Professor Alexander
Svolos of Athens University as the organisation's 'non-playing captain'.[36]
The telegram added for the first time: 'I believe Communists control
EAM unknown to most members.' From this date, if not earlier, it was
unmistakably necessary to handle the Greek situation with the utmost
delicacy.

Myers had already adopted two principles. One was to request, in a
telegram dated 24 January, that nothing having the 'remotest connection'
with military purposes should be infiltrated 'unless arranged or con-
fidentially approved by me';[37] but this request was not respected. The
other was to try to persuade the leaders of EAM to come out into the
open. They mostly showed little enthusiasm for taking to the mountains,
but on 21 February Myers reported that they wished to send representatives to Cairo.[38] He recommended that this should be agreed, and he
had already made provisional arrangements for their evacuation from
Greece (presumably by a clandestine sea route). Such a plan was consistent
with the proposal mooted at the same time by Leeper, the new British
Ambassador to the Greek Government in Cairo, who wanted 'to try to
bring together, both from Greece and the Middle East, representatives of
all Greek parties to meet in Cyprus or the Lebanon under British auspices,
in order to form the widest Coalition Government'.[39] But the plan hung
fire for a fatally long interval, in a mood of general indecision. Even the
KKE itself was in doubt about its own policy. Its plans, in the words of
an American historian, 'while crudely Marxist and pro-Soviet, were
vague and undeveloped'.[40]

Two questions divided the Communist leaders: whether power should
be sought by legal or revolutionary means, and whether the cities or the

mountains should take priority. Many regarded ELAS as less important than EEAM (the National Workers Liberation Front), especially after the latter's success in organising a general strike in Athens on 22 December 1942, and in frustrating the German plans for the conscription of labour in February–March 1943. Siantos continued to believe, even after he left Athens for the mountains, that the centre of power lay in the cities. Aris Veloukhiotis disagreed. Although he had been discouraged by the local committee of EAM in Lamia from taking part in the Gorgopotamos operation, and indeed had standing orders to the contrary, he had done so on his own initiative, no doubt to ensure that Zervas did not win all the credit.[41] In the wake of that success, he pursued a campaign of recruitment throughout Roumeli. His example was followed by Karagiorgis in Thessaly and by others (including Bulgarian Communists) in Macedonia. Once Aris was convinced of the opportunities, he hastened to Athens in February 1943 to persuade the Central Committee. He even urged 'the entire leadership of the party to come out to the mountains'.[42] Tzimas, the one leading Communist who shared his views, was allowed to go back to the mountains with him, with a mandate to set up a GHQ of ELAS, though still under tight control from Athens.

They had to act quickly if they were to succeed, for in the meantime Saraphis had established himself in Thessaly, with Kostopoulos under his command, and Psaros was expected soon in the area of Mount Parnassus. Saraphis had concerted his plans with Myers and Zervas, though the former was not greatly impressed by him; nor did either of them know that an officer accompanying him, Major Theodore Makridis (known as Ektor Politis) was in fact a member of the KKE.* On Saraphis's own initiative, which Myers accepted, Kostopoulos, Psaros and Zervas undertook to call their forces 'National Bands', and to operate under the direct control of GHQ, Middle East.[43]

Their hope was that ELAS would either be obliged to follow their example, or be cut off from British support. If EAM was to monopolise the struggle, therefore, a rapid reaction was needed. The first blow was struck by Karagiorgis even before Aris and Tzimas had arrived from Athens. On the night of 1 March, ELAS surrounded and disarmed the forces of Saraphis and Kostopoulos in a village of Thessaly, taking them

---

* Makridis was probably the ablest Communist officer in the Greek regular army. He became a member of the Central Committee of ELAS in the rising of December 1944 (*Levkí Vívlos*, p. 72). His fate in the 'third round' is obscure. He is said to have taken part in the planning in 1946 (Zapheiropoulos, p. 76), and was blamed for its inadequacy (Vlandas's MS, p. 68). But one account says that he refused to take part in the 'third round' and was allowed to emigrate (Kousoulas, p. 215n.); another that he was captured, tortured, driven mad and committed to a mental hospital (*Deuxième livre bleu*, p. 59).

both prisoner. There were threats that they would be tried for treason and executed, but on the arrival of Tzimas soberer counsels prevailed. After some days of humiliation both were released. Kostopoulos abandoned the struggle; but Saraphis, who had already formed doubts about his role and had become convinced that ELAS had the better cause, unexpectedly accepted an invitation to become Commander-in-Chief of ELAS. Myers, who arrived on the scene as these events took place, thought that his intervention had saved Saraphis's life; but in fact it was no longer in danger, nor was it correct to believe that Saraphis was converted 'at the point of a pistol'.[44]

From the point of view of the KKE, an important success had been achieved, because ELAS needed senior regular officers. They had made repeated approaches to Psaros, Saraphis, Zervas and others; but hostility to Communism had hitherto kept most of them at a distance. Each had his own political organisation; EKKA (National and Social Liberation) supported Psaros, AAA supported Saraphis and EDES supported Zervas. Being unable to convert them, the KKE sought to destroy them. Aris had threatened Zervas unsuccessfully in December within a few weeks of their co-operation at the Gorgopotamos. On 13 March a further ultimatum in opprobrious terms was sent to Zervas by another ELAS commander, threatening to 'drive him and all his forces into the sea'.[45] In May, with the sanction of Siantos, Aris attacked and disarmed Psaros as soon as he took the field. Saraphis, who had little sense of irony, then tried to persuade Psaros to follow his own example. But Tzimas more prudently explained to Myers that it was all due to a misunderstanding: Psaros would be allowed to re-form his band, and even given priority for supplies. There were thus to be three Resistance organisations enjoying equal recognition: EAM/ELAS, EDES (Zervas) and EKKA (Psaros). The change by EAM to a more co-operative relationship with the British was due to Tzimas's belief that there were better ways of monopolising the Resistance than brute force.

Attacks on rival guerrillas nevertheless continued throughout the summer of 1943, in a dual policy of aggression and reconciliation. Minor bands, such as those of Athos Roumeliotis and brigands like Karalivanos, were put out of action for good. Officers under Zervas's command who sought to establish themselves in new areas were similarly disbanded. Khoutas was repeatedly attacked, but vigorously defended himself. In Macedonia the forces of YVE (PAO) were dispersed and accused of collaboration with the enemy. There was some justice in the accusation, because Greek nationalists, like Mihailović in Yugoslavia, regarded the Germans as a less serious enemy than the Bulgarians or the Communists.[46]

But the label of 'collaboration' was attached by the KKE to anyone who was not in ELAS: they were all guilty of 'dividing the struggle', which came to the same thing. At the same time it was claimed by Tzimas that the policy of allowing 'traitors' like Kostopoulos to escape with their lives 'raised to a pinnacle the prestige of the KKE'.[47]

The KKE was sensitive about its reputation, which was suffering both in Greece and abroad from the impetuosity of activists like Aris. Opinion in the Central Committee was never unanimous and often confused. Hard-liners believed that there was no alternative to violent revolution. Others believed that events would move their way without force if they were carefully manipulated. The key factor was the unpopularity of the King, who was associated with dictatorship and defeat. When he retreated to Crete in 1941, it seemed natural to appoint a Cretan, Emmanuel Tsouderos, as his Prime Minister. But like a majority of Cretans, Tsouderos was a Venizelist and a republican. As he broadened his Government in 1942–3, more and more avowed republicans entered it, including the younger Venizelos. The Greek forces in the Middle East were also infected with republicanism, and even with Communism. A so-called Anti-Fascist Organisation of the Army (ASO), with branches in the other armed services, was formed on Communist initiative in October 1941, but it was later declared that 'there was no regular liaison between ASO in Cairo and EAM in Athens'.[48] Somewhat later (probably in 1942 or 1943) an organisation of right-wing royalist officers, the Sacred Bond of Greek Officers (IDEA), was also formed within the army in Egypt.

When mutinies occurred in the Greek forces, it was usual to blame the KKE, although at least once royalist officers were the culprits.[49] Communism was also blamed for other causes of anxiety, such as the determination of the Bulgarians to annexe Greek Macedonia, the provocation of German reprisals, and the threat of anarchy in Greece. As rumours from the mountains seemed to confirm the worst fears of patriotic conservatives, both republican and monarchist leaders intervened against the Resistance. Two of Greece's most senior Generals, the republican Pangalos and the royalist Papagos, both discouraged army officers from fighting in the mountains. The attitude of the Greek Government in exile was similar: their earliest emissaries to occupied Greece gave no hint of contemplating guerrilla activities.[50] In February 1943 a document came into Zervas's hands containing a warning to loyal officers from the King's Government against EDES as well as ELAS.[51] In this case the effect was unexpected. Zervas clearly could not withdraw from the struggle, and he resented the insinuation. But he had come to think that Communism was a greater danger than the monarchy, and he was aware of the British

Government's attachment to the latter. Fortuitously, it was suggested to him that he might send a friendly message to the King on the occasion of Independence Day (25 March). In fact he went much further. On 9 March he sent a long telegram to the Greek King and Government which contained a new statement of policy on the constitutional question:

> If King returns here result free opinion our people we will be first to welcome and consider Greece constitutional quarrels ended. If England for wider reasons and even without people's wishes wants return of King we fighting for liberation will not oppose at all.[52]

Zervas thus recanted his life-long republicanism, which he used to attribute to an incident in his youth when King Constantine I had humiliated him at the Officer Cadets' School.[53] The change precipitated a crisis within EDES, since Zervas told no one (not even Pyromaglou, his Second-in-Command) what he had done.[54] But it also, as was his intention, brought him into accord with British policy, which was to achieve the maximum resistance to the Occupation without compromising the future position of the King. The policy was a pragmatic compromise between the views of the military authorities and those of the Foreign Office, which expressed the two minds of the British Government in their directives to SOE. At first there had been no clear directive looking beyond the attack on the Gorgopotamos bridge, because the dramatic expansion of resistance which followed it had been unexpected. When a long-term policy had to be formulated under pressure of circumstances, it was at first confused.[55] There seems to have been no consultation in the process with the Greek Government, which was in a state of crisis at the time. But there was strong insistence by Churchill on the protection of the King's position, since he had proved himself a loyal ally and remained the only possible source of constitutional power, even if — which was not certain — he was temporarily unpopular among Greek politicians.

British policy towards occupied Greece does not command admiration, even allowing for the lack of first-hand knowledge on which it was based. A sympathetic American historian has argued, after examining all the available options, that there was no other practicable policy so far as the Resistance was concerned.[56] But that does not excuse the obstinacy with which incompatible objectives were pursued. In part the inconsistency was due to divided responsibility. Below the Cabinet, decision-making was shared between the Foreign Office, the Chiefs of Staff, and the Ministry of Economic Warfare, to which SOE was directly responsible. The staff of SOE, in contrast with those of SIS, were amateurs who had to learn on the job: there could naturally be no trained professionals, as in espionage, for a task which only existed in wartime.

The main handicap of SOE in Greece was faulty direction, not practical incompetence. It was required by a directive from the Chiefs of Staff in November 1942 'to give all-out support to guerrilla warfare, even to the extent of prejudicing the activities of secret groups'.[57] But it was also required to safeguard the position of the King, which could only have been done by ensuring that there was no resistance at all. Such an alternative was illusory in practice, since resistance had already begun, mainly on the initiative of anti-monarchists, before any British officers arrived in Greece; and it was certain to grow whether they wished it or not. The implications of this dilemma had to be carefully worked out. Meanwhile, SOE was obliged to take urgent action on the directive of November 1942. Since that ran counter to the cautiously exploratory plans on which action had so far been based, the first responses to the directive were somewhat hasty and ill-conceived.

For a start, SOE cancelled the original intention to evacuate the majority of the British parachutists who had taken part in Operation Harling (the Gorgopotamos viaduct). Instead of a small liaison group of two or three men, all twelve were obliged to stay in Greece, and Myers was ordered to draw up plans for widespread activity. Hence the British Military Mission came into being. A second change of plan was to parachute new teams into various parts of Greece, particularly Thessaly and Macedonia, whose officers were not immediately placed under Myers's command. One of these officers, Major Sheppard in Mount Olympus, was quickly taken in hand by Karagiorgis, who successfully concealed his Communist affiliations. Sheppard became an enthusiastic mouth-piece for EAM, and hence unwittingly for the KKE. Myers severely criticised Sheppard for allowing himself to be persuaded that EAM was 'purely a military resistance movement' which had 'no political aims whatsoever'. At the same time Myers was himself unjustly criticised by one of his own officers for being unable 'to understand how dangerous they were'.[58]

The clumsy policy of SOE was partly inspired by a continuing suspicion of Zervas. It was even thought in Cairo that Zervas had Myers's group of officers under his control. At the same time SOE was itself under suspicion of pursuing policies of its own in Greece, without too close a regard to the policy of the British Government. These suspicions were partly due to the fact that SOE was responsible not to the Foreign Office but to the Ministry of Economic Warfare. The outcome of a reconsideration of policy towards the Greek Resistance was a new formula drafted in London in April 1943, which required that SOE should be 'closely guided by the Foreign Office' as well as maintaining 'close contact with Commander-in-Chief, Middle East'.[59]

The Joint Planning Staff of the Commanders-in-Chief in Cairo reacted critically to these words, on which they commented that 'operational rather than political considerations are at present paramount'.[60] The plain inference was that the short-term military requirements and the long-term political requirements were in conflict, but there was a deep reluctance to admit it. In SOE there were already those who foresaw civil war after the liberation of Greece, and put forward recommendations for forestalling it as early as September 1942.[61] But Foreign Office officials commented that 'the assumptions were improbable and the recommendations impracticable'. They preferred to trust to British arms and prestige when the time came to avert such an upheaval. At the same time they recognised that by encouraging resistance, and in particular by supporting republican leaders, SOE was laying up trouble for the future; and they would have preferred what they called 'an inactive sabotage policy'.[62] Those responsible for military planning, however, took an opposite view.

In their argument with the Foreign Office, the planning staff of the Commanders-in-Chief invoked a recent directive from Churchill himself, which laid it down that while SOE should favour monarchist forces, others should not be disregarded if they were militarily effective.[63]

The directive to Myers which emerged from the conflict of views was necessarily a compromise. In effect, it was a licence to support both Zervas and ELAS; and the former had gained no special advantage from his message to the King on 9 March. The directive concluded that in the circumstances 'after the liberation of Greece, civil war is almost inevitable'; but Myers replied that it would not be so if the King could be persuaded to declare that he would not return to Greece until invited by a free plebiscite.[64]

No such undertaking was forthcoming, and both Zervas and ELAS continued as before. Both gained some advantage from the circumstances created by the new directive, which Myers had received in the last week of April 1943. There was a greatly increased flow of officers to join Zervas, but in sheer numbers of rank and file ELAS had a huge advantage. Zervas's force was virtually a private army, dominated by a single personality and limited to his native territory in north-west Greece. Its strength probably did not exceed about 5,000 throughout 1943. ELAS was a nationwide force built up by expert organisation on the basis of years of clandestine experience. It grew from rather less than 5,000 men in the spring of 1943 to between 35,000 and 40,000 people strong six months later.[65] The accession of Saraphis opened the prospect of building a regular force, professionally trained and staffed, in the place of guerrilla bands; and that was his own ambition. But at first he was not successful in attracting the officers he needed. The circumstances of his conversion were open to suspicion. Tzimas insisted that Saraphis should therefore visit Athens to clear himself with the Central Committee of EAM and with his former colleagues in AAA. Among the latter, Grigoriadis and Papandreou appeared to be sympathetic. Both Tzimas and Saraphis gained the impression, mistakenly as it turned out, that Papandreou would soon take to the mountains himself to assume a political role in the Resistance, even perhaps as head of a 'government'.[66]

When Saraphis and Tzimas returned from Athens to the mountains, they joined Aris in establishing the first GHQ of ELAS on 20 May. The site already chosen for the GHQ (though it was not set up there until July) was Pertouli in Thessaly, where Saraphis had family connections.[67] Like each subordinate HQ of ELAS it consisted of three equal members: a political adviser (Tzimas), a military commander (Saraphis) and a *kape-tánios* or popular leader (Aris). All three had to decide unanimously on any operation, a rule which handicapped co-operation with other Greek organisations and with the British Military Mission. An immediate instance of the difficulty occurred when the BMM wished to mount another major attack on the railway line through Greece. As the railway ran wholly through territory dominated by ELAS, it was impossible to enlist Zervas's forces. But the target selected by Myers, the bridge over the River Asopos, was declared by Saraphis to be impracticable. In the event a small group of British officers attacked and destroyed the Asopos bridge unaided on 24 June, while ELAS carried out a substitute operation devised by Saraphis, which consisted of blowing up a railway-tunnel at Tyrnavos. The destruction of the Asopos bridge was of some importance, but the Tyrnavos tunnel was closed for only two days, at the cost of 92 Italian and 160 Greek lives.[68]

Saraphis deceived himself that the operation he had mounted was as gratifying to Myers as to himself. Their different accounts of it are ironically revealing.[69] But Saraphis's obstinacy was symptomatic of his merits as well as his weaknesses. He did not wish ELAS to become a mere instrument of the British, least of all one whose units acted under the orders of British officers, most of them only wartime soldiers. He wanted a regular army under his direct command, responsible only to the British Commander-in-Chief in the Middle East. A regular army presupposed an established state and government: and since that was what the KKE also wanted, the aims of Saraphis and Tzimas coincided. The two men spent the summer of 1943 co-operating to impose their conception of the role of Resistance on Myers and the British Military Mission, whose instructions were different. The British authorities wanted not a regular army but a loose confederation of independent guerrillas whose operations they could control through British Liaison Officers. The crux of the protracted struggle between Myers, Tzimas and Saraphis was the concept of National Bands, which Saraphis himself had originally propounded, but which he had abjured on joining ELAS.

All three men wrote accounts of their tussle, which are generally accurate and complementary.[70] It lasted from April to July 1943. The opening gambit was a draft agreement, presented by Myers, on the conduct and control of the National Bands. They were to respect and co-operate with each other, to permit free recruitment in each other's areas, and to receive orders and supplies from GHQ Middle East through the British Liaison Officers. Tzimas saw that the British did not want a mass movement but a few small bands controlled by reliable Greek or British officers. He took the draft to Athens and returned with a rival draft, approved by his Central Committee, which differed in two major respects: it proposed firstly to eliminate the predominant role of British officers, restricting them to mere communication; and secondly to establish a Joint GHQ comprising three members of ELAS (because of their tripartite system of command) and one each from the other recognised organisations (such as Zervas and Psaros) together with Myers. On reference to GHQ in Cairo, Myers was told the revised draft was unacceptable.

He was under pressure, however, to obtain co-operation from ELAS as well as from Zervas in a major series of operations in June and July. Operation Animals was designed to create the impression on the enemy that the landings planned against Sicily were really directed at Greece. It was obviously necessary to wrap the purpose of the plan in extreme secrecy, especially as the security of the Resistance organisations (except for the KKE) was poor.[71] To obtain the necessary co-operation without revealing the real purpose, Myers felt compelled gradually to retreat from the position originally taken up towards ELAS, since without ELAS most of the intended targets would be unattainable. Unknown to him, Tzimas was also under strong pressure from Siantos to obtain a signed agreement at almost any price. Tzimas wrote later:

> Signature was much required politically in the towns to neutralise the campaign of reactionary bourgeois circles and collaborators with the enemy, that by the guerrilla movement we were making no worthwhile contribution to the allies, but only causing damage and

inflicting on the population the torments and reprisals of the occupation.[72]

In other words, EAM desperately needed the respectability of British recognition as an allied force.

Conciliation happened also to be the theme of Soviet policy towards the Western Allies at the time. On 22 May 1943 it was announced in Moscow that the Comintern had been dissolved (with effect from a week earlier). The Central Committee of the KKE welcomed the decision in a resolution dated 2 June, which stated with some uncertainty that

> while awaiting the final goal of socialism, the party of the proletariat, the KKE, fights today for national liberation, but after the war will fight for a people's democracy, when it must be transformed into the party of the broad working masses, a party of millions of members, a party of a people's régime in Greece.

The resolution also declared that the people's democracy 'will at the beginning have a parliamentary form'. It was criticised later from opposite points of view. The Yugoslav leader, Tempo (Svetozar Vukmanović), was indignant that the KKE would attempt to establish a people's democracy only after the war; Papandreou was equally indignant that the parliamentary guise would be only a temporary bluff.[73] Already, in fact, a tactical division was emerging between the Yugoslav and Greek Communists. The former had had a sharp brush with their Soviet allies as early as February 1943, though the occasion was no more than a decision to parley with the Germans over prisoners of war.[74] The KKE, however, was still completely subservient to Stalinist policy, as indicated by the dissolution of the Comintern. In the same spirit, on 28 May 1943, ELAS GHQ issued an extraordinarily conciliatory order about conduct towards other National Bands.[75]

Tzimas even persuaded Saraphis that ELAS should co-operate in Operation Animals as if the draft agreement with the BMM had been signed, even if it had not. In retrospect it seems that Myers could have risked taking a more unyielding stand. It is also arguable that the operations were not sufficiently important to justify the high price eventually paid for them. The operations were a once-for-all blow; the price was continuing recognition. Once again there was conflict between the military and political priorities. GHQ Middle East was insistent upon the operations, but although they were in the end expressly approved by Eden in London, he gave his consent only with reluctance.[76] In the event,

Tzimas and Saraphis had their own way. The military agreement was signed, virtually as they had drafted it, on 5 July 1943, when the operations were already in progress and nearing their climax. They obtained agreement to the Joint GHQ and the down-grading of the role of British Liaison Officers. There was also an open-ended commitment to finance the guerrillas at the rate of one gold sovereign a month *per caput*, and another for the maintenance and relief of their families.

The circumstances in which the financial decision was taken are not altogether clear from the only first-hand account available.[77] Some such arrangement seems to have been first discussed between Myers and Saraphis as early as February, when the latter was still independent.[78] It was apparently intended that the money should be used to buy food for the guerrillas, their families and other destitute Greeks. Since the mountain areas could never be self-supporting, this seemed to be the only way to attract supplies from the more fertile plains. Greek paper currency was suffering from uncontrollable inflation, so that apart from barter (for example, with parachute-silk) the gold sovereign was the only acceptable unit of exchange. It had the purchasing power of about five pounds sterling, which suggests that in the circumstances the provision was not lavish. The total of sovereigns brought into Greece by various British agencies during the Occupation (though not attributable exclusively to the Military Mission) reached about two million.[79] The influx aggravated the inflationary spiral; it created an attitude of mind which became embodied in the contemptuous slogan of the 'Golden Resistance'; and it gave the guerrilla organisations an incentive to recruit without limit and to inflate their strength with spurious names. Since it had always been Zervas's practice to pay for goods and services, the chief beneficiary of the new system was ELAS, which had hitherto relied on forced contributions, and probably continued to do so. The sovereigns were retained for other purposes.

The main success of Tzimas's diplomacy, however, was to have obtained British recognition of ELAS as an allied force under the command of GHQ, Middle East. It was confirmed in a flattering message, dated 22 June 1943, from the Commander-in-Chief, General Wilson, who always regarded ELAS as militarily the best force available.[80] A less sanguine view was taken in the Foreign Office of the consequences of recognising ELAS, but for the present military necessity prevailed. British military commanders did not regard themselves as overmuch concerned with political consequences, provided that they had diplomatic advisers to take care of them; and the Foreign Office sometimes seemed to regard military successes as of secondary importance in comparison with post-war considerations. From this division of purpose the KKE benefited. Communist leaders attached extraordinary importance to British recognition, and constantly complained that the successes of ELAS were insufficiently publicised. Tzimas therefore regarded the signature of the agreement in July 1943 as a turning-point of great importance, which he believed that Soviet diplomacy had indirectly helped to bring about.[81]

The KKE's motives in agreeing to co-operate with the BMM were misunderstood by their enemies both at the time and afterwards. It was widely supposed that the main motives were to obtain arms and money; but these requirements played only a secondary part in the decision. Supplies of arms from British sources were never large. Communist figures give, for example, a total of 3,300 rifles and light automatics supplied by the British, as against a total of 41,500 surrendered early in 1945. Even allowing for distortion and miscounting, the difference in order of magnitude is unmistakable.[82] Their other sources of supply are not entirely speculative. Apart from enemy booty and purchases on the black market, it has been alleged that by June 1943 ELAS had acquired control of 'the greater part of the light arms which the Greek Army had avoided surrendering to the Germans and Italians, and had hidden all over the Greek countryside'; and another large accretion was to follow in October 1943, when the arms of the Pinerolo Division (which were said to include reserve stocks for double the establishment of the Division) were seized after the Italian capitulation.[83] Compared to equipment on this scale, British supplies were a drop in the ocean. The supply of sovereigns was more important, especially when it was accompanied by an injudicious message from General Wilson on 18 July 1943 requesting the guerrillas to remain passive for the time being but to 'concentrate on further selective recruitment'.[84] Much was to be made by Communist propaganda of this open-ended invitation. But the greatest prize they gained was allied recognition and consequent respectability.

Although Siantos and Tzimas were pleased about the agreement, other Communists later expressed a more unfavourable view. Dimitrios Vlandas, who rose to prominence in the 'third round', said in his reminiscences that the subordination of ELAS to the British GHQ, carried out by 'the then leadership of the KKE behind the back of the Central Committee', was one of 'the specific acts of treachery which led to our defeat'.[85] Zakhariadis declared in 1950 that during the Occupation the KKE failed to give EAM correct guidance, as a result of which ELAS became a tool of British policy.[86] The Yugoslav leader, Tempo, attributed this subservience to 'the supremacy within the leadership of paid agents' of British imperialism.[87] He blamed the leadership of the KKE for other shortcomings: for giving priority to national liberation rather than revolutionary struggle, for treating partisan warfare as an incidental activity, for avoiding battle in order not to provoke reprisals, for basing their military organisation on local recruitment, for admitting too many of the officer corps into ELAS, for concealing from the rank and file that they were really Communists, for compromising with the bourgeoisie, and so on.[88] In particular, he argued that the military agreement only benefited the British and 'Zervas's quisling forces'. On many of the above points an almost exactly contrary view was argued by an old member of the KKE, I. Petsopoulos, whose fate was to be expelled from the party in 1946.[89] If all these various analyses of the situation had been known to the British authorities at the time of the negotiations, they might well have concluded that they had been more successful than they thought, and that with a little more resolution they could have largely neutralised the revolutionary elements in EAM.

At least, however, they had secured the co-operation of ELAS in the cover plan for the allied landings in Sicily (Operation Animals). The success of the operation is testified by German sources; and since the Germans were convinced that an allied landing on the west coast of Greece was imminent, the role of Zervas's forces was just as important as that of ELAS, if not more so.[90] But Zervas himself was disappointed by the political developments. Having already made his own accommodation with the Greek and British authorities, and having accepted the National Bands agreement in its original form, he now had to be cajoled into accepting the successive modifications of it as negotiated between Myers and Tzimas. With some reluctance, he signed the final text a few days after ELAS, and agreed to attend the first meeting of the Joint GHQ on 18 July at Pertouli in Thessaly. But he sensed that the atmosphere of co-operation was unreal; he accused the British of letting him down; and he began to reconsider his own position. The accusation that he entered into a secret understanding with the Germans at this time was premature. But he was becoming increasingly separated both from his republican associates in the field, especially Pyromaglou, and also from those in Athens, such as Gonatas, who were more unscrupulous about collaborating with the enemy in order to defeat the Communist danger.[91] Eventually Zervas was persuaded by the former to disown the latter; but the crisis in EDES was never resolved.

There was a crisis within EAM as well as within EDES in the summer of 1943, though it was better concealed. Pyromaglou noted that there appeared to be a conflict in the upper levels of the KKE 'between the moderate and uncompromising elements'. Many familiar dilemmas remained unresolved: whether to concentrate on the cities or the mountains; whether to emphasise or conceal the organisation's Communist basis; whether to aim at revolution or constitutional change; whether to co-operate with the British or oppose them. Desertion became common among the officers and other ranks of ELAS, many of whom preferred to join Zervas or Psaros.[92] Several leading guerrillas were hostile to the policies of the Politburo – among them, Aris Veloukhiotis, Orestis and Markos Vaphiadis, all of whom were later expelled from the KKE.[93] It was later noted that 'not a single man who joined the Party from the Resistance was admitted to the top échelons of the Party leadership'.[94] In fact, an attitude of suspicion prevailed among orthodox Communists towards the whole concept of resistance, as was to be observed in other East European countries after the war. But the instinctive discipline of Communism was sufficient to keep such friction out of sight. EAM continued to present a monolithic front to the world.

By the later summer of 1943, the Resistance had become a major factor in Anglo-Greek relations and the politics of war. Outside Greece, particularly in monarchist circles and the Foreign Office, it was regarded as a wholly troublesome factor. Inside Greece, opinions were divided between fear and admiration. Through EAM, the KKE was on its way to creating an alternative state, for which it was already seeking a respectable leadership, by overtures to such men as Papandreou and Svolos. It had an armed force for which Saraphis was developing a professional backbone: his memoirs spoke of a general staff, training schools, medical services, communications, courts martial and a Supreme Army Council. In other words, the transition was being made from guerrilla to conventional warfare. At the same time, the excesses of ELAS had earned it an unsavoury reputation, which enabled the Germans, with the help of prominent Greeks like Pangalos and Gonatas, to form the Security Battalions to combat the Resistance. Papandreou recorded that at the end of the year Athenian crowds actually cheered the Security Battalions as they paraded through the streets.[95] Equally discreditable in the eyes of patriotic Greeks were the political connections of EAM with Communist Parties abroad.

These connections were real but remote. The KKE probably had no contact with Moscow, except through Tito, until the summer of 1944. But in June 1943 a major gathering took place at Tsotyli in Macedonia, which was attended by Tempo on behalf of the Yugoslav Partisans, and by an Albanian Communist, but no Bulgarians. Tempo (Svetozar Vukmanović), a Montenegrin whom Tito had put in command of operations in Yugoslav Macedonia at the beginning of 1943, had little respect for the Greeks. He aimed at the incorporation of Greek Macedonia with his own country, as he wrote frankly in a letter to the Central Committee of the Yugoslav CP in August 1943.[96] The proposal to establish a GHQ of all the Balkan guerrillas, which he advanced at Tsotyli, had this object in view. It was suspected by the ELAS leaders, who had no intention at the time of being party to the cession of Greek territory. Saraphis rejected Tempo's proposal on the ground that ELAS, being under the command of the British GHQ in Cairo, could not also subordinate itself to a Balkan GHQ. Tempo was indignant at this attitude of purported loyalty to the British, who were still supporting the Partisans' enemy, Mihailović. The Albanian representative confined himself to discreet pleasantries.

Myers, who was present at Tsotyli, was conscious of distrust between the Greek, Yugoslav and Albanian leaders.[97] Of the public speeches on 29 June which he reported, only that by Tzimas was revealing. Tempo delivered a conventional attack on Mihailović, and the Albanian representative another on King Zog. Karagiorgis extolled ELAS and the Yugoslav Partisans, regretting that the latter were not supported by the British. In private, but in Myers's hearing, Tempo proposed 'an independent Macedonian Resistance Movement', which the Greeks received coldly.[98] The only public reference to Macedonia was by Tzimas, who accused the Germans of 'promising Bulgaria part of Macedonia and Yugoslavia part of Albania' in order to split the Balkan countries. He emphasised that EAM must desist from its 'past intolerance of other organisations', and must 'deal most tactfully with our minorities, particularly in Macedonia'. He even spoke of a 'higher command' of all the Balkan countries, and added that ELAS had been invited to send a band into Yugoslavia and another into Albania.

Evidently EAM was under some pressure from the Yugoslavs at this time. Tempo urged the Greeks to sanction the formation within ELAS of self-contained units of the Slavo-Macedonian National Liberation Front (SNOF), a pro-Tito organisation. Nor were Tempo's energies employed solely on the Greeks: he had visited the Albanian CP on his way to Tsotyli, and afterwards went on to visit the Bulgarians in pursuit of his plan for a Balkan GHQ.[99] But ELAS GHQ was his most important target, and he found the Greek Communists divided. Tzimas, Siantos and Ioannidis all met him before the conference at Tsotyli. Siantos expressed his usual reservations about guerrilla warfare in the mountains. 'He who ruled Athens ruled Greece,' Tempo quoted him as saying; and he added that 'the Athenian workers would be organised into military formations, so that at the moment of liberation they could seize the city.'[100] Tempo was not impressed, and Tzimas sympathised with him.

There was also the dilemma between giving priority to co-operation with the British and also with the other Balkan Communists. Again Tzimas favoured Tempo's plan, but Siantos and Ioannidis overruled him.[101] Still, Tzimas gained something from his friendly relation with Tempo, whom he persuaded to refrain from preaching Communism publicly in Greece. This was in accordance with Stalin's notions of resistance in the Balkans, but not with Tito's or Tempo's. It is also possible – so Tzimas believed – that the mere presence of a Yugoslav Partisan in Greek Macedonia influenced the British to reach a settlement with EAM over the terms of the military agreement.

It was plain, however, that the KKE was playing second fiddle to the Partisans, who had been active in the field a year longer and owed nothing to the British. A Balkan GHQ would have been dominated by Tito, and would have facilitated the eventual absorption by Yugoslavia of both Greek and Bulgarian Macedonia. Surprisingly, Tempo's plan was repudiated both by Tito, as 'a mistake and even harmful', and by Stalin as 'basically wrong'.[102] Both insisted that the organisation of Resistance should be limited by existing national boundaries. The KKE was therefore left to go its own way, despite Tempo's indignation and contempt for ELAS. At Tsotyli, and at a further conference which followed it a week later at Kastania in Thessaly, these under-currents were concealed. Myers, however, was conscious of the independent attitudes of the Communist leaders both towards their allies and towards each other. He detected among them a 'determination to set up independent regimes' after the war, 'unfettered to or by any major power'.[103] These words, implying that the Yugoslav Partisans would prove just as unamenable to Soviet domination as EAM to British domination, were written just when the British Government was on the brink of transferring its support from Mihailović to Tito. They made a prescient forecast.

That British policy towards the Balkans in the summer of 1943 was still determined primarily by wartime considerations was clear from the decision to give undivided support to Tito and the Partisans. Political consequences in Yugoslavia were to take second place. Over Greece opinions were more divided. On 9 July 1943 (the day on which Sicily was successfully invaded) SOE commented adversely on a warning from the British Mission in Greece about the 'post-war embarrassment' liable to be caused by the continuing policy of arming the Greek Resistance.[104] The warning had concluded: 'Am increasingly disturbed by possibilities of post-war uses (of) weapons now being provided.' The comment by SOE was that 'maximum effort' would be required for the operations to liberate Greece, and that 'post-war considerations must not prejudice its success'. Such a reaction was surprising at a time when Italy was clearly about to collapse, and when Myers's report on the conference at Tsotyli had shown how grave and far-reaching the post-war consequences might be. It was still, however, the view expressed by General Wilson at the end of the year.[105] The Foreign Office profoundly disagreed.

No special attempt seems to have been made to view British policy towards Greece and Yugoslavia in relation to each other. Nor was any made when the policies began to diverge in the autumn of 1943. In both cases there was a suspicion in London that SOE had been withholding important information from the Foreign Office, and even pursuing an independent foreign policy. The presumptions of bias over Greece and Yugoslavia were, as it happened, mutually contradictory, since it was necessary to postulate a pro-Communist bias in the one case and an anti-Communist bias in the other. But bewilderment led to suspicion, and suspicion to increased interest in the Balkans at the level of the Cabinet. Here again there was some division, since Churchill concentrated his attention mainly on Yugoslavia and Eden mainly on Greece. Each arranged within a few weeks to send a personal emissary into the field with a mandate to report at the highest level. Major David Wallace was sent to Greece in June 1943; Captain F. W. Deakin to Yugoslavia in May, followed by Brigadier Fitzroy Maclean as head of a Military Mission to Tito in September.

The implied lack of confidence in SOE was borne out by the reports of the new British representatives. Wallace's reports were damaging to ELAS, those of Deakin and Maclean favourable to the Partisans. There was justice in the contrast, for the achievements of the Partisans far exceeded those of their Greek comrades. The Partisans had been fighting in the mountains for at least a year longer than ELAS, and even if they had achieved no single coup of the importance of the Gorgopotamos or Asopos operations, they had held down much greater enemy forces. While the Greek guerrillas were withdrawing into the Pindus mountains on 26 November 1942 after their first major victory at the Gorgopotamos bridge, the Partisans were assembling on the same day for the first meeting of the Anti-Fascist National Liberation Council of Yugoslavia (AVNOJ) in liberated territory at Bihać – an event which the KKE could not emulate until eighteen months later. The military value of the Partisans had been proved, moreover, without any help from their allies. The British still concentrated their resources on Mihailović until mid-1943; and the Soviet Government, although it had regular wireless communication with Tito from February 1942, sent him no material help, little encouragement and much unwelcome advice.[106] German records show beyond doubt the value of the Partisans to the allied cause. They also suggest that the value of ELAS was greater than appeared at the time, though not to be compared with the Partisans.[107] More important, however, was the contrast between the decisions taken by the British Government on its assessment of the two situations. In essence, the decisions were to move towards meeting the political aspirations of the Partisans in full, but to resist those of EAM at almost any cost.

Superficially, these conclusions might be regarded as contradictory. Later, indeed, Churchill virtually admitted a contradiction: 'In one place we support a King, in another a Communist – there is no attempt by us to enforce particular ideologies.'[108] To the Greeks and Yugoslavs, who saw ELAS and the Partisans as cognate manifestations of Communism, the British attitude was puzzling. The Communists were naturally trying to equate Zervas with Mihailović, once the latter was discredited; but the facts were against them. Some attempts had been made by Zervas to establish contact with Mihailović; but the latest of these was in early May 1943, shortly before the British had made contact with the Partisans and abandoned Mihailović, from whom in any case no response was ever received.[109] It was possible for the British to abandon Mihailović, but not to abandon Zervas – the victor of the Gorgopotamos, whom they had themselves induced to take the field, and who had loyally fulfilled their every wish. It followed that there must be different policies towards the Communist Resistance movements in Yugoslavia and Greece. From that contrast flowed serious consequences in the post-war era, especially with regard to Macedonia.

The Communists also had their problems. The gathering at Tsotyli in June 1943 signalled the re-emergence of Macedonia as an issue which might divide Communists from each other, just as much as it divided other Greeks, Bulgarians and Yugoslavs. The Greek Communists handled the problem with extreme caution. Although the KKE had called on the Slavo-Macedonians to join the Resistance as early as January 1942, its spokesman, Zevgos, was careful to emphasise in July 1943 that the Slavophones were comparatively few in number.[110] Having conceded Tempo's request to allow the formation of Slavophone units within ELAS, they thought they had found a reliable leader for the purpose in a Macedonian Communist, Ilias Dimakis, also known in Greek as Gotsis;* but he proved to be a whole-hearted autonomist, much to the embarrassment of the KKE.[111] Their strictly cautious approach belies the accusation that the KKE was prepared to cede Greek Macedonia to an autonomous state, whether under Yugoslav or Bulgarian domination, though that was certainly the object of the Yugoslav and Bulgarian Communists. The two

---

* The name appears in Serbo-Croat as Goči, and in Bulgarian as Gotchev.

Slav CPs were in fact in bitter rivalry over the issue, and many of their
manoeuvres (such as Tito's creation of a Central Committee of the
Macedonian CP in July 1943) were really directed against each other.

The Comintern, which normally supported the Bulgarian CP over
Macedonia, had decided in 1941, on an appeal from Tito, to allocate
responsibility for resistance in Macedonia to the Yugoslav Partisans, evidently because of Stalin's respect for existing national boundaries. This
ruling was not superseded by the dissolution of the Comintern in May
1943. But the position of the KKE was hard to defend before Greek public
opinion, which saw them as betrayers of Greek territory. Much publicity
was later given to a document purporting to have been signed on 12 July
1943 at Petrich by Ioannidis, on behalf of the KKE, and a representative
of the Bulgarian CP, in which it was supposedly agreed that a Balkan
Soviet Federation would be set up after the war, including the whole of
Macedonia as an autonomous unit.[112] The story seems implausible and the
document doubtfully authentic. German intelligence officers, who first
saw the text when it was published by EDES in May 1944, were puzzled by
it, and therefore presumably did not forge it themselves.[113] Forgery being
a common instrument of Greek parties against each other, some cases (of
which this is one) provoke suspicion by being literally too damning to be
true.

Whatever may have been the case when Zakhariadis was in control, or
in times of extreme crisis in the KKE, the party's normal stance was one
of hesitation over Macedonia.* As Greeks, they recognised that the
majority of the population of Greek Macedonia was Greek in sentiment,
even including many whose first language was not Greek; and that the
northern frontier, however anomalous when it was established, had become as nearly complete an ethnic division as any in the Balkans. Their
determination to eliminate nationalist organisations like YVE (PAO) was
in the interests of monopolising the Resistance, not of betraying Greek
Macedonia. In this way they were never completely successful, because
suspicion of their motives was ineradicable. New nationalist bands
emerged against them in 1943-4, under Tsaous Andon (Antonios
Phosteridis) in eastern Macedonia and under Mikhalagas (Michael Papadopoulos) in the west; and endless troubles lay ahead for the Communists
in their attempts to assimilate the Slavo-Macedonians to ELAS. But to
Tzimas, with his roots in both nationalities, the problems did not seem
insoluble.

For a time, his optimism seemed justifiable. The Greek Communists

---

* Tzimas expressly assured me in 1969 that any attempt to detach Greek Macedonia, even if all the
countries concerned were under Communist rule, would have resulted in war between them.

were conscious in the summer of 1943 of riding on the crest of a wave, in the wake of their agreement with the British and the success of Operation Animals. Other Greeks were puzzled: not only Zervas, but also those in Athens and the Government and armed forces in exile. The disarray in Athens contrasted painfully with the self-confidence of the Communists. Republican politicians continued to send clandestine messages out calling for a clear statement by the King on his future position; Sophoulis wrote a letter to Tsouderos in this sense on 22 April. In July a senior Liberal, Exindaris, arrived in Cairo from Athens with a strong message that the return of the King without a plebiscite would be unacceptable. Monarchists in Athens were, by contrast, almost silent. Only General Papagos persuaded four of his fellow-generals to sign a declaration of loyalty on 20 May; but he was arrested soon afterwards, and deported to spend the rest of the war in Germany.

Most politicians in Athens preferred to wait and see. A few, including three successive Prime Ministers under the occupation (Tsolakoglou, Logothetopoulos and Rallis), felt it their duty to collaborate in order that the state and people might survive. Others collaborated more wholeheartedly, on the ground that Communism was more deadly than the Germans. Yet others, including such outstanding figures as Archbishop Damaskinos and Colonel Evert, the Chief of Police, carried out their official duties under the occupation while secretly helping the British and their agents. One of the most perceptive observers was Papandreou, who wrote a powerful memorandum in July 1943 to the Greek and British Governments on the threat posed by the KKE.[114] But neither he nor anyone else had a convincing policy to recommend against the threat, apart from insisting that the King must not return to Greece after the liberation until a plebiscite had been held on the constitution. The Communists alone went their own way, untainted by collaboration and seemingly indifferent to casualties, provided that their ends were achieved. In sincerity, ruthlessness and selfless dedication, they stood apart.

The Government in exile was in a state of natural perplexity. Its position was weak, and wholly dependent on British goodwill. It was a prey to rumours and hyper-sensitive to rebuffs. In December 1941 it had been horrified to learn from its Ambassador in Kuibyshev — mistakenly, as it turned out, but that hardly mitigated the effect — that Eden had discussed with Stalin in Moscow the cession to Turkey, as a reward for neutrality, of Chios and Mytilini, as well as the Dodecanese and Bulgarian territory.[115] Early in 1943 Eden inflicted a more substantial affront on Greek opinion by making a statement on the post-war independence of Albania.[116] Later in the same year the Greeks were again upset by the acceptance of the

Italians as 'co-belligerents'. Repeated mutinies in the Greek forces, particularly at the end of 1942 and in July 1943, weakened their prestige. The King's position was undermined by evidence of republican sentiment in Greece; even his own Prime Minister, Tsouderos, remained at heart a republican. Reluctantly, the King at last accepted his Cabinet's advice to clarify his position, but he would not agree to a plebiscite. On 4 July 1943 he issued a statement admitting that the Metaxas dictatorship had been illegal, confirming that the constitution of 1911 was still in force, but conceding no more than that elections to a Constituent Assembly would take place as soon as possible after the liberation of Greece. The implication, which Tsouderos confirmed, was that he would return with his troops.[117] This was precisely what the republicans would not accept; and the Communists, as the King's most vocal enemies, were the chief beneficiaries of his stubbornness.

3

War on Two Fronts
August 1943–April 1944

IN AUGUST 1943 the latent rivalry was suddenly brought to a crisis. Myers had organised the construction of a landing-strip for aircraft in Thessaly – the first in enemy-occupied Europe – to facilitate communications with Cairo. He agreed to take a small group of Resistance leaders with him on the first flight out of Greece, on the night of 9–10 August. Although he had the authority of SOE for doing so, several things had gone wrong. Because of overloaded wireless traffic, no one in London or Cairo knew in detail of the intention in advance, and the Foreign Office suspected that it had been deliberately misled by SOE. Myers had intended until the last minute to be accompanied only by one delegate from each of the recognised Resistance organisations. These were to have been Tzimas from EAM, Pyromaglou from EDES and Kartalis from EKKA. But his hand was forced by Siantos, who arrived at the landing-ground on 8 August to insist that EAM must have multiple representation. He claimed to have received a telegram through Cairo authorising EAM to send as many delegates as it wished. This was untrue, but at the time Myers felt obliged to give way, because otherwise Siantos would not allow even Tzimas to go.[1]

In the event, Myers was accompanied by an official party of seven. It consisted of Major Wallace (Eden's personal emissary); Tzimas, Tsirimokos, Despotopoulos and Petros Roussos, on behalf of EAM and associated organisations; and Pyromaglou and Kartalis on behalf of EDES and EKKA respectively. Pyromaglou, an intimate of Plastiras, had remained loyal to the original principles of EDES, but was losing faith in Zervas since the latter's attempt at reconciliation with the King.* Kartalis, a wealthy intellectual, fluent in English, French and German, was a former Populist who had veered towards republicanism. He and Pyromaglou became brothers-in-law after the war. They stood apart from the four

---

* Zervas often warned me that Pyromaglou had 'Communist leanings'; and he did in fact join the left-wing party EDA, a front for the Communists, after 1950. Pyromaglou later wrote of Zervas that his 'centralisation of power ... proved to be unwarranted and injurious' (Pyromaglou, *I ethniki antistasis*, p. 167).

representatives of EAM, all of whom except Tsirimokos were Communists. But all six delegates shared one common viewpoint towards the monarchy; and as soon as they arrived in Cairo, they gave emphatic expression to their republican views in a manner which caused consternation.

Several first-hand accounts, and many at second-hand, have been written of the delegation's visit to Cairo.[2] Of the first-hand accounts, those of Leeper and Tsouderos aim at self-justification. That of General Wilson shows limited understanding. The best are those of Myers and Pyromaglou, which complement each other. Together with Richard Clogg's study of the British Foreign Office papers, they provide a clear picture of this fateful episode in Greek history, which it is unnecessary to recapitulate in detail. The crux of the matter was that on 17 August a document was jointly presented by the delegation to the Greek Prime Minister, calling for an 'authoritative statement that the King will not return to Greece before the People has expressed itself on the form of the Constitution'. It was signed by Tsirimokos, Pyromaglou and Kartalis on behalf of the three Resistance organisations; by the three Communists, Tzimas, Despotopoulos and Petros Roussos; and also by Exindaris and Kanellopoulos as party leaders who had left Athens during the Occupation. The most uncompromising of all, according to Pyromaglou, were the non-Communist Republicans, particularly himself and Kartalis.[3] Two days later the whole of Tsouderos's Cabinet endorsed the declaration. Since the Prime Minister was a known Republican himself, the King was virtually confronted with a unanimous ultimatum.

The King consulted Churchill and Roosevelt by telegram before replying to the démarches. His telegram to Churchill referred to 'the lines we agreed upon before I left England' (of which Tsouderos later recorded that he had no information) and suggested that he ought to return to Greece with his Army even if he were later to leave for the time being.[4] Encouraged by a message on 29 August from Churchill (who was strongly supported by Smuts), and by a similar message from Roosevelt on 7 September, he resolutely refused to give way. Churchill's message expressly looked forward to 'your return to Greece at the head of your army and remaining there until the will of the Greek people is expressed under conditions of tranquillity', though until that moment the Foreign Office had not contemplated the King's return with the liberating forces.[5] Roosevelt's message, though less far-reaching, was also encouraging to the King. He had already agreed on 4 July to submit his position to the verdict of a Constituent Assembly after his return; he would not now agree to postpone his return until after a plebiscite.

Although he was forced to retreat further and further during the next eighteen months, each concession was made too late to stem the tide of republican hostility. The King never believed that his unpopularity was as great as it was made out to be. His handful of courtiers assured him that it was all invented by a handful of Communists. He was further persuaded that since the crisis had been precipitated solely by the ineptitude of SOE, and particularly by Myers, it could be overcome by sending the delegation back to Greece, but without Myers.

An objective view of the crisis was that taken by the US State Department. Roosevelt's support for the King was given against his officials' advice.[6] Their dissent from the British view of the constitutional issue had been explicit since December 1942, but in August 1943 they were compelled to give way. The US Ambassador to the Greek Government in Cairo was instructed to support his British colleague, Leeper, in deprecating any fresh statement by the King in response to the pressures of the Resistance delegation. On 22 August, at the Quebec Conference, Roosevelt joined Churchill in expressing satisfaction that the King 'was prepared to return to Greece as soon as possible and submit the question of the Royal House to plebiscite' at some unspecified later date. Later, on 8 October, the State Department formally notified the British Embassy in Washington that it had no further objection to the return of the King with his government, 'unless it should become clear during the military operations that such return would be overwhelmingly contrary to the wishes of the people and could only result in civil warfare'. Curiously enough, this victory for the King was followed fairly soon by a change of attitude in London, though not in the mind of Churchill himself.

The British authorities were divided over the crisis. The Embassy in Cairo and the Foreign Office shared the King's view, for without him there would be no constitutional basis for the future government of Greece. Churchill also had a sense of loyalty to the King, of which Myers was the natural victim. Although the King showed no personal hostility to Myers, the Foreign Office treated him with undisguised disapproval.[7] The military authorities considered that he was being unjustly victimised, and that ELAS, whatever its political colouring, was the most effective instrument of resistance. SOE, under severe criticism and shaken by internal convulsions, was in no position to assert its views. There was some hesitation before a final decision was taken. On 22 August the Resistance delegates were despatched to an Egyptian aerodrome, under strong protest, but their departure was cancelled at the last minute. They finally returned to Greece, by the same means as they had left, on the night of 16–17 September. With them were the first American officers to join

what now became the Allied Military Mission,* and also two Greeks who
had escaped from Athens some time before: Bakirdzis, the original
Prometheus; and Peltekis, who had rescued his successor, Prometheus II
(Koutsogiannopoulos), after his capture by the Germans. Bakirdzis, who
was a close friend of Psaros, surprisingly did not intend to join him in
supporting EKKA but to go to Macedonia to take up a senior command
under ELAS. Peltekis proceeded to Athens, where he established one of
the most successful organisations for secret intelligence and sabotage in
occupied Europe.

Myers did not return to Greece, though it was not until mid-November
that he was formally replaced in command of the Allied Military Mission.
His replacement was more welcome to Zervas than to ELAS.† At the
same time a radical reorganisation took place in SOE. The significance of
these changes was that, in future, considerations of long-term policy
would take precedence over short-term military requirements. A diametrically opposite reversal took place at the same time in Yugoslavia,
where the full weight of British support shifted from Mihailović to Tito.
No less significant were the changes in ELAS. Tzimas on his return from
Cairo made it clear that the delegation was extremely angry at its treatment, and that trouble would follow. What was not at once apparent was
that he himself would be a victim of the trouble. In the first half of
October Siantos personally took his place at ELAS GHQ, and shortly
afterwards Tzimas was sent on a mission to make contact with the Yugoslav Partisans. It was an ominous turn of events, which troubled the British
as much as the replacement of Myers troubled the Greek Communists.
The 'first round' of the civil war was the direct result of these changes.

Although some attempt was later made to conceal the fact, there is no
doubt that ELAS was the aggressor in October 1943. The fact that
clashes broke out simultaneously between ELAS and the nationalist
guerrillas all over Greece, from Epirus and Macedonia to the Peloponnese,
is evidence that the decision was taken by the only organisation which had
a nationwide system of control. The architect of the 'first round' was
Siantos, known to the Greek Communists as 'the Old Man'. His role
inescapably brought him into conflict with the British, but Siantos was
not anti-British, any more than he was a 'British agent', as Zachariadis
later called him. He assumed, like all Greeks, that Britain would remain
the major power in the Mediterranean, but he believed that Britain could

---

*The first ranking officer, Captain Winston Ehrgott of the US 7th Cavalry Regiment, was super-
seded in December by Major Gerald K. Wines.

† Saraphis at least once demanded my removal, as this would eliminate 'a cause of trouble between
us' (Saraphis, p. 84). He found Myers, as a fellow regular officer, easier to deal with. These attitudes
were not reciprocated (Myers, pp. 114, 149).

be compelled to accept a Communist Greece. He had been heard to speak warmly of Churchill: 'Ah! he knows people and things!' – a common expression of admiration in Greek, which he would have liked to hear applied to himself. But he was a man of limited imagination and no military experience. In launching the 'first round', he simply overplayed his hand, in a way that Tzimas would perhaps not have done. The cause of his failure was not treachery but miscalculation.

He underrated the strength of the factors opposed to him, both Greek and British; and he exaggerated the advantages of ELAS, which were considerable but not decisive. Possibly Saraphis and Aris misled him into over-confidence. The military staff had completed the reorganisation of the guerrilla bands into divisions, brigades and battalions, and the first 136 officers had graduated from the ELAS training school. In Saraphis's words, the enemy 'no longer had to do with guerrillas but with disciplined troops who knew how to fight'; and he tested them successfully with an operation in static defence at the pass of Porta Pazari into the mountains of Thessaly.[8] A section of his memoirs is entitled 'The Guerrilla Forces Transformed into Regular Army Units', and it was clearly written with special pride.[9] The front-line strength of ELAS was probably round about 15,000 men, with at least 20,000 reserves, whereas the strength of Zervas was barely 5,000 men and that of Psaros little more than 1,000. Moreover, Siantos had already held secret meetings with Psaros in August and early September, as a result of which ELAS could count on his neutrality in a clash with Zervas.

Another favourable factor for ELAS was a windfall of modern weapons as a result of the collapse of the Italians. Mussolini had been dismissed from office in July, and in August the new Italian Government asked the allies for an armistice. One of the first Italian formations to become 'co-belligerent' with the allies was the Pinerolo Division, with the Aosta Cavalry Brigade, stationed in Thessaly. By the terms of a local armistice, which carried the signatures of three members of the Joint GHQ (ELAS, EDES and British), the Italians were to retain their weapons and fight against their former allies as organised units.[10] It was only on these terms that the Italians would surrender to the guerrillas: without a British signature, they would have allowed themselves to be disarmed by the Germans instead, which was an unacceptable alternative. But by a series of *ruses de guerre*, ELAS isolated and disarmed them all on 15 October, a month after their surrender. The attack on EDES had already begun before this date, but it received an additional impetus from the acquisition of some twelve thousand small arms, together with mountain artillery, mortars and machine-guns.

ELAS could at last claim to be something like a regular army, properly equipped and organised, instead of a mere aggregation of unshod, ill-armed guerrillas. This was a crucial turning-point. To Saraphis, it was the fulfilment of a professional ambition, which had been cut short when he was stripped of his rank after the abortive revolution of 1935. He was now a Commander-in-Chief, though his army, in the words of an American historian,[11] 'was better organised on paper than on the ground, and as it gained in conventional organisation, it lost its effectiveness for the only type of fighting it was equipped to do'. Zervas resisted the temptation to make a similar transformation of his forces. Although he adopted the nomenclature of a regular army, his so-called battalions and divisions remained effectively guerrilla bands organised in flexible groups.

From the Communists' point of view, the transformation meant more than the satisfaction of Saraphis's professional vanity. It was part of the process of creating an alternative state in the mountains, which was to have all the familiar apparatus of sovereignty: an army, a navy, a police force, a youth movement, law-courts, taxation, communications, social insurance and so on. The climax was to be the establishment of an alternative government and legislature, such as the Yugoslav Partisans had already set up. The preliminary structure, based on ELAS, was now in being. The next step, due to take effect on 1 January 1944, was to set up 'people's committees for self-administration', followed by a 'Political Committee of National Liberation' (PEEA) in the spring. Linked with these ambitions was the proposal to construct a motor-road from Macedonia to Roumeli following the spine of the Pindus range, in order to improve military and administrative communications. Hitherto the mountains had only been intersected from east to west: a route from north to south would have been invaluable in the 'third round' of the civil war, though it served little purpose in a guerrilla campaign. The Allied Military Mission was asked, but declined, to provide assistance for the project.

Only the most perfunctory excuses were made by the Communists to justify the attack on Zervas. One story had it that an official of the KKE had been arrested by one of Zervas's officers in Epirus. This was the kind of episode that happened frequently, followed by complaints but no serious consequences. A myth, accepted by some non-Communists in EAM, was that 'someone pushed Zervas, so that the BBC could begin its attacks on EAM'.[12] None of these versions fits the fact that ELAS attacked its rivals simultaneously all over Greece. A graver allegation was that Zervas was guilty of collaborating with the enemy: he was said to have agreed to meet German officers to discuss a cease-fire. Evidence presented to the AMM by ELAS at the time suggested that the accusation was base-less, and documents published since the war, which appear to be genuine, have confirmed this view.[13] It is clear that the German HQ in Ioannina made approaches, with the help of the Bishop and a representative of the International Red Cross, both to Zervas and to the commander of ELAS Eighth Division in Epirus; and it seems that the latter went nearer to accepting the approach than Zervas. In the event no meeting took place between any German officer and either Greek organisation, since Zervas declined, and arrangements made with ELAS were overtaken by the civil war. But once the civil war had begun, German records leave no doubt that Zervas did make a secret truce for several months, in circumstances which he judged, quite improperly, to be not in conflict with his obligations to the allies.[14]

The unusual lack of caution shown by the KKE was probably due to Siantos's belief that Greece would soon be liberated from the Germans, so that the need for subterfuges was almost past. Tzimas did not share that belief, but his judgment was overruled. There was a conflict of view between the Communist delegates to Cairo, all of whom were relegated into insignificant positions, and those who had remained in Greece. Aris and Saraphis in particular were determined to finish off Zervas as quickly as possible. At one point Aris rebuked a subordinate commander of ELAS in writing for concentrating his forces against the Germans instead of against Zervas.[15] Saraphis was equally bitter on many grounds, personal and professional, not least because he held that Zervas's subservience to the British authorities and the King's government was an act of treason against Greece. Tzimas, though more level-headed, was compelled to conform. He himself signed the order to attack Zervas on 9 October, shortly before being relieved of his post at ELAS GHQ. The existence of a Communist plan to seize power in the autumn of 1943, and again in the spring of 1944 — both occasions when the liberation of Greece was wrongly thought to be imminent — was openly admitted some years after-wards.[16] German intelligence also had evidence of such a plan which may, for once, have been genuine.[17]

Siantos's belief that the enemy occupation was near its term was not unreasonable, for many events combined to support it. The allies had landed successfully in Italy, and the Italians had abandoned the war. The British had occupied several islands of the Dodecanese, and were calling for attacks by the Resistance on Greek aerodromes. It seemed to the KKE that the carefully planned operations in the summer had not been merely deceptive: at any rate, they had deceived many Greeks as well as the Germans. Even the British War Cabinet contemplated the possibility of an early evacuation of Greece by the Germans in the autumn of 1943.[18] The Germans themselves gave signs of being on the move in September. In fact they were re-grouping to make up for the Italians' defection, and preparing a counter-attack on the guerrillas. But by the time the blow fell, ELAS was committed to its miscalculation. The civil war had begun, but Zervas proved tougher than had been expected; the Germans assaulted both combatants simultaneously; and so far from being imminent, the liberation was in fact a year away. The British also reacted strongly to the civil war, especially after a New Zealand officer was killed by undisciplined ELAS troops. Military supplies to ELAS, but not to Zervas, were at once cut off.

During October and November, the German attacks on ELAS were devastating. Their main object was to re-open the east–west road from Epirus to Thessaly through Metsovo, which had been closed by Operation Animals. German successes forced ELAS GHQ to abandon its central position at Pertouli in Thessaly, retreating into the less accessible mountains further south in Roumeli. They were thus more isolated from the important region of Macedonia. During these operations, the Germans claimed to have killed 1,400 of the guerrillas, but Saraphis admitted only to 500 killed, and claimed 1,000 German casualties.[19] For a time then, from 15 October to 10 November, Zervas's forces were under simultaneous attack by both ELAS and the Germans.[20] But the fact that he was less severely mauled by the Germans gave some credence to the charge that he had an understanding with them. Their attitude towards him was ambiguous. On the one hand, he held territory close to the western coast, where they daily expected allied invasion: hence the thoroughness with which they destroyed villages in western Epirus.[21] On the other hand, they hoped to exploit his hostility against the Communists to seduce him from the western alliance. They succeeded in inducing him to accept a secret truce; but they were unaware that he had received orders from GHQ, Middle East, to abstain from offensive action during the autumn and winter in any case.[22] ELAS had received the same orders, but was less inclined to obey them.

German records show that they were sufficiently well informed about the feuds within the Resistance to exploit them skilfully. It is true that, like all intelligence services, those of the German high command were flooded with fantastic stories based on gossip, wishful thinking and deliberate fabrication, at which the Greeks were adept. Week in, week out, stories poured in about Russian officers with ELAS, Russian aircraft dropping supplies, plans for a Soviet Republic of Macedonia (and even of the Peloponnese), plans for a Communist rising, and so on.[23] Similar reports came in from low-grade agents about Zervas: he too had been meeting Russian officers; he had 2,500 Greek troops from the Middle East under his command; he had even, somehow or other, just been 'released from gaol', nearly two years after he took the field.[24] The Germans could recognise these as fantasies, however, because they also had high-grade agents in EDES, both in Athens and in the mountains. From these sources they regularly received documentary evidence on both Zervas and the Allied Military Mission, and on the relations between the two, and indirectly on ELAS. They were aware, for example, that Zervas's contacts with the Security Battalions and with other nationalist organisations like PAO and Mikhalagas's forces, were not treasonable but designed to wean them away from collaboration with the Occupation; and they were aware of the divisions within EAM and ELAS.[25] Good use of all this information was made in subversion and propaganda against the Resistance, particularly during the 'first round' of the civil war.

In these favourable circumstances, the Germans had no reason to help in the complete destruction of Zervas's forces, since to them a divided Resistance was preferable to one monopolised by the Communists. They soon left the rival armies to fight it out on their own. This first civil war was an inconclusive affair of little military interest. It fell into four brief phases. From October to the end of November ELAS pushed Zervas back into Epirus, west of the River Arakhthos, though both sides probably suffered more casualties from the Germans than from each other. In December there was a state of deadlock and stalemate, during which some allied observers mistakenly believed that Zervas had no hope of recovery. In early January 1944, Zervas counter-attacked with success, advancing far into Roumeli, while discussions were in progress for an armistice. At the end of January ELAS again attacked, and recovered most of the lost ground up to the River Arakhthos, before an armistice was concluded on 4 February. The significance of the four months of conflict lies in its effect on future relations between the Greeks, both inside and outside Greece. It was at this time that it came to seem patriotic to join the Security Battalions, and Resistance became discredited. Ever since then, both extremes of Greek opinion have agreed in identifying the Resistance with Communism. Their reasons were diametrically opposite – the extreme Right wishing to prove that all Resistance was evil, the extreme Left to prove that Communists alone resisted – but the conclusion for each was the same, and Greek public opinion has tended to accept it.

Feeling against the guerrillas ran especially high in the Peloponnese, where ELAS had been most successful in putting its nationalist rivals out of action. Consequently there was a strong flow of recruits into the

Security Battalions, which ELAS tried to stop by yet more bloody reprisals. These led to counter-reprisals of gruesome ferocity by the Germans. Their own war diaries tell the story with characteristic thoroughness: sixty-seven hostages taken in Old Corinth on 28 November, fifty hostages shot in Aigion on 4 December, fifty hostages hanged at Andritsaina on 5 December, twenty-five hostages shot at Gythion on 7 December.[26] In the same month came the crowning atrocity in the area of Kalavryta, where twenty-four villages were burned, three monasteries destroyed and 696 Greeks executed. This tragedy too was reputed by some to have been provoked by ELAS. Worse still was to follow when Aris Veloukhiotis took over command in the Peloponnese in the spring of 1944. Undeniably the Resistance contributed greatly to the sufferings of the population there, who have never forgotten it.* Equally terrible stories could be told of all parts of Greece. Everywhere people were to be heard laying the blame on the Resistance; and in Epirus at least, this was just as likely to mean Zervas, though still ELAS was held to be the more blameworthy.[27]

Mistaken though it might be to identify the Resistance exclusively with Communism, it was a fact that Communism was changing the face of mountain Greece wherever EAM was in control. The alternative state implied a new society. For the first time, as Aris put it, 'the villages learned what power was'. The old state had ignored them; the new state was in their midst. Its ethos was at once puritanical and modernising. In a sense puritanism was not new to Greece: a strict morality had always governed relations within the family; but no such public morality governed relations outside the family, where only the relation of patron and client was effectively binding.[28] War and enemy occupation were weakening the ties of the family; EAM was set to destroy the tradition of patronage and to substitute a modern habit in social relations. It was often a brutal process, impatiently imposed by urban revolutionaries on a rural proletariat.

The conflicts inherent in a modernising puritanism showed themselves in many ways. One was the treatment of women. Party doctrine insisted on the equality of the sexes: therefore women must have the vote and girls must be recruited into ELAS. Puritanism required that they should not be molested by their male comrades-in-arms, but the craving to be modern often prevailed against it. Saraphis, who was himself strictly conventional, hesitated to allow female units to take part in armed combat, even against Zervas. He and most of his colleagues would have been

* In 1971 friends in Kalamata apologised to me because a paragraph in a local newspaper referred to me as having been 'with the Resistance'.

shocked by the abandonment of sexual morality which seems to have become a matter of policy during the 'third round'.[29] But it was a direct
consequence of the psychological forces which they had let loose. Self-
discipline was hardly to be expected of people who had been shackled by
an archaic society. To be backward was one of the worst offences in the
eyes of EAM; but so was to be shameless.

In some respects modernisation meant not relaxing old disciplines but
imposing new ones. By time-honoured tradition, as a counterpart to the
habits of hospitality and generosity to strangers, thieving outside the
family or cheating the community had not been regarded as heinous
offences. This mattered less in the days when the state simply left the
villages alone. But now the state was EAM, and it was omnipresent. It
could also be brutal. Aris Veloukhiotis shot one of his own men for steal-
ing a chicken. He once claimed that he would rather execute ten innocent
men than let one guilty one go free. Men said that he was a sadist, and
incidentally a homosexual. Saraphis denied the sadism, yet there are many
eye-witness accounts of his readiness to kill and to witness killing.[30] He
gathered a bodyguard round him of men who differed in ferocity from the
rest of ELAS, some of them professional brigands. Allied officers saw Aris
or his bodyguard executing Italian prisoners, cattle-thieves, enemy agents,
with every appearance of enjoyment. Yet Tzimas, an ascetic intellectual,
could say of Aris that he was 'our paragon' (tò índalmá mas).

In time the corruption of brutality in the new society became widespread. Prisoners were tortured, particularly other Greeks; men and
women were mutilated after execution. The climax came with the formation of systematic execution-squads known as OPLA (Units for the
Protection of the People's Struggle), whose atrocities were notorious.
Years afterwards, in the presence of a younger Communist who had
fought in the 'third round', Tzimas admitted openly that atrocities had
been committed, though the younger man sincerely sought to deny it.*
He could not explain why it had happened. It was not inherent in the
circumstances of resistance, for no one ever accused Zervas, whatever his
faults may have been, of condoning organised atrocities. Part of the
difference lay in the much higher proportion of regular officers with
Zervas, who imposed a conventional discipline. The fearful discipline of
Aris and OPLA was something foreign to Greek custom; yet it was
associated with passionately held ideals.

In the end it led to disillusion, especially as each successive leader of
the KKE denounced his predecessors as traitors. Many Communists who
had joined the party in a spirit of idealism defected as the years went by.

* I heard this conversation at Ohrid, in Yugoslav Macedonia, in September 1969.

Despotopoulos signed a declaration of renunciation after the war. Niki-
phoros Dimitriou, a young officer cadet who distinguished himself at the
Gorgopotamos bridge and later found himself under sentence of death
as a rebel in the 'third round', afterwards lived to write a devastating
exposure of the moral and intellectual corruption of the KKE. Other
former Communists became prominent propagandists on behalf of the
military dictatorship set up in April 1967. A celebrated guerrilla leader,
Kapetan Orestis (Moundrikhas), defected after twenty years' service to
the KKE, and admitted later that he had been converted by his admiration
for the dignified conduct of the King. He was also impressed by the
personal qualities of the British officers who served with him in the
mountains, and whom he contrasted with the Balkan and Russian
apparatchiks, much as the Yugoslav Partisans were to do in 1944.[31] But
such disillusionment still lay in the future. In the autumn and early winter
of 1943 morale was still high and resilient, despite severe setbacks. EAM
had made bad miscalculations and ELAS had suffered a battering, but the
leadership was not shaken, and had little difficulty in keeping its forces
together.

The failure of the 'first round' in the mountains was evident before
Christmas. Zervas had survived and the liberation had not come. The
arrival of the first American officers to join the Allied Military Mission
had proved, after an early gleam of hope, to be a disappointment. A
number of Americans had been sent in by the Office of Strategic Services
(OSS) in the same way as their British colleagues by SOE; but they were
dependent on the British for communication and supply (though they had
their own ciphers), and the expectation that they could be relied on by
ELAS as an alternative source of help was delusive. Others were US Air
Force crews shot down over Greece, who joined the AMM when it
proved impossible to evacuate them during the winter, much as escaped
British prisoners-of-war had previously done. The Communists, particularly Tzimas, worked hard to detach their sympathies from the British,
in the hope of cultivating a rival American policy.

One of Tzimas's efforts proved particularly counter-productive for
EAM. He persuaded a young US Air Force officer, Lieutenant W. Hughling, that the British were deliberately frustrating his evacuation, and
that his return to Italy could easily be arranged from the territory of the
Yugoslav Partisans. Hughling agreed to accompany Tzimas on his journey
to the north in October 1943. It was an arduous and fruitless venture.
After penetrating far into Macedonia, and meeting both Yugoslav Partisans and probably also Bulgarians, Hughling separated from Tzimas and
returned to the headquarters of the AMM many weeks later. His account

of his experiences to the senior American officer, Major G. K. Wines, who had arrived in the meantime to become second-in-command of the Mission, provided the US authorities with their earliest first-hand knowledge of the character and strength of ELAS. The good sense of Wines ensured that there was no further risk of division between British and American policy in the field.

If the Western Allies could not be divided, new tactics had to be devised. With characteristic realism, the party line changed. Undismayed by the failures of the autumn and early winter, the EAM leadership addressed itself to its new tasks without repining. It had to liquidate the campaign against Zervas, to reconstitute its forces, and to recover the ground it had lost politically. All three tasks were accomplished with a skill which commands admiration. The first sign of willingness to make peace with Zervas was given to Wines on 11 December – an indication that the Americans were still regarded as neutral between the British and the Communists. Helpful contributions to the dialogue which followed were also made in Cairo by MacVeagh, the American Ambassador, who was anxious that his government should play a more active role; and even by Novikov, his Soviet colleague, whom Leeper furnished with detailed information from Greece. A cautious message advocating reconciliation was issued from Moscow on 4 January 1944.[32] Tsouderos, who was again working on a plan for a secret advisory committee in Athens under Archbishop Damaskinos, indicated willingness to consider broadening his government with representatives from Greece. In these more auspicious circumstances, after long-drawn-out exchanges and more than one fresh flare-up of fighting, a cease-fire was at last arranged on 4 February 1944. The rest of the month was occupied by an armistice conference attended by representatives of ELAS, EDES, EKKA and the AMM.

The military leaders – Saraphis, Zervas and Psaros – were all there; so were their political colleagues – Petros Roussos and Despotopoulos (EAM), Pyromaglou (EDES) and Kartalis (EKKA). But Siantos and Aris were both absent, and the KKE was not represented at the executive level. The discussions were inconclusive. Although there was talk of combining the guerrilla forces, many hours were wasted debating whether the result would be a united, unified or single army (enoménos, eniaíos or énas stratòs), which meant that it would never come about at all. Discussions of a single Commander-in-Chief (the nearest to a common choice being the republican General Othonaios) were fruitless for the same reason. The best that could be achieved was an armistice ending the civil war, which was signed at the Plaka bridge over the River Arakhthos on 28 February.[33] It contained a secret clause which committed the Resistance organisations to facilitating the entry of allied forces into Greece before the end of the Occupation. But the secrecy did not last long. Within three days a detailed record of the discussions was supplied to the Germans by an agent in Zervas's GHQ, and soon afterwards another record was published by the KKE in Cairo.[34]

At the same time EAM was busy reorganising its forces and extending them in new directions. Since power had failed to yield to a short, sharp tug-of-war, they had to spread a wider net and prepare for a long haul. Serious efforts were made to establish ELAS in the islands, including Crete, Samos and the Ionian group, though with comparatively little success. The Peloponnese was only slightly less difficult an area to organise, partly because there was a strongly monarchist and anti-Communist tradition in the peninsula, and partly because its network of communications was more complete, making guerrilla activity easier to combat. Both reasons combined to make the Peloponnese the area where the German-sponsored Security Battalions were most effective. It was not until the spring of 1944, when Aris Veloukhiotis was sent to take command there, that ELAS achieved any marked success in the Peloponnese. In Macedonia, on the other hand, the difficulties were of a different kind, and the urgency of re-establishing ELAS after the German onslaught was much greater.

The Greek Communists were in danger of losing the initiative in Macedonia. Apart from their mauling by the Germans, they were faced by a domestic war on two fronts. Already new nationalist forces were taking the field in place of PAO (YVE), which the KKE had virtually driven into collaboration with the enemy. In eastern Macedonia, there emerged an ex-sergeant known as Tsaous Andon (Antonios Phosteridis), and in western Macedonia the ambitiously named National Army of Mikhalagas (Michael Papadopoulos). Neither had any prospect of matching the power of ELAS, but their emergence was a symptom of patriotic opinion, which associated the KKE with treason.

The Slavophones were also increasingly active, and SNOF was becoming a serious rival to ELAS. Criticism of the Slavo-Macedonians was expressed at a Congress of the KKE in western Macedonia during August 1943, and in the same month the Central Committee of the Macedonian CP held a meeting near Lake Prespa, on the Greek frontier. Once SNOF had gained the right, through Tempo's intervention, to form self-contained units of their own under ELAS's general command, they did so with little regard for Greek susceptibilities or even for mutual co-operation. Some followed Naum Peios (in Macedonian, Pejov), whose sympathies were pro-Bulgarian. Others followed Ilias Dimakis (*alias*

Gotsis, Goči, or Gotchev), who looked to the Yugoslavs for support. The latent conflict between the different sections of the Communist Resistance in Macedonia was the main reason for Tzimas's mission to the north in October.

Most of the Slavophone inhabitants in all parts of divided Macedonia – perhaps a million and a half in all – felt themselves to be Bulgarians at the beginning of the Occupation; and most Bulgarians, whether they supported the Communists, IMRO, or the collaborating government, assumed that all Macedonia would fall to Bulgaria after the war. Tito was determined that this should not happen. The first Congress of AVNOJ in November 1942 had guaranteed equal rights to all the 'peoples of Yugoslavia', and specified the Macedonians among them. By implication, the guarantee could be extended to Pirin (Bulgarian) Macedonia and Aegean (Greek) Macedonia. The Communist Party of Macedonia, which had passed through a troubled time, first under a pro-Bulgarian leadership and then under pro-Yugoslav Macedonians, was taken in hand early in 1943 by Tempo, who formed a new Central Committee and informed it that it was now an integral part of the Yugoslav CP.

After suitable re-indoctrination, the Macedonian CP issued a pro-Yugoslav 'Ilinden Manifesto' on 2 August, the anniversary of a national rising in 1903. Tempo told them that they could look forward to unification and autonomy within a Yugoslav Federation. This prospect was confirmed by resolutions passed at the second Congress of AVNOJ, held at Jajce at the end of November. It was said to have the approval of Moscow, but this was untrue.[35] Stalin expressed indignation, and so did the Fatherland Front of Bulgaria (including, but not yet dominated by, the Communists), which urged a rival policy of 'an integral, free and independent Macedonia'. Tito in turn repudiated this policy in a message to Dimitrov on 24 January 1944.

Tzimas thus had an awkward task in his mission to the Yugoslav Partisans in Macedonia. He had to harmonise the interests of the KKE with those of the two Slav Communist Parties, which were at the same time increasingly hostile to each other. A Slavophone himself, he sought to bridge the gap by tact and persuasion, as well as by conciliatory gestures in the direction of SNOF. How far he went in his contacts with the Slav Communists is uncertain. It was alleged later that in January 1944, at a village near Edessa, he signed a pact with a representative of the Bulgarian CP which envisaged 'an autonomous Macedonian state of Soviet organisation which shall request to be placed under the protection of Russia'.[36] This document, together with the so-called Petrich agreement of July 1943, was said to have been 'retrospectively authenticated' by the Fifth

Plenum of the Central Committee of the KKE in January 1949.[37] But the story is extremely unconvincing.

Although Tzimas certainly met Bulgarian as well as Yugoslav Macedonians, his sympathies were with the latter. At the time the Bulgarian CP was much the weaker of the two. There was little reason for the KKE to make bargains with the Bulgarians, who had only minor resistance forces in the field. Tzimas would have been unlikely to make such concessions at a time when ELAS was itself again becoming a force to be reckoned with in Macedonia. There was need to present a respectable face to its followers, and none to sacrifice Greek interests. It is noteworthy that in the same month, January 1944, Zevgos reminded the Tenth Plenum of the decisions at the Sixth Party Congress in December 1935, by which 'the Party proclaimed afresh the Greek character of Macedonia and Greek Thrace', adding that 'its whole policy now revolves round the defence of our national independence'.[38] These words are inconsistent with the story of Tzimas's pact, which must be discounted.

ELAS's recovery of the initiative in Greek Macedonia was remarkable. Always a problematic area for the Greek Communists, its problems had now been greatly aggravated. To counteract them some of the ablest men in ELAS, both political and military, were sent to Macedonia. Outstanding among the senior officers was General Kalambalikis, who was appointed to command the Tenth Division of ELAS. A short, cheerful, patriotic professional soldier, who adhered to the social-democratic party, ELD (founded by Svolos and Tsirimokos), he saw it as his duty to act as a bridge between the left-wing guerrillas and the Western Allies; and he served them both well. But always at his side he had the political adviser of his division, Markos Vaphiadis; and this was a typical situation experienced by every regular officer in ELAS, particularly at the highest levels. Bakirdzis, too, as Corps Commander in Macedonia, similarly had Markos Vaphiadis constantly beside him when he took up his post in 1944. Over Markos in turn loomed the forceful personalities of Tempo and other Partisans of Yugoslav Macedonia.

Among nationalist Greeks it was already taken for granted that EAM was to be identified with the Slav Communists. Much evidence was collected, and later published, of collaboration between EAM and the Bulgarians; and the Slavophone Zisiadis (in Macedonian, Terpovski) was alleged to be the dominant figure of the KKE in Macedonia.[39] There was no disposition to distinguish between Bulgarians and Yugoslavs, or to recognise that they had rival aims. The differences between the Greek and Slavo-Macedonian Communists were also overlooked by nervous Greek patriots. They were more apt to be alarmed by such superficial symptoms as a proclamation by EAM after the Tehran Conference which declared that 'our orders come direct from Stalin', and added: 'What comes first now is to establish the independent Soviet Republic of Macedonia.'[40] Such effusions did not represent the considered policy of the KKE which had no wish to aggravate the Macedonian problem. Tzimas indeed had his work cut out alternately persuading ELAS to tolerate the existence of SNOF and bringing Gotsis back under ELAS control.

Later accusations of national treason against the Greek Communists extended also to their relations with the Albanians, with whom officially Greece was at war. But during the 'first round' the Albanians were less a source of anxiety to the KKE than they were to become in the civil war of 1946–9. Their impact on Balkan relations during the enemy occupation was relatively insignificant. They were a backward and divided people with only a brief history of independence. Their boundaries had little ethnic justification, for in the north many Albanians lived across the frontier in Yugoslavia, and in the south there was a Greek minority in Albania as well as an Albanian minority in Greece. This maldistribution had important consequences in both areas. In the north, the Albanian Partisans – the strongest element in the Resistance – were dominated by their Yugoslav colleagues. In the south, the Albanians in Greece – known as the Chams – collaborated readily with the enemy powers, and were eventually punished by being driven out of Greece by Zervas. But in this region the various territorial claims and counter-claims did not involve Macedonia, where Albanians (not being Slavs) were too few to be of any account. The Greeks, however, had claims on the southern part of Albania, which they called Northern Epirus and hoped to annex after the war, both on the ground that the population was partly Greek and because the Albanians had facilitated the Italian attack on Greece.

On these local antagonisms the KKE was cautiously silent, in the interests of harmony within the Balkan Communist movement. The Albanian Partisans represented a side-show in the Occupation. They could make little contribution to the Resistance, since lines of communication through Albania were not of major importance to the Germans; they were in a state of virtual tutelage under the Yugoslav Partisans; and no major issue divided them from their Greek comrades. The Albanian CP even contrived to neutralise the troublesome issue of Greek claims to Northern Epirus by the inclusion of Epirote Greeks in their first Anti-Fascist National Liberation Congress, held at Permet in May 1944, and also a Greek spokesman for the Northern Epirotes in their Provisional Government.[41]

The KKE naturally wanted the Albanian Communists to prevail over their nationalist rivals, as eventually they did. But there was no need and little opportunity for the KKE to help them do so, since Communism was relatively strong in southern Albania and the locus of the nationalist and royalist forces lay further north. The Greco-Albanian frontier area was therefore relatively inactive. At no time during the war did the Communist Parties on either side of the frontier call for its revision in either direction. This sterilisation of the frontier accorded with the policy of the major allies that both Greece and Albania should be restored within their pre-war boundaries. The Greek Government in exile disputed that policy, as also did the Greek nationalist Resistance; but the KKE had no reason not to acquiesce in it.

Contrary to popular assumptions, the KKE would probably also have been content with the status quo on the frontiers with Yugoslavia and Bulgaria. Although both before and after the war, circumstances compelled the Greek Communists to endorse Slav claims to a united and autonomous Macedonia, few of them did so out of real conviction. It was indeed impossible to make out any serious case for altering the frontiers in either direction on ethnic grounds. Minorities were to be found on both sides, but they were progressively dwindling as time passed since the unnatural frontiers had been drawn a generation before. Only on strategic grounds could a case for adjustments be argued; and on these grounds the Greeks, having been more than once invaded from the north, had the strongest case for adjustment, especially in the north-east, where the Bulgarian frontier was in places less than twenty miles from the Aegean Sea. On the other hand, the northern powers also had strategic claims to an outlet to the sea, which were mistakenly presumed to be backed by the Soviet Union; and the Yugoslavs and Bulgarians had rival claims against each other. If Communism were to prevail throughout the Balkans, grave problems faced the Balkan CPs in reconciling ideology with national interest. These had already risen to the surface during the winter of 1943-4.

The gravity of the potential conflict between the Balkan Resistance movements, which was not confined to Macedonia, at last compelled the Soviet authorities to intervene. For a long time they had ignored the Balkan problem, or treated it with indifference and incomprehension. Soviet propaganda continued, for instance, to urge the Yugoslavs to unite under Mihailović and contemplated sending a mission to him as late as October 1943, some months after the British had turned against him.[42] It was not until February 1944 that a Soviet Military Mission joined Tito's GHQ, where a British Mission had been established for nearly six months. The Soviet authorities were aware, from the message sent by Tito to

Dimitrov on 24 January 1944, that a grave dispute existed between the Yugoslav and Bulgarian Communists; but they had no ideas for solving it. In March Djilas was invited to Moscow as Tito's representative, and he spent most of the following two months there.[43] It became clear to him for the first time how ignorant Stalin and his entourage were of conditions in the enemy-occupied Balkans. But the Yugoslavs themselves, it must be said, were equally ignorant of conditions in Greece. Tzimas had as much difficulty enlightening his Slav allies as Djilas had enlightening his Soviet Allies. The winter of 1943–4 was crucial in bringing the latent Balkan conflicts to a head, almost unknown to the Western Allies who were in the end to derive uncovenanted benefits from them.

While Tzimas was in Macedonia dealing with EAM's Balkan relations, Siantos himself took charge of new initiatives in Athens and abroad. The turn of the year 1943–4 was a period of intense activity in the relations between Greece's divided parts. In all these relations the Communists held a dominant position because they were present everywhere and had good communications. The position of the Government in exile, on the other hand, was unenviable. Its writ ran nowhere except among the armed forces in the Middle East, and doubtfully even there. Its constitutional status rested simply upon the King's arbitrary mandate, unsupported by popular election. Many, if not most, of its members were antipathetic to the King, who found himself increasingly isolated, not yet being seen as the only alternative to Communism. His government had little hope of coming to terms with the forces in the mountains, with which they could not even communicate except through the good offices of their British allies.* Some kind of understanding between Athens and Cairo was imperative. There were signs of it becoming possible at the turn of the year, but the Communists had an interest in forestalling it.

The Greeks of Athens and those abroad had been brought closer together by events in more than one way. Their communications were improved, by wireless and courier, by sea and even by air. Many wireless links were now established in Athens, under British, American or Greek control. Sophoulis, for example, once sent substantially similar messages by three different routes within a few days: by an American and a British wireless, and by what was called 'the appropriate service in Athens', meaning presumably a link available to the Greek Government.[44] He also slightly varied the text to suit the interests of the different channels. But like most politicians in Athens, he was now conscious that what was going on in the mountains was not less grave, perhaps more so, than the

---

* In January 1944 they were obliged to appoint myself formally as their representative in negotiating with the Resistance leaders.

question of the King. Serious attempts were at last undertaken to form a common front between politicians inside and outside Greece in facing the threat to the nation, irrespective of their views on the monarchy. Even if they could not see the solutions, they recognised the needs: to broaden the Government, to bring the guerrillas under control, and to prepare the transition to liberation. At every point the obstacle seemed to be the King; and so once more the Archbishop of Athens seemed about to emerge as the nucleus of a compromise. Eden himself suggested to Tsouderos and his own colleagues in October that 'an authority' might be built up under the Archbishop, 'which could represent the Greek Government when the Germans withdrew'; and in November the British War Cabinet accepted his view.[45]

The confusion caused by the civil war was temporarily aggravated by a strange episode in Athens during November 1943. A New Zealand officer, Captain Stott, who had been one of the heroes of the attack on the Asopos viaduct, had made several visits to Athens during which he acquired valuable intelligence. On one visit, without authority, he used his con-tacts with the Mayor of Athens to propose a high-level meeting with the German authorities. His purpose seems to have been nothing less than to bring the war to an end. Neubacher, the senior German plenipotentiary in Athens, asked permission to meet the unknown British agent, but was allowed only to send a subordinate officer.[46] It quickly became apparent to the Germans that the approach was unauthorised, and contact was broken off. As soon as the British authorities learned of it, Stott was recalled. In the meantime the episode had become known in Athens, and was regarded by many Communists as an example of British disloyalty to the alliance. Soviet propaganda later so interpreted it. On the other hand, by revealing what they knew of the episode to the British through Despotopoulos, the conciliatory wing of the KKE showed that they genuinely wished to restore good relations.

Meanwhile appeals for unity were repeatedly addressed by radio to the Greek antagonists in the mountains: by the Greek Prime Minister and King; and by General Wilson, the British Commander-in-Chief, who was sympathetic towards ELAS and believed that if Myers were allowed to return to Greece, he could 'get them round to the right way of thinking'.[47] But the leaders of ELAS would only contemplate a cease-fire when their hopes of crushing Zervas were seen to be beyond fulfilment. Politicians in Athens were willing to help Tsouderos broaden his government, but the republicans continued to make conditions about the King. Pressure was put on the King to go beyond his statement of 4 July 1943, first by Tsouderos, and then by Eden and Churchill in Cairo on their way back

from the Tehran Conference. In response to Tsouderos, the King agreed
to write him a letter dated 8 November, which contained the words:

> . . . when the desired moment of liberation of our country comes,
> I will examine afresh the question of the date of my return to Greece,
> in agreement with the Government, in the light of the prevailing
> political and military conditions.[48]

The published version of his statement omitted the words 'of the date',
which led many in Athens and elsewhere to believe that the King had
agreed not to return without a plebiscite. The original draft, on the other
hand, omitted the words 'in agreement with the Government', which
Tsouderos insisted on inserting. Despite the date borne by the letter, the
final text seems to have been agreed only a few days before it was published
on 12 December.

Settling the King's position was only one of many concurrent problems.
The British Government had already begun to give thought to the future
of its Greek policy before the 'first round' began. Major changes in the
structure and staffing of SOE were made in the autumn, to bring it more
directly under the command of GHQ, Middle East. General Wilson still
complained that 'the diplomats were too strong for me'.[49] But matters
went even further. It was realised that, even if there were to be no major
invasion to drive out the Germans, British troops would be needed to
control Greece on liberation, possibly even before the end of the year.
On 29 September Churchill proposed a force of five thousand men,
equipped with armoured cars and Bren-gun carriers, whose function
would be to contend with 'rioting in the capital or incursion into the
capital from the countryside'.[50] The Chiefs of Staff agreed that the figure
was practicable.

The Foreign Office would have preferred two or three divisions – in
other words, something like the force which had to be sent, belatedly, in
December 1944; but it recognised that in 1943 such a force would be
considered impracticable. So seriously was the problem taken that in
November the War Cabinet agreed in principle to break with EAM and
to incorporate Zervas's forces into the Greek National Army, provided
that the Chiefs of Staff confirmed that ELAS was not of overriding value
and that the King would declare himself willing to await invitation from a
legally constituted government before returning to Greece. The Military
Mission had already been warned that it might be compelled to withdraw.

Pressure on the King continued, although the politicians in Athens
(including Gonatas, Papandreou and the Socialist Sophianopoulos) were

reported by Sophoulis to have welcomed his statement of 8 November.
At the beginning of December, in Cairo, Eden pressed the King to make
a further statement: 'I will not return to Greece until I am summoned to
do so by the clearly expressed desire of my people.' After consulting
Roosevelt, who was also in Cairo, the King refused.[51] Eden, having only
reluctant support from Churchill, did not press the matter. As a result,
the plan for breaking with EAM also lapsed automatically. Tsouderos tried
to make the King's refusal a ground for his own resignation, but this
too was refused. At the same time, discussions were in progress on
the establishment of a secret committee in Athens under Archbishop
Damaskinos, whose purpose would be to co-ordinate negotiations for the
enlargement of Tsouderos's government with men from inside Greece,
including the Resistance. An emissary from Cairo, Colonel Phrandellos,
was sent into Greece by parachute at the beginning of January 1944. He
returned in March with the news that EAM demanded an express declaration that the King would not return without a plebiscite, and that the
other politicians saw little need to broaden the Government but proposed
that the Archbishop should be appointed Regent. The King, who had
meanwhile returned from Cairo to London, once more curtly refused.[52]

A serious effort was now being made by the British authorities to
reconcile their political and military objectives. The burden of reconciliation fell chiefly on SOE in Cairo, because the primary objectives of the
Foreign Office and the military authorities were different. On the one
hand, it was judged essential that EAM should not be left with a monopoly
of power in Greece when the Occupation ended. Therefore Zervas's
forces had to be preserved in being, together with those of any other
nationalist leaders (such as Psaros and Tsaous Andon) who could be saved
from destruction. Evidence of this objective can be seen in a number of
episodes, besides the abortive plan for severing relations with ELAS and
incorporating EDES in the Greek National Army. A proposal from the
HQ of the Allied Military Mission, that if military operations were to
be effectively renewed against the Germans, it would be necessary to
abandon Zervas and make what terms could be negotiated with EAM, was
sharply rebuffed. Instructions were sent from Cairo to the AMM at the
Plaka Conference, that Zervas should be discouraged from allowing EDES
to be merged with ELAS under a single command, and that instead the
country should be divided into separate operational areas, the maximum
possible area being allocated to Zervas.[53] It was also decided to establish
American officers in Zervas's territory, as well as a more senior US officer
at the HQ of the AMM, so that ELAS should not appear to have a monopoly of liaison with the Americans.

On the other hand, the military assessment was that operations were still necessary against the Germans, and that by reason of its strength and geographical distribution ELAS was the only force capable of mounting them effectively. This view was upheld by the Commander-in-Chief, General Wilson, and the new Commander of SOE in Cairo, Brigadier Barker-Benfield. The plan of operations no longer envisaged an opposed landing in force, but only harassing operations against the Germans as they withdrew under pressure of events elsewhere in Europe. The operations, known by the code-name of Noah's Ark, were at first planned for April 1944, but this date proved premature. It was never realistic, and may have been devised only to occupy the guerrillas more usefully in planning operations against the common enemy instead of fighting each other. Although in the event Operation Noah's Ark was postponed until August, planning for it necessarily entailed the renewal of supplies to ELAS in the spring. This decision helped to revive the prestige and confidence of EAM.

One of the chief anxieties of the British and Greek Governments at the turn of the year was to avert the formation of any kind of authority in the mountains which might claim to be a rival government. It had been suggested as early as August 1943, by Pyromaglou, that the Government should be broadened to include EAM, and that a section (klimákion) of it should be established in the mountains.[54] The suggestion was unwelcome, and became more so when the Yugoslav Partisans set up an Executive National Committee in November 1943, in opposition to the royal government in exile. Consequently when Tsouderos proposed in December 1943 to reconstruct his government on a broader basis, the telegram in which his proposal was communicated to ELAS GHQ made it clear that the government would be reconstructed in Cairo.[55] It was for the same reason that Zervas was advised to oppose the formation of a 'single army' at the Plaka Conference, because that would presuppose a single political authority over it. There was independent evidence that EAM had precisely such an aim in view.

The leaders of the EAM in Athens were at work among the politicians, with no signs of the guilty conscience which everyone else thought they ought to feel. While Tsouderos's emissaries were seeking a basis for broadening the Government in exile, EAM was planning an alternative government in the mountains, to which they suggested that Tsouderos might send representatives. On 15 December 1943 they circulated a letter to a number of leading figures in Athens with a plan for political co-operation. Papandreou indignantly rejected it, and allowed his reply to be circulated.[56] He also sent a warning memorandum to the Greek

Government and the British GHQ. Few of the political leaders took the approach seriously, but a number of respectable figures who were less known in the political world accepted the proposal. Among the latter were Svolos and Angelopoulos, both professors at Athens University; and Bakirdzis and Mandakas, both senior officers who had been out of the army since the revolution of 1935. None of these men were Communists, though all were republicans.* The monarchy and Communism had now become the poles round which Greek politics gravitated. Both poles were more powerful to repel than to attract.

The Communists skilfully exploited the tensions between monarchists and republicans. They alone had active and able supporters in all the crucial places: in the mountains, in Athens, and outside Greece, in the armed forces and the merchant marine, as well as in political circles. The politicians were only beginning to appreciate that the question of Communism was more urgent than that of the monarchy. Tsouderos and most of those with any claim to succeed him as Prime Minister – Sophoulis and Papandreou in Athens, or Sophocles Venizelos within his own cabinet – were all liberal republicans in the Venizelist tradition. As liberals, they were unequally matched with the Communists; as republicans, they regarded the King as at best a handicap to the prospects of stability in Greece. The King himself was under strong but opposite pressures. His loyal friends criticised him for not dismissing Tsouderos and appointing a truly monarchist government; his critics, including his Prime Minister, were exasperated by his refusal to meet the republican opposition with adequate concessions.

In these circumstances the Communists assembled a reasonably impressive group of personalities to form their Political Committee of National Liberation (PEEA), which was established in the mountains on 14 March 1944. The provisional Chairman was Bakirdzis, who was shortly to be replaced by Svolos. Only two Communists – one of them Siantos – were included in the original membership. Although the Committee claimed, in its first message to Tsouderos on 16 March, to be merely a transitional body aiming at the establishment, with Tsouderos's co-operation, of a 'Government of General National Unity', it immediately assumed the functions of a government for itself. Each member was responsible for a department, with the title of Secretary; its collective decisions were to have 'the force of law'; and it was charged with the task

---

* Svolos and Bakirdzis were both alleged later to have close relatives in the service of the post-war Bulgarian Government. Svolos's wife was a member of the KKE; so was Mandakas's brother-in-law. None of these facts convict them of disloyalty to Greece, which from personal knowledge I would regard as improbable.

of organising the election of a National Council representative of the liberated areas of Greece. Its decrees were drafted in demotic Greek, which contrasted sharply with the *katharévousa* (purist) Greek always used by the legitimate government. Another innovation was that in the elections to the National Council women were to have the vote. In many respects PEEA was a replica of the Yugoslav Council of National Liberation. But it was at pains to create an air of moderation.[57]

On paper, at least, the alternative state was now in being. The KKE's position was once more very strong. Although it had not won a monopoly of armed force in the mountains, it predominated everywhere. There are discrepancies in the estimates of the strength of the various forces, but no doubt of the preponderance of ELAS. Saraphis later estimated that he had 48,940 men under arms, excluding reserves, though in a message to Tito which the Germans intercepted in January 1944 he claimed only 25,000 regulars and 40,000 reserves.[58] His corps of officers included 16 generals, 34 colonels and 1,500 other officers from the pre-war army.[59]

On the other side he estimated 100,000 German troops (though the Germans' own figure was 300,000 at their peak), together with 40,000 Bulgarians, 40,000 other foreign troops and 15,000 in the Security Battalions.[60] Saraphis would also have counted among the enemy the forces of Zervas, Tsaous Andon and Mikhalagas. The figures are uncertain, but British estimates of Zervas's maximum strength ranged from 5,000 to 12,000 (with up to 5,000 reserves), and the most authoritative German estimate was 7,000–8,000 (including 386 officers).[61] Tsaous Andon claimed 579 men;[62] those of Mikhalagas were certainly fewer. Psaros no longer counted among the enemies of ELAS: his force, which never exceeded 1,000 men, had remained neutral in the civil war, but he earned a tragic retribution when he was attacked by ELAS again, and captured and murdered on 16 April 1944. Numbers, in any case, were no longer of more than secondary importance. What mattered was superiority of armament, morale and initiative, all of which lay with ELAS.

To what extent the KKE planned the events which followed the establishment of PEEA is uncertain. They had reason to believe, from what they had been told of allied plans, that Greece might be liberated in April; and this belief could have encouraged them to take pre-emptive action. The murder of Psaros on 16 April, by an ELAS officer who had a personal feud with him, was probably unpremeditated, though it produced no sign of contrition from ELAS. It occurred at a moment when representatives of the guerrilla organisations were gathering for an operational conference in Thessaly, which Psaros was expected to attend. When Despotopoulos, the ELAS representative, was questioned about him, he

replied in laconic Latin: *'Fuit!'* According to some accounts, Despotopoulos had authorised the attack on Psaros's force at Siantos's express
order, but this did not mean that he intended the murder.[63] A more
plausible account has it that when Siantos first heard of Psaros's death, he
exclaimed: 'It's a catastrophe!'[64] It was, however, condoned. Saraphis
and Bakirdzis, who were personal friends and military colleagues of
Psaros, expressed perfunctory regrets. But no disciplinary action was
taken against their subordinates, just as none had been taken when a New
Zealand officer was killed by ELAS six months earlier. The tragic episode
showed that Saraphis had not in reality, as he claimed, a disciplined army
under his command, and that the Communist militants could assume a
freedom to exploit aggressively any opportunity that presented itself.

Unplanned opportunism is probably also the explanation of the upheaval which occurred in the Greek forces of the Middle East at the same
time.[65] By establishing PEEA, the KKE furnished the occasion but not the
cause. The theory that the mutinies in the Army and Navy in April 1944
were organised by the Communists in order to keep them away from the
scene of action at the time of liberation is implausible, not least because
PEEA quickly disowned the mutineers. There had in fact been fore-
bodings of mutiny in the armed forces since many months before. In
September 1943 Tsouderos had asked the British authorities to remove
fifteen suspect officers out of harm's way, but nothing was done. On
1 March 1944 he urged that the First Brigade should be sent to Italy, to
remove it from the disturbed atmosphere of Cairo. On 8 March, having
received Phrandellos's report on his return from Athens, he wrote to
warn the King of the difficulties which were about to arise, probably
beginning in Cairo.

All these events preceded the establishment of PEEA, after which
Tsouderos's fears were quickly realised. On 20 March, four days after the
first message from PEEA, Venizelos made a broadcast to calm the armed
forces. A week later Tsouderos was faced by a revolt in his cabinet, of
which he suspected that the ringleader was Venizelos. On 31 March a
committee of officers called on Tsouderos to resign. Two days later
Venizelos spoke of 'negotiating with the mountains', and proposed himself as Prime Minister. But he was mistaken in seeing himself as the man
of the hour. The Navy declared him unacceptable, and Tsouderos agreed
to continue in office until the King arrived in Cairo from London.

The outcome was very different from the expectations of any of those
involved. The King, arriving back in Cairo from London on 13 April,
accepted Tsouderos's resignation and appointed Venizelos Prime Minister.
But he lasted only a fortnight in power. During that time the mutinies

were suppressed, by British troops on land and by loyal Greek forces under Admiral Voulgaris, supported by the Royal Navy, in the harbour of Alexandria. In the meantime a new figure had arrived on the scene. Papandreou set out from the coast of Attica on 8 April, and arrived in Cairo on the 21st. On 26 April, two days after the mutinies were suppressed, Venizelos resigned and Papandreou was appointed Prime Minister. The real task of establishing national unity was at last to begin. The new Prime Minister had no doubt about the grimness of the task, on which he had already sent more than one powerful memorandum out of Athens to his predecessor.[66] He pointedly congratulated Admiral Voulgaris on suppressing the naval mutiny, and called on the British Government to 'cut off absolutely all moral and material support' to EAM if it persisted in its terrorist methods.

Unlike his predecessors, Papandreou could attack the Communists without being accused of being out of touch with public opinion under the occupation. Not only had he been living under the occupation himself until a few days before; he had spent three months in the Averoff prison in 1942, and had been in close touch with the Resistance, including EAM. His antecedents were impeccable. Educated in Germany, he knew the language and mentality of Greece's enemies; and his loyalty to the western democracies had been demonstrated in 1917, when he supported Venizelos against Constantine I and earned a CBE from the British Government. As early as July 1943 he had expressed the view that 'two world-wide fronts are taking shape: Communist Pan-Slavism and Liberal Anglo-Saxonism'.[67] A brilliant orator with a splendid presence and a magnetic smile, he was politically a shrewd manipulator rather than an administrator. But he had the qualities of courage and imagination needed to inspire the Greek people in their abyss of anxiety. Many sensed in April 1944 that he was the man of the hour, and that the hour had struck.

The 'first round' was finished. This designation has sometimes been confined to the mutinies of April 1944, but only by anti-Communists. No representative voice of the KKE ever expressly admitted responsibility, and Saraphis vigorously denied it, stating that 'PEEA and ELAS had had nothing whatever to do with the rebellion and that there had, in fact, been no communication'.[68] Although Saraphis would probably not have been made privy to a Communist plot if there had been one, what he said is likely to have been true. No evidence was produced at the subsequent trials of the mutineers to show that there had been any communication between them and the mountains.[69] The mutinies can reasonably be attributed to discontented republicans, abetted by individual Communists who took it upon themselves to exploit a revolutionary situation, under the title of 'anti-fascists', without express authority. The timing is consistent with this interpretation, for a deliberate plot, which had no chance of success under British guns, would have been out of phase with the current policy of the KKE in Athens and the mountains, where a return to legality was in progress. The ultimate aim of PEEA was a peaceful and not a violent accession to power. It was indeed later criticised by militant Communists, like Karagiorgis and Zakhariadis, for precisely that reason.[70]

Whatever the intentions of PEEA, however, it had unwittingly caused a polarisation of forces and attitudes. The armed services were drastically purged, some ten thousand officers and men being sent to concentration-camps because of their left-wing sympathies. A new Third Brigade, formed out of the relics of the first two, consisted wholly of men considered reliable; and the Navy and Air Force were similarly purged. Senior officers could no longer escape commitment one way or the other, sometimes against their real convictions. Just as republican officers like Saraphis, Bakirdzis and Mandakas became linked willy-nilly with the KKE, so other republican officers in Egypt, like Admiral Voulgaris and Colonel Tsigantes, became linked with the King as the sole guarantor of law and order.

It was the same with the politicians. Staunch republicans like Tsouderos, Kanellopoulos and Venizelos had served the King in exile: now they were joined by Papandreou, who called himself a Social Democrat and had signed the anti-monarchist declaration of 31 March 1942. Papandreou's main preoccupation seemed to be to destroy ELAS, for which purpose he would use any available force — EDES, the Greek Brigade, British troops — excepting only the Security Battalions.[71] At the same time others of a similar outlook who had joined PEEA, like Svolos, Angelopoulos and Askoutsis, were becoming no less committed to association with the KKE, which deliberately cut off their retreat by publishing their names as soon as they arrived in the mountains. The one major neutral was Archbishop Damaskinos; but he was angling for his own appointment as Regent — a fact which prejudiced Churchill against him.[72]

Thus the fateful lines were drawn. It was not only the formation of PEEA and the outbreak of the mutinies, however, which forced the Greeks to take sides. Some blame must also attach to the obstinacy of the King and Churchill. As Novikov, the Soviet Ambassador, remarked to MacVeagh, his American colleague, it was Leeper, as Churchill's agent, who was the real Prime Minister of Greece.[73] Neither Novikov nor MacVeagh played a significant role in the crisis of April 1944, though the latter would willingly have done so. Novikov's contributions were essentially negative. He barely reacted to the information supplied to him

by Leeper; he rebuffed an approach from Venizelos for Soviet help; he
failed even to call on Papandreou; and he told MacVeagh that Papandreou would be unable to solve Greece's problems.[74] Otherwise he
preserved a gloomy silence: only later in the summer did he receive
instructions to be helpful.

MacVeagh, on the other hand, was handicapped by the fact that the
State Department ignored his advice, while Roosevelt ignored that of his
Secretary of State. MacVeagh's despatches were excellent, but perhaps
almost too precise to be useful: an accurate but hardly illuminating
specimen described Papandreou as belonging rather to 'the right wing of
the leftist group than the left wing of the center'.[75] In the event, the only
American contribution to the crisis was a message of support from
Roosevelt to Churchill, which called on all Greeks to 'show a personal
unselfishness which is so necessary now and think of their glorious past'.[76]
It was by no means helpful at a time when many Greeks felt themselves
forced to choose between rival governments, rival armies, and even rival
allies. What is remarkable in the circumstances is not that tragedy
eventually befell, but that it seemed to be averted for so long.

PART TWO

The Second Round

4

Return to Legality
May–October 1944

PAPANDREOU'S FIRST decision was to convene a national conference in the Lebanon, to which all the Resistance organisations were
invited, along with the principal political figures in the Middle East and
others from Athens. It was encouraging that the KKE and its related
bodies – EAM, ELAS and PEEA – readily accepted. They had lately
carried through their own elections for a National Council, which met at
the village of Koryskhades in central Roumeli from 14 to 27 May. They
enjoyed the declared support of the Yugoslav Partisans, with whom an
agreement to co-operate was announced on 20 April. Although the attitude of the Soviet Government was more doubtful, its news agency, Tass,
regularly denounced the Greek Government in exile as 'fascist reactionaries'. In the western press there was already a tendency to eulogise EAM
and to criticise Churchill for his devotion to the Greek monarchy. With
the tide apparently flowing their way, the Communist leaders might well
have calculated that they only had to stand fast and wait for power to fall
into their hands on the day of liberation, like the Partisans in Yugoslavia.
That they did not do so argues that they were less confident than
appeared. There were both 'hawks' and 'doves' in the KKE, and some,
like Siantos, who were both in turn. The accession of respectable bourgeois figures such as Svolos into PEEA, together with Tsirimokos within
EAM, presumably encouraged the 'doves'. It is uncertain whether the
Communists received any directions from the Soviet Government at this
time; but if they did, such instructions would have enjoined caution,
because Stalin had no wish yet to antagonise the western powers. Even
Zakhariadis in 1945 emphasised the folly of challenging the British position in the Mediterranean, though in 1950 he denounced Siantos for
having adopted exactly that line himself.[1] The assumption that the British
would remain the preponderant power in the Mediterranean was still
unchallenged. Towards the end of May, the US Government indicated
that it had little interest in the area, and in June, Roosevelt acceded to
Churchill's request for a free hand in Greece, though with reluctance and

initially only for three months. Even so, he had to overrule his own Secretary of State, who demurred.[2] This arrangement was initially disapproved by Stalin, but a few months later, in Moscow, Stalin gave Churchill a virtual promise that he would not interfere. British policy in Greece thus had no more cause for anxiety from Moscow than from Washington.[3]

Within the KKE, the realists recognised the way the wind was blowing, whereas the hard-liners opposed it at all costs. Zakhariadis, who eventually aligned himself with the latter, wrote in 1950 that the KKE had failed to guide EAM correctly:

> The leadership of the KKE in fact interpreted the common allied struggle against Hitlerite fascism as an unreserved support not for the common allied cause but for British policy and British imperialist aims in the Mediterranean and south-east Europe.[4]

He criticised his colleagues for 'castrating ELAS' by subjecting it to British policy; for claiming that it had been impossible to foresee the 'British invasion and occupation' of Greece; and for destroying the 'pure revolutionary prospect'. He described this as part of the 'pro-British corruption' of the KKE for which Siantos among others had been responsible as early as 1937. In such extravagant language he criticised the composition of PEEA and the participation in the Lebanon Conference and its successors. At the time Zakhariadis was in a German concentration-camp, but at least some other Communists shared the views which he expressed in retrospect. Similar language was used by Vlandas in his reminiscences about all the decisions taken during 1943–4 by 'the then leadership' of the KKE, which was operating, according to him, 'behind the back of the Central Committee'.[5] His target was the Politburo, consisting of Siantos, Ioannidis, Partsalidis, Zevgos, Ploumbidis, Bartzotas, Stringos, Petros Roussos and Khrysa Khatzivasiliou. The result of the division in party counsels was a series of vacillations and compromises.

When the conference assembled in the Lebanon on 17 May, the British Ambassador was installed in a near-by hotel, and was in touch with the delegates throughout. His American colleague, MacVeagh, had declined a suggestion from the State Department that he should also attend. Had he done so, it would have helped both to promote his own wish that the US Government should play a more active role in Greek affairs, and also to offset the impression that the Lebanon Conference was stage-managed by the British authorities for their own benefit. In fact Papandreou was the dominant personality throughout. The delegation from EAM and its allies was impressive in appearance, but disunited. It consisted of Svolos,

Petros Roussos, Porphyrogennis, Angelopoulos, Saraphis, Stratis and Askoutsis. Of these only Roussos and Porphyrogennis were Communists, and the former was a weak man whose choice, according to Vlandas, was a 'deliberate act of treachery'. The rest were widely representative of the democratic left: Svolos and Angelopoulos from Athens University, Saraphis from the Army, Stratis a trade-unionist, Askoutsis a Cretan Venizelist. Other delegations were drawn mainly from the old political parties, apart from two other representatives of the Resistance: Pyromaglou (EDES) and Kartalis (EKKA). The last two were particularly vehement in denouncing ELAS, whom Saraphis, however, defended vigorously. Only the skilful chairmanship of Papandreou prevented an immediate rupture.[6]

After three days' debate a document known as the Lebanon Charter was signed on 20 May by all those present. Its eight points were based on a summary of Papandreou's final speech winding up the conference. They provided for the reorganisation of the armed forces outside and inside Greece, the end of the 'reign of terror' in the mountains, the relief of hunger and other needs, the restoration of order and liberty, the punishment of collaborators, and the post-war satisfaction of Greece's economic and territorial requirements.[7] The constitutional question was covered by the phrase that 'the political leaders . . . are understood to retain such views as they have already expressed'. Since the King would be obliged to accept his Ministers' advice, Papandreou regarded it as settled that the King would not return to Greece in advance of a plebiscite, and stated it publicly on 12 June. Meanwhile he proceeded to form his coalition government, in which he expected to include members of the KKE, EAM and PEEA. But although Svolos and his colleagues had all signed the Charter, their principals in the mountains repudiated their signatures and refused to nominate ministers. Saraphis and Porphyrogennis, who returned to Greece in June, were severely criticised by Siantos. Svolos, who did not return until later, wished to resign as President of PEEA; but, as so often in his career, he was unable to make up his mind. Meanwhile a heated exchange of telegrams took place between Siantos and Papandreou.

The leaders of EAM were suspicious on many points, in some cases accusing Papandreou of having misled them at the Lebanon Conference or of having himself contravened the Lebanon Charter. On 4 July they submitted through Svolos what they called their 'final terms' for joining the Government, which had been drawn up by Siantos. The document was somewhat confused and repetitive, but there were eight essential points: first, that all talk of 'dissolving ELAS' should cease; secondly, that accusations of terrorism against ELAS should be retracted; thirdly, that Zervas should be held to blame for the most recent clash between EDES and ELAS; fourthly, that the Security Battalions should be publicly denounced; fifthly, that there should be no executions of those tried for mutiny in Egypt; sixthly, that EAM and its associates should have (as promised in the Lebanon) six Ministers and an Under-Secretary in a Cabinet of fifteen instead of five posts out of twenty, which Papandreou now offered them; seventhly, that immediately after EAM representatives joined the Government, the King should himself make a statement that he would not seek to return until after a plebiscite; eighthly, that a section of the Government should be established in 'Free Greece', whereupon PEEA would be dissolved.[8] A particular requirement that PEEA, EAM and its associates should be separately represented was also emphasised in a letter sent to Papandreou on 9 July by Svolos, Stratis and Petros Roussos, which was plaintive in tone though reasonable and conciliatory in content.[9]

The points were of mixed validity and importance. It was probably true that Zervas had been responsible for the latest clash between EDES and ELAS at the end of June. It was unreasonable to expect Papandreou to reconstruct his Cabinet according to a formula dictated to him, though he later conceded another Under-Secretary to EAM. The requirement that the King should himself declare his willingness to await a plebiscite was not without substance. Although Papandreou could argue in reply that he had himself made the necessary declaration on the King's behalf on 12 June, it was a fact (whether known to EAM or not) that the King nevertheless, as he told MacVeagh, still regarded his position as unchanged.[10] On the whole, however, Papandreou interpreted Siantos's demands as calculated to be rejected. After analysing them in detail with his Cabinet, he replied: 'They ask us to surrender Greece: we refuse!'[11] Siantos remained obdurate for several weeks longer, even though officials of the Soviet Embassy advised the EAM delegates to join the Government. Possibly news from Yugoslavia stiffened his determination, for Tzimas was now at Tito's GHQ, which had been driven by German action to take refuge on the island of Vis, and was urging his colleagues not to give way. In June an agreement had been reached between Tito and Šubašić, head of the Royal Yugoslav Government, which practically assured Tito's control of Yugoslavia. This could be seen as a tempting precedent for the KKE.

But the collective leadership of EAM, which now had to carry with it men of a new and more moderate kind, was still undecided. Its assets and weaknesses were finely balanced. ELAS controlled more than half Greece and held its population to ransom. As Papandreou put it in a memorandum to Leeper on 21 April: 'EAM, of which the Communist Party is the head and backbone, today constitutes an organised armed minority which terrorises the great unarmed and unorganised majority of the Greek people.'[12] If the mutineers in Egypt were condemned to death, for example, EAM held nationalist officers of ELAS, who had rebelled against Communist domination in Macedonia, as hostages for them. But the leaders of EAM had less absolute control than Papandreou thought, and feared that they had less even than they had. In the mountains they were still faced by Zervas in the west and the Security Battalions in the south. The Germans were still capable of vicious reprisals: they executed 200 trade-unionists in Athens on 1 May, and massacred 270 inhabitants of Distomo on 10 June.[13] In Macedonia, EAM's control was disputed with the Bulgarian occupation, the nationalist guerrillas of Tsaous Andon and Mikhalagas, and the pro-Yugoslav forces of SNOF under Gotsis. Tempo and his Partisans were also believed to be poised to seize Salonika – so at least Zakhariadis alleged five years later.[14]

The Communists perhaps feared the forces available outside Greece even more. The Greek forces in Egypt, which had been purged and re-formed as the Third Mountain Brigade, moved into the line in Italy in September under General Tsakalotos and proved themselves formidable. Smaller but equally tough was the Sacred Squadron under Colonel Tsigantes, operating in the Aegean Islands. The Communists expected a large British force to occupy Greece, and looked upon the small commando-type units, both British and American, which were infiltrated into Greece in the summer under the terms of the Plaka Agreement, as forerunners of it. In fact, despite frequent adjurations and remonstrances from Papandreou, the British troops available for the liberation of Greece were inconsiderable and largely non-combatant. Papandreou repeatedly asked Churchill for more troops, on two occasions in personal meetings in Italy, but to no effect.[15] The exigencies of war and the assumption that the liberation of Greece would be bloodless prevailed over Papandreou's anxieties. But this was yet unknown to Siantos and his colleagues, some of whom were sincerely anxious to conciliate the British, and some regarded it as a regrettable necessity.

The latter group assumed that there was a conspiracy against them: Papandreou and the Security Battalions, Zervas and the Germans, were suspected to be in league together, with the British behind them all. Papandreou refused the KKE's request for a more explicit denunciation of the Security Battalions, on the ground that the matter was covered by the Lebanon Charter, which declared that 'severe punishment will be imposed on traitors and those who have exploited the misfortunes of the people'. He was inhibited from going further by awareness of a general feeling (shared, among others, by his own armed forces) that ELAS had proved a worse affliction to the people than the Security Battalions. It seemed to EAM that Papandreou was pre-disposed to believe anything to their disadvantage and nothing against their rivals. For example, he took it for granted that in any clash with EDES, ELAS was at fault, which was not invariably true. He also accepted accusations that ELAS was in collusion with the Bulgarian authorities, and protested accordingly to General Mandakas, as the military member of PEEA.[16]

The Communists were even more suspicious of Zervas, whose contacts with the Germans became known in the summer of 1944. Accusations of such contacts were freely exchanged at the time, many of them quite absurd. Saraphis, for example, later published a plan alleged to have been drafted by the Germans and EDES to transfer Zervas's troops from Epirus to occupy Thrace and Macedonia, which was logistically impossible.[17] Zervas alleged that the Germans deliberately left weapons and ammunition behind to be taken over by ELAS in Epirus, though this was denied in later years by General Lanz, the German commander concerned.[18] Zervas also came into possession of two documents purporting to record agreements signed by ELAS with the Germans and Bulgarians in Macedonia during September 1944; but again the texts are of doubtful authenticity.[19]

Contacts between the KKE and the Bulgarians, however, form a special case. No more than a shadowy line divided the Bulgarian CP from the occupation authorities, and some officials were members of both. When the Fatherland Front, which was at first a genuine coalition, seized power in September 1944 and switched sides in the war, the same services continued largely unchanged under the new government. Consequently the links between the KKE and the Bulgarian CP, of which the Germans themselves had abundant evidence, were indirectly also links with the Bulgarian occupation authorities, particularly as the liberation drew near.[20] At that time Bulgarian Communists took the initiative in declaring that they had liberated the areas which previously they had occupied, particularly Thrace and Macedonia. Ministers of the Fatherland Front toured Greek territory, assuming that it would continue to be retained by Bulgaria, and proclaiming their solidarity with EAM. Their attitude caused consternation, which was shared by the Yugoslav Partisans and many Greek Communists. This was why Markos Vaphiadis, an essentially patriotic Communist, decided to enter Salonika without awaiting orders, and the Greek nationalists facilitated his task. It also accounts for the authority alleged to have been given to a subordinate ELAS officer, to sign an agreement with the Germans not to harass their retreat if Salonika were handed over to ELAS.[21]

All the Resistance organisations were in touch with the occupying powers at various times, though the Communists managed it more discreetly than the rest. When Tsaous Andon signed an agreement with the Bulgarians at the end of the Occupation in order to expedite their withdrawal, he was bitterly denounced by ELAS, not least because his action was sanctioned by a British Liaison Officer.[22] Their greatest wrath, however, was reserved for Zervas. German sources show that such agreements as were made by the Germans with ELAS were 'isolated and strictly local' whereas with Zervas they had a 'general armistice' from December 1943 to July 1944.[23] There are many references in German records and memoirs to his 'co-operative attitude' or to a 'gentleman's agreement' with him. Roland Hampe, an archaeologist serving as a counter-espionage agent, spoke of negotiations in Salonika, and General Lanz, commanding the Army Corps in Ioannina, recorded negotiations there.[24] Neubacher's memoirs are imprecise in detail, but the German archives make it clear that he was expressly charged by Hitler, who was in constant fear of an allied landing in the southern Balkans, with the task of neutralising the Resistance by subverting one of the major organisations.[25] EDES was the natural target, both because of Zervas's known anti-Communism and because his force was located in the region where allied landings were to be expected. Neubacher's efforts to seduce Zervas were successful, though also in a sense gratuitous.

Much controversy has surrounded Zervas's dealings with the Germans. What seemed unaccountable was that for a period of more than six months there should have been no sign that the Allied Liaison Officers reprobated or even noticed the fact that Zervas's forces were abstaining from any action against the Germans. Neubacher himself observed the seeming tolerance of Zervas's 'English friends', though he mistook the reason for it.[26] The explanation is simple, for during the relevant period a suspension of offensive activity had been ordered by GHQ, Middle East.[27] Once it became clear that Greece could not be liberated until 1944, orders were sent to the guerrillas to 'lie low', with certain defined exceptions, between the operations in support of the invasion of Sicily (Operation Animals June–July 1943) and those in support of the liberation of Greece (Operation Noah's Ark, originally planned for April 1944, later postponed to August). The presumption must be that Zervas took advantage of the allied instructions to make a temporary truce with the enemy, of the kind that his ancestors used to call a *kapáki* in their wars with the Turks; and he denounced it on 20 August 1944, when he received orders from GHQ to launch Noah's Ark. The Germans, according to Zervas's reasoning, gained nothing significant thereby. But he did not tell either his allies or even his second-in-command, Pyromaglou, because he knew they would disapprove.[28] Such arrangements were of quite a different order from the systematic collaboration perpetrated by some of his associates in Athens, whom he eventually denounced under pressure from ELAS and the British.

For Zervas it was a matter of survival, and he knew that his survival was vital to Papandreou and the British. If his forces were eliminated in the summer of 1944, the KKE would have had little incentive to join the Government of National Unity. Saraphis and Aris had in fact laid plans once more to destroy Zervas, but they were forestalled by two events. On 19 June Zervas launched a pre-emptive attack on ELAS units established near Preveza – one of the few occasions when EDES took the initiative in aggression – and successfully cleared the area, thus opening up the west coast to supplies by sea from Italy. In July the Germans launched a major onslaught against ELAS in Macedonia, supported by diversionary attacks in Roumeli and the Peloponnese. Operation Steinadler, as it was called, was the severest ever mounted by the Germans in Greece: it cost ELAS some two thousand casualties, and captured very large stocks of ammunition.[29] More important it delayed Saraphis's plans for eliminating Zervas. Before these could be renewed, events took a new turn with the arrival in the mountains of a Soviet Military Mission under Colonel Popov on the night of 27–28 July.

A few days earlier the Soviet Ambassador to the Greek Government had been recalled from Cairo. The coincidence of events caused some alarm to the British and Greek authorities, but in fact both were symptoms of a more favourable turn of Soviet policy. Saraphis, while congratulating himself on the successful infiltration of Popov's mission without the foreknowledge of the British and Americans, pretended to expect that the Russians would join the Allied Military Mission, which of course they did not.[30] Both he and the KKE, however, were disappointed by the actual outcome. Colonel Popov's message was that there would be no material help from the Soviet Union, and that EAM must make its peace with the British.[31] Similarly Novikov, according to American information, had advised Svolos shortly before he left Cairo that EAM should join Papandreou's government; and his Counsellor was believed to have given the same advice to Angelopoulos, one of Svolos's non-Communist colleagues.[32] Evidently Stalin had at last decided on a strong intervention to restore order to an increasingly disturbed situation. These indications foreshadowed the famous bargain which was to be struck between Churchill and Stalin in Moscow on 9 October, and which had already been mooted by Eden in the middle of May.[33] Nevertheless, the Soviet Government gave no notice to the British of its intention to send in a military mission, which took Churchill and Eden by surprise.*

A degree of co-operation cost Stalin little since Greece was not, in terms of Soviet interests, the central arena. Further north, much more serious threats to Soviet policy were caused by the evolution of relations between the Yugoslav and Bulgarian Communists. There had been a marked change since the beginning of the year, for the Bulgarians had come to recognise the dominant position of the Yugoslav Partisans and Tito had learned to handle his neighbours more tactfully. Stalin was annoyed by the growing independence of Tito, particularly his disregard of the need for good relations with the British and his pursuit of a personal policy in the Balkans. Tempo, the Partisan commander in Macedonia, was privately discussing the formation of a 'united Macedonia' with the Bulgarian CP; he was later alleged to have been contemplating the seizure of Salonika when the Germans withdrew; and his activities were supported by the first Anti-Fascist Assembly of National Liberation of Macedonia (ASNOM) in August. Many pronouncements were made in the autumn in favour of Macedonian autonomy: for example, by the Yugoslav Djilas and the Bulgarian Kostov (who later paid the penalty of Titoism), as well as by the Macedonian Gotsis, of SNOF; and an article by the Yugoslav Žujović (who later sided with Stalin against Tito) even claimed that EAM had promised its agreement.[34] The Bulgarian Communists, while plainly intending to take over the occupied areas of Greece, acknowledged that Macedonian autonomy would be set in the framework of a Federation dominated by Yugoslavia; and in the autumn formal negotiations were begun to that end.

Reactions in EAM to these manoeuvres were mixed. On the one hand, Markos Vaphiadis showed himself a determined nationalist by the firmness with which he treated Gotsis as a mutineer and made sure that neither Tempo nor the Bulgarians should take over Salonika. On the other hand, loyal Communists in EAM supported the party line and were to be seen fraternising with officials of the Bulgarian occupation. More serious than the reactions of EAM, however, was the attitude of Stalin. Only gradually did the Yugoslav and Bulgarian Communists realise that their negotiations were contrary to his wishes. Although Tito visited Moscow in September, and Kardelj in November, they continued to discuss federation with the Bulgarians, apparently oblivious of Stalin's disapproval. At the end of the year he insisted on the transfer of the negotiations to Moscow, where they were systematically frustrated by Molotov. This peremptory

* During a temporary absence from Greece, I was staying with Eden when the news reached him on 30 July, and heard him telephone it to Churchill. It was clearly unexpected by both.

intervention was symptomatic of a mood which the Balkan Communists had misunderstood. What should have been the clearest indication of it was Stalin's policy towards Greece, where he was determined not to have a quarrel with the British. To that requirement, Macedonian autonomy and Balkan federation were secondary. His interest was a peaceful liberation of Greece, and that in turn required the entry of EAM into Papandreou's government.

There was still opposition to be overcome. Early in August EAM agreed to join the Government only under another Prime Minister, and Papandreou accordingly offered to resign; but Churchill forbade it. At last, on 2 September, six representatives of EAM entered office on the same terms that they had resisted since May. By this time Papandreou was acting on his own authority without reference to anyone but the British Ambassador and British Ministers. He agreed at their request to move his seat of government from Cairo to Caserta in Italy on 26 August, without consulting his Cabinet, three members of which consequently resigned. One of the three, Constantine Rendis, complained in a letter to Zervas on 4 September of the Prime Minister's 'personal government'.[35] It was suspected that Papandreou's idea of a Regency was now that he should occupy the post himself. With this suspicion in mind, the King deputed his brother Paul to act as Regent while he himself returned to London at the end of August. Paul hoped that he at least would be allowed to return to Greece in that capacity, even if the King was prevented; but neither British Ministers nor Papandreou would accept such a compromise. Everything seemed to assure Papandreou that he was the master of events. Two meetings with Churchill in Italy (on 21 August and 8 October), coupled with the acquiescence of Roosevelt and Stalin, and the adhesion of the EAM representatives to his Government, confirmed that his position was secure.

There remained, however, the problem of securing a peaceful and orderly liberation of Greece when the expected withdrawal of the Germans took place. The requirements that had to be met were an allied force of adequate size, and the co-operation of the Resistance organisations. On 17 August Churchill had asked for logistic support from the Americans for a force of ten thousand men to be sent to Athens; on 26 August Roosevelt had agreed; and on 23 September Stalin expressed his approval.[36] But it was difficult to detach so large a force, especially of combatant troops, from the Italian campaign. It was therefore all the more necessary to secure the co-operation of the guerrillas. The starting-point was the Plaka Agreement of 29 February, which had sanctioned the infiltration of 'special British and American units' to take part in the liberation. These would be insufficient by themselves to establish order without the help of the guerrillas; besides, it was necessary to regularise the relationship between allied and guerrilla units. At the Plaka Conference the guerrillas had been unable to agree on a Greek Commander-in-Chief, but it was thought that they would accept a British General. Accordingly Saraphis and Zervas were invited to the allied GHQ at Caserta in the late summer, to meet Sir Ronald Scobie, who had been appointed General Officer Commanding the British forces destined for Greece.

Zervas was accompanied to Caserta by Pyromaglou and his bodyguard, Saraphis by Despotopoulos and his batman. The latter were joined on arrival by the Communist Zevgos, now a Minister in Papandreou's government, who took charge of the discussions on the side of ELAS and treated Saraphis as little more than a technical adviser.[37] But it was Saraphis who had to sign the resultant agreement, much against his will, on 26 September. The Caserta Agreement placed the guerrilla forces under the orders of the Greek Government of National Unity, which in turn placed them under General Scobie.[38] It also contained detailed provisions for the maintenance of law and order. Saraphis's one success was to secure the omission of the phrase 'to restore' law and order; but the troops he was supposed to command were already systematically disobeying the provision which forbade guerrilla units 'to take the law into their own hands'. Precisely how much authority Zervas and Saraphis had resigned into Scobie's hands was not clear, and was to be bitterly disputed a few weeks later in Athens. Meanwhile Scobie appointed Spiliotopoulos (formerly chief of the 'Six Colonels') as Military Governor of Athens and Attica. As compensation to ELAS in return for their concessions, General Othonaios, whom they respected, was nominated as the future Commander-in-Chief in place of Vendiris. But many Communists considered that the subordination of ELAS to Scobie was a fatal surrender.

Papandreou was later criticised from the right for admitting EAM to the Government just as severely as Siantos was criticised by Karagiorgis and Zakhariadis for allowing his colleagues to join it. Papandreou's justification was that if EAM were not included in the Government, ELAS would seize control of Athens as the Germans left. In the climate of international opinion at the time it would then be impossible to dislodge them; and in any case, the British could not provide sufficient forces to do so.[39] The essential condition, he argued, was to have the Communists within the Government so that they would be faced by the dilemma: to disarm or revolt. Their dilemma would be enhanced by the fact that their colleagues in PEEA now included moderate men like Svolos who would not easily sanction rebellion. In this line of argument he had the support of his predecessor, Tsouderos, who wrote him a letter on 24 July encouraging him to persist in his efforts to draw EAM into his government.[40] Kanellopoulos also agreed that in the unsatisfactory circumstances (for which he blamed the British policy of supporting ELAS) there was no alternative open at the time.[41]

The British authorities inclined on the whole to support a similar line of reasoning, though there were divided counsels among them. General Wilson, now the Commander-in-Chief of the Mediterranean Theatre, still regarded ELAS favourably; and a visit to the mountains by Brigadier Barker-Benfield, the commander of SOE in Cairo, helped to delude ELAS that they might still win the day by dividing the British. On the other hand, Churchill was again considering an open breach with EAM and a withdrawal of the Allied Military Mission, though at the same time he and Eden were urging EAM to join Papandreou's government and pressing Papandreou to make it easier for them to do so by a more explicit denunciation of the Security Battalions.[42] Another uncertainty loomed over the fate of the mutineers in Egypt, twenty-four of whom were condemned to death (though eventually all were reprieved). The prospect of a bloodless liberation hung in the balance. Although the Germans were a spent force, they were still capable of atrocities which invited equally savage reprisals against their collaborators. Their withdrawal, beginning in September 1944, was harassed only by the guerrillas and small allied units, with support from the air. Considering that the Greeks only wanted to see the last of them as soon as possible, the harassing operations were unexpectedly effective.

Some German units, however, particularly those from the outlying islands, had the impression that they were being allowed to escape unhindered, if not 'under the protection of allied guns'.[43] Though certainly false, this impression was linked with the suspicion (which had remained alive since Captain Stott's unauthorised mission to Athens in the previous winter) that the British were willing to make a secret accommodation with the Germans to the disadvantage of their Soviet allies. Both German and Communist propagandists delighted in spreading such rumours. Another story of the same kind gained currency, that General Scobie sought to make contact with Neubacher, the German plenipotentiary in Athens, to obtain help in averting a Communist take-over.[44] Neubacher recorded that he was willing to co-operate, but the proposal 'was immediately and decisively rejected' by his own superiors. The story is not only improbable and out of character, but in conflict with a message sent by General Wilson through Archbishop Damaskinos on 10 October, which was later published by EAM, to the effect that there could be no negotiation whatever with the Germans 'except in the event of unconditional surrender'.[45]

Undoubtedly the rumoured approach by Scobie was an attempt to make mischief. There is evidence in the German archives of a calculated policy of using contacts with enemy agents to disrupt relations both within the Resistance and between the British and Russians.[46] Opportunities to do so occurred both in Epirus and in Athens, where Generals Lanz and Felmy respectively received approaches from agents of SOE and did not rebuff them. In each case, however, discussions of a general surrender were forestalled by German orders to withdraw from Greece.[47]

Felmy in particular was suffering a crisis of conscience over his orders, which required him to carry out a policy of 'scorched earth' in and around Athens. He was determined to disobey these orders, even if he could not arrive at some understanding with the British.[48] He allowed Roland Hampe to undertake negotiations with a number of Greeks in order to save Athens from destruction. Clearly all depended on the attitude of ELAS, which was cautious and ambiguous. A secret emissary to Saraphis brought back word that ELAS would not attack the retreating Germans, and copies of an order to that effect, signed by Saraphis, were widely distributed. Immediately there followed a counter-order from the Central Committee of EAM stating that 'no German soldier must leave Greece alive'. Another emissary to Siantos brought an oral reply that 'the Communists will adopt a passive attitude towards the Germans'.[49] Felmy thereupon took the risk, on 10 October, of making a unilateral undertaking to treat Athens as an open city. The allies, including ELAS, respected the declaration, but did not regard it as applying to Piraeus. Minor sabotage of a token character therefore took place in the port. The Marathon Dam was only saved from destruction by a unit of ELAS with an Allied Liaison Officer. On 12 October, the final day of departure, the Germans laid a wreath on the tomb of the Unknown Soldier 'as a token that they had not set foot in Greece as enemies of the country'.[50] The Germans were thus eliminated as a factor in the period of transition.

A precarious balance of forces was left behind them: or rather, a confused multiplicity of forces, for they did not form two opposing sides except in the imagination of EAM. In numbers ELAS was much the strongest, with some 70,000 men under arms, this including reserves. The British force under Scobie numbered initially little more than 4,000, who were mainly non-combatants, though by November it was to rise to nearly 23,000 men. The Greek Third Brigade was not available at first, being engaged in action in Italy from 8 September, where it won honour by the capture of Rimini. The forces of Zervas, Tsaous

Andon and others were too remote from Athens to play a significant role. Other forces were too small, or unreliable, or otherwise impossible to use.

The Security Battalions tried to put themselves at the Government's disposal, and Saraphis feared that they would be allowed to do so, when he received orders from Scobie to require them to fight the Germans, or failing that to intern them, but not to attack them. Another force, active only in Athens, was an organisation of irregular but disciplined street-fighters formed by Colonel George Grivas (later well known as the leader of EOKA in Cyprus), under the name of X (the Greek letter *Khi*). They engaged in nightly conflict with EAM in Athens, fortunately much of it limited to shouting slogans and abuse through megaphones. Finally, it was alleged that arms, money, and even a small task-force were smuggled into Athens from Italy to strengthen the hand of General Spiliotopoulos.[51] But the scale of such reinforcement cannot have been large.

If EAM had wished to seize control of Athens as the Germans withdrew, nothing could have prevented them. As Papandreou later admitted, an opposed landing of British forces against them would then have been 'politically impossible'.[52] At the beginning of October it was still uncertain what would happen. Scobie had ordered that ELAS should not enter the capital, and the largest available force, under the *kapetánios* Orestis, was instructed by ELAS GHQ to obey. There was, however, a large number of ELAS reserves in civilian clothes already in Athens, estimated at over three thousand by an ELAS source but reported by American sources towards the end of the month to amount to a full division.[53] They would have had no difficulty in taking over the city, as some activists wished to do. According to Bartzotas in 1950, 'the direction of the KOA (Communist Organisation of Athens) decided to prepare for armed insurrection in the course of two meetings held at the beginning of the month of September'.[54] Others who favoured drastic action included professional soldiers, such as Mandakas and Makridis, besides Saraphis, who was eager for a final show-down with Zervas.[55]

Aris Veloukhiotis, who had wreaked vengeance in September on the Security Battalions and all others whom he identified as collaborators in the Peloponnese, was back at GHQ in Lamia talking menacingly of 'new battles' and trying to recruit support for a revolt against any concessions. Among those trying to restrain him was Markos Vaphiadis. Markos's conduct was somewhat inconsistent, for he had himself (with Bakirdzis) occupied Salonika without orders, and lost no time in attacking the forces of Mikhalagas and Tsaous Andon, though neither was completely liquidated until December. EAM in Macedonia had in fact openly denounced the Lebanon Charter.[56] The advocates there of an uncompromising line had a strong supporter in Tzimas, who was now with Tito. From the Partisans' GHQ on the island of Vis, he had first paid a flying visit to Caserta, where he sought to stiffen the EAM members of Papandreou's government, and then accompanied Tito to Belgrade. It is doubtful whether Tito paid much attention to him, but that did not deter him from sending messages to Athens urging opposition to the British.

The official leadership of the KKE, however, was more cautious. Their mood was one partly of conciliation, but partly also of indecision. Study of their publications has revealed a strain not only of moderation but also of staunch nationalism.[57] Intercepted communications between the KKE, EAM and ELAS show that there was real anxiety about the possibility of being attacked, but the precautions ordered were essentially defensive.[58] This is not to say that the leadership of the KKE was unanimously committed – though Siantos genuinely was – to co-operation with Papandreou: Ioannidis, to take one example, certainly was not. But the activists who were spoiling for a fight were for the present under control. They were not inhibited from making contingency plans, which might be and eventually were put into operation when the party line changed. The conciliatory policy was then bitterly criticised – by Zachariadis as folly and treason, and by Vlandas as 'playing the game of British and Soviet imperialism'.[59]

The paradoxical identification of British and Soviet policy, implied in Vlandas's criticism, was indeed correct. It was this simple but unexpected fact that so confused Communist policy. Zachariadis himself acknowledged in 1945 that Britain and the Soviet Union were 'two poles' around which Greek policy had to revolve.[60] When Churchill stopped briefly in Caserta on 8 October on his way to Moscow, Papandreou made urgent representations to him about the continued Bulgarian occupation of Macedonia and Thrace. As a result Churchill obtained from Stalin a peremptory order to the Bulgarians that they should withdraw totally and at once from Greek territory.[61] Some members of EAM, who had already begun fraternising with the Bulgarian turncoats, were taken by surprise; others, of a more nationalist outlook, including Markos Vaphiadis and Bakirdzis, were relieved.

Unhappily, similar considerations did not apply to the situation in Athens. By 1950, Zachariadis had come to think of the liberation as 'the British invasion'.[62] He castigated Partsalidis for saying (in 1946) that 'no one could imagine that the Greek people ... would find themselves under British military occupation'. Similarly Siantos was reported to have said (also in 1946) that 'the British fooled us', by which he presumably meant that he had expected a much larger British force, against which ELAS would have been powerless; and when only a small force came, he assumed that it would not resist a Communist bid for power.[63] Zakhariadis denounced Partsalidis for stupidity and Siantos for treachery. In his view virtually every decision taken by the KKE in 1943–4 contributed to a state of unnecessary subservience to the British. He criticised the composition and policy of PEEA, the organisation and political orientation of ELAS, the signature of the Lebanon Charter, the subordination of ELAS to the British GHQ and the Caserta Agreement. But all this was said with the wisdom of hindsight. In the autumn of 1944 Zakhariadis was still in a German concentration-camp, and no one even knew whether he was alive.

The substance of Zakhariadis's retrospective complaints was that it was folly to give Papandreou and the British the credit for acting in good faith. It should have been assumed, he argued, that they intended to strike down and destroy ELAS, and therefore ELAS should have struck first. Even at the time, among the divided counsels of EAM, there were those who took that view: Saraphis, for example, thought that the object of the Caserta Agreement (though he signed it himself) was to break up the unity of ELAS with a view to eliminating it later.[64] Others with fighting experience, like Makridis, Mandakas and Aris Veloukhiotis, thought the same. It is not easy to say which view was right, because there were equally divided counsels on the British side. The composition of General Scobie's force was based on the assumption of a peaceful liberation: its code-name, Operation Manna, implied as much. The British official history argued that its main object was 'to prevent, not to counter' a seizure of power by EAM, yet the military planners gave no sign of believing such an attempt likely.[65] Both the King and Papandreou considered the force inadequate. The former believed that Churchill had promised two or three divisions; the latter begged again and again for more British forces, and for their deployment throughout Greece up to the northern frontiers.[66] He also urged the early return to Greece of the Third Mountain Brigade from Italy, and the Sacred Squadron, which was operating in the Aegean under Colonel Tsigantes; but neither could be made available for some weeks.

In a situation where each side distrusts the other and believes itself to be in danger of attack, it is impossible to distinguish between precaution and provocation. Each side would have regarded its own instructions as purely defensive, but if the other side had known them at the time it would have regarded them as aggressive. On the side of the returning forces, the Greeks were more distrustful than the British. An illuminating note was recorded by General Tsakalotos, Commander of the Third Mountain Brigade, shortly before his own return to Athens:

The secret orders of the government are categorical: no trust in ELAS or EAM and no co-operation (with them) in the preservation of order. Unfortunately some senior officers do not obey, taking the view that since five EAM Ministers are members of the government, their forces too should be used to keep order ... The Security Battalions are in a most difficult position, since they have been denounced as traitors by the government. But the Military Governor (Spiliotopoulos) has given them appropriate instructions, with an undertaking, which is not correct, that they will be pardoned. They are needed to counteract EAM, which is insistently demanding their disbandment.[67]

If the leaders of the KKE could have seen that note at the time, they would have taken it as confirming their worst apprehensions. On the other hand, the British attitude is well described by an American historian: 'The British military authorities were prepared for defence, from at least August 1944 ... and these defence preparations became intensified as danger from the Left appeared to grow in the month of November.'[68] *Mutatis mutandis*, the same assessment could have been made by a sympathetic historian of EAM.

So it was with great wariness, as well as ostensible harmony, that the two sides confronted each other on 17 October, when a small Anglo-Greek armada arrived off Piraeus, accompanied by Papandreou, Scobie, Macmillan and Leeper. The King had been persuaded at last to absent himself. Some Greek Ministers had already arrived in Greece, only to find how powerless they were. Kanellopoulos had been a helpless witness of Aris's atrocities against the Security Battalions and other so-called 'reactionaries' in the Peloponnese. Other Ministers had been despatched to the north, only to find that the guerrilla leaders were acting as their own masters. In Epirus, Zervas was drastically solving the problem of the Chams, many of whom had collaborated with the enemy, by driving them out of Greece into Albania; in Macedonia, Markos had dealt similarly with Gotsis, and was rounding up the remnants of Mikhalagas and Tsaous Andon. It was already evident that in the provinces the writ of the Government did not run, and the rule of law meant the will of the Resistance. But in contrast with these bloody episodes, the liberation of Athens was peaceful. On the day of the allies' arrival, the Politburo of the KKE passed a resolution welcoming 'the brave children of Great Britain, our freedom-loving ally'.[69] Only in one instance did the KKE take control without authority, but also without violence: Porphyrogennis, as Minister of Labour, was able tacitly to facilitate the occupation of the premises of the General Confederation of Trade Unions by EEAM.[70] For the rest, the formal restoration of legitimate government on 18 October was undisputed.

Seen from the point of view of the Resistance, the conduct of the Greek and British authorities was not entirely conciliatory. On arrival in Athens, Papandreou reconstructed his Cabinet with a decided inclination towards the right wing.[71] In the parade which marked his entry into the capital, no place was found for representatives of the Resistance. Scobie's headquarters were installed in the same building which the Germans had recently vacated. His staff officers immediately began discussing how to 'disarm' the Resistance forces, without any consideration of using more tactful terms such as 'demobilisation' or rewarding them with decorations. It was as if a deliberate effort were being made to disregard all that had happened between April 1941 and October 1944. Many people were indeed trying to forget; others felt as if they were being liberated from the Resistance as well as from the Occupation; but others resented being thrust aside. Restlessness took the form of daily demonstrations, organised by Communists or Royalists, chanting 'Popular Democracy' (*laokratía*) or 'Greater Greece' (*Megáli Elláda*) respectively. Papandreou ingeniously combined both slogans in his speeches.[72]

Liberation was thus welcomed with a combination of joy and anxiety. The ordinary people, starved and decimated, survived amid ruins and fear. For the ruins the blame lay on the Germans, but the causes of fear lay with the Communists and even the British. It was widely believed that the threat of Communism in the autumn of 1944 was due to errors of judgment by the British during the Occupation, and that if those errors continued, the KKE would take over power in Greece. Later formulations of the argument took on a more far-reaching character: if the British had not armed ELAS, there would have been no threat of Communism; there would also have been no rising in Athens in December, and no civil war between 1946 and 1949; neither the first nor the second nor the third round, on this hypothesis, would ever have occurred. There is a logical basis for the argument, but the logic is not so simple as it is represented.

There was bound to be resistance in any case. Only the nature of it was in doubt. As a Greek military historian wrote:[73] 'The Second World War showed the necessity of liberation movements, in the course of which it was evident that no social class and no political group stood to lose anything from them if it fought whole-heartedly and with determination against the Occupation.' This lesson was learned by the Communists but neglected by other Greek leaders. Before the British had made any direct contact with the Resistance on the Greek mainland, ELAS was already actively in arms; but almost no nationalist Greek had yet taken the field except Zervas, who did so only on British instigation.[74] All sources agree on the woeful dilatoriness of nationalist leaders and senior officers to recognise their opportunity, which was also their duty. Colonel Khrysokhoou described the vigorous activity of the Communists in Macedonia during the summer of 1942, while respectable Greeks ('merchants, bankers, industrialists, lawyers, teachers and other people of importance') did nothing to counteract them.[75] General Tsakalotos, who was in Athens at the same time, wrote that 'the nationalists proffered the greatest help to the KKE . . . by their follies and divisions.'[76] The memoirs and biographies of many politicians and soldiers are eloquent of their hesitations.

The point was well made by others who did not hesitate over their duty. Pyromaglou, for example, wrote that 'the senior political and military leadership which remained in occupied Greece never took part in the Resistance throughout the Occupation, and from the middle of 1943 reacted against it for fear of its own elimination after the liberation'.[77] Zervas's most ardent supporter, Dr Khoutas, wrote equally emphatically in the same sense.[78] The difference between the Communists and the rest was that the Communists did not wait to be instigated. The British did not create ELAS: they found it in existence; the only question for them was whether to use it or boycott it. The latter course would have involved a serious diminution of activity against the Occupation. Post-war examination of the German records has shown that guerrilla activity, principally by ELAS, was more valuable than was appreciated at the time.[79] It can be argued nevertheless that success was bought at too high a price: it would have been better, many believed, to have given ELAS no material support at all.

The exact scale of British material aid to ELAS, and hence to the KKE, is not easy to assess. There are discrepant figures given by different sources; and allowance has to be made for the fact that neither ELAS alone nor the guerrilla movement as a whole was the only recipient in Greece, nor was SOE the only source. The total number of sovereigns infiltrated into Greece has been estimated as high as two million (by the Bank of Athens) and as low as 1·23 million (by SOE itself);[80] but these two figures are not necessarily inconsistent, because the former includes importation by the Occupation authorities. Receipts by ELAS therefore perhaps fell between three-quarters and one million. In the case of material supplies by sea and air, there are again different estimates. An American source quotes a figure of 2,514 tons dropped by air, but gives no figure for sea-transportation; SOE's own estimate was 4,090 tons by sea and 1,706 tons by air.[81] A striking fact about SOE's figures is that eighty-five per cent of the tonnage is attributed to food and clothing: arms and ammunition accounted for less than 1,000 tons. It was also estimated by SOE that ninety per cent of the sovereigns infiltrated were spent on food and maintenance, but that is an over-simple conclusion. It rests on the assumption that the sovereign was equivalent to two pounds sterling, which is a gross underestimate; and it overlooks ELAS's practice of confiscating supplies from Greek merchants without payment. More seriously, since there is no doubt that ELAS had far more weapons than the British ever supplied, it is probable that a considerable surplus of sovereigns was built up and expended by the KKE on purchases of arms and ammunition from the enemy.

Most difficult of all to assess accurately is the scale of supply of weapons, though the orders of magnitude are fairly clear. Communist sources tend to give both higher figures for the total armament of ELAS and lower figures for the British supplies than do British sources, the implication being that the whole of the difference was accounted for by booty captured from the enemy. An interesting comparison can be made between the quantities of weapons actually surrendered by ELAS in February 1945, according to a Communist source, and the quantities promised under the terms of the armistice agreement (the latter figures being given in brackets): artillery pieces, 100 (32); mortars 219 (163); heavy machine-guns 419 (315); light machine-guns 1,412 (1,050); light automatics 713 (650); rifles and pistols 48,953 (41,500); anti-tank rifles 57 (none specified).[82] From later evidence it is known that although ELAS handed in more weapons than it promised, many more were retained and hidden. With these figures should be contrasted the Communists' estimate of what they received from the British: 10 mortars, 30 machine-guns, 100 light machine-guns (Brens), 300 light automatics (Stens) and 3,000 rifles.[83] The figures are no doubt under-estimated, but when they are set alongside SOE's own estimate that less than 1,000 tons of arms and ammunition were supplied to the whole of the Greek Resistance, it is plain that the Communists' estimates were not exaggeratedly low and that only a small proportion of their armament came directly from British sources. In purely material terms, SOE obtained resistance at a cheap price, though it is difficult to say precisely how cheap it was.

To quantify the value of the guerrilla operations against the Germans is even more difficult. An American summary concludes that the guerrillas 'did perform valuable military services for the Allied cause', without attempting to measure them mathematically.[84] A British official historian gives figures which must be regarded with caution.[85] On the railway system the damage is said to have amounted to 117 trains derailed, 209 locomotives and 1,544 wagons destroyed, the equivalent of 28 kilometres of track destroyed in hundreds of different places, 5 tunnels and 67 bridges demolished (including two of the largest viaducts in Greece). On the roads the destruction amounted to 854 motor vehicles, plus 136 bridges and the equivalent of 12 kilometres of telephone wire. Miscellaneous destruction included 17 ammunition and petrol dumps, 1,560 tons of petrol, 16 tanks, 5 aircraft on the ground (and also 2 shot down in the air). Among stores captured were 102 motor vehicles, 12,000 cases of explosives, 870 rifles and 10,000 rounds of ammunition, 80 machine-guns and mortars, 36 heavy machine-guns and 220 horses. Although these figures are said to have been authenticated by British officers, they almost certainly include some double-counting and even more exaggeration. It must also be remembered that much of the damage was inflicted not merely on the Germans but on the Greek national economy, to the detriment of post-war reconstruction.

The last reservation has to be made even more emphatically in assessing the balance of human losses. Again there are discrepant figures.[86] German casualties are estimated at a total between 5,000 and 15,000 dead, wounded and missing; and that excludes the Italians, thousands of whom died in the mountains after their surrender in September 1943, as well as the Bulgarians. Guerrilla casualties are variously estimated. A low figure for ELAS alone is 4,500 dead and 6,000 wounded; but German statistics (which may be exaggerated) yield a total of 20,650 killed and 25,728 wounded for all forces between June 1943 and September 1944 alone. The same statistics show 4,795 executed, but civilian casualties from reprisals were certainly much higher than that. They have been estimated at 70,000, nearly equal to military casualties in the Albanian War. Deaths due to starvation and other circumstances of the Occupation were very much higher still, though these would have taken place in any case and were not due to the Resistance. On balance, however, there can be no question that the ratio of human as well as material losses was heavily adverse, and that a substantial proportion of both was directly attributable to the Resistance. Only imponderable factors can be set in the scale on the other side: that Greek philótimo would have permitted no other course; that the demoralisation of abject surrender would have been a national disaster that could never have been retrieved; that a Greece which did not resist the Occupation would have ended up like Bulgaria or Rumania. These things are true, but they are at best doubtful quantities.

It would be wrong, however, to give too much weight to the contention that the Western Allies gained nothing at all of military value by supporting ELAS. An exaggerated version of this view holds that 'in the task of organising rebel bands, the KKE was helped in preference to all other bands by Britain with arms, money, material of all kinds and British instructors, because they were misled by false promises that the rebel organisations would fight against the Occupation'.[87] It is false that ELAS was given preference; it is probable that arms directly supplied by the British amounted to barely ten per cent of the equipment of ELAS; and the implication that ELAS did not fight against the Occupation is refuted by German records. The evidence of Generals Loehr, Lanz and Speidel leaves no doubt of the nuisance value of the guerrillas, by which term they meant principally ELAS;[88] for Zervas's forces, though more compact and controllable, were much smaller, and their main value was simply that they existed in a strategically sensitive area. On the other hand, the exaggerated claims of Saraphis about the achievements of ELAS must equally be discounted, even though they seem to have influenced the British official history.[89] Only a small fraction of the armed man-power of ELAS was ever in action against the Germans. The rest were reserved for purposes of political control. But those who fought, fought well; and they detained about three hundred thousand enemy troops in Greece.[90] It is perhaps reasonable to describe them as a 'running sore', which is not a negligible function under enemy occupation.[91] In any case, the balance of gain and loss is not one that can be determined arithmetically.

The British official histories, both diplomatic and military, are unhelpful in the task of assessment. *British Foreign Policy in the Second World War* was based entirely on Foreign Office documents, without regard to SOE material, much of which was available in the same files.[92] It therefore endorses the prejudices of the Foreign Office. In the relevant volumes of *Grand Strategy*, one historian accepted grossly inflated estimates of the successes achieved against the retreating Germans in Operation Noah's Ark; another, going to the opposite extreme, heightened the contrast between the Yugoslavs and the Greeks by writing that the former made 'excellent use' of the weapons supplied to them, but 'as for the unhappy Greeks, how many of their weapons were used against the Germans and how many against each other is a question no historian is ever likely to resolve' – which is true, but equally true of the Yugoslavs.[93] In effect the latter historian followed Churchill in implying that after July 1943 the Greeks failed in their duty to fight the Germans, and only fought each other.[94]

The truth is more complex. The Greek guerrillas were under orders from GHQ, Middle East, to refrain from offensive activity, with occasional specific exceptions, for the greater part of twelve months from July 1943. Nevertheless, the continued existence of the guerrillas and the allied missions with them helped to sustain the Germans' fears, right up to September 1944, that an allied invasion of the Balkans in force was being planned. This is evident from Hitler's War Directives as well as other German sources.[95] Considerable German forces were thus detained in Greece, and frequent operations were undertaken to eliminate the guerrillas. Apart from occasional reprisals in all parts of the country, nine operations sufficiently serious to warrant code-names were launched in northern Greece between September 1943 and August 1944.[96] In most cases the target was ELAS, which was the organisation least inclined to obey the orders to refrain from the offensive. These facts do not wipe out the stain of the first civil war, but they help to redress the balance.

Resistance must be judged as a totality. A high proportion of the Greek Resistance was ineffective from the allied point of view, because it was primarily directed to securing other political ends; but the smaller proportion which was effective could not have been used, nor even have existed, in isolation from the totality. There were other aspects too of the Resistance which depended in an invisible way from the organisations active in the mountains. There were, for example, the escape routes, which returned to the allies thousands of ex-prisoners of war and hundreds of airmen shot down over Greece. There were intelligence and sabotage networks in the towns, among which that of Peltekis (Apollo) was one of the most brilliantly successful in any capital city of occupied Europe. There was the National Workers' Liberation Front (EEAM), which frustrated the conscription of labour: this too, like ELAS, could not have existed without the KKE behind it. There was the clandestine press, which again depended wholly on the political organisations. Many would have liked to have one or another of these assets without the rest of the Resistance. But they were simply inseparable.

There are naturally different approaches to the assessment of the Resistance among Greeks, as well as between Greek and British writers. Greek historians sympathetic to the Resistance, like Gatopoulos and Enepekidis, are apt to measure its value by tabulating lists of incidents as though the mere statistics of activity were conclusive. They also throw into the balance the heavy casualties and material damage suffered under the Occupation, which other Greeks regard as evidence against the Resistance rather than in its favour. Allied assessments attach more importance to the tactical results of operations in relation to overall strategy. They give more weight to the location and timing of operations than to mere numbers. In this respect the determination of ELAS GHQ, in contrast with Zervas, not to submit to allied guidance in the detailed execution of allied requirements was unfortunate. An extreme example of useless effort and waste of life was the attack on the Tyrnavos railway-tunnel in May 1943, in which Saraphis took such pride.[97] By way of contrast, an accumulation of quite small operations directly related to allied strategy could have a disproportionate value, as when the Germans were deceived into thinking that Greece rather than Sicily was the next target after the North African campaign.[98] But the Greeks did not always see the point of such carefully orchestrated plans, because they naturally supposed that the allies' first priority was the same as their own — the liberation of Greece. Some even argued that since the Germans were bound to be defeated eventually in any case, there was no point in Resistance, which would merely open the door to Communism.

It is true that the Resistance contributed little to the liberation of Greece, as distinct from the harassment of the Occupation. Greece was liberated by the indirect effect of forces operating elsewhere in Europe: principally by the Red Army advancing from the East, and secondarily by the Western Allies advancing through France and Italy. The Germans withdrew from Greece not because they were driven out but in order to avoid being entirely cut off from their home-base, as their garrison in Crete actually was. It follows that the Resistance requires justification on grounds other than the liberation of Greece. It was, of course, a psychological necessity for the Greeks: they would not have been Greeks if they had not resisted the barbarians; they were temperamentally incapable of passive non-resistance. This vein of temperament was skilfully tapped by the Communists, and less skilfully by other Greeks who lacked their conspiratorial experience.

There can be no certainty in hypothetical arguments about past events. But it is clear that EAM and ELAS would not have ceased to exist if the British had boycotted them or had not been there at all: they would only have been more uncontrollable. As Myers observed to Pyromaglou in the summer of 1943, 'You must not forget that EAM, with all its force and self-sufficiency, was already in existence and in operation before I ever arrived in Greece.'[99] If the British had tried to support Zervas while boycotting ELAS, the latter would have attacked EDES earlier. Up to the spring of 1943 Zervas would have had scarcely more chance of survival than Saraphis or Psaros. In that case ELAS would have been the only armed Resistance left in the field, and the seizure of power by the KKE when the occupation ended would have been hard to forestall. An American historian went so far as to conclude that the survival of EDES was by itself sufficient justification for 'every effort of every Allied liaison officer sent to Greece'.[100] It is true that if a decision to boycott ELAS had been taken, the Communists would have been less well supplied: there would have been no British sovereigns and no Italian arms from the Pinerolo Division. But neither of these relative deficiencies would have been decisive. The probability is rather that ELAS would have been more dependent on the Yugoslav Partisans, and the KKE more subservient to Tito.

The arguments are finely balanced and hard to settle definitively. In the circumstances of mid-1942 – a date which proved to be barely half-way through the war, and might have been much less – it would have been unreasonable for the British authorities to reject anyone prepared to fight the Germans; and this the Communists were certainly prepared to do, at any rate after Hitler's attack on the Soviet Union. Once it had been decided to support ELAS as a fighting force, which entailed support of EAM as a Resistance organisation, it would have been difficult to reverse the decision, even if it had been desirable. It can be pointed out that such a reversal was in fact carried through in the case of the anti-Communist Mihailović. In that case the reason was that Mihailović refused to fight the Germans, which could not reasonably be argued (although, unreasonably, it was) against ELAS. The most that could be said against the leaders of ELAS was that fighting the Germans was a secondary, but not a negligible, consideration compared to acquiring power in post-war Greece; and that they would fight the Germans only at times and in ways of their own choosing.

The conclusion to which these arguments point is clear but paradoxical. It is true that there would probably have been no December rising and no civil war from 1946 to 1949 if the British had withheld all support from ELAS between 1942 and 1944. But it is true only because in that case the KKE would have been already masters of Greece in 1944, and it would have been 'politically impossible', as Papandreou saw, to force an allied landing against them.[101] Public opinion in the West, skilfully nurtured by Communist propaganda, was sympathetic to all Resistance movements, particularly to those with left-wing affiliations. If ELAS had fought alone, or as a component of Tito's Partisans, that sympathy would have been even stronger. The consequences can hardly be doubted. To say this is not to condone the many tactical errors of British policy. It is only to assert that the British intervention in occupied Greece made one contribution to Greek history that could not have come about in any other way. Instead of a *fait accompli*, it left the Greek people with a choice. Unfortunately, they chose civil war.

It is customary to excuse the Greek people on that score by shifting the responsibility elsewhere: to Hitler or Stalin, Churchill or King George II, or their various agents. All of these certainly bore some of the blame for the tragic climax of December 1944. Without Hitler there would have been no Occupation and therefore no collaborators; no Resistance and therefore no Security Battalions. Stalin, paradoxically, carried the least burden of direct responsibility, though his doctrines inspired the KKE and his inscrutable indifference did nothing to restrain it. The combined stubbornness of Churchill and the King was a proximate cause of the tragedy. If they had accepted at the beginning of 1943 the realities which they were compelled to accept at the end of 1944 – in particular, that the King could not return to his throne as if nothing had happened – then the December events might not have occurred. But even if those particular events had not occurred, it is a delusion to suppose that nothing else would have taken their place. The Greek people were too deeply divided to have simply resumed their history where it had broken off in 1941, or even in 1936. The KKE would hardly have allowed a peaceful transition from occupation to liberation without contemplating some such future action as took place in Czechoslovakia in February 1948.* Those Greeks whom the KKE called 'reactionaries' – that is to say, at least everyone to the right of Papandreou, who called himself a Social Democrat – would still have been determined to destroy EAM. Different scenarios can be imagined, but none could have taken place without bitterness and probably bloodshed. This is not an accusation against the Greek people, to use Aris's expression. It is merely a recognition of fact.

* Papandreou made this point in an article in *Kathimerini* on 2 March 1948, which drew the conclusion that 'December (1944) may be regarded as a gift from the Almighty'. Text reproduced in Papandreou, pp. 292–301.

5

The December Events
November 1944–February 1945

THREE WEEKS after the Germans left Athens, the state of Greece was tense but uncertain. Neither side had formed any aggressive intentions, but each suspected the other. Siantos and Partsalidis imposed a co-operative policy on ELAS, as did Macmillan and Leeper on the Greek authorities. The latter had no resources except what the British provided, and the British would not divert man-power from actual operations in Italy to forestall hypothetical dangers in a friendly country. Nor did any encouragement to militancy come from any external source. The Americans were ostentatiously neutral, taking no part except in relief operations. It was not until December, when the Americans supported the idea of a Regency, that their policy was anything but non-committal. Mac-Veagh was therefore obliged to adopt an attitude of 'detached interest', as Macmillan called it; with which may be contrasted the Soviet authorities' attitude, equally well described as one of 'gloomy disinterest'.[1] There is no evidence of any incitement of EAM by the Soviet Government: quite the contrary. The Yugoslavs seemed just as indifferent. Tzimas, who had entered Belgrade with Tito on 27 October, could see for himself that the Yugoslavs were in no position to support aggressive action.

If violence were to occur in Greece, therefore, it would arise from within. The danger was greatest in Athens. Elsewhere there was no similar confrontation between rival forces, except to a limited extent in Salonika, where control was shared by ELAS, under Markos Vaphiadis and Bakirdzis, with a British–Indian Division; but in Macedonia ELAS's freedom of action was still hampered by tension with the Yugoslav Partisans.[2] In a few other towns, principally ports such as Preveza, Patras, Volos and Kavalla, small British units were also present, chiefly for non-combatant duties connected with supply, communications and relief. The rest of the mainland was under the control of the guerrillas: Zervas, with his HQ at Ioannina, holding most of Epirus; ELAS, with its HQ at Lamia, holding Macedonia, Thessaly, Roumeli and the Peloponnese. The islands were controlled partly by EAM and partly by the Greek authorities, supported by the Sacred Squadron; with the exception of Crete, where the main centres remained in the hands of the Germans until their final surrender in May 1945. This patchwork of control left EAM still in a dominant position, with three-quarters of the territory and one-third of the population at its mercy. By contrast, the writ of Papandreou's Government ran only in Athens, Patras and Salonika.[3] But all eyes were on Athens, where it was clear that the fate of Greece would be settled.

The central issue was simple. It was no longer the question of the King: that had been eliminated for the time being by his enforced absence. There were a number of subsidiary issues, such as the treatment of the Security Battalions and others accused of collaboration; but on these there were no fundamental differences in principle between Papandreou and EAM. In any case all such subsidiary issues would be settled by the outcome of the struggle for power. What was crucial, and could not continue indefinitely, was the co-existence of two armed forces, each acknowledging separate political authorities, which were only nominally united in the Government. One or other or both would have to be disarmed, and each was unwilling to yield its suspicions of the other. For Papandreou, the critical test would be the agreement of the EAM Ministers to allow ELAS, with its armed ancillaries, such as the National Civil Guard (EP) and the Units for the Protection of the People's Struggle (OPLA), to be disarmed and selectively re-enlisted in the Government's forces. For EAM, the critical test would be the agreement of Papandreou and the British to demobilise the Third Mountain Brigade and other government forces as well as ELAS, and to reconstitute a new army on equal terms; or alternatively, to retain roughly equal units of both sides intact, and to integrate them under a single command.

Most of November was spent in wary manoeuvring to achieve one or another of these outcomes without a resort to force. At what point force became inevitable, and who was to blame, are questions on which opinions will always differ. Some historians regard the arrival of the Mountain Brigade in Athens on 9 November as the fatal moment; and in that case the blame would lie primarily on Papandreou and the British authorities.[4] But a case can be made for an earlier or a later date. No reconstruction which laid the blame exclusively on one side could stand close examination. A pessimistic historian might argue that all prospect of a peaceful outcome vanished at the confrontation in Cairo during August 1943, which preceded the 'first round'. An optimistic one might argue that the prospect had not finally vanished even after the first shots were fired on 3 December 1944. All that a diary of events can reveal is a deteriorating trend, marked by fluctuations and conflicting sub-trends, throughout November.

At first Papandreou did not expect any great difficulty. On 2 November he outlined his plans to Leeper. He proposed to call up the class of recruits born in 1915 on 20 November to form a new National Guard. This would replace the old gendarmerie and EAM's National Civil Guard (EP), which would be dissolved on 27 November.[5] On 1 December all guerrilla forces would be dissolved, and four new classes would be called up on 10 December, which would (together with the Mountain Brigade and other existing units) constitute the new National Army. There was some fluidity about the proposed dates, for Papandreou's account gives 24 November as the date of the first call-up for the National Guard and 1 December as its date of take-over.[6] He also records a separate decision of the Cabinet on 5 November that ELAS and EDES should be dissolved on 10 December; and that date was announced by Scobie two days later.[7] Since the EAM Ministers were parties to these decisions, there was a presumptive justification for the optimism which Papandreou expressed to Leeper on 9 November and to MacVeagh on the following day.[8] To the latter he also spoke of the probability that some collaborators would have to be executed – a prospect satisfactory to EAM.

Leeper was unconvinced by Papandreou's optimism. He had recorded in his diary on 7 November that he did not expect the façade of unity to last, and that 'ever growing acts of lawlessness by EAM in Athens' were taking place.[9] On the same day Churchill wrote in a note to Eden: 'I fully expect a clash with EAM and we must not shrink from it, provided the ground is well chosen.'[10] He added that 'we should not hesitate to use British troops to support the Royal Hellenic Government under M. Papandreou'. The evidence of EAM's intentions at that date is less clear. Papakonstantinou, an ex-Communist, quotes a number of phrases from internal documents at the time which vaguely suggest aggressive notions: for example, an oath prescribed on 4 November to achieve 'the complete liberation of Greece from the foreign yoke'; and a proclamation on 7 November calling on ELAS to 'plunge into the final battle'.[11] Other communications at the same time presupposed co-operation with the Government. For example, on 6 November, at the Government's invitation, the KKE called on subordinate commands to submit names for inclusion in a list of potential candidates for administrative appointments.[12]

The KKE was also preoccupied with its foreign relations. It was uncertain how the Americans would behave in the event of a clash, but no opportunity was missed of dividing them from the British. On 4 November, *Rizospastis* declared that the US Ambassador had expressed disapproval to Leeper of the military measures that were being taken; but no trace of such a remonstrance is recorded by either Leeper or MacVeagh.

The Soviet authorities were silent to the point of embarrassment. Not a word of sympathy could be quoted by the KKE, even on 7 November, when the anniversary of the Bolshevik Revolution was celebrated by the Communists in Athens. Still more disquieting was the news received by the KKE from Macedonia, on 4 November, that there had been a clash between ELAS and Slavophone bands north of Florina.[13] Tempo was reported to have threatened that if the KKE were not careful, it would find itself alongside the British in conflict with the Partisans and the Soviet Union. In these paradoxical circumstances, EAM was unlikely to pick a deliberate quarrel with the British as well. The more militant tone of the KKE's internal communications from 9 November onwards must be attributed to the supposition of a threat, rather than to a decision on aggressive action.

On 9 November the Mountain Brigade arrived in Athens, at the request of Papandreou and with the approval of Scobie and Leeper, but against the express disapproval of the EAM Ministers. Its strength was nearly 2,800 men including just over 200 officers.[14] The ecstatic welcome accorded to the Brigade, when it marched through the city on the following day, showed that it was regarded as a protector against ELAS. The public of Athens, haunted every night by menacing slogans chanted by the reserve ELAS through megaphones, could not be blamed for regarding with suspicion an organisation which had steadily declared for two years that anyone who did not support it was a traitor; which had condoned the murder of Psaros, among many other less well-known figures, and the massacres by Aris Veloukhiotis in the Peloponnese; and which had systematically destroyed all its nationalist rivals in the Resistance except Zervas, who survived only by a hair's-breadth. It was true that lately the leadership of EAM had adopted a reformatory course, and probably the reform was genuine; but the Athenian middle classes were not to know that.

Equally, on the other side, with the arrival of the Mountain Brigade, suspicion mounted among the leaders of EAM. With the 2,800 men of the Brigade and a British force now augmented to about 8,000, the authorities had a distinct superiority of force, since ELAS (other than reservists) had so far observed the order to remain outside Athens. On 9 November Siantos sent out a general message to subordinate commands warning them that 'Reaction aims to create conditions favourable to a coup and dictatorship', and declaring that ELAS 'will disband only when the forces from Egypt are disarmed and a new army is formed under the command of men enjoying the confidence of the fighting people.'[15] The latter point became critical on 11 November, when the new Commander-in-Chief, General Othonaios, asked that Saraphis should be appointed his Chief of Staff. Since Papandreou would only allow Saraphis to be appointed as Assistant Chief of Staff, Othonaios resigned on 13 November.[16] Scobie summoned Saraphis on the same day to warn him against acts of terrorism by ELAS, and threatened the use of British forces against ELAS if they continued.[17] According to Saraphis, Scobie told him to 'bear it in mind that a guerrilla army is not able to face a modern army with heavy arms, tanks, aircraft and a fleet at its disposal'.

If Scobie indeed used those words, he exaggerated his own immediate strength. A precautionary reinforcement was already taking place from Italy, so that by the end of November he had nearly twenty-three thousand troops under his command, not all of them combatants.[18] But he still had few heavy weapons and no tanks in Greece, and it would take time to acquire them. Aircraft could be flown in more rapidly, and it seemed desirable that they should do so at once if only to create an impression. On 17 November two RAF squadrons and a Greek squadron flew into the main Athens airfield, to be greeted by the Prime Minister in person; and three more RAF squadrons arrived by the end of the month. MacVeagh noted that the Greek Air Force personnel were 'notably Rightist in sentiment', as a result of the purges since April.[19] The gesture indicated a growing anxiety among the allied authorities. On 15 November, Leeper had information of concentrations of ELAS near Athens; on 16 November Scobie repeated his warnings to Saraphis; on 17 November, accompanied by Leeper, he repeated them again to Svolos, Siantos and Zevgos, the last of whom reacted angrily; and on 18 November Vendiris was reappointed Commander-in-Chief in place of Othonaios.[20] It was true that ELAS was making preparatory dispositions, but they were still ostensibly defensive. Siantos held a press conference on 15 November, at which his tone was notably moderate; and on 20 November Aris received a stern warning from the KKE against his provocative attitude in Lamia.[21]

By the middle of November the allied authorities were over-reacting to a situation which was in turn made worse by their reactions. The behaviour of the Communists, however, was consistent with the suspicion that they intended to seize power, even if in fact that was not yet their intention. Porphyrogennis used his position as Minister of Labour to consolidate the KKE's power-base in the trade unions by setting up a Provisional Committee of the General Confederation of Greek Workers (GSEE) in anticipation of elections, which were announced for 1 December.[22] The Provisional Committee was drawn entirely from EEAM, which in turn was dominated by the KKE; so there could be no doubt in whose hands lay the power to call a general strike. The KKE also showed its power to organise demonstrations by a spectacular ceremony on 20 November to celebrate the twenty-sixth anniversary of its own foundation. 'Hundreds of thousands in Athens and Piraeus' took part, according to *Rizospastis* on the following day. One of the walls of the British Embassy was painted red, according to Leeper.[23] Siantos made a speech demanding that all 'volunteer units which were organised at home and abroad' – by implication including the Mountain Brigade and the Sacred Battalion, as well as ELAS and the EP – should be dissolved. He also accused the Government for the first time of planning a civil war.

Both sides were mistaking their own perceptions for reality, as they continued to do in retrospect. Siantos's speech on 20 November could be taken in conjunction with his secret order two weeks earlier, to imply an intention to use force after first putting the other side in the wrong. The same interpretation could be put on Churchill's instructions to Eden on 7 November and Scobie's warnings to Saraphis on 13 and 16 November. Leeper wrote in his diary on 13 November that 'it is possible, though not probable, that we shall have to use force'; and Saraphis, writing five years later, interpreted those words to mean that 'the British were already at this time contemplating the use of force against ELAS'.[24] Far-fetched though Saraphis's interpretation may be, it was no more far-fetched than Leeper's own interpretation of the rhetorical outbursts of *Rizospastis* and the crafty ambiguities of the Communist leaders, such as their talk of preparations for 'the final battle' and 'complete liberation from the foreign yoke'.[25]

Papandreou himself was by no means in a militant mood. He was prepared to make concessions to placate EAM, but they must be within limits of his own choosing. He agreed to replace Spiliotopoulos as Military Governor of Athens by Colonel Katsotas, a man more acceptable to the left; and he gave EAM an extra post in the Government when the Under-Secretary for War resigned. The latter post was filled by General Sarigiannis at the request of ELAS. These and other appointments show Papandreou's confidence in his own control over the Cabinet, which appeared to be beyond challenge. No signs of a split had yet occurred, though there were forces outside the Cabinet which should have put Papandreou on his guard: the old political leaders like Sophoulis and Tsaldaris, who watched his every move with cynically critical eyes; others like Venizelos and Rendis, who had resigned from his government in protest at Papandreou's personal domination; and the more militant Communists, who disagreed with the policy of reconciliation. But up to the last week of November, nothing had happened that seriously threatened disaster.

Tension increased as the dates drew near for the demobilisation of EP

(1 December) and of ELAS and EDES (10 December). Siantos and Saraphis repeatedly asserted that they would not disband ELAS unless the Mountain Brigade were also disbanded. They were less intransigent about EP, at least in appearance. Siantos's orders issued on 22 November were that when the first class was called up for the new National Guard, members of the KKE 'must be the first to join'.[26] Those already in ELAS must hand over their weapons to ELAS (not to the Government); those in EP must also hand over their weapons to ELAS; and the remaining members of EP, 'after handing over duties to the National Guard, must join ELAS with all their arms and equipment'. In other words, although EP would be dissolved, ELAS would be stronger than before. Nothing was said of OPLA, the execution-squads which had earned themselves such a horrifying reputation in the last months of the Occupation. But in any case the future of OPLA and EP was of secondary importance compared to that of ELAS, which could only be resolved in the context of a settlement of the future of the armed forces in general. The subject was lengthily and bitterly debated in the Council of Ministers on 22 November and the following days.

It has been asserted that on 22 November Papandreou made a statement that 'all volunteer units' would be demobilised, and that his phrase was understood to include the Mountain Brigade and the Sacred Squadron.[27] It is hard to see how such a statement could reasonably have been applied to the Brigade without a clear explanation to that effect. It is certain, however, that he made no such statement publicly, for no newspaper in Athens reported it on 23 November or any subsequent day. A year later, in an article published on 5 December 1945 in the newspaper *Makhi*, Professor Svolos wrote that 'in a draft agreement with the Left, which Papandreou initialled on 22 November, he himself expressly provided that the Mountain Brigade would also be effectively disbanded by granting indefinite leave to its men'. Svolos was in a position to know, being a member of the Government. But he did not speak of a public declaration; and he perhaps failed to realise that there was a wide difference between indefinite leave and demobilisation, since men on leave could be quickly recalled. Even his diluted version of the story, however, is not convincing. No such document bearing Papandreou's initials has ever become public. If he did indeed initial such a commitment, it would also have been known to the editorial offices of *Rizospastis*, through the Communist Ministers in his government. Yet the columns of *Rizospastis* during the week after 22 November reveal no such knowledge, and in fact contain many paragraphs which would have been phrased differently if it had been known at the time that Papandreou had made such a commitment.

On 23 November, the day following the supposed commitment, *Rizos-pastis* carried a leading article opposing the disbandment of ELAS and a report that 'the disbandment of volunteer forces was not discussed at yesterday's Council of Ministers'. Further statements insisting that ELAS must not be disbanded without a corresponding disbandment of the Mountain Brigade appeared on the following days, without any hint that Papandreou had already conceded the demand. Only on 30 November, by which date matters had already passed a further critical stage, did the first hint of the supposed concession appear in *Rizospastis* in an editorial written by Karagiorgis. His words have sometimes been interpreted as claiming a commitment to demobilise the Brigade. But if they are read carefully – and Karagiorgis always used words carefully – it is clear that they imply the opposite:

> But we ask Mr Papandreou and all the Ministers of the Right cate-gorically: Did or did not the Government's statements of its pro-gramme (*programmatikès dil 'seis*) promise explicitly that *all volunteer bodies* would be disbanded and that the basis of the future national army would be *regular* recruitment? Who then is going back on his word?
>
> How many days have passed since the Prime Minister put his signature to an agreement that the Mountain Brigade too should be sent on indefinite leave? How many days have passed since there were official declarations that the Gendarmerie will be disbanded and disarmed? Who then is recanting?

Papandreou never replied to these questions, nor did he ever subse-quently admit to having made such commitments. The presumption that 'all volunteer units' included the Greek forces from the Middle East was first asserted by Siantos in his speech on 20 November, but never accepted by Papandreou. The passage quoted above shows that the KKE was aware of this fact. The editorial would not have relied merely on 'the Govern-ment's statements of its programme' if it could have quoted a statement by Papandreou himself as recently as 22 November; nor would it have referred to an agreement that the Brigade should merely be sent on 'in-definite leave' if it could have quoted one that it should be demobilised; nor would it have quoted a declaration merely that 'the Gendarmerie will be disarmed and disbanded' if it could have quoted a corresponding decla-ration about the Brigade. Clearly the whole campaign was an exercise in verbal ingenuity with no basis of substance. Even a year later, when Kara-giorgis published a selection of his editorials from *Rizospastis* in book-form,

dating from 15 November 1944 to 16 February 1945, there is no trace in
that publication of the allegation that Papandreou had made a binding
commitment to disband his only regular forces, whether on 22 November
or any other date.[28] The absence of evidence has not, however, prevented
historians repeating each other on the subject for many years.[29]

It is another question whether Papandreou ever contemplated such a
concession. Svolos's story and the later accusations by the KKE appear to
have rested only on rumours and gossip, but these were certainly current
at the time. The first to allege openly that Papandreou had seriously
thought of demobilising the Mountain Brigade was the senior Liberal
politician, Kaphandaris, who did so in the presence of both Papandreou
and Siantos on 27 December.[30] Neither Papandreou nor Siantos made any
comment. The same story appears in the account written in 1946 by a
British journalist, who added that Scobie 'disapproved' of Papandreou's
intention.[31] Saraphis, writing also in 1946, gave a substantially similar
account:

> The British would not accept in any way that the Mountain Brigade
> and the Sacred Squadron should be disbanded, (which) Papandreou
> had agreed should be demobilised simultaneously with ELAS.[32]

He quoted Svolos's article in *Makhi* as evidence that Churchill himself had
overruled Papandreou. First-hand British accounts only speak of 'generous
leave'.[33] There is no mention of 'demobilisation' or even of 'indefinite
leave' being conceded by Papandreou in any memoirs of the time: neither
in his own nor those of Tsakalotos, the Commander of the Brigade; nor in
those of Leeper, Macmillan, Eden and Churchill; nor in the relevant
volumes of the British official histories.[34] No evidence of a commitment
being undertaken by Papandreou, in any of the terms suggested, is to be
found among the British official papers in the Public Record Office, nor
in the Greek archives.[35]

What the British documents reveal is something different. The British
authorities were anxious that Papandreou should not agree to disband the
Brigade, and feared he might do so; but unless he was lying to his allies,
he never did so. On 15 November Leeper reported to the Foreign Office
that at Papandreou's request he had met Svolos and urged him to stop
pressing for the disbandment of the Brigade, because it would cause 'an
acute political crisis'.[36] He thought that Svolos accepted his argument.
On 19 November Churchill minuted to the Foreign Office that 'the disbandment of the Greek Brigade would be a disaster of the first order'.[37]
Since the Foreign Office proposed on 20 November that this minute

should be transmitted to Leeper, the Prime Minister's view must at some stage have reached Papandreou. Even if it reached him only after 22 November, when he supposedly made the fatal commitment, it is scarcely credible that no record should have survived in the British documents either of the commitment or of its reversal. It is more probable that Churchill's intervention forestalled any possibility of such a concession by Papandreou, even if he had ever contemplated it. On 26 November Leeper reported that Papandreou 'gave General Scobie and me an assurance that the Mountain Brigades (sic) would remain intact'.[38] Again it would be incomprehensible that there should be no reference to a specific commitment being reversed.

The leadership of EAM had indeed little reason to misread Papandreou's intentions, however much it might resent them. During the arguments which followed the Lebanon Conference, Siantos complained that Papandreou had introduced a phrase about 'the abolition (katárgisis) of ELAS' which was not in the Lebanon Charter. Papandreou replied that the phrase was consistent with the decisions of the Conference, to which the representatives of EAM, ELAS and PEEA had all subscribed.[39] Whichever may be thought to have had the better case in logic, EAM finally joined the Government without having compelled Papandreou to withdraw the phrase. The same reasoning may be applied to the Caserta Conference. Saraphis maintained subsequently that the Caserta Agreement placed ELAS on equal terms with the Mountain Brigade, and did not empower Scobie to order the disbandment of ELAS. Such power rested only with the Greek Government, he argued; and no doubt he reflected to himself that the EAM Ministers could be relied on, if necessary, to frustrate it. But the EAM Ministers had already allowed Papandreou to announce on their behalf, early in November, that the guerrilla forces would be disbanded in December. Saraphis later claimed that the long-term purpose of the Caserta Agreement had been to 'eliminate' ELAS; but he had himself signed it.[40]

Such debating points could not diminish the anxieties of EAM, which were reflected in the headlines of Rizospastis towards the end of November. 'War criminals retain arms', and 'Resistance to be disarmed', it declared on 22 and 23 November; 'The Fifth Column survives in the midst of Athens' on 25 November, above paragraphs showing that the reference was to Khí, the Gendarmerie and the Security Battalions. On the same day the Central Committee of EAM met, so Rizospastis reported on 26 November, though without further details. For the next three days there were persistent attacks on the Gendarmerie, which suggested that it was to be made the scapegoat for whatever might follow. An editorial on 28

November violently attacked Zervas as a 'mercenary' and 'lackey of Glücksburg'. It has been said by some writers, not all of them hostile to the KKE, that it was during these very days that a decision to resort to force was taken. The evidence is partly hearsay and partly circumstantial, and the significance of it is disputed by historians.[41] But it is clear at least that a very sharp and possibly decisive change of attitudes took place some time between 25 and 29 November. A crisis which appeared to be fatally imminent on 26 November, and then to be averted on the 27th finally reached the point of catastrophe on the 30th. In the last analysis, the reasons can only be a matter of speculation.

Scobie had three abortive interviews with the guerrilla leaders on 26 and 27 November.[42] At the first he requested them to countersign an order disbanding their forces on 10 December. An officer representing Zervas at once agreed, but Saraphis (who was accompanied by Mandakas) requested time for consideration. At the second meeting Zervas was present in person and confirmed his agreement, but Saraphis claimed that he could only accept such an order from the Greek Government. Scobie produced a letter from Papandreou endorsing his order, but Saraphis said that was insufficient. At the third meeting on 27 November, Scobie reported that the Cabinet had been unable to agree unanimously to issue the order, but he nevertheless requested that Zervas and Saraphis should accept it on his authority. Saraphis again refused. But on the same day a more encouraging development occurred.[43] Zevgos, Tsirimokos and Svolos called on Papandreou with a draft decree by the terms of which a national army would be established consisting of two brigades of equal numbers: one composed of the Mountain Brigade, the Sacred Squadron and a unit of EDES, the other drawn wholly from ELAS. All other units of all kinds would be disbanded. Papandreou agreed to submit the proposal to the Council of Ministers, and announced on 28 November that the decree would be signed by all Ministers on that day. During the same day Scobie told Saraphis that he 'could leave for Lamia', and he did so on 29 November believing that a compromise was still likely to be achieved.[44]

In fact, however, the compromise had already broken down in obscure circumstances for which each side blamed the other. Papandreou stated that on 28 November Zevgos alone called on him to withdraw the proposal submitted on the previous day, and to substitute a proposal that all the armed forces of whatever kind should be disbanded, including the Mountain Brigade and the Sacred Squadron. This was a reversion to the intransigent demands of a week earlier. When he published the two proposals later for comparison, Papandreou drew both texts from the *EAM White Book*, so that there could be no argument about the change of front.[45]

The contention of EAM at the time was that Papandreou had nullified the compromise by making a statement which implied that the Mountain Brigade and the Sacred Squadron would be left outside the newly constituted force, which would consist only of 'a brigade of ELAS and a proportionate unit of EDES'; but no source was quoted for this alleged statement. Even the words quoted as Papandreou's own in *Rizospastis* on 29 November could as easily have been construed to be consistent with the agreed formula as to be inconsistent with it, though it is true that Mac-Veagh also managed to misunderstand them.[46] The change of attitude took the KKE's associates by surprise, for neither Svolos nor Tsirimokos accompanied Zevgos on his second visit to Papandreou. In fact they almost brought themselves to the point of a final breach with EAM on 29 November, but changed their minds again at the last moment. Visiting Papandreou alone on 30 November in a state of great agitation, Svolos told him that he was quite powerless.[47]

What had really happened to change the attitude of the KKE remains obscure. The recollections of Tzimas and Orestis suggest that Tito had something to do with it.[48] Tzimas was in Belgrade with Tito, and was joined there by Petros Roussos in a special mission from the KKE. In Tzimas's presence, Roussos asked whether the KKE could count on Yugoslav support in the event of a conflict with the British. Tito replied affirmatively. Despite Tzimas's reservations, based on first-hand knowledge of the limited resources of the Partisans, the encouraging reply was immediately relayed to Athens, where it arrived on 27 November. It is impossible entirely to discredit this account, though it smacks too much of the 'conspiracy theory' of history to be convincing. It may be doubted whether Tito gave very close attention to relations with the KKE at this time, when he was preoccupied with the more serious problem of reaching agreement with the Bulgarian CP over a Balkan Federation and Macedonia's place in it.[49] Tempo had not eased matters by managing to quarrel simultaneously with the Bulgarians as well as the Greeks. Changes of mood in the tense atmosphere of the KKE leadership can only be a matter of speculation, and were certainly not always rational. There is a case for the view that the leadership of the KKE, having been argued into concessions by its political allies, was argued out of them twenty-four hours later by some of its militant activists. It seemed to be incapable of taking the initiative, and to be searching desperately for someone else to do so.

Although some preparations were made for the use of force, they remained essentially defensive. On 28 November Siantos sent out a general order to 'be ready to repulse any dangers'; and similar orders were repeated on the following two days.[50] No attempt was made to prevent officers and men of the Gendarmerie passing through territory controlled by ELAS on their way to Athens. Saraphis described a state of confusion on his arrival at ELAS GHQ on 29 November, until the Central Committee of ELAS was reconstituted. Even then plans had to be improvised, because ELAS had been actually preparing to demobilise.[51] At the same time there were one or two more ominous signs.[52] On 30 November Mandakas (a member of ELAS Central Committee) ordered supplies of explosives, mines and automatic weapons to be sent to the Division nearest Athens. On 1 December a Communist who visited two of the KKE offices in Athens, including the Party HQ, found both of them stripped and evacuated. When he asked the only man he could find where everyone had gone, the only reply he could get was 'underground' (stìn paranomía). These episodes took place while the EAM Ministers were still members of Papandreou's Government.

It was becoming hard to argue that the measures taken by the KKE were merely precautionary. They had taken no decision, and made no specific plan, but they were daily giving the impression of both. There comes a point when precautions tend to provoke the very actions against which they are intended as a safeguard. That point had now been reached in Athens, and unfortunately it had been reached on both sides. On 1 December Scobie issued a proclamation declaring the intention of the British authorities to protect the Greek people and its government 'against any attempt at a coup d'état or act of violence which is unconstitutional'. On the same day, which was the date fixed for the dissolution of the EP, Papandreou invited his colleagues to sign an order to that effect, stating that he would treat it as an issue of confidence.[53] All the EAM Ministers except Sarigiannis refused to sign, and resigned collectively at midnight. Svolos and Tsirimokos decided that Papandreou was to blame for provoking the crisis.[54] At this point it is impossible to judge who was provoking whom; but if intentions are measured by the efficacy of the preparations made by either side to impose its will by force on the other, neither had any firm intention because neither made any adequate preparations.

But neither side would believe this of the other. One of Papandreou's Ministers later advanced, as proof of long preparation by the KKE, 'the speed and efficiency of the operation' in December.[55] Macmillan and Leeper also believed that there had been a deliberate planning, beginning at the latest in the last week of November.[56] British officers shared this view, especially those who had access to intercepted wireless traffic. On the other side, a member of the Central Committee of the KKE advanced,

as proof of Scobie's aggressive intentions, his concentration of 'tremen-
dous forces' in Athens, including Indians and 'dwarfs from Uganda'.[57] It
is true that more than half the British forces finally deployed in Greece,
including an Indian brigade, were there before the end of November. As
evidence of Papandreou's determination to provoke a civil war, the same
Communist cited the failure to harass the German retreat, the refusal to
demobilise the Mountain Brigade, the concentration of the Gendarmerie
in Athens from all over Greece, and the retention in camps of the Security
Battalions. All these accusations were beside the point. Scobie had no
operational plans, as was plain from the dispersal of his forces, including
an RAF Headquarters at Kiphissia, on the outskirts of Athens, almost
without means of defending itself. Nor had the KKE any operational plans,
apart from the inflamed intentions of a few hotheads. The first orders
which Saraphis received from Siantos on 2 December seemed to him confused, exasperating, and an affront to his professional competence.[58]

The prospect slightly improved from Saraphis's point of view when the
Central Committee of ELAS resumed its responsibilities on the same day.
Even then Siantos was still the dominant figure, and the only experienced
soldier with him, General Mandakas, had held no command for nearly ten
years. The first order received from the Central Committee of ELAS informed Saraphis that ELAS GHQ would be subordinate to it; the second
informed him that Zervas was expected to transfer his forces to Athens
and asked ELAS GHQ to take 'the necessary measures'.[59] Zervas was
naturally a welcome target for ELAS GHQ (which meant primarily Aris
Veloukhiotis and Saraphis), but the forecast of Zervas's intention was
wide of the mark. He had returned to Epirus on 1 December, travelling
to Preveza on a British corvette. His departure was reported on 2 December by *Rizospastis* (which had not mentioned that of Saraphis two days
earlier) under a vindictive but inconspicuous headline: 'The Fifth
Column'. The brief report said that Zervas 'declared that he was going to
Ioannina to carry out the orders of the government'. Taken with other
movements reported in the same paragraph (including that of Tsigantes to
the Aegean islands), the implication was that the intention was aggressive
against EAM. But it would have been impossible for Zervas to move his
forces to Athens without logistic support from the British on a large scale.
The notion that Scobie would have been willing to provide such resources,
even if he had them available, illustrated the incomprehension prevailing
between EAM and the British.

Saraphis added, no doubt correctly so far as his own responsibility was
concerned, that up to the receipt of Siantos's instructions on 2 December,
'not a single ELAS unit had been transferred and no step had been taken

which could be construed as preparation for an offensive'.[60] On 2 December, apart from various other dispositions, he recorded that 'we had given orders for certain movements in the direction of Epirus'.[61] A more aggressive gloss is put on these orders by the purported text of a second telegram from Siantos, expressly ordering Saraphis to attack Zervas with three divisions as soon as his preparations were complete.[62] That is in fact what Saraphis did, though it took almost three weeks to complete the preparations. But the authenticity of the latter telegram is doubtful; and in any case Saraphis needed no urging against Zervas. He was in fact more aggressively minded than Siantos at the time. On the same day that Siantos's first orders arrived, Saraphis sought permission to attack 'all British forces scattered over the whole of Greece', so that 'they would not be used against our men on the Athens front', but to his disappointment he was instructed 'to do nothing more than follow the movements of the British'.[63]

As Saraphis's request implied, he took it for granted that ELAS would have to fight the British in Athens as well as the Greek authorities. He offered to allow any ELAS officers who could not face that prospect to withdraw, but none did so.[64] Siantos, on the other hand, was making no such assumption. He still spoke of the British as 'our allies'. Orestis, commanding the ELAS Division nearest to Athens, issued orders on 2 December that his troops should 'avoid provocation and try to persuade the British to stay out of the conflict'.[65] As late as 17 December, according to Zachariadis's accusations in 1950, Siantos committed the blunder of allowing a British regiment to enter Athens unopposed.[66] In order not to become involved in a battle with the British, if it were avoidable, Siantos decided that the Central Committee of ELAS should control operations in Athens and northwards to a line from Thebes through Domokos to Khalkis, leaving the firebrands of ELAS GHQ to deal with the less troublesome and sensitive problems of eliminating Zervas, Tsaous Andon and any remaining independent Greek forces in the northern provinces.[67] The implication was clear: cooler heads were needed to deal with the diplomatic conundrums likely to arise in Athens.

EAM showed few signs of having decided what to do next after withdrawing from the Government. On 2 December an emergency meeting of the Central Committee was held, after which a General Strike was proclaimed for 4 December and a demonstration at 11.00 a.m. on the preceding day (a Sunday). There was little that the Government could do about a strike, given the total control which EAM exercised over the General Confederation of Workers. But it could forbid a demonstration. Unfortunately, Papandreou chose the worst possible course. On the morning of 2 December, when EAM asked permission for the demonstration in Constitution Square, he allowed his depleted Council of Ministers to agree because, as he later wrote, 'it was not yet known whether the KKE would resort to revolutionary action immediately'; but later in the day, when he realised that the demonstration was to be followed by a General Strike, a refusal of the Civil Guard to hand in its weapons, and the re-formation of the Central Committee of ELAS, permission for the demonstration was withdrawn.[68] Another account gives the additional reason that Leeper was due to address a meeting at the same time as the demonstration in a building near the Square.[69]

The EAM leaders claimed that it was too late by then to cancel the demonstration, and they made no attempt to do so. On the contrary, *Rizospastis* on 3 December carried as headlines: 'Everyone today at 11.00 a.m. to EAM Demonstration in Constitution Square! Down with the Government of Civil War! Forward to Government of REAL National Unity!' By way of contrast, it may be noted that on 2 December, *Rizospastis* had been able to include at very short notice a stop-press announcement of the resignation of the EAM Ministers, so the plea of insufficient time was scarcely tenable. It is also notable that *Rizospastis* was the only newspaper in Athens which did not carry the news on 3 December that the demonstration had been banned: *Elevtheria*, for example, had it in a front-page headline.

Since the demonstration had been forbidden, the police were posted at the entrance to Constitution Square on the morning of 3 December to prevent a crowd assembling. They were armed, though fortunately most of them only had blank ammunition. Among the demonstrators, according to the youthful Mikis Theodorakis, 'bearing arms was strictly forbidden'; though he qualified that recollection by adding that 'only a few dozen cadres, charged with keeping order, had been authorised on this point, in order to avoid all provocation'.[70] In such circumstances shooting was inevitable, as the KKE must have foreseen. When the shooting began at about 10.45 a.m., it was impossible to say for certain who fired first. Papandreou later said that the demonstrators were armed and 'attacked' first (though he did not say 'fired'); but an Assistant Military Attaché at the American Embassy thought they were not armed.[71] The British Ambassador, who watched one group of demonstrators marching past his house, thought that he heard light automatics and hand-grenades when they were out of sight, but before they reached the Square; the American Ambassador thought he heard 'bombs' further up the same street, but he was not sure; and the Greek Government's subsequent enquiry reported that 'the first shots were fired by armed demonstrators, who were also supplied with hand-grenades'.[72] Colonel Evert, the Chief of Police, put it on record several years later (in 1958) that he had personally decided to break up the demonstration by force, with Papandreou's consent, but only after one of his men had been killed by a hand-grenade.[73] Many journalists, who were also eye-witnesses, gave many other accounts, mostly hostile to the police. It is at least certain that all the casualties from fire-arms were civilians in the crowd, though some policemen were lynched in the aftermath.

The Square was cleared in the early afternoon by a company of British troops without the use of force. The number of civilian dead has been estimated as low as seven and as high as twenty-eight, and the total casualties from about a dozen up to over a hundred.[74] Clearly the police lost control of the situation; whether the KKE either had or lost control is harder to say. Experience since those days has shown how effectively a small number of determined men, tactically placed, can turn a peaceful crowd into a violent mob. That there was some degree of Communist guidance in the crowd is apparent both from Theodorakis's reference to 'a few dozen cadres', and from the most reliable American account, which emphasised that 'the crowd made a definite effort to distinguish between the American and British policy', by chanting 'Roosevelt, Roosevelt', and carrying 'vast numbers of American flags' as well as 'many Greek flags, a few Russian, but no British'. Since an Athenian crowd would hardly have made such distinctions spontaneously, the presence of a guiding hand seems clear. But the predominance of the American flag over the Russian perhaps also signifies that the intention was pacific; for the red flag alone would have been construed as aggressive, whereas the stars and stripes may have implied an appeal to the only acceptable mediator. MacVeagh took the point, and continued his efforts to induce his government to intervene.[75]

After the affray of 3 December, the violence was slow to escalate, except against the police. It was alleged, quite untruthfully, that the police fired again into the crowd attending the funeral of the victims on 4 December.[76] Attacks on police-stations in Athens continued on 4 and 5 December, causing a number of casualties. A brigade of ELAS, 2,000 strong, was moved into the capital from the Peloponnese during the night of 5-6 December. Attacks were extended to government buildings on 6 and 7 December, but care was still taken by ELAS to avoid clashes with British forces and even with Greek troops of the Mountain Brigade. Reactions on the part of Scobie and his forces were also restrained, despite a strong directive from Churchill on 5 December charging Scobie with responsibility 'for maintaining order in Athens and for neutralising or destroying all EAM–ELAS bands approaching the city'. The directive contained the ominous words: 'Do not hesitate to act as if you were in a conquered city where a local rebellion is in progress.'[77] Churchill also encouraged Scobie to be ready to use the Mountain Brigade if necessary. But Scobie did hesitate, as he had good reason to do. Although his troops were hemmed in by ELAS in different quarters of the city, at first no attempt was made to launch an attack on them, nor even for several days on the Mountain Brigade either.[78]

Continuing exchanges between Scobie and ELAS accompanied the slow escalation of the battle. Both sides evidently wanted to avoid a collision, but each insisted on its own terms. On 4 December Scobie sent Saraphis an order to withdraw ELAS from the vicinity of Athens, but in reply Saraphis merely referred him to the Central Committee of ELAS. Two days later, and again on 9 December, the Central Committee complained formally to Scobie that his forces had fired on ELAS.[79] On 7 and 8 December Scobie and Saraphis exchanged pained and argumentative telegrams, the latter still expressing the hope that 'as allies and friends, you will remain neutral'.[80] The hope was not entirely groundless, for a number of indications during the first few days of the rebellion came to encourage EAM. First, there was an internal crisis in the Government, which caused Papandreou on 4 December to offer his resignation; but Churchill opposed it, and the King refused to accept it.[81] Secondly, the Americans made clear their neutrality, of which many petty indications exasperated the British.[82] Stettinius, the Secretary of State, made two unhelpful statements on 3 and 5 December; Admiral King ordered that American ships should not be used to supply the British forces in Athens; but it was noted that the American Embassy did not refuse to have its rations delivered by British troops. Only Hopkins and Forrestal, of the President's close associates, intervened to help Churchill. Finally, a bitter debate in the House of Commons on 8 December severely shook the British Government.

Still no open, general battle had been joined between the British and ELAS. An editorial in *Rizospastis* on 4 December complained that no one would have expected the British to intervene with tanks and armoured cars and *arapádes* (meaning Indian troops) armed with clubs and wearing British uniforms. In reality they had not fired a single shot, nor had any been fired against them. Outside Athens, the Central Committee of ELAS had ordered no more than that British units should be told that 'all movement was forbidden and that, should they make any attempt to move, they would be forcibly prevented'.[83] Most of them had already been withdrawn to Volos, Patras, Athens or Salonika unmolested, though at the sacrifice of much of their equipment. In Epirus, where definite orders to eliminate EDES had been issued by the Central Committee to ELAS GHQ on 6 December, Zervas was forbidden by Scobie, through his British Liaison Officers, to take the initiative in attacking first.[84] In Athens, while ELAS continued to attack Greek targets – police-stations, government buildings, the hastily formed National Guard, and eventually the Mountain Brigade itself – British troops were not yet subject to direct attack. On 8 December there were rumours of 'peace feelers' from ELAS, which Churchill ordered Scobie to reject if they offered 'anything less satisfactory than the terms agreed upon before the revolt took place'; but the rumours were fictitious.[85] By 10 December ELAS was believed to be wearying of the conflict, though in fact the worst was still to come.[86]

Armed clashes were thus limited for nearly two weeks to sporadic incidents.[87] On 4 and 5 December ELAS units moving towards Athens met British units on the road, but not a shot was fired between them. In some cases arms were surrendered by ELAS to the British. Saraphis moved ELAS GHQ out of Lamia to a near-by village in conformity with Siantos's orders to avoid a clash. On 5 December Scobie's troops occupied the HQ buildings of EAM and ELAS in Athens without force, since they had already been abandoned. British patrols cleared many areas of the city by day, but could not prevent ELAS units moving back into them at night, usually in civilian clothes. So far it was an almost silent, almost bloodless test of wills. Only on 7 December did ELAS for the first time fire deliberately on the Mountain Brigade, while still refraining from attack on the British troops.[88] The first serious clash between ELAS and the British occurred on 12 December, when a force in British battle-dress entered the HQ of the British Armoured Brigade and took over a hundred prisoners, before finally being driven out after twelve hours of fighting. The attack was not part of a general plan, nor was it followed up. Even five days later, Siantos allowed a British unit to enter Athens unmolested.[89]

Fortuitous circumstances combined to increase the bitterness of the struggle. One of the earliest targets for ELAS was the Averoff prison, where a number of accused collaborators were held to await trial. The prisoners were deliberately released by the Greek and British authorities, to save them from being lynched. Others were captured and executed by OPLA. Many ex-collaborators of a lower grade, including former members of the Security Battalions, were recruited into the new National Guard, which was being hastily formed at the beginning of December. By the end of the month it numbered some nineteen thousand men organised in thirty-six battalions under the command of Tsakalotos.[90] They were undependable troops of low morale, and some of criminal reputation.

Scobie prudently decided that in no circumstances should they be used to attack ELAS. They were confined to patrolling and guard-duties, but as such they were vulnerable to attack and to execution if captured. Next to the National Guard and the Gendarmerie, the principal targets of ELAS were the *Khites*, adherents of Colonel Grivas. Incidents between ELAS and the British continued to be sporadic and almost accidental, though increasingly serious after the middle of the month. There was particular resentment of the presence of non-white troops, which was also criticised in the House of Commons.[91]

How serious the predicament of the British troops in Athens had become was not appreciated at first, because ELAS was content to isolate them in different areas without launching direct attacks. On 11 December, however, Field-Marshal Alexander and Harold Macmillan arrived in Athens from Italy and formed a very grave assessment of the situation.[92] Alexander quickly reached two decisions: to send further reinforcements to Athens, and to replace Scobie and many of his staff. A myth has grown up in Greece that Scobie saved Athens in December 1944, but the truth is that he almost lost it: the city was saved by Alexander's new appointment, General John Hawkesworth.* How seriously Scobie had lost control of the situation, and his state of pessimism, chiefly based on shortage of supplies, can be judged from the fact that he contemplated a plan to withdraw his troops to the port of Phaliron, which would have meant the complete surrender of Athens.[93] There were other signs of defeatism among his staff, which justified Alexander's severe decision. Macmillan and Leeper, however, successfully argued to Alexander that the removal of Scobie would destroy Greek morale, since his name had become a symbol of British protection. It was therefore decided to leave him at his post, in order to conduct any further negotiations with ELAS, but to bring in Hawkesworth with a new staff to take command of the impending battle.[94]

Reinforcements from Italy were successfully introduced between 13 and 16 December, at some risk because of the distance from Athens to the nearest available harbours and aerodromes. Hawkesworth, who arrived on 15 December, then had a force of some fifty thousand men at his disposal. Fortunately no clashes were to take place with ELAS anywhere outside Athens. The good sense of local commanders, both Greek and British (including Bakirdzis and Markos Vaphiadis in Salonika) prevented any additional catastrophe. Nor did the reinforcement of Athens represent in full a corresponding reduction of the forces available for operations against the Germans in Italy, for it proved possible to divert to Greece a division which was already on its way by sea from Italy to Egypt.[95] (It was

---

* Hawkesworth died in 1946 and his name is unknown in Greece.

being conveyed in American landing craft, but Admiral King's ban was circumvented by substituting British crews for Americans and transferring the ships to the British flag.) The result of these reinforcements was, in Tsakalotos's words, that the tide turned against ELAS between 13 and 14 December; and ELAS officers also recognised the 13th as a critical day.[96] In fact the Communist ex-Minister Porphyrogennis had visited Scobie secretly on 12 December to seek terms. The terms offered were exactly the same as at the beginning of the month. On 16 December Porphyrogennis returned with a reply that they were unacceptable unless the Mountain Brigade were also withdrawn from Athens as well as ELAS, together with other conditions which Scobie rejected.[97]

Only on 15 December for the first time did ELAS make a concerted attack on British units in Athens; only on 20 December did it overrun the RAF HQ at Kiphissia; and the attack on Zervas in Epirus began only on the following day. The unexpectedly protracted delays in launching decisive operations were due partly to the time needed to complete preparations, which Siantos had underestimated, and which Saraphis later adduced as evidence that there was no plan of attack prepared in advance. They were also partly due to the Communists' anxiety, not shared by Saraphis, to avoid a conflict with the British. But another conclusion which appears from the conjunction of facts in mid-December is that the Central Committee of ELAS overestimated the superiority of its own strength and thought that it still held the initiative. The failure to gain a decisive advantage from the initial surprise was fatal, as ELAS's officers admitted, especially because of the lack of reserves to support a prolonged struggle.[98]

The battle of ELAS against the British was thus lost before it really began. By 18 December the main road from Athens to Piraeus had been cleared by British troops, and 'the enemy were gradually being pushed back'.[99] On 22 December another approach was made by ELAS to Scobie, offering terms for a cease-fire, but again a number of concessions were demanded in return. The new offer was never formally rejected, because it was overtaken by political events of great importance. Churchill had become restive during December for a number of reasons, both military and political. Among the military reasons was a crisis in the war against Germany, for the German counter-attack in the Ardennes, beginning on 16 December, had done great damage to allied plans, and even threatened Brussels and Antwerp; while in Italy the allied campaign was making no real progress. A disquieting appreciation came from Field-Marshal Alexander on 21 December, that the most he could undertake with the available troops in Greece was to clear the area of Athens and Piraeus, but not to destroy ELAS throughout the country.[100] In other words, there was no military alternative to making terms of some kind with ELAS. To this unwelcome information Churchill had to add other considerations, not least the hostility of public opinion in Britain and the USA. There had been a second critical debate in the House of Commons on 20 December. American hostility was aggravated by a simultaneous crisis in allied relations over the composition of the Italian Government.

At the centre of the hostility was the feeling that the trouble could have been averted if Churchill had not been so devoted to the King. This view was now shared not only by President Roosevelt's advisers, but also by Churchill's own colleagues, including Eden, Macmillan and Leeper.[101] From all quarters, beginning with Leeper on 10 December, came advice once more to establish a Regency under Archbishop Damaskinos. As successive voices joined the chorus, Churchill found by 23 December that the only opponents of the idea were himself, the King and Field-Marshal Smuts. His own reluctance to accept the advice was based partly on the King's repeated refusal to agree, partly on his own suspicions of the Archbishop's motives, and partly on an objection from Papandreou that to appoint a Regent at this juncture would be interpreted as a sign of weakness. But when even Roosevelt, urged by MacVeagh and Stettinius, joined in supporting the proposal for a Regency, Churchill recognised that drastic action was required, and that only he could take it. On Christmas Eve, with dramatic suddenness, he decided to go to Athens himself with Eden. They arrived in the afternoon of 25 December, and were joined by Macmillan and Alexander from Italy.

Churchill at once summoned a conference, which met on 26–28 December, including all the chief personalities in Athens, among them the leaders of the KKE, EAM and ELAS (Siantos, Partsalidis and Mandakas). Allied representatives included the American Ambassador, the French Minister and Colonel Popov, in addition to all the principal British figures. Churchill addressed the first meeting, pointing out that the British presence in Greece had the support of both Roosevelt and Stalin. He and the other allies then withdrew, leaving the Greeks to settle their own problems. The Archbishop presided throughout.[102] Although it was helpful that broken contacts had been resumed, no conclusions emerged from the conference. But Churchill, who left Athens on 28 December, was at last convinced of two things: that a Regency must be established, and that the Archbishop was, after all, acceptable. Back in London, he pressed the King once more to agree, supported by a personal telegram from Roosevelt on 28 December.[103] His discussions with the King were painful and stormy, and in the last resort brutal.[104] Under extreme coercion, the King finally appointed the Archbishop as Regent on 30 December, having refused to do so at least four times earlier in the month. On the following day, again with Churchill's agreement, the Regent accepted Papandreou's resignation, and on 3 January, after some hesitation, he entrusted the task of forming a new government to General Plastiras, who had arrived in Athens from France on 13 December.

None of these events materially affected the course of the fighting. Plastiras, who had been the titular head of EDES, was a fiercely anti-Communist republican. He would have liked to conduct a war of extermination against ELAS. But the matter rested in other hands. Hawkesworth was only ready for a limited but decisive offensive on 27 December, while the conference was still sitting under the Archbishop. The Central Committee of ELAS had prepared itself for the worst by ordering, on 24 December, the abduction of hostages. During the last few days of the year, as Hawkesworth gradually forced ELAS northwards out of Athens, many of the hostages were murdered, and others were taken on forced marches to the hills which caused hundreds more fatalities. The justification given for the atrocities was that the British held thousands of mutineers in the Middle East in concentration-camps. Saraphis could point out that from the moment the hostages 'reached GHQ's zone, not a life was lost', but his silence on the rest of the grim story only confirms what numerous eye-witnesses, photographers and other investigators established, and even Communists later admitted.[105]

On New Year's Day, while ELAS was conducting a stubborn retreat, the Communist Zevgos visited Scobie to discuss terms once more, but again Scobie insisted on the same terms as before, without qualifications. By this date Aris and Saraphis had completed the defeat of Zervas's force, which was evacuated in Greek and British ships from Preveza to Corfu on the last day of 1944. Various accounts of the débâcle of EDES have been published,[106] both hostile and sympathetic, but all tend to obscure the simple point that one side was willing, and the other was not, to fight fellow-countrymen. Three divisions of ELAS were thus released for operations elsewhere, but it was too late to transfer them to Athens, where they might have been decisive if they had not been preoccupied with Zervas throughout December. By 3 January Hawkesworth was able to begin his advance from Athens, and two days later he could declare the whole area of Athens and Piraeus clear of the enemy. On 6 January Scobie withdrew the terms which he had previously offered, partly because of the abduction of hostages, and partly because the terms had required only the evacuation of Attica and the surrender of arms in Athens, both of which objects had been overtaken. On the following day the Mountain Brigade joined in the advance from the capital.[107] On 8 January Saraphis, returning from his victory over Zervas, met the Central Committee of ELAS in Lamia and offered to take command of the operations against the British, but he was told it was too late. Three days later four representatives were sent to Scobie to accept his terms, and on 11 January an armistice was signed, to take effect at one minute after midnight on the night of 14–15 January.[108]

Much remained to be settled, amid continuing bitterness. The Greek authorities, particularly Plastiras and the Regent, resented Scobie's failure to insist on the immediate release of the Greek hostages held by ELAS. Scobie had given way on this point, on Leeper's advice, because otherwise it was feared that ELAS would again break off the negotiations; and in any case, 'what we now demanded and could not get, would soon follow'.[109] Saraphis stated that the hostages were in fact all released immediately after the armistice, but if that were strictly true there would have been no need to refuse to include their release in the armistice agreement. Saraphis in turn was indignant that the British continued operations after the armistice was signed (though before it took effect) in the hope of capturing ELAS GHQ, which had withdrawn to the comparative safety of Trikkala.[110] According to Leeper, the three-day interval between the signature and the cease-fire was really provided at the request of ELAS, in order to give time for all units to be notified. Such was the small change of distrust and confusion.

A month passed before the cease-fire could be converted into a permanent settlement. During that time much of the foreign sympathy which EAM had enjoyed, particularly in Britain, was dissipated by revelations about the atrocities and abduction of hostages. The British Government included details of atrocities in a White Paper published on 31 January.[111] That might not have been decisive but for the almost accidental part played in the destruction of illusions by British trade-unionists. Their involvement, under the leadership of Sir Walter Citrine, General Secretary of the TUC, arose from the confusion into which the General Confederation of Greek Workers had fallen.[112] The appointment by the Communist Minister of Labour, Porphyrogennis, of a new Secretariat and Executive Committee, drawn entirely from EEAM, was declared illegal by the new Minister of Labour in Plastiras's government on 3 January, on the grounds that it had been made under a wartime decree of October 1942 which had never been promulgated. The appointments were therefore cancelled and replaced by Reformist nominees, whose appointment was in turn denounced by the Communists in EEAM. Inevitably the dispute was interlocked with the battle which was still raging in Athens.

On 10 January, just before the cease-fire was agreed, a new development occurred in the dispute. A group of seventeen trade-unionists visited the British Embassy to denounce the Communist control of EEAM and to invite a mission from the TUC to Greece. The invitation was accepted, and Citrine arrived with four colleagues on 22 January. They stayed in Greece for twelve days, during which they met leaders of EEAM in Levadia. Citrine succeeded in organising a round-table conference between the rival leaders. Agreement was reached on almost every point except the timing of fresh elections to the Executive. The TUC mission returned to London on 3 February, having agreed to send out a new mission under Citrine's deputy, Vincent Tewson, to supervise the elections. Citrine had done more, however, than trade-union business. He had talked to British troops and investigated stories of atrocities. His report, *What we Saw in Greece*, was published by the TUC in London on 8 February. The evidence of atrocities which he had found increased the sense of anger against the KKE and opened the eyes of many left-wing sympathisers in Britain. His report hardened the attitude of those who had to negotiate the final terms with ELAS.

This was one of a number of factors which adversely affected the Communists during the period of negotiation after the cease-fire. Another was the intransigence of both the Regent and Plastiras. The Regent held a press conference on 12 January, at which he criticised the abduction of hostages; Plastiras made it clear that he wanted a punitive expedition against ELAS rather than a peace conference.[113] Still more troublesome to the KKE was the outcome of the Yalta Conference early in February, at which Churchill thanked Stalin for having refrained from interfering, and Stalin made it clear, apart from a few questions for information, that he had no interest in Greece. It was unrealistic, however, to talk of destroying ELAS by force, as Macmillan and Alexander had already recognised. The point was brought home to the Athenian public by the publication of a map in *Elevtheria* on 16 January, which showed that ELAS still held three-quarters of Greece, including the whole of the north except Salonika and most of the Peloponnese except for the northern belt. In other words, as an ex-Communist later put it, 'the KKE had decisively lost the battle of Athens, but the national government . . . had not won the battle of Greece'.[114] The British authorities were in any case opposed to a hard line. Eden had been willing, even during December, to contemplate the inclusion of EAM representatives in the Government; Macmillan laid most of the blame on the stubbornness of the King; and both he and Leeper were resolved that the 'red terror' should not be followed by a 'white terror'.[115]

Negotiations in these circumstances were bound to be protracted, the advantages not being all one-sided. They began on 2 February in a villa at the sea-side resort of Varkiza, and lasted ten days. No complete first-hand account has been published: those by Leeper and Macmillan are only concerned with the closing stages.[116] The Government delegation was led by Plastiras's Foreign Minister, Sophianopoulos, a left-wing republican who had some sympathy with EAM. His statement of the Government's demands satisfied Leeper, who added: 'I need hardly say that he had gone through very carefully with us in advance the proposals he was going to make.'[117] Siantos led the EAM delegation, accompanied by Partsalidis and Tsirimokos. Technical discussions on military questions took place simultaneously but separately. One question was the quantity of weapons to be surrendered; another was the release of prisoners, over which EAM was represented by Tzimas, who had returned from Belgrade to Trikkala and been sent on to Athens by Siantos.[118] Two matters particularly preoccupied the EAM leaders: the terms of amnesty, and the inclusion of their own representatives in a new government. By tenacious argument they were able to gain the first point in part, but they were defeated on the second.

ELAS did not regard itself as a beaten army suing for peace at any price. Its forces were largely intact, its GHQ was safely installed at Trikkala, and it still controlled most of the country. Nor had its leaders a guilty conscience: as Mandakas summed up their attitude a few years later, 'We could not do otherwise.'* The KKE's mastery of propaganda was unshaken. *Rizospastis* had continued to be produced in Athens until 24 December, after which the editorial staff withdrew to Trikkala, where production was resumed in January.[119] Karagiorgis's final editorial in Athens contained words which foreshadowed retreat but not defeat: 'Eternal thanks from the Nation to the heroic fighter, the unconquered Elasite!' Although both Plastiras and Scobie believed that if the cease-fire had been postponed a few days, a final victory could have been won, Alexander and Macmillan knew better. Macmillan had told Eden on 21 December that he was 'certain that there is a large amount of sympathy with EAM in Greece'.[120] It was symptomatic of this feeling that although ELD officially broke away from EAM on 17 December, and condemned the folly of ELAS in fighting the British and taking hostages, nevertheless Tsirimokos agreed to join the EAM delegation at Varkiza.[121] When Macmillan and Leeper were invited to join the conference on the last day to help break a deadlock, their intervention was on the side of concession and compromise.

* In conversation with myself in June 1950.

The final terms signed at Varkiza on 12 February were not ungenerous to the defeated side.[122] Several clauses were presented in a form which could be represented as meeting the express demands of EAM: for example, article 1 guaranteeing the 'free expression of the political and social opinions of all citizens', and restoring 'trade union liberties'; article 2 on the raising of martial law; article 3 guaranteeing an amnesty; article 5 on the National Army, from which by implication members of ELAS were not to be excluded; articles 7 and 8 on the purging of the civil service and the security services. Article 9, proposing a plebiscite on the constitution and parliamentary elections, in that order, 'within the current year', was also welcome to EAM. Other clauses were more onerous to them, and embodied a public sense of bitterness against them. Article 4 required them to release all hostages, even those alleged to have collaborated with the enemy (who were to be tried by the state); and article 6 required immediate demobilisation of all armed forces under the control of EAM, and the surrender to the state of all requisitioned supplies. The total of weapons agreed to be surrendered under this clause was 41,500 rifles, 2,015 automatic weapons, 163 mortars, and 32 pieces of artillery. The totals actually surrendered were more than was agreed but much less than ELAS possessed.[123]

Despite appearances, the agreement was no more than partially welcome to the Communists. It was judged on the Government side that they had two primary aims – to conceal as much equipment as possible and to protect their followers from punitive action.[124] In the first aim they were thought by Leeper to have failed, since even if they did not surrender all their weapons, 'what they had concealed was discovered by the British troops after the agreement'. This view of the outcome was in essence endorsed by Karagiorgis when he wrote to Zakhariadis on 18 March 1948: 'It is unfortunate that the important decision of the leadership on hiding weapons was not technically accompanied by another decision, that those who hid them should leave the country.'[125] The leaders of the KKE were also blamed for achieving only partial success in their second aim, for the amnesty was effective only to protect themselves and not their rank and file. Article 3 provided that 'common-law crimes against life and property' should be excluded from the amnesty unless they were judged 'absolutely necessary' to the political aim for which they were committed; and it did not apply at all to crimes committed prior to 3 December 1944, the day of the rising. Article 2 also, although it ended martial law, continued the right of arrest without warrant throughout the country except in Athens, Piraeus and the suburbs (where the Government was thought to be sufficiently in control), until the demobilisation of ELAS was complete.

From the point of view of the KKE, the best justification for the Varkiza Agreement was that advanced at the Sixth Plenum of the Central Committee in October 1949, that it was 'the indispensable manoeuvre for the reconstruction of the popular democratic forces'.[126] But there was much heart-searching before that conclusion was reached. When the Communist negotiators, led by Siantos, returned to ELAS GHQ at Trikkala after signing the agreement, they were coldly received. Aris Veloukhiotis led the faction which argued that 'the war should continue'. He agreed, however, to join Saraphis in signing the final Order of the Day to ELAS on 16 February. This order, which gave effect to the article on demobilisation, was repugnant to Aris, and he did not intend to honour his own signature.[127] According to his biographer, his motive was loyalty to the party and a desire to avoid civil war within ELAS.[128] Soon afterwards he left Trikkala for Lamia, called his friends together and declared that 'We have been betrayed!' Rhetorically he asked to whom the KKE belonged: 'is it the personal affair of Siantos and Ioannidis?' Others were to ask similar questions later, but for the present Aris, like Trotsky before him, was ahead of his time. He wanted the 'third round' to begin at once, but the party line was that of Siantos. Ostensibly, at least, ELAS was to be stood down. But when the final Order of the Day was published in *Rizospastis* on 20 February, it bore no signature.

6

The Bitter Truce
February 1945–January 1946

THE VARKIZA Agreement left the Greek people temporarily numbed. All were relieved, but few could see what was to be done next; most were content to leave fresh initiatives to the British. Only very gradually were the first steps taken back towards political normality. Some of the traditional parties were reformed: the Liberals under Sophoulis, and the Populists under Constantine Tsaldaris. New combinations were also formed. In March 1945 Gonatas formed a party called the National Liberals, to which Zervas adhered; and EDES was formally dissolved towards the end of April. Later in the year, Papandreou, Kanellopoulos and Sophocles Venizelos moved together to form the National Political Union, which aimed to rally the moderate Centre. These were temporary alliances, likely to dissolve once Parliament was restored.

More significant were the developments on the left. In April Svolos and Tsirimokos made their breach with EAM final and formed a new coalition, the Union of Popular Democracy and Socialist Party of Greece (ELD/SKE), in which they were joined by Askoutsis and Stratis, both former members of EAM. A statement of policy by ELD blamed both EAM and Papandreou for the disaster of December, but added that 'criticism of the December events and the severance of *organisational* links with other parties of EAM do not indicate a turn to the Right or to the Centre'.[1] The reconstruction of EAM as 'a purely political coalition of parties' was announced on 25 April.

How to interpret the disaster greatly perplexed the Communists both in Greece and abroad. Leading articles in *Rizospastis*, now published at Trikkala, were at first cautious. On receiving a summary of the Varkiza Agreement, Karagiorgis wrote on 14 February: 'we see that EAM ... did what was possible to put an end to the internal disturbance'. Two days later he had no more to add except that 'Varkiza safeguards ideological freedom in the ranks of the new army'. Others openly or by insinuation condemned the agreement. Tzimas argued from the first that the British could have been defeated; Vlandas took a similar line, at least in his later reminiscences.[2] Some even thought in terms of an early renewal of the conflict. Everywhere ELAS tried to preserve its coherence even while the specified number of arms was being surrendered. 'Almost all the structure of ELAS survived, if only in skeleton,' wrote a British observer at the time.[3] The younger Grigoriadis, a regular officer in ELAS, later confirmed that the reconstruction of its armed force began at once after the armistice, and that at least 40,000 personal weapons had been retained.[4] The justification was that irregular forces of the Right remained under arms. In the north, where ELAS was undefeated, the militant mood remained strong. The EAM Committee of Salonika passed a resolution immediately after the cease-fire stressing the need to be ready for a renewal of armed conflict, which it said had stopped 'only temporarily'.[5] An ELAS band was re-formed in the field in Macedonia by a Communist schoolmaster, who called himself Ypsilantis, as early as May 1945.[6]

One man more than any other was prepared to translate threats into action: Aris Veloukhiotis. While *Rizospastis* dropped hints of trouble to come, which only masked indecision, Aris tried to precipitate another round of violence by refusing to accept the consequences of Varkiza. Although he had signed the last Order of the Day on 16 February, he had no intention of obeying the call to surrender. From Trikkala he set out westwards into the Pindus range with his band of devoted guerrillas, and thence northwards through Epirus up to the Albanian frontier, which he was allowed to cross. But he was not warmly received in the north, and once there he could find no way of renewing contact with the KKE. Others followed his example without any concerted plan. Various estimates have been given of the numbers of ELAS who escaped beyond the northern frontiers. Perhaps the most reliable figure is about 8,000 Greeks and also about 8,000 Slavo-Macedonians in the first phase, followed by nearly 20,000 more people later in the year.[7] Karagiorgis later expressed the opinion that many more should have been sent north, taking with them their arms.[8]

Aris re-entered Greece early in May, probably encouraged by the news that Zakhariadis had been found alive in the Dachau concentration-camp.[9] He moved south again with his tiny force through Epirus to Roumeli, where he had first taken the field three years earlier. There he learned from *Rizospastis* of 31 May that Zakhariadis had upheld the Varkiza Agreement in a published statement, declaring that 'if anyone from within our ranks, in the cities or the mountains, continues to resist, we will attack him openly and expel him'. The reference to Aris himself was clear and brutal. It was followed on 12 June by a formal denunciation, published inconspicuously on the back page of *Rizospastis*. Zakhariadis took the opportunity to remind his readers that Aris had signed a *dilosis* or declaration renouncing Communism under Metaxas. The description of his revolt as a 'suspect and opportunist action' is proof that the party line had been confirmed by the return of Zakhariadis: it was to be one of acquiescence in the failure of the 'second round'. Zakhariadis later blamed 'advice from Tito and his band' for Aris's breach of the Varkiza Agreement.[10] After roaming the hills of Roumeli in despair for a few days longer, hounded by the National Guard and betrayed by villagers, Aris shot himself on 16 June. His severed head, with that of one of his men, was displayed on a pole in Trikkala.

His revolt was treated by the KKE as an inexcusable deviation from the party line, though other Greeks chose to regard it as symptomatic of a general intention to start a 'third round' immediately. There was a state of confusion and indecision within the KKE, which Zakhariadis's unexpected return aggravated. On balance the 'doves' were in the ascendant over the 'hawks'; and Zakhariadis's weight was thrown on the side of the former. But he also increased the confusion by some of his early utterances. At his first press conference on 1 June he said that the KKE would oppose any attack on Albania (Northern Epirus), which was rumoured at the time to be contemplated by the Greek Government. A week later, having consulted the Politburo, he allowed an amendment to be issued, stating that if the majority of the people favoured such an expedition, the KKE would 'submit to the decision of the majority', while still declaring its disagreement. This was an extraordinary statement for a Communist, who would normally assert the identity of the will of the people with the views of the party. Zakhariadis himself later admitted that it was a 'fatal concession to bourgeois nationalism'.[11]

Having been a prisoner for nearly ten years, he was out of touch with the feelings and experiences which contributed to determining the party line. Little or no guidance came from abroad, Stalin having agreed with Churchill to leave Greece alone, and Tito being preoccupied with internal problems. Later recriminations within the KKE showed that the Central Committee was in a state of irresolution, for which Zakhariadis was later blamed and for which he equally blamed others. Apart from the confusion over Northern Epirus, Zakhariadis was criticised in 1950 by Tempo for a statement made on 6 June 1945:[12]

> The KKE has never been in favour of a social revolution. The KKE has always striven, and still strives, to attract a majority of the nation.

These words implied, according to Tempo, a lack of revolutionary determination amounting to defeatism. But again in 1950, Zakhariadis was accused by Bartzotas of the opposite offence of Titoism, because at the Twelfth Plenum of the Central Committee on 25–27 June 1945 he had spoken of Britain and the Soviet Union as the 'two poles' round which Greek policy must revolve.[13] To place the two great powers on the same footing was to take an anti-Soviet line. Zakhariadis himself acknowledged at the Seventh Plenum in 1950 that he had exaggerated the necessity of Greece's dependence on Britain.

The pressures on Zakhariadis to adopt an aggressive policy came especially from those with Macedonian connections, like Tzimas and Markos Vaphiadis, for it was in the north that Communism was on the crest of the wave. The Slavo-Macedonian Communists had already reorganised themselves as NOF (National Liberation Front, without the 'Slavo-Macedonian' prefix).[14] Tempo was scathing, both then and later, about the failure of the KKE to continue the struggle, which he contrasted with Lenin's refusal to surrender to foreign intervention and Tito's refusal to compromise with Mihailović and the royalists.[15] Despite the Varkiza Agreement, ELAS continued to dominate large areas of Macedonia, but without encouragement from Zakhariadis, who had no more control over the dissidents than did the Government over its own agents. The limit of his boldness was a resolution of the Twelfth Plenum, which said that Varkiza had provided 'a mere breathing-space'.[16] Few of the city-based members of the Central Committee would have pressed him to go any further, whatever the views of those more accustomed to guerrilla warfare in the northern mountains. Support from the north had already proved an illusion.

It was widely held within the KKE that the Yugoslavs had let them down in December 1944, after making promises of help. Zakhariadis later said so with great bitterness, especially in an article in the *Cominform Journal* on 1 August 1949 and in his address to the Third Party Conference in October 1950.[17] Possibly Tito had a guilty conscience about the reproach. At least the Yugoslavs (as well as the Albanians and Bulgarians) made no difficulties over allowing Communist Greeks and Slavo-Macedonians to take refuge within their borders after Varkiza. The first refugee camps were formed during 1945: at Tetovo, near Skopje; then at Novis Iva; and most important, at Bulkes in the Voivodina. Others were established at Rubik, near Tirana in Albania, and near Petrich in Bulgaria.[18] But these were not training camps for armed activists. The new People's Democracies in the north had too many problems of their own in 1945 to take such risks. In some of them it was still uncertain whether the Communists would prevail over the United Fronts of the war period; in others it was uncertain whether power would settle in the hands of the Communists who had spent the war in Moscow or those who had stayed at home. Everywhere 1945 was a year of transition.

Even more uncertain was the attitude of the great powers during 1945. It was assumed that the British would not readily give up their interests in Greece, and their limitations were not yet appreciated. Stalin continued to show little interest in Greece beyond an occasional curiosity. He refused even to consider taking part in the proposed supervision of the Greek elections, which he criticised as constituting an interference in the internal affairs of the country. The attitude of the United States Government was also still just as detached. Although it contributed generously to relief through UNRRA, and agreed to help in supervising the elections, it did not wish to be further involved. A Greek observer in Washington described the Americans, even as late as January 1946, as still behaving like 'a somewhat distant third party trying to smooth out, or rather to gloss over, the Anglo-Soviet differences'.[19] Their reward was to be exempted for some time yet from criticism in the Communist press. The 'murderous terrorism' which was daily denounced in *Rizospastis* and *Elevtheri Ellada* was still confined to the British and the Monarcho-fascists.

The year was also marked by a conscious effort to re-establish the respectability of the KKE, or at least of EAM, in the eyes of the Western Allies. On the day before the Varkiza Agreement was signed, Siantos was already referring to the events of December and January as an 'unfortunate misunderstanding' with the British.[20] He thanked the British ('his friends and allies') effusively for helping to bring about the agreement.[21] A pamphlet published by Zevgos in April 1945 admitted that the KKE had in fact committed murders, but it pointed out that others had also done so, from Kolokotronis in the War of Independence to Pangalos in the 1920s.[22] In support of the conciliatory line, numerous delegations composed of individuals likely to create a favourable impression were sent abroad to Britain, France and the USA. Karagiorgis attended the founding conference of the United Nations in San Francisco as a journalist, and succeeded in obtaining a resolution from a meeting of Greek–Americans in June condemning 'monarchist terrorism'. Partsalidis visited Paris and London, and claimed to have had a friendly reception. In October a delegation of the Communist youth movement, EPON, attended a World Congress of Youth in London. On the whole these visits had an encouraging response. The Communists were equally eager to receive visitors to Athens from western countries, particularly British Labour MPs.

There was much emphasis on 'democracy' in the propaganda of the day. The alternative use of the Greek term to mean 'republic' was subtly used to create antagonism against the monarchy. *Rizospastis* on 8 April called

for 'a Democratic Front to save Democracy', and on 16 May 'for the
suppression of dark forces, for the democratic reform of the country'.
The true significance of these vague terms was spelled out by Zevgos at the
end of April, in a postscript to his account of the December rising:

> Let all the democratic, anti-fascist forces, to whatever party they
> belong, unite in an all-powerful democratic, anti-fascist front to
> solve the first great problem of the new Greece, to annihilate fascism,
> and monarchism first of all, which threatens the country with the
> coming of Glücksburg.[23]

Such rhetoric could be interpreted to mean that if the restoration of
the monarchy were averted, the KKE might be willing to acquiesce in a
constitutional evolution of Greek democracy. Siantos and Ioannidis continued to believe in a 'normal democratic development': it was Aris's
chief accusation against them.[24] Zachariadis defined his aim as 'the
smooth progress to a free expression of the people's will'.[25] These phrases
were in contrast with the more belligerent language which often accompanied them.

The salient impression, reinforced by the return of Zachariadis, was
one of confusion rather than guile. So irresolute had the KKE become that
at times it almost seemed to want the Government to provoke it into a
decision. The Communist press was full of complaints that the Varkiza
Agreement was being infringed. Within a month of its signature, deputa-
tions of protest to various authorities were presenting themselves several
times a week: on 22 February to Sophianopoulos, the next day to the
Regent, on 27 February to Plastiras, on 7 March to Leeper, on 11 March
to MacVeagh. The first documented protest in writing was presented over
Partsalidis's signature on 3 March.[26] Regular participants in the protests
were Siantos, Partsalidis, Zevgos and Porphyrogennis; but sometimes
they had non-Communists like Askoutsis and Tsirimokos to accompany
them. The most powerful protest was addressed jointly to the Regent and
Prime Minister on 4 April, over the signatures of twelve former members
of PEEA and Papandreou's government, only four of whom were Communists, with Svolos's name at the head.[27] At the same time the Communist press was daily filled with horrific headlines and stories of atrocities:
'Returning Elasites arrested and maltreated', said *Rizospastis* on 1 March;
on 8 March its headline denounced 'The Pogrom Against ELAS'; and on
13 March an article on infringements of Varkiza made open reference to
the KKE's hopes of Stalin's support: 'The great Georgian, the Titan of
Titans . . . hears our sighs and groans!' But Stalin was silent.

The implication of the KKE's propaganda was that an indiscriminate campaign of 'white terror' was being launched against their adherents. They made no distinction between the official organs of the state and the unofficial agents of the right wing, or even common criminals. On 12 May 1945 *Elevtheri Ellada* published figures of outrages committed in the first ten days of the month which included, among many others, 19 murders, 25 attempted murders, 100 convictions, 645 assaults, 10 arrests of women, 1,183 illegal arrests, 437 house searches, 100 thefts from pharmacies and so on. Such a miscellaneous catalogue of complaints, some of them against the police and judicial authorities, and some against the adherents of rival organisations or of no organisations at all, must obviously have defied investigation. It was nevertheless the standard method used by the KKE for rousing public opinion under the pretence of seeking redress. Another such catalogue, exactly a year later, contained almost the same hotch-potch of official and unofficial misdeeds.[28] The intention was evidently to create the impression that the Government, the police, the National Guard, *Khí*, the ex-collaborators and Security Battalions were all in league together to persecute the former adherents of ELAS, who alone were identified as having belonged to the Resistance.

Certainly there was very strong feeling against ELAS after the events of December, and there were many examples of private vengeance. Some official discrimination—but in the eyes of anti-Communists, not nearly enough—was practised against them in the reorganisation of the security forces. The National Guard was recruited exclusively from men with an anti-Communist reputation.[29] According to *Rizospastis* on 24 March, twelve hundred members of the town police were retired and sixty placed under arrest for holding 'democratic views'. But with the express approval of Plastiras, officers and NCOs of ELAS were not excluded from the new Second Division of the army, formed from the nucleus of the Third Mountain Brigade.[30] In the provinces ELAS was far from being an extinct force. Large areas of Greece were still under left-wing control for several months after Varkiza. In the Peloponnese, although 'royalist slogans were everywhere', and jubilant crowds shouted for the King, nevertheless EAM was maintaining part of its hold by threats and propaganda.[31] In some towns of Macedonia, notably Naoussa and Verria, EAM still had its offices open.[32] It was the discovery of hidden arms dumps and the graves of dead hostages that kept bitterness against the KKE alive, rather than any deliberate provocation on the part of the Government. The terrible facts of Communist atrocities were too well attested to be concealed or palliated.[33]

At the highest level, vindictiveness against the Communists evaporated fairly quickly. Martial law was ended, and an amnesty bill introduced, two days after the signature of the Varkiza Agreement. The three Prime Ministers who held office for more than a few weeks in 1945 and early 1946 (General Plastiras, Admiral Voulgaris and the aged Sophoulis) marked a descending scale of hostility. Sophianopoulos, who served all three as Foreign Minister, was not unsympathetic to the KKE. Only the Regent was implacably hostile. Plastiras, who was openly contemptuous of politics and politicians, at first wanted to launch a punitive expedition against ELAS, but he was soon persuaded that it was impracticable.[34] His first statement of policy was firm but not uncompromising. He spoke of reconstructing the armed forces, punishing collaborators, reviving the national economy and holding elections and a plebiscite (in that order) under allied supervision. He added that although crimes committed under the occupation would be punished, there would be 'no proscription'.

The question was not whether he would be as good as his word but whether, under anti-Communist pressure, he could be. An early setback was the resignation on 20 February of the Minister of the Interior, Pericles Rallis, who had been one of the signatories of the Varkiza Agreement barely a week before. He resigned in protest at Plastiras's decision to appoint a junior Minister of Security in his department; and in consequence the post had to be given another name to placate liberal consciences. A more encouraging development was the appointment of a Constitutional Committee for Foreign Affairs, with representatives of all parties including the KKE. But in early April Plastiras himself was forced to resign. Ostensibly the reason was the publication of an indiscreet letter which he had sent to the Greek Ambassador at Vichy in 1941, criticising Greece's continuation of the war. In reality the Regent had simply lost confidence in him.

His successor was Admiral Voulgaris, who had suppressed the naval mutiny at Alexandria a year before. Although in the past he had been a staunch republican, he was at once denounced by the KKE as a 'monarcho-fascist'. But his brief administration was marked rather by weakness than repression. He drew his Cabinet mainly from the political Centre, the outstanding member being Professor Varvaressos, the Minister of Supply. Varvaressos introduced a bold and imaginative programme for economic recovery in June, which included devaluation of the drachma, controls over wages and prices, heavy direct taxation and measures to regulate distribution and to eliminate the black market. But the state had not the means to enforce his plans, nor had the Government the will, when confronted with the antagonism of the civil service and the commercial classes.

Similar weaknesses frustrated the enforcement of public security. The new National Guard, which moved out into the provinces in April, and the Gendarmerie, which began to resume its functions in July, were unable to impose order or even, in many cases, to discipline their own men. Their shortcomings were due to circumstances rather than malice. A second amnesty in August increased the numbers of former members of ELAS at large, against whom many private scores remained to be bloodily settled. Hostility to the KKE took many forms of armed violence, ranging from outright banditry to the tolerated excesses of Grivas. The Communist press linked all of them together as 'monarcho-fascist terrorists'. Tsouderos added a new ingredient to KKE propaganda when he revealed in April the existence of a 'military league' of royalist officers, formed within the army in the Middle East during the war. This was IDEA (the Sacred Bond of Greek Officers), of which more was to be heard in later years.

Government after government watched helplessly as control slipped out of its hands. Much of the criticism of successive Ministers was unjust. They were blamed for things for which they were constitutionally responsible but had not the physical resources to manage, like security and the economy. They were equally blamed for things in which they had the means to interfere but not the constitutional responsibility, such as the trials of collaborators under the Occupation and criminals in the Resistance. These were matters for the courts, but the Government was blamed for the manner in which the courts handled them. Using the existing criminal code as they were obliged to do, the courts showed greater tolerance to collaboration with the enemy than to crimes by the Resistance. The trials of the principal collaborators, including three Prime Ministers, began on 21 February and lasted until 31 May. In a series of scornful reports, the Communist press dismissed the proceedings as farcical, but did not fail to report prominently the embarrassing evidence of Sophoulis in defence of the Security Battalions, the revelations of Tsolakoglou about his contacts with Papandreou and the allegation that Rallis, the last German-appointed Prime Minister, had supplied arms to Zervas. In the event, only three collaborators were condemned to death (none of whom was executed) and five to life sentences. On the other hand, death sentences were freely passed during the same period on former members of ELAS and particularly of OPLA; though of these, too, in the end, few were executed.

The main force making for moderation at this time was the British presence. Leeper wrote that 'even before the fighting was over, I was painfully aware that it would be our difficult task to prevent the red terror from being followed by a white terror'; and he rightly claimed that the leniency shown to EAM was 'largely due to British advice'.[35] Apart from Leeper and the service commanders, much of the credit belonged to Macmillan, who made several visits to Athens in the early months of 1945 and exercised a restraining hand on Plastiras at more than one crucial moment. Macmillan later recorded in his memoirs that he himself agreed with those Greeks who criticised the mildness of British policy. He attributed it to the lack of sufficient forces to complete the suppression of 'revolutionary Communism', together with the failure of the American Government and British public opinion to appreciate the truth about the KKE.[36] On the other hand, a less highly placed observer in the field wrote that the inability of the Greek Government to enforce a policy of conciliation and toleration gave 'considerable substance' to left-wing protests; and the British presence 'could make us appear as accomplices of the acts of injustice and revenge that were carried out'.[37] Both extremes of opinion thus held the British to blame.

That Britain, not the USA, would remain the predominant power in the Mediterranean, was still taken for granted. This assumption underlay Stalin's reluctance to antagonise Churchill, and his acceptance of the 'percentage agreement' in October 1944. True, he linked the Americans with the British when he justified his attitude later to the Yugoslavs by pointing out that, unlike the two Western Allies, 'we have no navy'; but in 1944 his main motive was 'not to frighten the British', without reference to the Americans.[38] That the same assumption was made by the KKE formed one of the main themes of Zakhariadis's later criticism of party policy in 1944. ELAS, he complained, was unnecessarily subordinated to 'British policy and British imperialist aims in the Mediterranean and south-east Europe'; and he bitterly blamed the British (though quite erroneously) for preferring that Tito should have Salonika rather than ELAS.[39] The assumption persisted in allied thinking, if in an attenuated form, even when it began to appear hollow. An American observer in 1947 wrote that, from 1942 onwards, 'London made most of the political decisions concerning the eastern Mediterranean, while Washington furnished much of the actual power needed for their enforcement.'[40] This was also the view expressed in an important article on 'The American Position in the Mediterranean' in an academic periodical during the same critical summer.[41]

The doctrine of British supremacy in the Mediterranean naturally died hardest in Britain. Churchill embodied it, and Bevin assumed his mantle on becoming Foreign Secretary. His Minister of State, Hector McNeil, once described Greece as 'an Egypt without a Cromer', taking for granted

The planners of the Gorgopotamos Bridge operation, General Zervas and Brigadier Myers.

At ELAS GHQ: Despotopoulos, Wines, Aris, Woodhouse, Saraphis.

Mountains of Albania, seen from Epirus.

Transport of supplies to the guerrillas.

EDES and ELAS guerrillas in a mixed group.

Political platform: Karagiorgis on left, Siantos second from right.

The Plaka Bridge, scene of the armistice ending the First Round, February 1944.

George Papandreou.

Demonstration in
Athens, December
1944.

British troops operating in Athens, December 1944.

King George II.

Constantine Tsaldaris
and Themistocles
Sophoulis, Prime
Ministers during the
Third Round, 1946–9.

Field-Marshal Papagos.

King Paul and Queen Frederika at Lamia, 1948.

Markos Vaphiadis,
Commander-in-Chief
of the Greek
Democratic Army.

Sentry-post on Mount
Lykabettos, December
1947.

Captured guerrillas.

Greek Army artillery in action on the Bulgarian frontier, 1948.

Captured guerrilla weapons.

Greek Army entrenchments, Karpenisi, 1948.

Final assault on Vitsi, August 1949.

Bust of General Van Fleet, unveiled at Kastoria, 1951.

its status as a British protectorate.[42] A British journalist could still make the same assumption even in 1949, when he wrote that 'those who would injure England can safely injure her in Greece'.[43] Even a less romantic observer wrote in 1954 that 'a friendly Greece was demonstrably as essential to the British Commonwealth in the middle of the twentieth century as it had been in the nineteenth'.[44] Up to 1947 the British Government appointed and dismissed Greek Prime Ministers with the barest attention to constitutional formalities. British experts dictated economic and financial policy, defence and foreign policy, security and legal policy, trade union and employment policy. The memoirs of Leeper and Macmillan show how readily, though with occasional outbreaks of Greek obstinacy, this relationship was taken for granted on all sides. Of all the organs of the Greek state, the courts were perhaps the most successful in maintaining their independence, and the politicians the least successful. But on the whole Britain's illusory power was used benevolently, if not always wisely.

The most constructive efforts to promote reconciliation were made in the field of trade-union organisation. This problem went to the heart of Greek politics, for the General Confederation of Greek Workers (GSEE) was divided on essentially political lines.[45] The leadership of EEAM, though dominated by the Communists Theos and Nepheloudis, also included Reformists like Kalomoiris and Stratis, and even supporters of right-wing parties like Photis Makris. Outside EEAM there were both Reformists and survivors of the paternalist organisation of the era of Metaxas. After Citrine's mission at the end of January had made some progress in healing the divisions left open by the December events, he agreed to send a further mission under his deputy, Vincent Tewson, to complete the task. Tewson arrived in Athens towards the end of February, expecting to supervise the election of a new Executive and Secretariat, but he found a state of embittered deadlock. The elections were never held. Instead, Tewson negotiated a second agreement on 25 February, and left behind his junior colleague, Victor Feather, who negotiated a third agreement on 28 February. The effect was to recognise the new provisional Executive and Secretariat which had been installed by Plastiras's Minister of Labour in January. But although all the agreements were given legislative sanction by the Government in March, they were not recognised by the Communists, who still dominated the trade unions outside Athens.

The political importance of Greece was shown even more emphatically by the visits of Churchill twice, Eden three times, and Macmillan at least half a dozen times in the first six months of liberation. The financial problems of the country attracted the services of several outstanding officials from the Treasury. In many other official and semi-official fields – for example, the British Council and the Press and Information Offices – personal appointments were made which were appreciated by the Greeks as a recognition of their standing in the allied world. On the other hand, the narrow mediocrity of the staffs available to Scobie and Leeper, at least until it was too late, was in striking contrast. It suggested that Greece had not been expected to present either military or diplomatic problems, which was a serious error of judgment.

A wide range of technical missions operated in Greece. Military Liaison, under a British general, co-ordinated relief supplies until UNRRA could begin operations. There were training and supply missions to each of the armed services. There was a police mission, a financial mission, a Co-operative Society mission and later a legal mission. All of these aimed to make possible a peaceful reconstruction of Greek life, avoiding recrimination and revenge. They consistently discouraged all provocation of the Left. The police mission, for example, declined to allow the Greek police to be armed – although the head of the mission came from the only armed police force in the United Kingdom, the Royal Ulster Constabulary. British troops frequently intervened to curb the excesses of anti-Communist bands. Eden admitted in the House of Commons on 11 April that there had been such excesses; but even *Rizospastis* at least once, on 21 July, gave credit to the British for arresting a group of 'monarcho-fascist bandits' near Larisa. More often the Communist press abused the British for tolerating breaches of Varkiza by the 'military league and monarcho-fascist terrorists'. Comparison of *Rizospastis* and *Elevtheri Ellada* with other newspapers, particularly those that were anti-monarchist as well as anti-Communist, like *Elevtheria*, shows that the campaign was exaggerated.

It appeared to become even more violent after Zakhariadis resumed control in June. Leeper, who went on leave in that month, found the Communists 'a good deal bolder' on his return, though MacVeagh detected a favourable shift.[46] There was a brief pause when the British Labour Government came into office on 26 July under Attlee – an event which *Rizospastis* said on 2 August 'creates joy and hope among the peoples of Europe'. But the hopes were abruptly shattered by Bevin's first speech as Foreign Secretary, in which he indicated that there would be no change of policy towards Greece. *Rizospastis* expressed on 22 August 'a certain spontaneous feeling of sorrow'. It reported Zakhariadis on the same day as having said in a speech at Kavalla that 'Bevin's statements are contrary to the will of the Greek people', and more arrogantly that 'we shall reach understanding with England as equals' – a phrase repeated in the headlines. The ordinary tone of *Rizospastis* was much blunter. 'Is Greece a

British colony?' it asked on 6 May; on 5 June it reported Zakhariadis attacking the British presence in Greece; at the beginning of October it reported formal denunciations of the British by the Seventh Party Congress, which was held openly in Athens; and on 11 November it began publishing intercepted telegrams of the British Military Mission to the Resistance, under the headline: 'Light on the Intrigues of the Tories in Greece.' By demanding Cyprus on 5 June and accusing the British on 16 June of encouraging the secession of Crete, *Rizospastis* was also able to strike a patriotic note.

During the latter half of 1945 a more active militancy could be detected on the part of the KKE; yet the appearance could have been delusive. Communists bands were reported to be re-forming in Macedonia, but they were spontaneous and uncoordinated.[47] Zakhariadis used strong words but took no action. At his first press conference on returning to Athens he had spoken of the possibility of 'a new armed struggle'; at the Twelfth Plenum of the Central Committee held on 25–27 June – the first since his return – he called for 'mass self-defence'; and many of his other statements could mean much or little, according as they were read literally or metaphorically. So far from encouraging violent reactions to 'monarcho-fascist terrorism', the overt actions of the KKE were often strikingly conciliatory – inexcusably so, in the judgment of militant Yugoslavs such as Tempo.[48] On 11 August, for example, the district committee of EAM in the village of Lerina actually deplored the murder of two policemen and urged the public to denounce the perpetrators to the authorities. An example of 'popular self-defence against monarchist bandits' was reported in the same spirit by *Rizospastis* on 9 October: villagers at Khalastra, near Salonika, had arrested them and handed them over to the police. There was no determination yet to oppose 'monarcho-fascism' with force, though much of the KKE's propaganda suggested that there was.

In this period of hesitation the KKE was anxious to be seen as both democratic and patriotic; and this was clearly Zakhariadis's policy. As proof of patriotism, he declared in Salonika on 24 August that 'Macedonia is and will remain Greek!' On 25 October he publicly denied that the KKE had ever supported an independent Macedonia. He brought a libel action against a right-wing newspaper, *Ellinikon Aima*, for accusing him of having undertaken not to support Greece's frontier claims. His pretensions to democracy continued in the same vein, when he denied that the KKE had ever supported social revolution. On 17 June *Rizospastis* reported the party's new programme under the headline: 'Unity – Order – Tranquillity – Work – Reconstruction.' On 30 June the Twelfth Plenum was reported to have called for 'a popular-democratic way out from the present internal disorders'. On 23 July the Politburo demanded a new coalition government, to include the KKE. In August, when the Government banned an EAM demonstration in the Athens Stadium, the ban was quietly accepted, under protest. The phrase 'representative government' occurred almost daily in *Rizospastis*. There was some justice in Tempo's acid conclusion that the KKE really fought 'for the participation of Communists in a bourgeois-democratic government, with the bourgeoisie in the key position'.[49] Still worse, in Tempo's opinion, the KKE was wasting its time in a struggle to capture the 'mass organisations' while the bourgeois reactionaries were 'working systematically on the building up of their State machine and their military force'.

These fraternal criticisms were not beside the point, but they could be answered. The new policy of the KKE was consistent with a campaign of political subversion from within. Some indication of the method of operation can be seen in the trade unions, where the Communists were more strongly entrenched; and the 'mass organisations' were not so unimportant as Tempo implied. After the breakdown of the agreements negotiated by Tewson and Feather, and the nomination of a new provisional Executive of the General Confederation by the Government, the Communists formed a new trade-union organisation of their own called ERGAS, which soon commanded a large following.[50] Some time was to elapse, however, before its strength could be tested by elections. In June the Government assumed power by law to reconstruct the General Confederation and to assign a time-limit to the provisional Executive. Later in the same month a fresh agreement was reached, with the renewed help of Victor Feather, to hold elections in September. Again the decision was hotly disputed by the Communists, now strongly re-established in the framework of ERGAS.

Although the Government ratified the latest agreement by decree on 3 July, no trade-union elections were in fact held in September. A succession of decrees in September and October was required in order to legitimise the continuation of the provisional Executive, and by December foreign intervention was found to be necessary again. The French trade-unionist, Saillant, was sent to Athens on behalf of the WFTU, with Feather to assist him. As a result of a further conference under Saillant's chairmanship, a new decree was issued on 8 December giving the Minister of Labour fresh power to reconstruct the provisional Executive; and on 16 January 1946 another decree validated all the ministerial orders made since the expiry of the original time-limit in September. This last technical precaution was prudent, but as it turned out ineffective in law, for it was later to be overruled by the Council of State. The battle between the Communists and anti-Communists in the trade unions was thus engaged on two fronts, political and juridical. During 1946 ERGAS was to win the former but lose the latter; and its defeat in the courts was probably among the causes which led in the end to the Communists' conviction that they could not come to power by constitutional means.

The same conviction was prompted even before the end of 1945 in other fields. However successful the Communists may have been in the 'mass organisations' (meaning principally the trade unions and co-operatives, but also youth movements and cultural and sporting organisations), their efforts to penetrate the Government were unsuccessful. Their pressure for a coalition or representative government had no effect so far as their own participation was concerned. The succession of governments in the second half of 1945 showed a slight shift towards the left Centre, but the KKE was ignored in the process. By July Voulgaris's government had begun to crumble. Sophianopoulos resigned as Foreign Minister on his return from the founding Conference of the United Nations at San Francisco, and began to urge the formation of a political government and early elections. Varvaressos's economic plan began to break down in August, frustrated by intense opposition from commercial interests, and he resigned on 2 September. Sophoulis attacked the Government for failing to maintain security. The Regent, on a visit to London in September, found the new British Government in an uncompromising mood. Fierce arguments raged over the dates and priority of the elections and the plebiscite on the monarchy, leading in the end to a severe crisis in the Greek Government.

The decision to reverse the order laid down in the Varkiza Agreement, and to hold the elections first, was taken in London during September. It is not clear who took the first initiative to bring about the reversal. It accorded with the wishes of EAM; it was advocated by the American authorities as early as 16 June, though opposed at that time by the British Government; but it was supported within a short time by Leeper.[51] The reasoning was that if the elections came first and if (as the British Government hoped) the parties of the Centre were successful, then the fate of the monarchy could be decided in a calmer atmosphere; but if the plebiscite came first, it would be regarded as simply a contest between the monarchy and Communism. The subsequent elections in the latter case, it was argued, would then follow the same pattern as the plebiscite, by throwing up a government of the extreme Right or the extreme Left as the case might be. It was a logical but futile ratiocination in an emotional and irrational atmosphere. It was supported, according to monarchist sources, by the Regent himself as a device for prolonging his tenure of power.[52] Eventually the decision was taken by the three western powers, with the

Soviet Government dissenting. On 19 September it was announced that the elections would be held first and would be observed by a joint British, American and French mission. But it still remained to fix the date and to convince the Greek politicians.

After prolonged wrangling, Voulgaris announced on 5 October that the elections would take place on 20 January 1946. Three days later, confronted with general opposition, he resigned. For three weeks no one was able to form a new government, and the Regent took the chair at the Council of Ministers himself. Sophocles Venizelos tried and failed to form a government on the last day of October; Kanellopoulos tried on the first day of November, but lasted less than three weeks in office. Bevin's Minister of State, Hector McNeil, arrived in Athens and insisted on the formation of a political government drawn from the Liberals and the left Centre. Sophoulis therefore took office on 20 November, with Tsouderos as his deputy and Sophianopoulos again as Foreign Minister. A number of personalities from the Resistance (but no Communists) were also included in the Government. The King protested at the postponement of the plebiscite until after the elections, and the Regent accordingly offered his resignation.[53] But both were eventually persuaded to yield: the King coldly acquiesced, and the Regent withdrew his resignation.

Kanellopoulos later attributed the appointment of Sophoulis's government to the prejudices of the British Labour Party and its contacts with the left-wing Resistance.[54] Certainly the composition of the Government caused surprise, especially as it was thought to have been selected by Leeper, who was regarded in Athens, quite mistakenly, as biased to the right.[55] Anti-Communists were angered by the immediate announcement of a further amnesty (the third of the year) and the introduction of a new law in December, on the advice of the British Legal Mission, to 'decongest' the prisons by releasing many of those held without trial. The reactions of the KKE were mixed. Having been excluded from the Government once again, the Communists could not support it, but they agreed, adopting a phrase from parliamentary convention, to 'tolerate' it. During November leaflets even briefly circulated in Macedonia praising the conduct of the British Government.[56] But the mood quickly changed. Early in December *Rizospastis* began to attack the new government, and on 8 December Zakhariadis published a virulently anti-British article. Decongestion of the prisons was criticised as inadequate: a full amnesty and a coalition government were again demanded. On 11 December the KKE withdrew its 'tolerance' of Sophoulis.

Some historians have supposed that the decision to revert to force was taken at this date, and that it was taken on the initiative of the Soviet

Government. Professor Kousoulas wrote of a new drive by the Soviet Union in the direction of the Mediterranean and the Persian Gulf, in which 'the KKE had a task to perform'.[57] Other writers have attached importance to the story of a meeting of Greek, Bulgarian and Yugoslav Communists at Petrich on 15 December, at which the Yugoslavs (among them, Ranković) were said to have promised material aid to the KKE and to have co-ordinated plans for active war.[58] Such a meeting may well have taken place, but it is noteworthy that one of those who reported it (a French journalist, one of whose informants was probably Tzimas) also stated that no message was received at Petrich from Stalin, who was more interested at this date in Azerbaijan than in Greece. It was perhaps significant that on 19 January 1946 an EAM delegation arrived in Moscow, ostensibly to discuss its political claims with the Soviet Government; but the significance of it should not be exaggerated. If the KKE were receiving instructions to organise revolution, they would have been conveyed secretly. An overt meeting in Moscow at such a time, being bound to provoke suspicion, would presumably have been avoided. The interpretation of Soviet policy is still a matter of speculation.

At the Yalta Conference in February 1945, Stalin had tacitly confirmed his agreement with Churchill, originally made in Moscow in October 1944, not to interfere with British policy in Greece. So matters continued for some time. Then the international situation was dramatically changed in the four months between the beginning of April and the end of July 1945, by the final defeat of Germany, the deaths of Mussolini, Hitler and Roosevelt, and the fall of Churchill's government. Stalin might have been expected to assume that the balance of power had shifted decisively in his favour, not foreseeing that Truman, Attlee and Bevin would prove tougher antagonists than their predecessors. His calculations may also have been affected by the advent of the atomic bomb, which ended the war with Japan in August; but more probably he would in any case have followed his habitual policy of caution. He missed no opportunity to extend his security zone, but his general attitude, while tactically aggressive, was strategically defensive, particularly in south-east Europe. Where the war had left a vacuum, as in Rumania, Bulgaria and Albania, he would fill it; but where his wartime allies stood firm, as over Trieste and later over the Turkish Straits, he would not push matters to a dangerous extreme. Yugoslavia was a puzzle which he still did not understand, but he persisted for the time being in trying to treat Tito as just another satellite. Of his wartime allies, the French were still negligible, and the Americans seemed anxious to withdraw from Europe as soon as possible. The British appeared to be a more formidable obstacle than in fact they were.

It was in these conditions that the Potsdam Conference in July 1945, and the Foreign Ministers' Conferences which followed it, were conducted. Stalin and his spokesmen advanced a number of claims, but pressed none of them in the face of opposition. At Potsdam Stalin expressed a wish to obtain a naval base in the Aegean, hinting at Salonika, Alexandroupolis or the Dodecanese; and he also spoke of the need for a revision of the Montreux Convention on the Straits. At a meeting of the Foreign Ministers in London during September, Molotov asked for the trusteeship of Tripolitania, but agreed that the Dodecanese should go to Greece, and refused to discuss Northern Epirus. He also took the opportunity to protest at breaches of the Varkiza Agreement and to call for a 'democratic' government in Greece. *Izvestia* denounced 'the terrorism of Greek reactionaries, monarchists and overt Fascists' on 22 August, and also criticised the idea of foreign observers at the Greek elections. At the next meeting of the Foreign Ministers, held in Moscow in December, there was little discussion of Greece, but more of Turkey and the Straits. In the meantime the Soviet Government had agreed to send an Ambassador, Admiral Rodionov, to Athens, although nine months earlier Molotov had warned Sophianopoulos at San Francisco that they would not do so unless the Greek Communists were included in the Government. So far as south-east Europe was concerned, the Cold War had scarcely yet begun.

Despite the growing tension between the USA and the Soviet Union elsewhere, the KKE could still reasonably hope that the Americans would remain neutral in Greece. The first sign of interest that they showed after Varkiza was a proposal from President Roosevelt on 21 March that an international commission should be established to develop the Greek economy.[59] This was the kind of initiative that was welcome to MacVeagh; but as Churchill insisted that the commission should be exclusively Anglo-American, Roosevelt dropped the idea. Soon afterwards, when Plastiras was replaced as Prime Minister by Voulgaris, the Americans mildly hinted that they would have liked to be consulted.[60] These straws in the wind were unknown to the KKE, but they greatly prized American sympathy. When Truman succeeded as President on Roosevelt's death, his first speech was greeted by *Rizospastis* on 17 April with the headline: 'Important Speech by Truman – Duty of Great Nations to Serve the Peoples and not Tyrannise over them.' For some months the new American administration remained gratifyingly uncommitted. But its officials were aware of the possible dangers. Warnings of the threat of Macedonian autonomy had been sent from Washington to diplomatic posts in London, Moscow and the Balkans in late 1944.[61] MacVeagh, in a long despatch dated

15 January 1945, spoke of the role of 'international communism' in Greece, forecast the possibility of 'mountain banditry', and concluded that 'the prospects for the future cannot be considered as other than dubious still'.[62]

Only gradually, however, did the mood harden in Washington, and then chiefly for reasons related to other parts of Europe rather than Greece. The agreement to join Britain and France in observing the elections was a more important turning-point than was realised at the time. Other indications were more tentative.[63] In July, after a series of incidents on the Greek–Yugoslav frontier, the US Government offered to join in sending an international mission of investigation, but did not press the proposal against opposition. In the same month it made a credit of twenty million dollars available to the Greek Government. A slight retreat from growing responsibility came in September, when the US Government rejected a proposal by Bevin that UNRRA should extend its functions to a virtual control over the Greek economy.

The Communist press was quick to notice any changes from a neutral stance. An article in *Rizospastis* on 22 September, headed 'Problems of the Mediterranean', speculated on US interests there; another on 1 October discussed Soviet–American rivalry. At the Seventh Party Congress, held in Athens from 1 to 6 October, while the British were regularly denounced, little was said about the Americans. Later in the same month President Truman sent Mark Ethridge, a publisher and personal friend, on a tour of the Balkans, which led to a report criticising Soviet activities. There followed a speech by the President in New York on 27 October which was construed as a veiled attack on the Soviet Union; and on the 30th *Rizospastis* compared Truman unfavourably with Roosevelt. Still, when the USS *Providence* visited Piraeus in December, the occasion was not generally seen as anything more than a gesture of good will.

The lines of great power conflict in the Balkans were thus not yet firmly drawn during the course of 1945. The tentative character of the great-power divisions was reflected within south-east Europe itself. The so-called 'people's democracies' had not yet fallen into the well-drilled harmony which caused them to become known in the west as satellites of the Soviet Union. Greece's relations with her northern neighbours varied for historical reasons. Yugoslavia was a wartime ally, Bulgaria a wartime enemy; and Albania, though looked on by the Greeks as an enemy, was regarded by her allies as a victim of Italian occupation. The Greeks therefore had territorial claims against Albania, which the Constitutional Committee on Foreign Affairs in June urged the Western Allies to invite Greece to assert by force. They also had claims against Bulgaria, which

Voulgaris's government reaffirmed in the same month. The KKE was cautious and confused in opposing these claims.

Although all Greece's northern neighbours were undergoing the imposition of Communism, the process was uneven and not unopposed. In both Albania and Yugoslavia relics of the nationalist resistance still survived. They were relentlessly crushed, but it took time. Since Albania was too remote for foreign intervention, the Communist Party was free to impose itself at leisure. It was at first a Yugoslav rather than a Soviet protectorate. When there was thought to be a danger of Greek aggression on Northern Epirus, it was Yugoslavia that signed a treaty of alliance with Albania in July 1945; and when the Albanians mined the Corfu Strait in 1946, it was Yugoslavia that provided the mines and technicians. To the dismay of the Greeks, the western powers eventually recognised the Albanian Communist Government in November 1945.

In Bulgaria, where an Allied Control Commission was established, some temporary restraints could be enforced on the Fatherland Front. Protests by the British and US Governments in August 1945 compelled the postponement of elections which had originally been fixed for September; but they were held all the same in November, without the opposition parties and with predictable results. In the same month Dimitrov, the former Secretary-General of the Comintern, returned to Sofia from Moscow to assume power. Yugoslavia, in contrast, followed a more uncertain course, hindered and harassed not only by the surviving remnants of the forces of Mihailović (which were not finally liquidated until the spring of 1946), but also by the suspicions and hostility of the Soviet authorities.

There was already in 1945 much friction between the Yugoslavs and their Soviet allies. The Partisans had been offended by the conduct of the Red Army during its passage through Yugoslavia, as well as by the assumption of senior Russian commanders that the country owed its liberation to them. When Kardelj and Šubašić visited Moscow in November 1944, Stalin spoke disparagingly to them of the Partisans; and when Tito and Djilas were invited to Moscow in April 1945 to sign a treaty of friendship, Stalin deliberately offended Tito by his crude jokes.[64] The Yugoslav CP also resented Stalin's interference in its dealings with the Bulgarian CP. At the end of 1944, when Kardelj visited Sofia, there was talk of a 'defensive alliance' between the two countries, and plans for a further meeting later to discuss federation; but Stalin insisted that the discussions should be transferred to Moscow, where Vyshinsky presided and deliberately obstructed further progress.[65] In May Stalin further offended Tito by refusing to support his claims on Trieste. In June came a Soviet rebuke to

Tito for a vigorously nationalist speech delivered at Ljubljana, in which he said: 'We demand that everyone should be master in his own house.' Kardelj, however (according to the Soviet account), assured the Soviet Ambassador in Belgrade on 5 June 1945 that Yugoslavia still looked forward to becoming 'one of the future Soviet Republics'.[66] There was no question yet of an open breach between the two Communist countries.

The repercussions of this tension between the Soviet and Yugoslav CPs on the relations of both with the Greeks in general, and with the KKE in particular, are still obscure. Although Stalin remained indifferent to Greece, the Soviet press and radio attacked the 'monarcho-fascist' government no less virulently than did the Yugoslavs. But some restraint was put on Yugoslav claims to Macedonia. Private assurances of a qualified character were given to the British Government in January 1945 that the Yugoslavs had no designs on Greek Macedonia.[67] On 23 April *Rizospastis* published an official Yugoslav statement made in New York on 19 April, which was designed to allay any such fears. But other public statements, both official and unofficial, gave a different impression. On 21 June *Borba*, the Yugoslav CP newspaper, spoke of a 'separate Macedonian nationality'. During the Potsdam Conference the Yugoslav Government submitted a memorandum to the three major powers, and a protest to the Greek Government, alleging persecution of the 'Macedonians of the Aegean', whom it described as 'our co-nationals'.[68] The Yugoslavs also obtained support at a Pan-Slav Congress in Prague during October 1945 for a resolution stating that 'the Slavs of the Aegean coast still live under a foreign yoke: it was decided to raise the question of the liberation of the Macedonians of Aegean Macedonia'.[69]

More important than these challenging phrases was the attitude of Tito himself. His plans for federation with Bulgaria clearly had implications for Macedonia. Although his diplomatic communications with the western powers were relatively conciliatory, his statements for domestic consumption were less inhibited. On 8 July 1945 he spoke of the oppression of 'Slav minorities' in Greece, which was compelling 'democratic Greeks and Slavo-Macedonians' to take refuge in Yugoslavia.[70] On 11 October he made a speech which was widely interpreted as laying claim to 'Aegean Macedonia',[71] though on the 13th *Rizospastis* published a subtly different version of his words:

There are some who have the idea — and these ideas come from abroad — that Yugoslav, Greek and Bulgarian Macedonia ought to be united in one great Macedonia. There are adherents of this idea even in Bulgaria. The men who say this are the men who burned the

villages. Men from abroad whispered it in their ears. We know it,
and we know it is not the wish of the Bulgarian people. If there are
Macedonians who suffer in Aegean Macedonia, that causes us emotion.

It is impossible to be sure exactly what Tito said, no doubt carried away
by his own rhetoric. But it was embarrassing to the KKE, which was trying to re-establish a patriotic reputation. Tito did not much care whether
he embarrassed his Greek comrades or not.

Later records of this period leave no doubt that the Yugoslav Communists regarded the KKE with little respect. Tempo's criticisms of the party's
policy after December 1944 represent just about all the attention given to
the Greek Communists by any senior Yugoslav leader. In the nationalist
mood of Communist Yugoslavia, there was little room for internationalist
sympathy. Vladimir Dedijer's panegyric on Tito, published in English in
1953 as *Tito Speaks*, mentions no Greek Communist by name except
Tzimas and Zahhariadis. The Partisans would hardly have regarded the
KKE as a dependable ally in the task of detaching Macedonia from Greece.
Nor was the time ripe for such a collaboration. December 1945, the
month in which the Yugoslav, Bulgarian and Greek Communists were
reputed to have met at Petrich, was also the month in which the Greek
and Yugoslav Governments agreed to establish diplomatic relations, and
in which Admiral Rodionov arrived in Athens as Soviet Ambassador. It is
unlikely that at such a moment either the Yugoslavs or the Bulgarians
were encouraging the KKE to subversive action. The Bulgarians, with
Dimitrov again in power, would have known that Stalin wanted no such
action. They had no resources to offer in support of the KKE; and in the
circumstances of 1945, they knew that they must lose any competition
with the Yugoslavs for control of Aegean Macedonia if it were to be
detached from Greece. The Yugoslavs, though less subservient to Moscow,
had no more reason to incite the KKE to subversive action.

It seems probable, therefore, that if the meeting at Petrich actually
took place in December 1945, it was an occasion at which the KKE be-
wailed its predicament rather than one at which the Balkan Communists
plotted a rebellion in Greece. The same may be said of the visit of the
KKE deputation to Moscow, led by Partsalidis, which was coldly received
there in January 1946.[72] Soviet policy at the time was one of open diplomatic action in the Balkans rather than subversion and revolution. To say
that Soviet policy was open, however, is not to say that it was friendly.
Stalin could not afford to miss any opportunity for advantageous propaganda. Hence the Soviet appeal to the UN Security Council on 21 January,
calling for the withdrawal of British troops from Greece, which the KKE

obediently supported with a manifesto issued on the same day.[73] The application was a riposte to the complaint of the western powers at the continued presence of Soviet troops in Iran, where autonomous governments had been set up in Azerbaijan and Kurdistan. The Soviet complaint, which incidentally comprised the British presence in Indonesia as well as Greece, was to be regarded as a gambit in great-power politics rather than a declaration of changed intent towards Greece itself. But it led to the final resignation of Sophianopoulos as Foreign Minister, because he disapproved of his government's instructions to support the British case unreservedly at the UN. It naturally also caused great uneasiness among the Greeks.

But these developments in international relations, whether between the great powers or within south-east Europe, did not constitute the decisive impetus to the renewal of civil war in Greece. There are strong reasons to doubt whether there was any such external impetus in 1945 at all. The only effective source of support for a revolutionary policy on the part of the KKE would have been Yugoslavia, since the Albanians were virtually satellites of the Yugoslavs and the Bulgarians were completely subservient to Moscow. Yugoslav policy alternated between obedience to the dictates of Stalin, which were to leave Greece undisturbed, and a purely selfish nationalism aimed at annexing Greek Macedonia. Neither policy offered an acceptable role for the KKE, nor any encouragement to expect Yugoslav support for a revival of the Communist rebellion in Greece. The origins of the 'third round' must lie within Greece itself, not in foreign incitement. At the same time, it is doubtful whether even the internal conditions of the country led to a positive decision by the Communists so early as the end of 1945. The evidence suggests that, bad as things were, in terms of a deliberate decision the hour of the 'third round' had not yet struck.

Conditions in Greece, unlike the other occupied countries, actually became worse during 1945. They were already terrible enough. It was estimated that eight per cent of the population – well over half a million out of roughly seven million – had been killed in the war or died under the Occupation, as compared with a death-rate of 0·8 per cent in the case of the United Kingdom.[74] The Paris Conference on Reparations in 1946 assessed the physical destruction in Greece at the sum of 8,500 million dollars, or well over a thousand dollars per head of population. In 1947 the International Labour Office somewhat belatedly reported that Greece had suffered more severely during the war than any other allied country except the Soviet Union.[75] But this fact was not recognised in the early operations of UNRRA: in its first two years Greece ranked only fifth among the recipients of aid by value, after China, Poland, Yugoslavia and Italy. Perhaps the most serious aspect of the physical damage was the disruption of communications, which hindered both economic recovery and public security. Railways and rolling-stock were almost totally destroyed; main roads and bridges hardly less so; and coastal traffic was handicapped by the sabotage of harbours and losses of shipping. The most important island, Crete, was not only beyond regular communication but still under enemy occupation until the final German surrender in May 1945.

Athens was more than ever isolated from the provinces, and yet was regarded more than ever as the hydrocephalus of Greek life. Whereas the capital had suffered more than the provinces from shortages under the Occupation, it suffered relatively less in 1945 because supplies could be imported through Piraeus. Without an efficient system of distribution, a large proportion of UNRRA goods passed into the black market, to the benefit of the most anti-social elements in Greece. After the failure of Varvaressos's reforms and his resignation on 1 September 1945, the economic situation was judged to be even worse than four months earlier.[76] The KKE, operating through ERGAS, had no difficulty in organising strikes and demonstrations against rising prices, inadequate wages and economic policy in general. There were momentary signs of relief: the British financial mission briefly halted the spiral of inflation by importing sovereigns for the Bank of Greece to sell at fixed prices; and in September, for the first time, an American loan was forecast. But the loan proved abortive and the financial measures eventually unavailing. Since almost all Greece's means of earning foreign exchange had been cut off, the country was wholly dependent on foreign aid; but it lacked the physical and administrative means of putting the aid to good use. Of the two tasks defined in the title of UNRRA, Greece almost alone was left in the phase of Relief while the rest of Europe proceeded to Rehabilitation.

Misery and hardship naturally found an outlet in violence, especially as the provinces were burdened by several thousand unemployed ex-guerrillas whose only training was in the use of arms. The Communist press frequently predicted that more bloodshed would be the outcome. Less convincingly, it insisted that the Government was deliberately provoking it. Indirectly the British and UNRRA were also held to blame, on the assumption that they could easily have remedied the economic ills of the country if they chose. These accusations were groundless; but so were the counter-charges that the KKE was deliberately aggravating economic misery to provoke disorder. The genesis of violence in 1945 was of a more spontaneous and familiar kind. Brigandage, long endemic in the

Greek mountains, had been subsumed in the Resistance for four years: now it found its habitual outlets again, with no more than an incidental flavouring of politics. It owed little to economic causes, and less to Communism or monarcho-fascism, but a great deal to the tradition of anarchy and vendetta. Political organisers from X (*Khi*) on the one side, and the KKE on the other, stepped in at different stages in different areas to impose policy and control. But in most areas what they were seeking to exploit was already spontaneously there.

The first evidence of recurrent violence shows no evidence of a calculated plan on either side. Both the left-wing and the right-wing press regularly reported what were clearly sporadic and insignificant episodes from March 1945 onwards. Apart from the lone rebellion of Aris Veloukhiotis, which ended with his death on 16 June 1945, authentic cases of bloodshed showing any degree of organisation were rare until the late summer. In April a right-wing band led by Sourlas was reported to be active near Stylis, and later again near Verria; a similar band under a muledriver called Kalambalikis was active near Volos; and in May left-wing bands were said to be re-forming in Macedonia.[77] By 17 May *Rizospastis* was able to report incidents caused by Sourlas and others in Roumeli, Thessaly, Epirus, Macedonia, Thrace and the Peloponnese; but these were obviously exaggerated. The earliest incident of a political character reported by a newspaper that was neither pro-Communist nor promonarchist (*Elevtheria*, on 26 May) was the kidnapping by 'nationalists' of a doctor from Lamia who had been a member of EAM. Nothing equivalent to the 'reign of terror' regularly reported by *Rizospastis* ever appeared in *Elevtheria*. But the beginnings of a serious deterioration were apparent in July, when the Government introduced a new law against brigandage and issued a statement on the 'disorderly situation'. The London *Times* first reported terrorism by right-wing bands on 24 August.

Careful reading of the press leaves no doubt that up to the end of 1945 at least, so far as political labels could be attached to the perpetrators, the blame for bloodshed lay primarily on right-wing forces, particularly Grivas's *Khi*, and on anti-Communists exacting vengeance for earlier atrocities. The first episode indubitably caused by a left-wing band was the ambush of a British truck between Florina and Edessa on 16 July, in which one man was killed: the local Communists admitted responsibility and pleaded a mistake.[78] On 4 October Zakhariadis predicted to the Seventh Party Congress that 'if this mess continues, every Greek will have to take to the hills'; and more and more were doing so. On 30 October *Elevtheria* reported a clash in Phthiotis between two soldiers, accompanied by a civilian, and a band of six armed men, one of whom was killed; but the paper balanced the news on the following day with a report of a Communist killed in Piraeus. So the story went on, getting neither better nor worse, up to the end of the year. It is unnecessary to take seriously the figures published by *Rizospastis* on 14 November of the victims of 'monarcho-fascist terror' throughout Greece: 780 killed, 5,677 wounded, 28,450 tortured, 70,528 arrested; the highest figures being in the Peloponnese. In December, on the other hand, the Minister of Justice published figures showing nearly 18,000 people held in prison (not all were of the left) and charges pending against nearly 50,000 members of EAM and ELAS.[79] At the turn of the year the pattern was unmistakable, but it was essentially one of unofficial persecution. Grivas's *Khítes* were viciously active, especially in the Peloponnese; Communist meetings were regularly broken up, especially in Athens and Macedonia. On 20 January 1946 a revolt of monarchist bands, which seized Kalamata, led to a temporary proclamation of military law in Messinia.

The KKE had a legitimate grievance, given that they were still a legal party, however justifiably unpopular. The agents of the Government were unable to protect them from vengeance, and did not exert themselves to do so. The Communists responded at first with strikes and demonstrations rather than with organised violence. Although their public statements were couched in inflammatory language, they could be interpreted metaphorically just as well as literally. It was always implied that anything the KKE did would merely be by way of reacting to its antagonists. On 18 October *Rizospastis* declared that 'any coup by monarcho-fascism will be the signal for a general popular struggle by all methods in towns, villages and mountains'. This could be construed as a forecast of what was to follow from 1946 to 1949, but it might equally have been mere rhetoric. Other recurrent phrases pointed to the north as the seat of danger. Zakhariadis declared that Greece was being used as a base for preparing attacks on Albania, Bulgaria and Yugoslavia; and on 13 January *Rizospastis* reported on the persecution of the Slavo-Macedonians. But Leeper formed the impression at the turn of the year that there were no signs of trouble on the northern frontier.[80] Although the Ministry of Public Order admitted on 28 December that there were disorders in many areas, including Thrace, Mesolonghi, Trikkala and Corinth, only the first of these adjoined the frontier.[81]

The likeliest diagnosis is that the KKE was still suffering from divided counsels. It had barely finished its orgy of self-criticism over the events of 1944. The final verdict of the Politburo, reached on 8 November but not published in *Rizospastis* until 25 November, was to approve 'the heroic armed resistance of the entire people in December', while criticising the party's errors at the Lebanon and Caserta conferences, the underestimate of British policy and other forces, the lack of political flexibility, the taking of hostages, 'and so on'. It was vaguely added that the KKE must be ready 'to lead the people in new struggles', which could have meant much or little. The general impression is one of indecision and playing for time. Typical was the reaction to the announcement by the Government on 20 January that the first post-war elections would be held on 31 March, under the supervision of allied observers from the USA, Britain and France. The immediate response of the KKE was to urge its supporters to register to vote. A few weeks later the decision was reversed; and between the elections and the plebiscite it was reversed again. Zakhariadis was anxious to keep his options open, even at the cost of appearing schizophrenic.

PART THREE

The Third Round

7

Disorder into Guerrilla War
February 1946–March 1947

IT IS as difficult to say exactly when the 'third round' began as to say
when Resistance began under the Occupation. A common tradition has it
that the decision to start the civil war was formally taken at the Second
Plenum of the KKE Central Committee on 12 February 1946, and the
first blow was struck at Litokhoro on the eastern slopes of Mount Olympus on the night before the General Election, 30–31 March. The full decisions of the Second Plenum became known only in retrospect. At the
time little was published except Zakhariadis's opening speech, in *Rizospastis* on 17 February, and the decision to abstain from the elections,
announced on 22 February. In his reported speech Zakhariadis spoke of
'popular self-defence' (*Aftoámyna*), of a general strike and armed resistance,
of heroism and determination and self-sacrifice; and he demanded that the
British should go. None of this was new. Allowing for Communist rhetoric, and for the fact that he was speaking on the first anniversary of the
Varkiza Agreement (12 February), it could hardly be taken as a declaration
of war. But apparently a more far-reaching event took place on the same
day, which was revealed only at the Sixth Plenum in October 1949. In his
speech on the latter occasion, later published as a pamphlet under the title
New Situation, New Tasks, from which extracts were broadcast by the Free
Greece Radio on 6 December 1949, Zakhariadis stated that the decision
'to proceed to the organisation of the new armed struggle' had been taken,
with Tito's support, on 12 February 1946.[1]

Similar stories were repeated later by different speakers, with or without the claim to Tito's support. At the Seventh Plenum of the Central
Committee in May 1950, Zakhariadis again said that the Second Plenum
'in effect decided that the new armed struggle should begin'.[2] At the
Third Conference of the KKE in October 1950, Dimitrios Vlandas described the attack on Litokhoro as 'the beginning of the revolution'.[3]
Most specifically of all, Markos Vaphiadis stated some years afterwards
that Zakhariadis himself gave orders for an attack to be launched in
Macedonia on the day before the elections; that Markos and Kikitsas (a
former *kapetánios* of ELAS) chose Litokhoro as the target; and that the

operation was commanded by Ypsilantis.[4] If this story were wholly true, it would be decisive. But Greeks have a habit of remembering what historically ought to have happened rather than what did.

No contemporary account – not even the Communist press – names Ypsilantis as responsible for the attack on Litokhoro; nor was it treated at the time as an exceptional event in the growing wave of violence. Foreign observers writing during and even after the civil war ignored Litokhoro. It passed unmentioned in the works of McNeill (1947), Voigt (1949), Leeper (1950), Chandler (1959) and O'Ballance (1966). The best American source mentioned Litokhoro, but by implication did not regard it as a deliberate initiation of the civil war.[5] If it had been so intended, a supporting campaign of propaganda would have been launched by the Communist press; but there was none. The earliest reference to the incident at Litokhoro as a prelude to war appeared only nineteen months later, in the Communist newspaper *Exormisi* on 28 October 1947.[6] It was repeated in another Communist article in 1948.[7] But according to Markos's later account, Zakhariadis told him a few weeks after the incident that it had been intended only as a bluff to frighten the Government into making concessions.[8] He spoke of his intention to cause a 'thunder-clap', apparently meaning an isolated incident.[9] If it was to be the beginning of a storm, why did no storm follow? When it happened, the KKE seemed to be as much taken by surprise as anybody else.

It is undisputed that at the Seventh Plenum in May 1950 Zakhariadis said that the Second Plenum 'in effect decided that the new armed struggle should begin'. But he also used other words which suggest a substantial qualification.[10] Some of those present at the Second Plenum, he said, wanted to continue the 'submissive line' which had been adopted since Varkiza. Others wanted an 'immediate transition to armed struggle'. But the majority rejected both extremes. It was therefore decided to continue to press for reconciliation, but

> to hasten and complete the technical-organisational military preparation for the progressive reinforcement of the armed struggle of the people. During the session of the Plenum a special conference of the military cadres of the KKE also met and dealt with this question.

In fact, counsels were divided and the decision was a compromise. The KKE was not to initiate aggression but was to be ready, if reconciliation failed, to meet force with force. The assumption was that the decisive aggression would come from the other side. Since mutual assaults were a matter of daily occurrence, either side could have acted on that assumption at any time.

This interpretation of the events of the Second Plenum is confirmed by the later reminiscences of Dimitrios Vlandas, who was present.[11] He wrote that nothing was decided beyond the political resolutions mentioned by Zakhariadis. The so-called 'military conference' which took place during the session lasted barely an hour. All that happened at it was that Zakhariadis asked how many arms and men were available in the provinces. It was simply recognised that 'the Reaction will not permit any possibility of democratic development through political forms of struggle, and that an armed confrontation will become inevitable'. Vlandas expressly adds: 'However, the Plenum did not take a decision on armed confrontation.' He makes the surprising assertion that 'the Central Committee of the KKE concerned itself with the armed struggle for the first time seventeen months after the Second Plenum' — that is to say, at the Third Plenum in September 1947, 'when the outcome of the armed struggle had in effect already been decided against us'. This contention forms part of Vlandas's consistent distinction between the Central Committee and 'the then leadership', which he identifies with the Politburo.

In his view, the leadership was to blame, by its silence about the purely political decisions taken by the Plenum, for giving the impression 'that an armed rising had been decided upon, when in fact no such decision had been taken'. Nothing, therefore, changed as a result of the Second Plenum.

Equally, there was little change on the side of the Government. Sophoulis's policy towards the Left was conciliatory, since he still hoped for universal participation in the elections. He was criticised by the right-wing press for the policy of 'de-congestion' of the prisons, which had released many men with criminal records and old scores to be settled against them. Another complaint, emphasised in *Kathimerini* on 15 February, was that his decision to close the police-posts at the entrances to towns, which had been taken under Communist pressure, simply allowed armed bandits to circulate freely. On the other hand, the Communists took as a sign of intended repression the creation of a Supreme Military Council in March 1946. The Council was to comprise the Prime Minister in the chair, together with the Minister of War, the Chiefs of Staff and the heads of the British missions. So far from being an instrument of repression, it proved an ineffective body, which eventually had to be abolished before the rebellion could be defeated. In any case it was not until several months after its creation that a Greek army could again be said to exist in effective form. Meanwhile the control of disorder was regarded as a police function, but the Gendarmerie was unequal to it.

Violence continued in all parts of Greece, provoked both from the Left and from the Right. Comparison of right-wing newspapers like *Kathimerini* with left-wing newspapers like *Rizospastis* shows an almost equal incidence of violence during the first three months of 1946, with a diametrically opposite attribution of the blame. Geographically, the incidence was probably still graver in the south, where the Communists were less strong and therefore the lesser offenders. In the Peloponnese the bands of X (*Khi*) organised by Grivas were chiefly to blame; in Macedonia responsibility was more confused. The National Guard alienated almost all but the most devoted Royalists by its conduct, but justified it by pointing to the provocation inherent in the very existence of offices of the KKE in towns like Naoussa. A British observer in Macedonia reported that political opinion was primarily royalist in Kozani, left-wing in Naoussa and right-wing in Verria; but the violence was motivated by revenge as much as by politics.[12] Again and again bitterness was exacerbated by the discovery of recent graves containing the victims of atrocities, whether of the Left or the Right.

Yet there was still thought to be some hope of reconciliation; and even the faintest hope had to be nourished so far as was possible. Many Greeks of all parties believed that a postponement of the elections could help to promote reconciliation, often though they had been postponed already. Even the Communists were said to be contemplating a reversal of their decision to abstain, on the advice of foreign Communists and emissaries from abroad.[13] This advice had been conveyed by the CPSU through Partsalidis and by Dimitrov through Petros Roussos; and Zakhariadis, on a visit to Prague in March, had similar advice from Thorez and Togliatti. An influential minority within the KKE (including Siantos, Zevgos, Tzimas, Partsalidis, Karagiorgis and Khrysa Khatzivasiliou) was thought to be in favour of taking part; and Zakhariadis himself later judged that abstention had been a mistake.[14]

In the hope that the Communists would have second thoughts, Sophoulis pressed the British authorities for another delay. Even *Khi* asked for a week's postponement. But the British Government had grown weary of Greek manoeuvres: besides, it was recalled that at Varkiza the agreement had been to hold the plebiscite before the end of 1945 and the elections as soon as possible thereafter. The time-table had slipped already to a point that was becoming ridiculous; and the Allied Mission for Observing the Greek Elections (AMFOGE) was on the point of readiness. No postponement could therefore be allowed. Accordingly the left-wing leaders of ELD and Sophianopoulos announced their intention to abstain along with the KKE. The Populists under Tsaldaris duly won.

Whether or not guided by deliberate policy, events then moved inexorably towards disaster. On the night before polling day, 30–31 March, an armed band descended from Mount Olympus on Litokhoro. First reports put its strength at more than a hundred, but the figure was reduced on the following day to sixty. Two left-wing *kapetánioi* (Xinos and Smolikas) were named in the national press as the leaders, but next day two different names (Photeinos and Tzavellas) were given. Common to all reports were the damage and casualties: many buildings were burned to the ground, including the police-station; eight people were killed, including six soldiers and gendarmes, a civilian and a woman; at least seven soldiers and gendarmes were missing. Those missing were at first thought to be buried among the ruins, but several of them turned up on the following day, having been captured and then released. In the circumstances polling had to be postponed until a week later than in the rest of the country. Other details in various accounts included the identification of seven of the bandits as natives of Litokhoro. What made the affair exceptional was the large size of the attacking force and the report that they were armed with mortars as well as hand-grenades. The presence of two *kapetánioi* (even if the names were confused) suggested a joint operation by two bands, averaging thirty men each. All these alarming facts seemed in retrospect to justify the belief that the civil war began that night.

Yet it was not so seen at the time. There had already been almost equally serious incidents in the preceding month, on which tradition might just as well have fastened retrospectively. Against the background of what preceded and followed it, Litokhoro seems to be part of an irregular cascade rather than a final watershed. As early as the first week of March, Sophoulis had publicly confirmed rumours of 'Bulgarian terrorists' co-operating with left-wing bands in western Macedonia.[15] A week before Litokhoro five men were killed and eight wounded in an attack by a left-wing band on a village near Volos.[16] Nationalist newspapers, both left of centre like *Elevtheria* and on the right like *Kathimerini*, generally printed such stories inconspicuously on the back pages; and the latter expressed the opinion on 17 February that both the Government and the left-wing were exaggerating them to justify a postponement of the elections. Their attitude did not change until long after 31 March. Even those historians who later accepted the tradition that the civil war began at Litokhoro were unable to identify any further incident worth calling a battle until July.[17] Most contemporary accounts agree in depicting the descent into civil war as a gradual deterioration, which took its gravest turn much later in the year. The Communist press was no exception.

Considering that *Rizospastis* was edited by Karagiorgis and directly controlled by Zakhariadis, its reactions were confused. No report of the episode appeared on the immediately following day, 31 March, which was election day.[18] The first report, which was based not on the KKE's own information but on a government statement, appeared on 1 April under the headline: 'Authorities and Bandits Stage So-called Attacks by Communists.' The terms of the report are revealing:

> The Government, which through the mouth of the Prime Minister has continually denounced the Fascist character of the state mechanism and the alliance of the security forces with the terrorist bands of the Right, has not hesitated in its final moments to become the apologist of murderers of the democratic population. The Ministry of Public Order, before beginning the announcement of the results of yesterday's coup d'état, which was characterised by brutal force and fraud on the part of the monarchists, took care to provide the press with various lies and provocations to create an impression exactly the opposite of the reality. Thus it was announced yesterday that on 30 March a Communist band attacked the police-station at Litokhorion (Katerini), causing the death of ten gendarmes and soldiers, together with other provocative lies about alleged attacks against the Right. As we have frequently reported, it is precisely in the area of Katerini that the monarchist band of Galis is operating, and precisely in the last few days that it has run amok against the democratic population of the whole area.

The impression that *Rizospastis* had little idea what in fact had happened is reinforced by the use of the unusual form Litokhorion (with its different accentuation and pronunciation) for Litokhoro: the correction was made only on 9 April. Further evidence of confusion appeared in *Rizospastis*'s issue of 3 April, when the interpretation of the incident had changed. The cause of the trouble was no longer a right-wing band but the appointment of 'hardened criminals to the command of the Gendarmerie', and in particular of 'a human monster as Adjutant'. It was added that according to the local military commander, when the attacking band left Litokhorion, 'the majority of the inhabitants followed it'. In other words, the attackers were no longer monarcho-fascists but oppressed democrats.

The rank and file of the KKE were confused as well as taken by surprise. Only later were the leaders of the attack on Litokhoro definitely identified as their comrades, Photeinos and Tzavellas. At the time they might well have been taken for any of the uncommitted outlaws at large in Macedonia. The same state of indiscriminate lawlessness persisted until July. Frequent and bloody clashes between rival bands were reported in the press, for which the Government blamed the Communists and the KKE blamed 'monarcho-fascist terrorism'. But no co-ordination could yet be detected on the Communist side. The reports came from all over the country – from the Peloponnese as much as from Macedonia – and the incidents showed no pattern or purpose.

There were also signs of indecision within the KKE. Several prominent figures, including Kapetan Orestis (Moundrikhas), were expelled from the party in April. Markos Vaphiadis was said to be urging armed action, Zakhariadis to be hesitating and telling Markos that he did not understand the Central Committee's intentions. Zakhariadis had visited Prague in March, and was reported in *Rizospastis* on 3 April to be in Belgrade on his way back; so he was out of Greece when Litokhoro was attacked. Although Greek Communist accounts say that he personally gave the order, Yugoslav sources present him as trying to avoid an armed struggle but being forced into action by Markos and others from the rank and file.[19] Other visits were exchanged between East European leaders soon afterwards: Hoxha to Belgrade, Tito and Dimitrov to Moscow. It seems hardly likely that these resulted in giving the KKE any licence to fight with general Balkan backing. *Rizospastis*'s slogans during the summer were still 'self-defence' and 'reconciliation'.

Such slogans might be common form for a Communist Party even if it were planning revolution; and there is no doubt that planning continued on the basis of the decisions taken at the Second Plenum. But a decision to plan for war is not a decision to make war. No reliable source dates the formation of local headquarters in the field earlier than June 1946, nor the departure of Markos Vaphiadis for the mountains earlier than August. There was in fact grave doubt within the KKE whether a revolutionary situation yet existed. The elections on 31 March were not encouraging to the KKE, and the plebiscite on the monarchy, fixed for 1 September, was likely to be still less so. Although the Communists claimed that all those who abstained from the vote on 31 March must have been their supporters, the report of AMFOGE estimated politically inspired abstentions at less than ten per cent. This was the first general election in Europe which had ever been subjected to international scrutiny and to the statistical technique of 'sampling'; but the outcome was far from unquestionable.[20] What was most significant, however, was that even on the figures quoted by *Rizospastis* on 10 April 1946, abstentions were notably lower in the northern districts, where the KKE counted on most support, than elsewhere in the country. The map of abstentions published by *Rizospastis* showed that of the northern constituencies, only Florina and Ioannina appeared among the ten highest in the list of abstentions; and the Macedonian constituencies of Kavalla, Serrai, Drama, Rhodopi and Khalkidiki were (with Athens) at the bottom of the list.

These could not have been encouraging results for a party bent on revolution and relying on support from the north. Undoubtedly they caused heart-searching within the KKE. Some argued that abstention had been a mistake, presumably on the premise that even if the KKE would not have won many votes, it could have claimed that its supporters were prevented from voting by force or fraud. Karagiorgis even believed that it might have won a majority.[21] Zakhariadis reflected the confusion by first demanding the annulment of the elections of 31 March, then instructing his followers to register for the plebiscite on 1 September, and finally denouncing the Plebiscite Bill as fraudulent when it was published in June. The columns of *Rizospastis* during the summer often suggested uncertainty of purpose in the KKE. There were constant comparisons of the state of Greece to Germany under Hitler, and accusations of collaboration with the Germans were freely made against nationalists like Zervas and Tsaous Andon. Monarcho-fascism, it was said, was driving Greece to civil war (a phrase first used in *Rizospastis* on 13 July). But still the KKE exercised restraint, as if doubtful of public opinion. Years later Markos Vaphiadis claimed, in a letter to the Central Committee in 1957, that he had told Zakhariadis in May 1946 that he could put twenty-five thousand men into the field; but Zakhariadis still hesitated.[22] Vlandas's reminiscences confirm that Zakhariadis had not yet committed himself to civil war: he regarded armed action merely as 'an ancillary method of forceful pressure on the enemy, to make possible a peaceful evolution'.[23]

The KKE had good reason to be doubtful about public opinion, and Zakhariadis had much less reason for confidence in the possibilities of subversion in the towns. Although he was later to claim success in capturing the mass organisations as a basis for the seizure of power, there was little sign of it in the summer of 1946. The traditional Communist demonstration on May Day was notably ill-attended in Athens, though in part the weather was to blame. It formed a striking contrast with the enthusiastic reception given by the Greek public to the US battleship *Missouri* on a goodwill visit to Piraeus during April, which even *Rizospastis* felt obliged to welcome. A few weeks later a one-day General Strike was called by the KKE in protest against the passage through Parliament of a Security Bill on 18 June. *Rizospastis* claimed that the strike had been successful, but even its own figures were not impressive: less than fifty per cent of the workers in Piraeus and barely forty per cent in Athens came out.

This was hardly a revolutionary reaction to a law which was on paper very severe. It set up summary courts with powers to pass capital sentences for several new offences, including membership of armed bands advocating 'autonomy' or subversion; and it gave to the Government powers to ban public meetings and strikes, and to the police powers of search without warrant and detention without trial. Almost as remarkable, however, as the muted reaction from the Left was the restraint with which the Government used its powers. The new courts were initially set up only in Macedonia; the Communist press was not banned until October 1947, nor the KKE outlawed until the end of that year; the power to ban strikes was not used until December 1947; and martial law did not become general until late in 1948. Both sides seemed in fact determined to maintain the forms of legality until the eleventh hour.

Even the crucial struggle for the control of organised labour was conducted in constitutional form on both sides, at least on the surface. It was crucial because the trade unions were by far the most important of the mass organisations on which, according to Communist theory, the success of the revolution depended. If power could be won in the industrial towns – which meant, in effect, Athens, Piraeus and Salonika – then no armed struggle in the mountains and provinces would be necessary at all. Zakhariadis, as usual, wavered, while others were more consistent; but they were consistent in holding opposite views. Siantos resisted any idea of transferring the leadership from Athens to the mountains again; Vlandas, speaking in Piraeus, denounced those who took to the mountains as cowards for avoiding 'the real revolutionary struggle of the towns and the factories'; Bartzotas deliberately delayed the despatch of men and funds out of Salonika.[24] 'The daily struggle of the proletariat', in Zakhariadis's phrase, still took precedence over guerrilla warfare. Here lay the original conflict between Zakhariadis and Markos Vaphiadis, for the latter shared the view later formulated by Tempo, that the struggle should have been transferred to the mountains much earlier. In Tempo's judgment, the KKE committed two cardinal errors: first, in giving priority to the towns over the mountains; and secondly, in fighting the battle for the mass organisations on constitutional lines.[25]

The story of the constitutional struggle for the control of the trade unions is an intricate one, which need only be summarised.[26] After the intervention of British and French trade unionists during 1945, elections to a National Congress of the General Confederation of Greek Workers (GSEE) were at last held in February 1946, and were won by candidates of the Communist-controlled ERGAS. But the Reformist unions, led by Photis Makris (a former member of EEAM, now a supporter of the Populist Party) disputed the validity of the elections. The Council of State invalidated the ministerial orders under which the elections were held, but without pronouncing on the elections themselves. The Minister of Labour thereupon installed a new Executive and Secretary-General of his own choice, which the Council of State invalidated in its turn on the grounds that only the courts had power to take such action. Finally the courts appointed an Executive, which the left-wing unions refused to recognise. It was not until 1947 that a compromise was reached and confirmed, even then without the participation of ERGAS. The Government was accused (by Ministers of the British Labour Government, among others) of political interference, but it was able to point out that the intervention had been only by the courts. To the Communist-controlled unions, however, the distinction between the Government and the courts was a fiction. They felt themselves driven back into underground activity.

Underground was indeed where most Communists felt most at home. The so-called *Aftoámyna* (self-defence) provided them with the means. The *Aftoámyna* was ostensibly created for protection against 'monarcho-fascist terrorism', meaning the acts of revenge which the Government was powerless to prevent. Clashes involving prominent Communists became common in the summer. Tzimas was set upon, with Partsalidis, in more than one Macedonian town during May, and was forcibly expelled with other colleagues from Salonika in July. The Communist press made the most of 'atrocities' of widely varying seriousness with such indiscriminate fervour as to lose much of its effect. The most serious case was the murder of Costa Vidalis, a well-known Communist journalist, in August; but *Rizospastis* would use equally impassioned language over an attack on a restaurant in Ioannina by Zervas's men, or a break-in at the house of a leading Communist (Porphyrogennis) in Athens. These and countless other incidents of violence were matched by just as many committed by left-wing bands. The *Aftoámyna* killed three gendarmes near Larisa in April. In June it was announced by the Government that seventeen gendarmes and three soldiers had been killed in less than three months. The press on both sides was full of exaggerations, and yet what the press imagined was in many respects less serious than the reality.

The reality was that banditry was turning into guerrilla war. The *Aftoámyna* itself began to go underground, becoming part of the KKE's illegal apparatus in the towns. In the traditional manner of Communist Parties, it was organised in securely segregated cells which met in the strictest secrecy, their *rendezvous* being known by the Russian term *yavka*. In the countryside a new pattern began to emerge. There were three elements in what appeared to be a deliberate plan: to force the Gendarmerie out of its smaller posts, compelling it to concentrate in the towns; to cut the lines of communication between certain towns; and to eliminate a number of frontier-posts in the north. The effect would have been to isolate Macedonia from the rest of Greece and to open up contact with the neighbouring Communist powers. These tactics led to the first direct clashes between Communist bands and the Greek army.* The National Army, consisting of three Infantry and four Mountain Divisions, became operational only in May, when it took over from the National Guard.[27] It was first in action in the first week of July, at Pontokerasia in the north-east. The object of the Democratic Army, once established as such, seems to have been to establish a stronghold of 'free territory' round Grevena in southern Macedonia, a traditional centre of Greek guerrillas. It was esti-mated that by the late summer the rebels had about sixteen hundred men under arms, normally organised in bands from five to twenty strong, but often grouped in larger units.

The significance of Grevena can be seen from the map. It occupied a strategic point on the most convenient of the few motor-roads which connected Athens with the critical area of West Macedonia. From the point where the roads from the capital divided in the plain of Thessaly, the alternative routes available to motorised traffic were either by the longer way of Larisa, Elasson, Servia, Kozani and Siatista; or by the shorter way of Karditsa, Trikkala, Kalambaka and Grevena.† The two routes joined up again at Grevena, which thus had the advantage of road communications in two directions, north and south. Other roads leading into the moun-tains of West Macedonia, besides involving longer journeys from Athens, also had the disadvantage of terminating in towns from which there was no alternative way out for motorised traffic, such as Pendalophos and Konitsa. So although it was necessary that the National Army should retain posses-sion of such towns, it was even more essential to hold Grevena. In at-tempting to isolate the town, the Democratic Army was showing a grasp of strategy which marked a new phase.

Newspaper reports, however, were slow to suggest any change of character or tempo in the course of violence. Apart from the Communist press, they usually confined such incidents to small type on the back pages. The cumulative impression given by such reports did not show much difference between 1946 and 1945. There were occasional exceptions:

* The terms 'National Army' and 'Democratic Army' will henceforth be used for the opposing forces, since that is what each called itself.

† The route on the west of the Pindus range by way of Ioannina did not yet extend from Epirus into Macedonia.

for example, *Kathimerini* published a leading article on 25 April headed 'The Rule of Law', which denounced armed assaults by the Communists in several specified places; but the incidents themselves were of a familiar and minor kind. A graver note soon began to be sounded: on 8 May, *Rizospastis* published a letter from a Communist 'somewhere in the mountains', in which he wrote, among other melodramatic phrases, 'we have found weapons and formed our band'. The letter-heading was almost suggestive of a military communiqué, and was attacked as such in the nationalist press. The phrase did not reappear until October, but in the meantime the terminology of war became more frequent. 'The Government insists on Civil War,' declared *Rizospastis* on 13 July; and on 11 August Karagiorgis published an editorial headed: 'The Greek–Greek War.' Meanwhile *Rizospastis* ominously began a series of articles on Central Macedonia in July, and another series followed in October with a date-line 'somewhere in Thessaly'.

The threat from the Communists was now much more serious in Macedonia than elsewhere. Law and order were threatened everywhere, but the lawless elements were primarily right-wing in the south and left-wing in the north. Figures collected by a British observer showed that in a single week of July in Macedonia, ten murders could be attributed to bands of the Left, six to the Right and five were uncertain; in another week the record for the whole country was twenty-three by the Right, sixteen by the Left and two uncertain.[28] The balance of guilt in Macedonia and in the rest of Greece showed an unmistakable disparity. Similarly, when the first executions took place under the Security Act in the same month, nine out of the first twelve men executed were from Macedonia. It was also in Macedonia that the first serious threat of mutiny in the National Army took place. Three brigades of II Corps in the neighbourhood of Kozani were affected in July: three hundred men were arrested for complicity and fifteen hundred more disarmed as unreliable.[29] Insufficient care had been taken to screen Communists or ex-members of ELAS in the call-up; and the conspiracy was detected only just in time.

Clearly there was widespread and genuine discontent. It has been conventionally supposed that the civil war was inspired from Moscow, down channels through the Communist Parties of the Balkans to the KKE and the Slavo-Macedonian minority, and thence to a relatively passive Greek population, which was drawn into rebellion by deception and force. Some warrant for this version of events could be found in the outward conduct of the Soviet Government. Much significance has been attached to Stalin's bellicose speech in the Soviet elections on 9 February, which a former member of the KKE called 'the declaration of the Cold War', and a more sober Greek historian called 'an answer to the Great Enigma straight from the mouth of the Sphinx'.[30] But these were no more than rhetorical metaphors, no more reasonable than the similar terms applied by Communists everywhere to Churchill's speech at Fulton, Missouri, a month later (on 5 March), when he visualised the descent of an 'Iron Curtain' from Stettin to Trieste. It is equally possible that the Soviet Government was merely reacting to what it saw as the hostility of the western powers, and to situations in the Balkans which it had not directly provoked and was unable to control. Stalin was not the absolute master-mind of events.

Certainly there were some troublesome influences which were working downwards from south-east Europe. Stalin wanted an outlet to the Mediterranean; Tito and Dimitrov both wanted Greek Macedonia; many of the Slavophones wanted autonomy; and the KKE wanted power. But there were also influences who were working upwards. The conventional scheme would ignore the rivalries between Tito and Stalin, Dimitrov and Tito, Greeks and Albanians, Slavo-Macedonians and Greeks, and many other cross-currents. It would also overlook the sheer impossibility of controlling events from outside the Balkan countries. A striking example was the first attack on British destroyers in the Corfu Strait, which were fired on from the Albanian coast in May 1946. It is most unlikely that such an incident was desired by the Soviet Government, yet later evidence showed that both this incident and the mine-laying in the Strait, which severely damaged two British destroyers in October, were contrived by the Albanians with the help of Yugoslav and Greek Communists.[31] Such people were simply beyond Stalin's control. So were the bands of outlaws which were already active in Greece long before any kind of higher command was imposed on them. Even unsympathetic witnesses admitted that they had real grievances and that 'there was, at least initially, a great deal of sympathy' for them.[32] Neither Greek nor Yugoslav Communists went into action at Stalin's behest. Indeed, they had difficulty in guessing what his behest was.

The function of the KKE was thus rather that of a catalyst in an atmosphere of indecision. Tito was not the instigator any more than Stalin: he had to be persuaded to translate aggressive speeches into action. Up to mid-1946 he had only provided a site at Bulkes for a camp where the scattered refugees of ELAS could be assembled (though not trained), and made available Yugoslav officers to advise on tactics. But he knew, from his visit to Moscow in June 1946, that Stalin was in a cautious mood over Balkan problems. Stalin treated Tito with flattering cordiality on that occasion, but gave him no encouragement towards expansion: he thought the Albanian Communists unreliable, and appeared to be trying to force a rift between the Yugoslav and Bulgarian CPs.[33] This was also the occasion when the formation of the Communist Information Bureau (Cominform) was first mooted by Stalin; but its first targets were to be France and Italy, not Greece; and one of its undisclosed purposes was to limit Tito's freedom of action. Where the Western Allies were determined to stand firm — for instance, over Trieste or the Turkish Straits — Stalin drew back from challenging them; and he no doubt assumed that Greece was such a case. Djilas's account is categorical: 'The Soviet Government took no direct action over the uprising in Greece, practically leaving Yugoslavia to face the music alone in the United Nations.'[34] Apart from verbal support by Moscow radio and the Soviet press, the Greek rebels were left to prove themselves. If Tito and Dimitrov did rather more, it was for reasons of their own, in spite of Stalin's wishes and not because of them.

A plausible account of Stalin's attitude can be read, making allowance for national bias, in Tempo's analysis of the civil war.[35] In 1950 he wrote that:

The leadership of the Soviet Union had no interest whatever in the victory of the people's revolutionary movement in Greece, because Greece was geographically remote from the Soviet Union (hence intervention of the Soviet Army was out of the question), and because it was outside the sphere of interest of the Soviet Union (by agreement between the Governments of the Soviet Union and the western imperialists).

In support he referred to the agreement of October 1944 between Stalin and Churchill on 'percentages of interest' in the different Balkan countries. As a result, not only had the British been given a free hand but for several years after the war Soviet propaganda ignored Greece altogether, even in the inaugural resolution of the Cominform. Faint-hearts within the KKE, such as Zakhariadis, had taken their cue to adopt a quasi-legal policy instead of a revolutionary one. They continued, according to Tempo, to see Greece in terms of social-democratic conceptions, as a bridge between East and West under an all-party coalition. Even as late as May 1947, Zakhariadis wrote to the Yugoslav CP about the KKE's aims as comprising free elections, a general amnesty, equal friendship with all the great powers and a guarantee of neutrality for Greece under the protection of the United Nations.[36] To the Yugoslavs this was outright defeatism; but there is no evidence that they themselves were giving the KKE more than moral support and advice in the early days.

They were also inhibited by the hesitancy of Zakhariadis. Some years

afterwards Markos gave to a French journalist an account of the instructions he received from Zakhariadis in July 1946; and although his account
was tendentious, much of it was plausible. Zakhariadis insisted, first, that
recruitment must be exclusively voluntary; secondly, that no defection by
complete units of the National Army should be accepted; thirdly, that the
rebels must attack only 'monarcho-fascist bands', not the regular forces;
fourthly, that the Democratic Army must remain on the defensive; fifthly,
that reconciliation must remain the party line.[37] The object was only to
bring pressure to bear on the Government, not to promote a Communist
revolution from the mountains. Vlandas confirms that the leadership forbade mass desertions, although a clear majority in most infantry units had
left-wing sympathies.[38] He also says that the services of regular officers,
even those who had been in ELAS, were not wanted, and they were
allowed to be exiled – a blunder for which Vlandas blames Theodore
Makridis, the only regular officer on the Central Committee of the KKE,
whereas Zakhariadis blamed Siantos for treachery.[39] All these confused
instructions show how ill at ease Zakhariadis was in the role of an organiser
of guerrilla warfare. Markos was little inclined to pay attention to his
instructions, and soon went beyond them. But he had not yet the resources to undertake major operations. Zakhariadis and his colleagues saw
to it that he was kept under restraint by limiting his supplies of manpower
and money. From the point of view of the KKE, the mountains were still a
side-show.

The early operations of the Greek rebels were therefore necessarily on
a small and tentative scale. Such planning as they evinced was rudimentary,
and of a political rather than a military character. Few professional soldiers
other than foreign advisers were associated with the rebellion, even when
the Democratic Army was established in the autumn of 1946. Vlandas says
that there was no military member of its original GHQ at all.[40] Makridis
is said to have been responsible for the initial plans;[41] but he achieved no
notable reputation, nor did any more senior officer of the regular army
openly join the rebellion. In September eighty-six senior ex-officers of
ELAS were arrested and deported to islands by the Government, among
them Saraphis, Bakirdzis and Kalambalikis. It is doubtful whether any of
the last three would in any case have fought in the civil war, though
Bakirdzis (who committed suicide in 1947) may possibly have been under
strong pressure to do so. The most senior deserter known to have been
trying to join the Democratic Army was Lt-Col Koukouras, who was
court-martialled and shot in June 1947. Altogether twenty-seven officers
deserted from the National Army during the civil war, but none attained
any prominence in the Democratic Army.[42] From first to last the rebel

leadership in the field was in the hands of civilians, with at most the training of reserve officers and experience of guerrilla warfare under the German occupation.

In the summer of 1946 they were at about the same stage of development as ELAS had been in the autumn of 1942. After a year of individual
brigandage, in which political motives were only incidental, the phase of
true guerrilla warfare was about to begin; but a professional structure
such as Saraphis had imposed on ELAS was still far off. Although larger
units began to be reported – up to two hundred strong in Macedonia –
there was still no tactical co-ordination.[43] Among the active leaders before
Markos took the field were veterans of ELAS like Ypsilantis, Lassanis and
Kikitsas in Macedonia, and Goussias (George Vrondisios, who eventually
succeeded Markos as Commander-in-Chief) in Roumeli. All were still
operating on their own. At this relatively early stage the rebels were
scarcely vulnerable to the counter-measures of the Greek Army, which
was as little qualified to fight guerrillas as the Germans had been.

The first of what were known as 'clearing operations' were launched in
Mount Vermion and Mount Olympus during July 1946, with indifferent
success. On 3 August *Rizospastis* contemptuously referred to the use of
'rocket-firing aircraft, Spitfires and tanks', which were indeed little suited
to the task. In a mixture of metaphors, it might be described as using a
sledge-hammer against a needle in a haystack. The rebels emerged virtually unscathed to attack the small town of Naoussa, on the eastern slopes
of Vermion, which they besieged for three days, 6–8 August. In the
following weeks other parts of Macedonia came under attack: a village
near Florina in early September, Deskati on the borders of Thessaly three
weeks later, Pendalophos in early October and Ritina in Pieria a week
later. For a time in the autumn practically every road in Western Macedonia was cut, except those leading to the north.

In these operations there appeared for the first time signs of a directing
brain, which was presumably that of Markos. Simultaneously, in September, the road from Athens to Salonika was mined, the road from
Kalambaka to Ioannina was cut by demolishing a bridge, and the bridge
across the River Venetikos south of Grevena was captured and held. Although other roads remained passable, the rebels were in a position to
control traffic between Thessaly and Macedonia by issuing their own
signed passes.[44] It was a greater degree of independence than ELAS had
ever been able to assert in the days of the German Occupation. It was also
very costly to the allied authorities. In a single month between mid-
October and mid-November, about 250 men were killed in Central
Macedonia.[45] They were classified as 95 nationalists, 25 soldiers and 8

gendarmes on the one side, and 110 bandits, 4 Communists and 8 unknown on the other. These terrible figures showed that the writ of the Government was ceasing to run. At the same time anti-British feeling was growing on both sides. The Government's reaction was first to deport suspected Communists on an increasingly massive scale to remote islands of the Aegean. July 1946 was the month in which foreign aid to the rebels in Macedonia became unmistakable; and in which also the Greek Government first appreciated that it might have to turn to the USA for the material aid which the British were no longer able to supply.[46]

Although the first tactical objective of the rebels was to isolate Macedonia from the rest of Greece, they were also anxious to represent their movement as nationwide. To make Macedonia the primary target had the advantage of securing communications with the north; but it had the disadvantage of implying treasonable intentions with regard to Greece's territorial integrity. So the Communist press did its best to draw attention to disorders elsewhere. *Rizospastis* reported terrorism in the Ionian Islands on 21 May; disorders in Thessaly on 9 June; bandits in Ioannina on 26 July; fear and terror in Lakonia on 2 August; clashes near Sparta, Tripoli, Agrinion and Khalkis on 15 September. But it could not be concealed that the principal scenes of conflict were in the north. General Tsakalotos lists ten major operations in the course of 1946, all in Macedonia or Thrace.[47] No major actions were fought further south until 1947, though the National Army carried out a number of sweeps in Thessaly and Roumeli during the last three months of 1946 without making any significant contact; and similarly in Mount Pelion in October, Mount Ossa in November and Evrytania in December.

At this early date the disparity between the rebels and the national forces was not great, but they were difficult to compare because their assets and weaknesses did not correspond. In many respects no confrontation was possible between them. Most of the strategic factors favoured the Government, but tactically the rebels held the initiative and many of the advantages. Actual combat could take place only on land, but the other arms had a negative importance. Although the national forces had complete command of the air and sea, they gained little benefit from it in the first year.[48] The Royal Hellenic Air Force started with only 58 obsolete aircraft and 291 pilots; it had no experience of anti-guerrilla operations, and could find no targets worth attacking. The Royal Hellenic Navy had emerged from the Second World War stronger than ever before, but its initial role was also essentially negative. Against the German occupation the Communists had mobilised a useful fleet of motor-caiques, known as ELAN. In 1946 they had little access to the sea-coast, and in any case they faced a much more formidable navy than the Germans could ever deploy in Aegean waters. The first time that all three services were used in conjunction was in mopping-up operations on Mount Olympus in July 1946; but it was little more than a show of force.[49] Later both the air and the sea were to play a substantial role. In the beginning the conflict was only between two armies, themselves of disparate character.

In numbers and equipment the advantage on land also lay wholly in favour of the national forces, but circumstantial and psychological factors prevented them from exploiting it. Estimates of the rebels' strength in the field vary widely, in part because during 1946 they were still in the process of bringing under control numerous independent bands which were anti-Government without yet being pro-Communist. But all accounts agree on a great increase between the summer of 1946 and the end of the year. At the earlier date careful estimates vary between 1,500 and 2,700, at the later date between 8,000 and 13,500; and in addition there were about 12,000 more in camps outside Greece, chiefly at Bulkes in Yugoslavia.[50] During the same period the Greek Army reached 90,000 and the Gendarmerie approached 30,000. To their numerical superiority must be added the fact that only the national forces had heavy and mechanised equipment: tanks, armoured cars, artillery, heavy machine-guns, motor transport. But for a variety of reasons they were unable at first to exploit their superiority. They were like a fire brigade which always arrived too late, and could never prevent a fire from breaking out.

Morale was a major factor. In the opening stages of a guerrilla war, the initiative always lies with the rebels. Theirs was in essence a total war: they were not seeking to win a military victory, but to undermine the state, politically and economically. They therefore avoided direct confrontations. With the advantages of surprise and flexibility, they struck where they chose and then disappeared. Against such an enemy it was impossible to use the equipment of a conventional army; nor was a conventional army trained to meet such tactics. The British Army Mission was training the Greek Army on orthodox lines, as if to form a small integral component in a larger allied force for the kind of war recently fought against Germany. The equipment supplied was not only unsuitable for counter-guerrilla operations but largely obsolete. The men called up for service were mostly of the pre-war classes (since these were at least partly trained), and they were weary after six years of war and discontented at seeing their juniors left at home or installed in safe occupations in the rear. Among the discontented were many ex-members of ELAS who had been called up into the National Army indiscriminately.

The natural deficiencies of an army trained and equipped for the wrong purposes were compounded by errors of policy and leadership. Senior commanders were at first generally inadequate. Their sense of discipline was undermined by the knowledge that they were serving under men of no greater seniority or experience than themselves. Both appointments and operations were subject to political interference. The insistence of influential Deputies that their constituencies must be protected led to a policy of static defence instead of aggressive pursuit. Unsuitable officers were promoted as a reward for their political affiliations – republicans under Plastiras and Sophoulis, royalists under Tsaldaris. The Army and Police Missions also insisted for too long on a complete separation of the roles of their respective services. Only in September 1946 was it appreciated that the Army would have to give priority to operations over training, and the Gendarmerie would have to be brought under the Army's command. By then the morale of both was very low.

So the disparity of numbers was illusory. The rebels had a potential 'fifth column' in the Greek Army as well as the clandestine organisation of the *Aftodmyna* in the civilian population. The latter was, according to General Tsakalotos, 'the most formidable organisation and the chief instrument of action' of the KKE.[51] Its tasks included intelligence, political propaganda, terrorism, sabotage, mine-laying, subversion of morale, murder, recruitment and supply. The strength of the *Aftodmyna* is not easy to calculate, but it was pointed out that, towards the end of the civil war, operations in the Peloponnese which put out of action 3,600 guerrillas in the field also produced 1,600 surrenders in the neighbouring towns.[52] Clearly the clandestine supporters of the rebels were a large addition to their strength, and one which could not be eliminated by the methods in which the new Greek Army was being trained. But the chief value of the *Aftodmyna* may have lain only in the fears which its existence caused, for Vlandas describes it as poorly orientated and no more than a 'pale shadow' of ELAS.[53]

The rebels also had the advantage of familiar and difficult terrain to neutralise the material superiority of the enemy. The Greek mountains had at that date few roads accessible to motor-transport or armoured vehicles; and since the rebels themselves possessed neither, they could mine the roads freely with devastating effect. The conformation of the Pindus range, running through the centre of Greece from north to south, gave the rebels the advantage of interior lines, while the Greek Army was confined to the coastal routes and the few roads which crossed the mountains from east to west. Apart from the Peloponnese, where a more elaborate system of roads radiated from the central town of Tripoli as well as round the coast, there were few motor-roads connecting eastern and western Greece. Read from north to south, there was the long route running across Macedonia from Florina through Salonika to the Turkish frontier, but not at that date connected with Epirus; there was the route from Epirus to Thessaly through Metsovo; there was the uncompleted route across Roumeli, which connected Karpenisi with Lamia but not yet with Agrinion; and there was the route along the north coast of the Gulf of Corinth to Athens. All these roads, as well as those from north to south, were in serious disrepair.

These circumstances offset the National Army's logistical advantages. Nor were the rebels initially at a disadvantage in matters of supply. The Democratic Army had no need at first of a large supply organisation. Its men travelled light and lived off the country. Essentially they were light infantry, and their tactics made it impossible for the enemy to use anything more than light infantry against them. As such, there was no great disparity in equipment between the two sides. The rebels were not short of arms and ammunition: their disadvantages were only lack of standardisation and inadequate maintenance. In these respects the National Army, with obsolescent equipment, most of it captured from the Italians and Germans or supplied from British war-surplus stocks, was not at first in much better case. The two sides were evenly matched in their weakness rather than their strength. But it was evident that the National Army would be in a better position to win a protracted struggle unless the rebels could establish a continuing source of military supply. Hence the importance of contact with the Communist states to the north, and the need to control the frontier areas of Macedonia.

Once Macedonia was identified as the main centre of disaffection, it was natural that nationalist Greeks should detect the bogey of autonomism at work again. Tsaldaris denied it in his speech on the Security Bill, preferring to attribute the disorders to 'anarchist elements' instead; but to most Greeks this was a mere euphemism. Zakhariadis faced the real accusation boldly in a speech in Salonika on 17 June: 'any autonomist movement in Macedonia is absolutely inconsistent with the policy of the KKE and EAM'. The same was true, he added, of the Slavo-Macedonians: 'full equality of rights' was their only claim. He went so far as to say that 'no Communist Party of Macedonia exists'; but across the border the Macedonian CP controlled by Tito was actively spreading its influence in Bulgaria and would not be likely to neglect potential adherents among the Slavophones in Greece. The KKE could only try to play down the awkward facts by insisting, as *Rizospastis* did on 8 July, that Greece's northern neighbours had no territorial claims. But between the beginning of August and the middle of October 1946, both Yugoslav and Bulgarian claims to 'Aegean Macedonia' became so frequent, open and aggressive, that their official inspiration could not be in doubt.[54]

Evidence available to successive Greek governments, both before and after the General Election of 1946, seemed to leave no doubt of the reality of the threat.[55] On 28 February the Athens press reported that the Government was to protest in Belgrade about the formation of an army of former members of ELAS on Yugoslav territory, which shows that the camp at Bulkes was already known, although Communist sources later stated that guerrillas did not begin to move out of it to cross the frontier until the autumn.[56] In the meantime frightening rumours still spread. On 4 March Sophoulis confirmed to reporters that 'Bulgarian terrorists' were co-operating with left-wing bands in Western Macedonia; and on 23 March a headline in *Kathimerini* simply announced: 'Autonomists killed in Northern Greece.' Conscientious efforts were nevertheless made not to give official sanction to accusations against the two northern neighbours. When the Governor-General of Macedonia published a signed article in June accusing the Yugoslavs of abetting Greek rebels, he was forced to resign, though not long afterwards he was restored to office. Greek attempts to be conciliatory seemed to lead to fiercer propaganda.

'Greek imperialists have no right to keep the Macedonians any longer under their yoke', declared the Yugoslav newspaper *Borba* on 26 August. Even if it could be contended that the press in Yugoslavia did not represent the Government officially – itself a challengeable proposition – there was no lack of similar pronouncements by men in authority. On 6 September Moša Pijade, speaking as the official delegate of Yugoslavia at the Paris Peace Conference, referred to 'Aegean Macedonia' as being under 'brutal oppression'. On 22 September Dimitar Vlahov, the Prime Minister of the People's Republic of Macedonia, said in a speech at Monastir: 'We openly declare that Greece has no right whatsoever over Aegean Macedonia.' On 10 October Dobri Terpechev, President of the Economic Council of Bulgaria, declared that 'there exist not three Macedonias but one single Macedonia stretching across Bulgaria, Yugoslavia and Greece, which will eventually become a single whole'. But the Greek Communists contrived to suggest at the same time that the autonomist movement was promoted and directed by the British.[57]

The intended inference was that any trouble over the frontiers arose solely from the claims of the Greek Government against her neighbours. At the Peace Conference, which opened in Paris on 29 July, Greece tabled territorial claims against both Bulgaria and Albania, as ex-enemy powers, but not against Yugoslavia, which was nominally an ally. Communist propagandists on both sides of the frontiers pretended to believe that the Greek National Army intended to invade its neighbours, as it had once before invaded Bulgaria in 1925. But the Army was incapable of such aggression, even if British troops had not been there in force to forestall it.

There was more substance in Greek fears of a repetition of past invasions from the north. Albania's existing frontier gave her access to a mountainous salient into Greece known as Mourgana; and also possession of a plain and valley south-west of the Prespa lakes, containing the natural route linking Greek Macedonia with Greek Epirus, which were otherwise separated by the northern Pindus range. The Greek claim to Northern Epirus also rested on conquest in 1940, and on a substantial Greek population in Korytsa and Argyrokastro. The Yugoslav frontier was crossed by two easy routes of invasion into Greece, the Florina and Vardar gaps; but no adjustment could eliminate that fact of geography. The Bulgarian frontier dominated north-eastern Greece along the Rhodopi range – a threat that could only be overcome by shifting the frontier inland to the reverse slope of the hills, which would in turn merely have reversed the direction of the threat.[58]

Greece's claims to such adjustments were supported with little enthusiasm at the Peace Conference by the British and American Governments, which feared that to meet them would only sow the seeds of future wars.[59] They were opposed by the Soviet Government and ridiculed by the Balkan Communists, including the KKE. *Rizospastis* reported in friendly terms on the Bulgarian delegation in Paris on 15 August, and on the Albanian delegation a week later. By the middle of October the Greeks' claims had been completely frustrated, their only territorial gain being the Dodecanese from Italy. Zakhariadis published a leading article in *Rizospastis* on 10 October gloating over the failure of Tsaldaris's foreign policy. Worse was to follow a week later, when *Rizospastis* on 17 October quoted Tito as saying in an interview: 'Our government raised the question of Macedonia and the Aegean, but the persecution of the Slavs by the Greek authorities continues, and if it continues we shall naturally take certain measures.' The outcome of the Peace Conference was thus to intensify hostility and suspicion between the Balkan neighbours, as well as between the great powers. What Churchill a few months earlier had called an 'Iron Curtain' now ran along the northern frontier of Greece.

But the Iron Curtain was impenetrable only to the enemies of Communism. If Greek aircraft accidentally infringed Yugoslav air-space, there were angry protests. On the other hand, it became increasingly clear that the rebels were obtaining supplies and recruits from across the frontier. The Greek rebel camp at Bulkes had become an open secret: it even published its own newspaper, which was quoted from time to time in *Rizospastis*. It was only one of several camps outside Greece, and perhaps not militarily the most important. A British journalist who visited Bulkes in 1947 found 'an entire Greek town' rather than a military camp; and a French journalist in close touch with the KKE later described it as no more than a holding camp, where men were selected for training and non-combatants were kept under control in a miniature police-state.[60] The latter stated that training took place mainly in Greece, under Markos's supervision, but other sources leave no doubt that there were training camps in Albania and Yugoslavia. Aid from the north also went much further. Often rebel operations near the frontiers were seen to be supported from neighbouring territory. A force of some seven hundred men attacked Skra from Yugoslavia on 13 November. Other examples were quoted in a memorandum from the Greek Government to the British and American Ambassadors on 18 November. Finally the Greek representative at the United Nations was instructed to request an investigation by the Security Council. Tsaldaris himself flew to New York to attend the debate in December.

The decision to invoke international intervention was the climax of a year in which the Greek Government had been increasingly isolated. It began with the Soviet reference to the United Nations in January, complaining of the presence of British troops in Greece. Although the complaint was successfully resisted, it was known that the British Government wished to withdraw its troops as soon as possible after the plebiscite in September, although police and service missions were to remain. By the autumn British troops had begun to concentrate in the north, leaving southern Greece undefended by allied troops. The British Government could not increase its supply of arms to the Greek Army, and refused to supply them for civilian use. In desperation, with British acquiescence, the Greek Government began to turn to the USA; and a high-level mission was sent to Washington in July under Venizelos. Meanwhile the Soviet Government became increasingly hostile. At the Council of Foreign Ministers, as well as at the Peace Conference, Soviet representatives opposed Greece's claims and insulted her government. In August the Ukrainian delegate at the United Nations again lodged a complaint in the Security Council. When the United States proposed in September that a commission of three impartial observers should be sent to Greece, the Soviet delegate vetoed the resolution. By this time the US Government was alert to the danger in the Near East, having seen the most cogent of many indications in a fresh Soviet demand for revision of the Montreux Convention on the Turkish Straits.

After every allowance is made for the correction of the record by revisionist historians, it cannot be disputed that greater blame for the Cold War rested with Stalin than with the western leaders. But what was true at the level of great-power politics was not necessarily true at the more parochial level of the Balkans. As the two sides in the Greek civil war became increasingly polarised, they naturally sought to identify themselves with the two major international camps; but the identification was to some extent forced. Less than two years earlier the Americans had been neutral with some sympathy towards EAM. The British, at any rate since the fall of Churchill in mid-1945, had little sympathy with the right-wing royalist government. They had earned the displeasure of many Greeks by insisting that Varkiza should not be a punitive settlement. In fact, the British authorities believed in 'reconciliation' more sincerely than the Communists. Just as it may be endlessly disputed on the great-power level which side started the Cold War, so it may be on the local level which side frustrated reconciliation. But a just allocation of blame would probably not be the same on the two levels. In the one case Stalin was more to blame than Truman, even in the light of revisionist interpretations; but in the other case the blame must fall more equally on the incompetence (rather than malignity) of the Greek Government and the determination of the Communists not to co-operate. Both were abetted by the bitter memories and inflamed emotions of a long-suffering public.

'Where are we going?' asked a headline in *Rizospastis* on 22 September: 'Reconciliation or War?' It was still possible to be in doubt about the answer. The period of the plebiscite on the monarchy, which took place on 1 September, had been the last opportunity for a compromise, for the Government then temporarily suspended the operation of the Security Law and the KKE finally recommended its followers to vote. What chance there was of a return to more peaceful conditions was destroyed by the action of the Yugoslav and Soviet Governments in recalling their diplomatic representatives from Athens towards the end of August. In both cases the reason given was the aggressive language of the Greek press, which was certainly scurrilous in its abuse of the Communist powers. But the latter must have known that the Greek press was literally uncontrolled, unlike their own. A more probable reason was their desire not to witness the restoration of King George II, which was certain, not because the plebiscite was to be faked, but because the majority of the Greek people saw the monarchy as the only bulwark against Communism. When the King duly recovered his throne as a result of the plebiscite by an overwhelming majority, with a deliberate significance the Bulgarian monarchy was formally abolished exactly a week later.

But no irreversible commitment to civil war was taken by the KKE before the plebiscite. Even after it there were still arguments for caution. In areas which the KKE counted as its strongholds, such as Piraeus, Salonika and Macedonia generally, the vote was surprisingly even. Although the King was regarded as the figurehead of 'monarcho-fascism', he might, as in 1935, prove to be conciliatory and even weak. The British troops, who were due for early withdrawal, might be compelled as a matter of policy to remain if violence passed out of control; and that would prejudice the Communists' plans. Tito was said to have promised support for a rebellion, but his word might again prove unreliable. Probably Zakhariadis still favoured keeping the options open, having no military experience himself and being jealous of colleagues who had won fighting reputations against the German occupation. Markos Vaphiadis, on the other hand, was determined to act. The order of the day establishing the GHQ of the Democratic Army was dated 28 October 1946 (chosen as the anniversary of Greece's defiance of Italy in 1940), though it was probably not drafted till some weeks later. Markos himself had been active in the mountains since September or earlier. He is known to have held an operational conference in the hills of Khasia (Thessaly) between 18 and 20 October. But still no public announcement was made.

The silence of *Rizospastis* was no doubt due to Zakhariadis, whether from caution or jealousy. The first mention of the HQ of the 'Democratic Army of Northern Greece' (not yet of its GHQ) appeared in *Rizospastis* on 21 November, when a communiqué was published over the signatures of Ypsilantis and Lassanis. The name of Markos (without the surname Vaphiadis) first appeared in *Rizospastis* on 18 February 1947, in connection with the news of a visit to his GHQ in Thessaly by a young British Labour MP, George Thomas.* Even then the Communist press contrived to give the impression of knowing little about this popular leader. When it published his 'autobiography' on 7 March, it did so as if he were hitherto unknown; and the published story omitted all reference to his important role in ELAS. Again the editorial hand of Zakhariadis can be detected. It was not long before the mutual antagonism between the two men became notorious. When the Ministry of Press put out a story alleging that Markos had accused Zakhariadis of being a Trotskyite and trying to remove him, *Rizospastis* simply reported it on 27 March 1947 without comment or denial.

Antipathy between the two men was not surprising. Both had been born in Anatolia under the Ottoman Empire, Zakhariadis in 1902, Markos in 1906, but their careers were very different. Markos had become a

* Later a Cabinet Minister (1966–70) and Deputy Speaker of the House of Commons (1974).

tobacco-worker, and so belonged truly to the working class; Zakhariadis, a schoolmaster, did not. Both were in prison when the Second World War began, but while Zakhariadis spent the years of Occupation in a German concentration-camp, Markos escaped in 1941 and later won a high reputation in the mountains. He always stood out from other Resistance leaders. Even in appearance he did not seem like a Greek. With his unusual height, his gaunt features and lank brown hair, he might rather have been a Celt. Although a fiery temperament was betrayed by his blazing eyes, it was strictly under control. His language, though dogmatic and often ferocious, was restrained in delivery. He had not the flamboyance of Aris Veloukhiotis nor the intellectual distinction of Tzimas, but unlike Zakhariadis he would have been noticed in any crowd. Photographs of him during the 'third round' suggest that he had mellowed with experience. One taken in 1948 shows a man who had suffered more from his own party than from the Greek high command.[61] It was Zakhariadis rather than the Americans who prevented him from becoming the Tito of Greece.

The KKE, despite appearances at the time, entered the civil war in a state of doubt and division. Looking back in 1950, Zakhariadis claimed that conditions had been ripe for revolution in 1946, but personal failings had frustrated it. Markos had failed to ensure sufficient reserves, Siantos had failed to organise the secret network in the towns, Karagiorgis was a traitor in the service of American and British imperialists, and so on.[62] The leadership in his own absence – meaning principally Siantos and Partsalidis – had been wrong to sign the Lebanon Charter, wrong in its tactics in December 1944, wrong to accept the Varkiza Agreement. But, he went on, the decisions in 1946 had been right: Communism was then dominant in the trade unions and agricultural co-operatives, in the commercial and professional classes, in the Army, among the young, the intellectuals, the athletic clubs; the *Aftoámyna* was strong, the British were unpopular, the Slavo-Macedonians were overwhelmingly favourable ('despite the treachery of the Titoists'), Venizelism was dying among the refugees, and the foreign situation was encouraging.[63] It would have been a very naïve Communist who believed all these things; but this was how Zakhariadis chose to see the situation in retrospect.

Beneath the surface, the foreign situation was less favourable than he made out. The Communist Governments in eastern Europe were consolidating their power with much difficulty and mutual friction. Tito was becoming disillusioned with the Soviet Union, especially after Stalin failed to support his claim to Trieste. Stalin's foreign policy was exclusively concentrated on safeguarding his own security, regardless of the interests of his allies and satellites. There was a strong case for Yugoslavia and her neighbours to do the same; and this led to suspicion of each other as well as hostility towards Greece. Both in Albania and in Bulgaria there were dissensions within the ruling party, which turned on relations with Yugoslavia rather than with Greece. Yugoslavia had a large Albanian minority to keep quiet in the south-west, as well as ambitions to annexe Pirin Macedonia from Bulgaria. In their external relations Greece was of secondary importance during the later months of 1946. The Yugoslavs and Albanians were engaged in drafting a series of mutual treaties foreshadowing an almost complete economic integration; and the Bulgarians at the same time were occupied in securing the best terms possible in their peace treaty with the allies, which was finally signed on 10 February 1947. The three countries had not, and could not have, a concerted and unanimous policy for northern Greece. They were at one only in their hostility to the Greek Government. If Markos and his colleagues had a chance of overthrowing it, he deserved their help; but probably none of them looked sufficiently far ahead to see – still less to agree – what would happen thereafter.

In the wider international field the prospect was also doubtful. In retrospect, the Greek struggle is regarded as one of the catalytic episodes in the Cold War, because it led to the Truman Doctrine in March 1947. 'History took a new course', in the words of an American writer who took part in diverting its course.[64] That was exactly what Stalin feared, but the Greek Communists were slow to appreciate it. Until the middle of 1946 the Communist press treated the Americans as a secondary factor in the Mediterranean balance of power. A change of tone became noticeable in the late summer, as increasingly strong statements were made by President Truman, by Byrnes, his Secretary of State, and especially by Forrestal, his Secretary for the Navy. On 28 August *Rizospastis* complained of the presence of the American fleet in the Mediterranean, which Forrestal had made clear was to be permanent. The arrival of the USS *Roosevelt* in Greek waters in September was regarded with much greater concern than the visit of the USS *Missouri* in April. Although in the Communists' propaganda attempts were still made to imply a separation between British and American policy, on 3 November *Rizospastis* openly linked them in its headline: 'Blatant Anglo-American Intervention in Government Question!' But the KKE had not yet detected the connection between these developments and Britain's inability to continue supporting Greece alone.

The real symptoms were still concealed. In March 1946 came the first private indications of American willingness to provide more aid to Greece; in July Dalton, the Chancellor of the Exchequer, told Tsaldaris that British aid would need to be supplemented from the USA; in August Venizelos called on President Truman in Washington with a request for a large loan; in September the British Government agreed to continue financial support to the Greek forces until 31 March 1947, provided that the US Government would also help; and in the next few weeks American officers, both in Athens and Washington, gave hints that such help would be forthcoming.[65] Little of these exchanges was yet public knowledge. But the appearance in Athens in December of two Field-Marshals, Montgomery and Smuts, and a few weeks later of an American economic mission and a prominent American trade-unionist, were plainly significant. So was the succession of General Marshall to Byrnes as Secretary of State in January 1947. Yet still the American President gave no overt signs of a change of policy. His budget for the following fiscal year showed little increase in foreign aid, and Congress actually reduced the amount he proposed.

The Greek Communists, so far as they read the signs, appear to have concluded (though not unanimously) that if they acted energetically they could destroy the Government's resistance before the Americans were ready to act. As soon as the Democratic Army's GHQ was formed, there was a marked increase of operational activity, which was deliberately spread southwards. In November it was admitted in Parliament that the rebels held many villages in Thessaly, where they had set up their own courts, collected their own taxes, and operated their own telephone service. On 20 November Rizospastis claimed that the Democratic Army had established over a hundred guard-posts in the vicinity of Grevena. It named the village of Anthrakia, between Grevena and Kalambaka, as their headquarters; and it also named several of their leaders, but still not Markos. Zakhariadis found it timely yet once more to affirm, in an interview with a correspondent of the London News Chronicle on 12 December, that 'the KKE has always proclaimed unreservedly that it regards our present frontiers as sacred and inviolable'.

With the same object of distracting attention from the frontier area, the Communist press gave prominence to operations in the south. 'The shadow of Ibrahim falls on the Peloponnese,' wrote Rizospastis on 25 October, alluding to the Egyptian invader of 120 years earlier. On 10 December it reported the rebels about to enter Karpenisi, and on 31 December in Ypati. On 7 January 1947 it reported them active in the neighbourhood of Corinth, and even in Cephallonia and Mytilini; on 9 January near Atalanti, and on 14 January at Gravia. Many of these reports were exaggerated, but the Government itself admitted the situation in the Peloponnese to be critical. Independent bands of right-wing sympathisers were still active there, so that the National Army had to contend with two opposing sources of disorder. There was a major clash near Kalamata in mid-January, and another in the outskirts of Sparta a month later. Operations in the north at the same time were deliberately muted. This was the case not only in the Communist press but to some extent in reality.

The reasons for the quiescence lay in a decision by the UN Security Council on 19 December 1946 to send a Commission to investigate the Greek allegations of aid being supplied to the rebels from Albania, Yugoslavia and Bulgaria. Unlike later enquiries on behalf of the United Nations, this first Commission of Investigation had the support of all members of the Security Council, including the two Communist states, Poland and the Soviet Union; and its membership was drawn from all eleven member-states. Again, unlike its successors, the Commission was allowed access to the countries under accusation, and was even invited to the GHQ of the Democratic Army. The presumption is that the Communists felt they had little to hide; and that attention could easily be distracted from the little that had to be hidden in the north by escalating operations further south. They were also at pains to convince their visitors that there was no Slavo-Macedonian autonomist movement, and that they did not depend on supplies from their Communist neighbours.

A leading article in *Rizospastis* on 19 December, signed by Karagiorgis, denied that Tito had ever spoken of 'Aegean Macedonia', or that Yugoslavia had any territorial claims against Greece. Three days later he wrote another leader, welcoming the Commission of Investigation and hoping that it would visit Bulkes, where it would find 'a few thousand democratic Greeks, hounded out by the post-December Fascism, living in a civilised and serious atmosphere, enjoying self-government and working for their living, until conditions permit them to return to their own country'. British and American journalists were also shown evidence that the Democratic Army possessed British arms but none of Russian origin. A particularly valued witness was the British Labour MP, George Thomas, who met Markos at his GHQ in February 1947 and found him 'very friendly towards Britain ... quiet in his manner, extremely polite and clearly educated'. He too found no signs of foreign help, and concluded that 'the government's policy is the cause of the rebel movement'. This report appeared in *Rizospastis* on 18 February 1947, while the UN Commission was receiving evidence in Salonika. On 25 March *Borba* in Belgrade published another interview with Markos in which he spoke of the Macedonians as a 'minority', with no reference to self-determination.

Meanwhile the UN Commission was receiving evidence of a very different tenour from the Greek Government. Captured rebels and deserters testified at first hand that they had been trained in camps at Bulkes, Rubik and elsewhere, and had entered Greece under arms from across the northern frontiers. The evidence was later published in a book called *The Conspiracy Against Greece*. It was easy to question the validity of the evidence, especially as the earlier part of the same book (covering the years up to 1945) contained much fabricated material along with some that was genuine. Those who visited Bulkes, including both members of the UN Commission and foreign journalists, saw no signs of training being carried out there.[66] Yet the Communist members of the Commission were significantly unable to refute or shake the evidence of the witnesses they interviewed.[67] The most convincing line that they could pursue was that the rebellion was not caused by foreign intervention but by conditions of anarchy and persecution in Greece. In this argument there was some truth, though so far as the Greek Government itself was concerned the conditions were due to incompetence rather than vindictiveness.

The portrait of the rebellion presented by Communist witnesses was persuasive enough to divide the UN Commission on lines that were now familiar. They were also divided over the invitation to visit the GHQ of the Democratic Army, which was accepted by the Soviet and Polish members against the protests of the American and British members.[68] In the end only the first two carried out the visit, accompanied by Albanian, Yugoslav and Bulgarian liaison officers, and also by a Greek interpreter (Naso Zapheiridis) who elected to remain with Markos at his GHQ.* They met Markos and Kikitsas for a long interview on 20 March. Not surprisingly, the Commission was divided in its interpretation of the conflicting evidence submitted to it, and its eventual report (signed in May 1947) provided the Security Council with no basis for an enforceable decision. But in the meantime its work was overtaken by more dramatic events. By the end of 1946 the Greek Government, and indeed the Greek state itself, had almost reached the point of collapse. Within a few weeks the US Government had reached its historic decision to take over the desperate responsibility from Britain. The first definite indication that President Truman recognised it as inevitable came in a secret telegram from him to the Greek King on 18 October.[69]

The Greek National Army was now clearly incapable of a task for which it had never been equipped or trained. Its commanders recognised that drastic measures were needed. Spiliotopoulos, the Chief of the General Staff, flew to London in November 1946 to press for an increase in the

* Zapheiridis had been Myers's interpreter, and left Greece with him in August 1943. Evidence that he was an agent of the KKE became known soon afterwards, but probably remained unknown to the UN Commission.

Army's authorised strength from 92,000 to 135,000. He and Vendiris (who succeeded him in February 1947) planned and created several new kinds of troops: static Units for the Defence of the Countryside (MAY), mobile Units of Pursuit Detachments (MAD) and Commando units within the Army. But these could have no immediate effect. To eke out the Army's inexperience in guerrilla operations, men who had fought in the Resistance like Tsaous Andon and Mikhalagas were allowed to reform their bands under Army command. Even more necessary was an injection of courage and experience at the highest level. As Tsaldaris's last government crumbled at the turn of the year, a new coalition was formed around leading figures like Papandreou and Kanellopoulos, with the aged Populist Maximos as titular Prime Minister. The appointment of George Stratos as Minister of War proved effective; even more important was that of Zervas as Minister of Public Order.

One of the first actions of the Maximos government was to convene a meeting of the Supreme Military Council early in February. It met in an atmosphere of gloom approaching despair.[70] The politicians blamed the generals and insisted on changes in the high command. Spiliotopoulos predicted that the civil war would last three years. Perhaps because of his apparently defeatist attitude (though events fell little short of justifying him), Spiliotopoulos was replaced by Vendiris on 20 February. Tsakalotos, hitherto in command of III Corps, was appointed Deputy CGS. Another Corps Commander, who had made the unrealistic forecast that the war would be over in two months, was also replaced on the grounds of the low state of morale among his troops. The new high command was bold and energetic, but it was hampered in its turn by political pressures. Vendiris and Tsakalotos planned to clear Roumeli in the spring, but Ministers representing Peloponnesian constituencies pressed for priority to be given to the Peloponnese. In the event Zervas solved the dilemma by offering to clear the Peloponnese himself with the Gendarmerie alone. At least some signs of reviving morale could be detected.

Still all turned on the intentions of the American Government. Prompted by a series of almost panic-stricken telegrams from their representatives in Athens, as well as by the desperate appeals of Greek Ministers in Washington, President Truman and General Marshall moved steadily in the direction of intervention. Marshall's first speech as Secretary of State on 22 February forecast a more active role for the USA in foreign relations. On the same day, at the height of the worst winter of the twentieth century, the British Government published an economic White Paper[71] which The Times called 'the most disturbing statement ever made by a British government'. Two days later the British Embassy in Washington

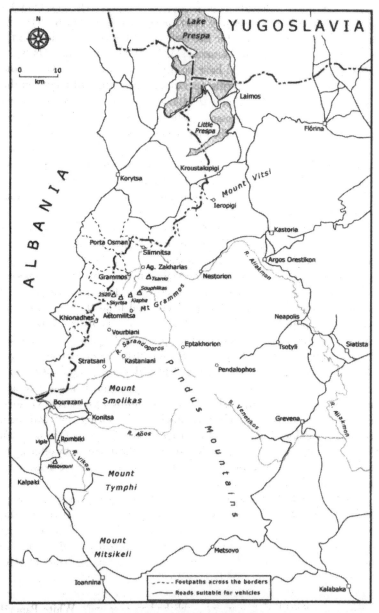

Northern Pindus (including Grammos Vitsi).

informed the American Under-Secretary of State, Dean Acheson, that the British responsibility for Greece would have to be terminated at the end of March. Under Acheson's leadership, with the approval of Truman and Marshall, a rapid reaction was organised by the State Department. The probability of American intervention became known almost at once in Athens: *Rizospastis* reported it on 1 March, and denounced it on the following day. On 3 March the Greek Government presented its formal request for aid in agreed terms.[72] After a series of meetings to secure the approval of Congressional leaders, the President delivered his historic address to both Houses of Congress on 12 March, asking for 400 million dollars to be shared between Greece and Turkey.

The outcome was not a foregone conclusion. Communists in Europe were well aware of divided counsels in Washington, and vigorously played upon them.[73] The earliest protest was addressed to General Marshall on 4 March by the 'National Committee of the Macedonian American People's League' in Detroit, all the signatories bearing Slavonic names. On the following day a telegram of protest was despatched by EAM to the Secretary-General of the United Nations. The fact that the UN had been by-passed was the subject of criticism from the left wing of the Democratic Party, led by the former Vice-President, Henry Wallace. But the criticism was not confined to fellow-travellers. Only the great influence of Senator Vandenberg availed to stave off Republican suspicions of the new policy. It was he who suggested to President Truman the device, which was belatedly adopted, of submitting the proposed action to the United Nations, while explicitly recognising that the organisation lacked the resources to carry it out.[74] Even with bipartisan backing, however, the programme was not assured of an easy passage through Congress.

Members of the Senate Foreign Relations from both parties were still sceptical. One of them asked Dean Acheson where the so-called 'Truman Doctrine' would stop. Acheson denied that it would apply to China, because the Chinese Government, unlike Greece, 'was not approaching collapse and facing defeat'; but he foresaw some unspecified expenditure over the next few years in Korea. He was asked what was the significance of the promise of support for free governments 'everywhere' which needed help against 'Communist aggression'. His answer was unilluminating, and the doubts remained.[75] The programme was finally approved by both Houses, though far from unanimously: by 67 votes to 23 in the Senate, and 287 to 107 in the House of Representatives, with much cross-voting between the parties in both cases. Perhaps in response to the doubts expressed, there was at first comparatively little stress on the military aspects of the programme. Soon after the Greek–Turkish Aid Bill was signed by President Truman (on 22 May), it was made known that Acheson was already at work on a programme of economic support for Europe in general, which emerged as the Marshall Plan in June. In these ways every effort was made to avoid presenting the Truman Doctrine as a kind of declaration of war: not unsuccessfully, for General Marshall, who was attending a Foreign Ministers' conference in Moscow at the time of the President's speech, heard no reproaches on the subject at all.[76]

In Greece, however, there was no doubt about the interpretation of the Truman Doctrine. The Communists were outraged, and the slogan of 'reconciliation' soon disappeared from their newspapers. On 13 March *Rizospastis* spoke of Truman's 'undisguised declaration of American imperialism', and on the following day it forecast the formation of an International Brigade, as in Spain a decade earlier; but this never materialised. The Government and its supporters acquired a new self-confidence, which often took ugly forms. Executions after summary courts-martial became almost weekly occurrences, despite appeals that they should be suspended while the UN Commission was in the country. Over 550 reputed Communists were arrested in Athens on 4 March on Zervas's authority. Later in the same month Zevgos, a member of the KKE Central Committee, was assassinated in broad daylight in the streets of Salonika. A right-wing band provoked a bloody clash near Gythion in Lakonia, as a result of which martial law was proclaimed there on 23 March. It was the last time that the state had to act against lawlessness on the Right. Effectively the civil war had reached the point of no-return, bringing with it the risk first of a new Balkan War, and ultimately of a third world war in its train. History had indeed taken a new course.

8

Guerrillas into Battle Order
April 1947–January 1948

IT BECAME clear in the summer of 1947 that American aid would take at least some months to materialise in sufficient quantity to turn the tide. The first shipments of military supplies began to arrive in Piraeus on 1 August. Later consignments were delivered direct to Salonika, as the nearest port to the area of operations, so that the psychological effect was lost on Athens. In the meantime more discouragements were in store. The sudden death on 1 April of King George II was a shock which gave rise to rumours about secret assassins in the royal palace.* On the same day a new financial year began under even more disheartening auspices, with a budget deficit of 287 million dollars and a prospective deficit on the balance of payments not far short of the same figure.[1] To complete the grim picture, UNRRA was due to cease operations at the end of June, before any alternative source of relief and rehabilitation had been established.

Energetic measures were already in progress to stave off disaster. Two weeks before the Bill for aid to Greece and Turkey was signed by President Truman on 22 May, Dean Acheson had made a speech foreshadowing new measures to fill the European dollar-gap, which would of course include Greece; and on 5 June General Marshall delivered the historic speech at Harvard University which led to the European Recovery Programme.[2] Although the Communist countries were invited to participate, it was assumed in advance that the Soviet Government would compel them to refuse, as it did. Nor was the effort to create a democratic bloc in Europe confined to the economic plane. On 14 May Churchill made a speech in London on the need for a United Europe, which was scarcely less important than his speech at Fulton on the Iron Curtain a year before. All these new initiatives should have revived confidence in Greece, but the Greeks suspected that in a collective European enterprise they would not enjoy a high priority. In the case of UNRRA, for example, they observed that their share had been not much more than a quarter of that allocated to their defeated enemy, Italy.

---

* Orestis (Moundrikhas) told me in 1969 that when he was in charge of the illegal organisation in Athens before the war, he had had three agents inside the palace.

They were also disappointed with the performance of the United Nations, which had supposedly been created to protect states against the kind of aggression they were suffering. When the US Government belatedly reported its intentions under the Truman Doctrine to the UN, a sharp debate followed, in which the Soviet representative, Gromyko, severely attacked the American proposals on 8 April. It was no doubt partly for this reason that opinion was divided on the Bill in Congress. At the same time the division of international opinion was reflected in the work of the UN Commission of Investigation in the Balkans. When the Commission completed its work on the spot and left for Geneva to write its report in April, a sub-commission was left behind in Salonika; but it was never again allowed to enter the territories of Greece's northern neighbours. The report itself proved contentious.[3] It was adopted only by a majority: the French as well as the Soviet and Polish delegates refused to sign it, and the Soviet delegate presented a minority report. Even the majority report disquieted Greek opinion by criticising the Greek Government for some aspects of its internal policy, as well as the Albanian, Yugoslav and Bulgarian Governments for supporting the rebels.

More disheartening even than the international dissension was the poor progress of military operations during the summer of 1947. Zervas was as good as his word in the Peloponnese, which he cleared with the Gendarmerie alone, but it was only a temporary success. At the beginning of April he announced that Lakonia was free of bandits; two months later thirty gendarmes were killed in a clash in the neighbouring province of Messinia. North of the Gulf of Corinth, the army conspicuously failed in its tasks. For the first time it was required to mount operations of a conventional kind against an enemy organised on a similar basis to its own. Code-names were assigned to its series of offensives, as in a regular campaign. Operation Terminus, beginning in April, was planned to clear Roumeli by a broad sweep from south to north. It was to be supported and complemented by a number of subsidiary operations moving successively further north: Operation Eagle in Agrapha and Tzoumerka from 5 to 30 April; Operation Hawk in Khasia and Antikhasia from 1 to 31 May; Operation Stork in Ossa and Pelion from 7 to 15 May; Operation Swan in Mount Olympus from 12 to 30 June; Operation Crow in Smolikas and Grammos from 26 June to 22 July. General Tsakalotos, who was in overall command of Operation Terminus, admitted in retrospect that the results were insignificant.[4] The rebels evaded encirclement, the National Army took few prisoners, and could only hold the ground recovered at an exorbitant cost in manpower.

The nominal strength of the National Army at the beginning of 1947 was 90,000 men, organised in seven divisions and seven independent brigades.[5] Only half of these were active infantrymen, many only partly trained and at least some of suspect loyalty. An increase of 15,000 had been authorised by the British authorities in November 1946, as a result of Spiliotopoulos's visit to London. A further increase of 15,000 was demanded by the Greek authorities in February 1947 and sanctioned by the Americans in April. But the full increase to 120,000 was not effective until late in the year, by which time still larger increases were being demanded. Meanwhile a series of reorganisations of the high command showed clear evidence of dissatisfaction and irresolution. There were three different Chiefs of the General Staff during the year – Spiliotopoulos, Vendiris and Giantzis.

The dispositions at the beginning of the year were based on the traditional assumption that the role of the Army was defence against external attack rather than internal subversion. In the north were stationed III Corps (three divisions and one independent brigade) to guard East Macedonia and Thrace, and II Corps (four divisions and two independent brigades) to guard Central Macedonia, Epirus and Thessaly. Thus initially only four independent brigades were available for southern Greece and the Peloponnese. I Corps was not formed until February 1947, and did not come under Tsakalotos's command until a year later. He had no more than a scratch force for Operation Terminus, which was intended to be only a side-show preliminary to major operations further north. This was a miscalculation.

The most serious of the Army's weaknesses was low morale. On 19 April, shortly after the beginning of Operation Terminus, *Rizospastis* published a secret report dated 5 February by General Petzopoulos, the Director of Military Operations (G1), containing a pessimistic appreciation of the situation in the provinces. The Government gave orders for the arrest of the responsible editor (Zakhariadis having temporarily vanished from Athens) on a charge of criminal libel, thus tacitly acknowledging the genuineness of the document. Petzopoulos had reported that the morale of the National Army was low for a variety of reasons: the lack of provision for soldiers' families, the exemptions from military service granted for political reasons to the rich and influential, the lack of adequate recognition of merit, the inadequacy of nationalist propaganda and the success of Communist propaganda. To these weaknesses later commentators added others: the demoralisation of the officer corps during the years of war with Germany, whether they spent them in Cairo or Athens; the lack of strong discipline and adequate staff training; the inadequacy of available equipment, particularly mountain artillery and aircraft.[6] To confirm the last point, on 22 May a Spitfire was shot down by the Democratic Army's anti-aircraft artillery.[7] During the whole war, a total of fifty-four aircraft were eventually shot down, in addition to 495 damaged by rebel action.[8]

Most important of the psychological factors was the conviction that the Democratic Army was winning. Petzopoulos's report left no doubt of the basis of this belief. His analysis of the enemy order of battle estimated that Markos Vaphiadis had available a total force of at least 11,000 and perhaps as much as 12,400 armed men in the field, excluding unarmed auxiliaries, the *Aftoámyna* and reserves in the northern Communist countries. These reserves themselves probably amounted to another 11,000 effective troops.[9] The distribution of the active rebel units in Greece was estimated to be: 1,150 to 1,350 in Thrace; 1,940 to 2,100 in Central Macedonia; 1,700 to 1,900 in West Macedonia; 5,800 to 6,300 in Thessaly; 400 to 450 in Roumeli; 400 around Mount Taygetos in the Peloponnese. The numbers in Thessaly were the most ominous, and it was there in Mount Khasia that Markos was said to have his GHQ, with Gotchev and units of NOF alongside him. *Rizospastis* reported on 22 March that the site of Markos's meeting with the UN delegates was Khrysomilia, near Kalambaka. Petzopoulos concluded that the Democratic Army was planning to seize an area comprising Kalambaka, Deskati and Domokos, in order to proclaim a state of Free Greece. His overall estimate of the Democratic Army's strength was not far wrong, since Communist figures show 10,800 in January 1947 rising to 14,800 in February, though they had less than half Petzopoulos's figure in Thessaly.[10] His assessment of their intentions was probably correct.

The National Army had a forlorn task in opposing the rebels' plans. Low morale caused a high rate of desertion: the figures for the whole war were 27 officers and 838 men, the majority of whom deserted in the early period of widespread defeatism.[11] Apart from morale, the shortage of manpower was crucial. On paper there was a superiority of about ten to one, but in practice it was impossible to exploit the advantage. As Tsakalotos pointed out, the National Army had to guard lengthy communications, to enable villages to sow and harvest their crops, to protect public services and urban centres, and to defend a frontier nearly four hundred and fifty miles long.[12] The Democratic Army, on the other hand, could strike at will and had no need to hold any particular piece of ground, until it chose to deprive itself of these advantages. The much greater strain on the National Army obliged it to place a time-limit on each particular operation in order to give the troops time to rest. During Operation Terminus a limit of seven days was imposed for clearing Mount Helicon, five days for Parnassus, seven days for Orthrys, and so on. In every case the limit was too short to be effective. Equally ineffective were the tactics, which consisted of an attempt to encircle the evasive forces of the Democratic Army in terrain where it was physically impossible to form a tightly closed ring.

A further reason for the failure of Operation Terminus was the tactical astuteness of Markos and his military advisers, in launching a major diversionary attack. In Petzopoulos's report, Epirus was a significant blank on the map, but it was not long to remain so. The credit for seeing the importance of the Mourgana salient, which jutted from Albania into Greek Epirus, was later claimed by Vlandas.[13] On 8 July units of the Democratic Army broke out of Western Macedonia to the south-west. The Greek high command had neglected this possibility, for two reasons. Firstly, the conformation of the Pindus range and the absence of motor roads made Epirus inaccessible from Macedonia for the National Army (except by the circuitous route through Thessaly and Metsovo), and the inexperienced Greek generals failed to see that the same inhibition would not apply to guerrillas, who were not dependent on motor transport. In the second place, it was thought that territory once dominated by Zervas could not be vulnerable; and in fact when Zervas, fresh from his success in the Peloponnese, hastened to Ioannina he was able to rally the demoralised national forces. But before his intervention the National Army had suffered a severe shock. For the first time the Democratic Army was operating not as a band of guerrillas but as a regular force.

Some Greek authorities considered that Markos could have seized both Konitsa and Ioannina at this time if he had pressed the attack home.[14] But after a tentative thrust at Konitsa, which was repulsed on 13 July, the rebels pursued other tactics. Their force divided into two parts, one advancing south-eastwards towards Grevena and the other southwards towards Ioannina. The eastern force was engaged in a severe battle for Grevena, the first such action on a major scale since the civil war began. It was repulsed on 25 July with loss to the rebels of 128 dead, 135 wounded and 90 prisoners. The western force reached a point only ten miles north of Ioannina, where the commanding general, in a state of panic, planned to evacuate the city. He had advised civilians to leave, before Zervas arrived to bring the situation under his personal control. In fact the rebels did not attempt to capture Ioannina. They by-passed it on both sides, moving into Lakka Souli to the south-west and Zagori to the east, before withdrawing towards Albania and establishing themselves in the mountain salient of Mourgana. But their freedom of movement was frightening. *Rizospastis* published a map on 27 July showing a vast area of Pindus, bounded by Konitsa, Ioannina, Metsovo, Grevena, Siatista,

Kastoria and Florina, under the Democratic Army's control. By 29 August, less convincingly, they had extended it on the map southwards to the Gulf of Corinth.

Although in practice it was impossible for the Democratic Army to control so large an area for any length of time, it could deny effective control to the Government. The Communists could not yet take over the functions of the state, but they could disrupt it. By the middle of 1947 the Government's writ had ceased to run over very large areas of the country, and the state was in danger of total collapse. At minimal cost to themselves, the rebels had almost achieved their object of causing the ruin of 'monarcho-fascist' Greece. The economic consequences can hardly be exaggerated. The national economy had always been poor; it had become much poorer as a result of the German occupation; and in contrast with the rest of Europe, the deterioration had continued since the end of the war. Industrial workers and peasants – never entirely distinct classes – suffered alike. The most severely affected were those in agricultural industries, such as tobacco and currants, which normally earned most of Greece's foreign exchange; together with mining, whose considerable potential could not be exploited in conditions of war. Unemployment among such workers not only caused hardship but provided a recruiting-ground for the KKE. Having once been active contributors to the national economy, their contribution was now negative or even destructive. It was in these circumstances that the International Labour Office in 1947 prepared a gravely pessimistic survey of *Labour Problems in Greece*, which was published eventually in 1949.[15]

Greece was never self-sufficient in food, and the destruction of road and rail communications made it difficult to distribute what supplies were available. The real value of wages in 1947 was lower than pre-war. Before the war, according to the ILO Report,

> the standard of living of Greek workers was inferior to that of the majority of wage-earners in other European countries. Today this standard of living is no more than a fraction of its pre-war level.[16]

On top of the general deterioration came the problem of refugees. Villages threatened by the civil war were voluntarily or compulsorily evacuated, with the result that the Ministry of Welfare had to take responsibility for a refugee population which exceeded 400,000 by the end of 1947, and reached nearly 700,000 by 1949. The misery was deepened by a further tragedy which was never completely explained: when in retreat from occupied areas, the Democratic Army was sometimes accompanied not only by adult recruits but by thousands of children without their parents. The Government said they had been kidnapped, the rebels that they had been rescued from the tragedy of war. Out of some 28,000 children taken out of Greece in this way, only some 10,000 were ever repatriated.[17]

The Greek authorities were showing signs of desperation. Between 9 and 14 July Zervas authorised many thousands of arrests in Athens: 2,500 were reported at the time, but Zapheiropoulos gave a total of 7,000 in Athens alone, and 10,000 in the whole country.[18] The total of executions became appalling, and led to international protests: on 30 August *Rizospastis* reported 24 executions in a single day, and a total of 462 since the Security Act became law. At the same time both the Government and the high command were in disarray. On 24 August Venizelos, Papandreou and Kanellopoulos all resigned, and Maximos at once followed suit. An attempt by Tsaldaris to form another Populist government failed; and on 5 September the aged Sophoulis took office at the head of the first Liberal–Populist coalition, formed under strong American pressure.

Stratos remained as Minister of War, to ensure continuity. A new series of operations was launched to restore the situation in the mountains: Operation Javelin in Smolikas (Macedonia) from 10 August to 10 September, and Operation Whirlwind in Vardoussia (Roumeli) from 19 September to 12 October. Neither was successful. At the end of the series a high-level conference of military commanders was held at Volos from 16 to 18 October, which had the character of a post-mortem. As a result Vendiris resigned as Chief of the General Staff and was appointed to what seemed the relative sinecure of Army Commander. He was succeeded by General Giantzis, who had preceded him in command of what was called the First Army (though in fact there was never more than one).[19]

Vendiris's supersession was due to political reasons, not to military failure. Being politically a Liberal, he was *persona non grata* to Tsaldaris, the Populist leader, on whose support Sophoulis depended. But in the event it turned out to be a blessing in disguise that Vendiris had become available as Army Commander. The forces available to the high command were now too large for operations to be effectively controlled without an intermediate HQ between the Corps Commanders and the CGS. A total of 120,000 men were organised in three Army Corps – I Corps based on Athens, II Corps based on Larisa and III Corps based on Salonika – with garrisons in the Peloponnese and the islands not organised into higher formations. Each Corps comprised three divisions; and to control the number of divisions necessary to operate a pincer movement in the northern Pindus from both east and west – sometimes as many as six – was

beyond the capacity of a single Corps HQ, especially given the primitive
and vulnerable state of communications overland. The Greek high command kept its Corps HQs mobile – I Corps under Tsakalotos, for example, operated successively in Roumeli, Epirus, the Peloponnese and
Macedonia, with different divisions under its command in each case; but it
was nevertheless desirable also to have the flexibility provided by an Army
HQ which could co-ordinate two or more Corps in major operations.
This was to be Vendiris's role after he relinquished the post of CGS.

Almost at once the new high command found the initiative seized
against them again. On the day the conference at Volos ended, the Democratic Army launched a determined attack on Metsovo, half-way between
Ioannina and Kalambaka. If the operation had succeeded, the motor-road
connecting Epirus and Thessaly would have been severed. The fighting
lasted over a week, and was later identified by Tsakalotos as the first true
'battle' of the civil war, though Zapheiropoulos gave priority to the
earlier battle for Grevena.[20] At Metsovo the tactics of the Democratic
Army were at fault in not capturing all the surrounding heights before
assaulting the town. Otherwise they would probably have succeeded,
with far-reaching consequences. Even though they finally had to concede
defeat, they had shown resilience in returning to the attack and in operating as regular troops. At the same time they were able to mount a number
of diversionary attacks to throw the National Army off balance: at Pendalophos in Macedonia; at Amphissa in southern Roumeli; at Delvinaki and
Zitsa in Epirus. They now had artillery at their disposal in the north,
supplied by the Yugoslavs, and also two battalions of Slavo-Macedonians,
supplied by NOF.[21]

The international situation was also becoming more menacing to the
Greek Government. In July the Soviet Government refused to take part in
the Marshall Plan and compelled the governments of eastern Europe also
to refuse. Later in the same month Tito and Dimitrov met at Bled, and on
2 August the Yugoslav and Bulgarian Governments signed a preliminary
pact with the ultimate object of forming the long-planned Balkan Federation. Unaware that Stalin disapproved of this initiative, and that the two
governments were still in disagreement about Macedonia, the Greeks
were alarmed. Within the month both the Yugoslav and Soviet Governments confirmed their fears by breaking off diplomatic relations with
Greece. In debates at the Security Council, on an American resolution
based on the majority report of the UN Commission of Investigation
which condemned the conduct of Albania, Yugoslavia and Bulgaria, the
Soviet delegate bitterly attacked Greece and the USA, and vetoed the
resolution. A month later, at the beginning of October, the Communist

Information Bureau (Cominform) was set up in Belgrade. Stalin's reason for locating it in Belgrade was in order to have a means of keeping a close watch on Tito's activities, which increasingly annoyed him. Like the rest of the world, the Greeks misunderstood the intention. The KKE resented being left out of the Cominform; and nationalists, regarding it mistakenly as a revival of the Comintern, assumed that it was a new threat to their liberty.

A mood of despair would not have been surprising in the autumn of 1947, but in fact there was more reason for optimism than the public realised. 'The operations of 1947 assured the salvation of Greece,' as Zapheiropoulos put it.[22] The Democratic Army had suffered crippling casualties in the year: 7,213 killed, 5,433 prisoners and – hardly less important – 5,222 deserters. On the Government side, the Ministry of Public Order announced on 30 September losses over a longer period (from October 1944) totalling 45,214 civilians killed and 3,031 Army and Gendarmerie casualties. A comparison of these figures was not advantageous to the Democratic Army in the short run; and in the long run things were bound to get worse for them. They were still able to recruit in excess of their losses, but the margin of increase was diminishing month by month. The problem of reserves was ultimately to prove fatal. Meanwhile the Democratic Army was developing into a conventional force, which made the need for reserves all the more imperative. Battalions and regiments needed staff and service troops on a different scale from guerrillas; and this led to an unsatisfactory policy of forced recruitment. The rebels were in danger of making the same mistake as ELAS four years earlier. It is said that Siantos and Markos both opposed this development; but Siantos died in peculiar circumstances in May 1947,* and Markos reluctantly acquiesced in the new policy. At the same time Tito, disappointed by the failure to capture Grevena, began to lose interest in the long-drawn-out campaign.

A report which Markos wrote on 4 August 1947, for submission to the Central Committee of the KKE in September, gave a realistic assessment.[23] On the one hand, he described the enemy as unwilling to fight, 'except for a small number of fascists'; and he emphasised the advantages of the Democratic Army in mobility and flexibility, 'always maintaining choice of place, time, action and surprise'. He claimed that by extending the conflict to the Peloponnese and Crete, 'we have everywhere succeeded in scattering the enemy's forces'; and also 'we have been stubborn in serious engagements against important centres in the hands of the

---

* He died in a clinic controlled by the left-wing Doctor Kokkalis. Rumours that he was murdered, either on the orders of Zakhariadis or the British, are not to be taken seriously.

enemy'. On the other hand, the rate of desertion from the National Army and of recruitment from the villages was not good, because of 'our failure to create a firm conviction in our victory and reliability'. Surprisingly, he added that 'great enemy propaganda and our own total lack of propaganda, due to weakness, and even to lack of an organisation which might work at raising the political consciousness of the men, are also contributory factors'. He deplored the lack of recruits from the towns, which Zakhariadis later blamed on Siantos and Tempo on Zakhariadis. Other sources confirm that at this date in Central and Western Macedonia ninety per cent of the Democratic Army were peasants and only ten per cent (not all of them workers) were from the towns.

Markos also admitted mistakes in 1947. He described many of his officers as lacking patience, tenacity and responsibility. After the war he criticised the hasty manner in which the guerrillas had been converted into a regular army, and admitted that from the middle of 1947 about ninety per cent of his recruits were obtained by force.[24] The reason for abandoning patient growth and thorough training was the fear of losing support from the north. To succeed, the rebel leaders would have to establish an alternative government on Greek soil as soon as possible; and that was virtually promised by Zakhariadis and Porphyrogennis when they attended the Congress of the French Communist Party at Strasbourg in July. In August Markos's GHQ began issuing 'legislative decrees'; on 8 October Zakhariadis's last editorial in *Rizospastis* (before he went underground) forecast a 'compact and extensive Free Greece with its own government'; and three days later *Rizospastis* announced the first elections in Free Greece, to be held in a group of seven villages in Mount Olympus. 'Free Greece' would require a more highly organised force to capture and hold the necessary ground. But such a force was inevitably more vulnerable to the tactics and weapons of the National Army. Once their brigades and divisions were confronted by battalions and regiments, their superior numbers and equipment were bound to be decisive in the long run.

According to Markos, 'the enemy succeeded in overcoming a series of weaknesses, was better organised, and as the war went on, gained experience of guerrilla war and successfully adjusted to its tactics'.[25] This was only true in part: it would have been more accurate to say that the Democratic Army made the more serious error of adjusting to its enemy's tactics. The one significant adjustment made by the National Army to guerrilla warfare was the creation of Commandos at the beginning of 1947. These were successful only within limits, and their successes were achieved at the expense of conventional units. Because many of the best men volunteered for the Commandos, they gained a sort of monopoly of the right to fight; but although effective as short-term counter-guerrilla units, they were not suitable for sustained operations or for holding captured ground. An American critic attributes the excessive effort put into forming Commandos to mistaken British thinking, based on the different experience of the Second World War.[26] The truth is that, after the critical years of 1940-1, British experience also found it preferable to train regular units in Commando techniques rather than to strip them of their best men for the benefit of a small, irregular élite.

The basis of the eventual improvement in the National Army's performance was less revolutionary. The conference at Volos in October 1947 concluded that what was necessary was to make better use of the equipment available, particularly air-power; to practise new tactics, such as an accumulation of sweeps in successive waves rather than attempts at encirclement; to take advantage of night and winter for surprise operations; and above all to put the stress on attack instead of defence. To facilitate a new policy of seeking out and destroying the enemy in the mountains, it was necessary to have a reliable force to hold and protect the liberated towns and villages. For this purpose a new National Defence Corps was established, and the makeshift units which had formerly constituted a sort of Home Guard of armed civilians (MAY and MAD) were embodied in it. It consisted originally of 40 battalions of 500 men each, but the authorised strength was soon increased to 100 battalions, though only 97 were actually mobilised. At the same time, with American approval, the strength of the National Army itself was increased from 120,000 to 132,000. With the arrival of American liaison officers in October and the formation of a joint US–Greek staff, a new spirit of resolution and methodical activity began to show itself. Many sources agree that the Americans from the first played a more active role than their British predecessors, even in front-line operations; and their engineers showed great energy in restoring communications.[27]

When the American Mission for Aid to Greece (AMAG) produced its first report in December 1947, there were already slight signs of encouragement. Some changes had been introduced into the original intention, which was that Greece should receive three-quarters of the 400 million dollars which were allocated under the Truman Doctrine, and the sum should be divided in roughly equal parts between military and civil economic aid.[28] It was clear that for the time being at least military aid must predominate. In fact during the first five months of operations the American Mission had furnished 74,000 tons of military supplies, with further consignments to the value of 100 million dollars placed on order for the Army and 13 million dollars on order for the Navy, as against a grand

total of 23 million dollars for civil relief. Commitments already undertaken for the future included the reconstruction of ports, roads, railways
and the Corinth Canal, which formed part of both the military and the
civil infrastructure; and there were allocations for rebuilding houses, for
irrigation and agriculture and for processing factories. All the latter
undertakings depended on restoring security, and of that there was at last
some hope. The AMAG Report concluded not unreasonably that Greece
had been saved from being 'plunged into national disaster'.

The Americans had also mobilised the moral support of the United
Nations on behalf of the Greek Government. It was not easily done, once
the negative vote of the Soviet Union had frustrated the attempt to secure
action by the Security Council on the recommendations of its Commission
of Investigation. After further fruitless debate the subject was taken off the
agenda of the Security Council on 15 September, and transferred to the
General Assembly. This had the advantage that no veto could prevent the
adoption of a resolution, but the disadvantage that it could not be made
mandatory to carry it out. On 21 October the General Assembly resolved
by forty votes to six, with eleven abstentions, to call upon the governments of Albania, Bulgaria and Yugoslavia to abstain from supporting the
guerrillas in Greece; and to call upon the four governments to establish
normal diplomatic relations, to agree on frontier conventions, and to
co-operate in solving the problems of refugees and minorities within their
jurisdiction. The resolution also established a Special Committee on the
Balkans (UNSCOB) to supervise the fulfilment of its recommendations,
and called on the four countries concerned to facilitate its work.[29]

It took time to bring UNSCOB into operation. Its national composition
was to be the same as that of its predecessor, the Commission of Investigation, but the Soviet and Polish Governments refused to take part.
Representatives of the nine participating countries arrived in Greece in
the last week of November, and set up their headquarters in Salonika on
1 December. Their first few weeks of operation were devoted to administration and planning, but they decided to establish teams of observers in
the field as soon as possible. Six zones of observation (later reduced to five)
were established along the northern frontier of Greece, divided by
parallel lines running roughly north to south. A succession of interim
reports began in the New Year, which established beyond doubt that men
and supplies were crossing the frontier in support of the Democratic
Army. But Albania, Yugoslavia and Bulgaria would not allow the observer
teams to set foot on their territory. The argument in all cases was that
UNSCOB had been illegally established, and that the General Assembly
was unwarrantably seeking to interfere in matters of internal jurisdiction.

The Greek Government took new heart from the evidence of American and allied support, and began to address itself to its disheartening problems with a fresh vigour. One of the acutest problems of the National Army, for which a solution had still to be found in 1947, was the disposal of Communist sympathisers who would otherwise have been called up into its ranks. The narrowly averted mutiny in the summer of 1946, and the large number of desertions to the Democratic Army, had alarmed the authorities. It was seemingly a matter of policy on the Communists' side not to deter their sympathisers from allowing themselves to be called up. In 1950 Zakhariadis denounced this as an error, for which he held Siantos to blame; but he contributed to it himself by his prejudice in favour of giving priority to subversive action in the towns rather than to guerrilla warfare in the mountains. Whatever the reason, the Greek authorities were confronted by the problem of large numbers of potential enemies in their own midst. Such men would be almost equally dangerous whether they were called up or left behind to operate in the *Aftoámyna*. Known Communists had to be placed under restraint, and detention-camps were established for them on two islands – Gioura (Giaros) for men and Trikkeri for women – as well as the use of Ikaria as a place of exile for more senior detainees. But there were also thousands of boys and young men who were guilty of nothing more serious than ideological sympathies with the Left. For them another treatment was needed.

A solution, which became highly controversial, was eventually devised in 1948 by George Stratos, the Minister of War, who formed a group of special camps on the islands of Makronisos and Leros. There a process of re-education was practised which a British observer compared to English public schools.[30] The camp on Leros was for younger boys, in whom King Paul took a special interest, and was influenced by the organisation of the Boy Scouts.[31] Less flattering accounts were put about by left-wing critics, who compared Makronisos with Nazi concentration-camps.[32] First-hand accounts, such as Mikis Theodorakis's autobiography and Philip Geladopoulos's *Makronisi*, confirm that for those who resisted 'rehabilitation' the treatment was severe. Yet it is a fact that out of about thirty thousand young Greeks who passed through the camps on Makronisos, something like seventy per cent eventually abjured Communism. Three battalions of troops drawn from the camps were recruited into the National Army, though there were some desertions from them.[33] About ten per cent remained convinced Communists, and twice as many were regarded as permanently suspect. The success of the operation as an experiment in re-indoctrination must be considered doubtful. It could not be compared with the success of the KKE's own political commissars.[34] But judged as a

practical expedient for eliminating a serious source of subversion from the
body politic, Makronisos was on balance a success. Perhaps only a government of markedly liberal complexion could have dared to introduce it.

Sophoulis, a man of generous instincts but capable of ruthlessness,
showed a characteristic combination of clemency and severity. He first
introduced an amnesty for one month (later extended to two months) on
taking office; and then in October passed a law against seditious newspapers, which was used immediately to suspend publication of *Rizospastis*
and *Elevtheri Ellada*. The Amnesty Bill, introduced by the new Minister of
Justice, Ladas,* was offered as a sop to liberal opinion. But its outcome
was to attract many more surrenders from the remnants of right-wing
bands than from the Democratic Army, which thus showed how strong a
grip the KKE still had on its followers. Suppression of the Communist
press was a corresponding concession to the Government's right-wing
allies (or even, according to the last issue of *Rizospastis*, to the Americans).
But it was not followed by any kind of censorship on the legitimate press,
nor even by the immediate outlawry of the KKE. Leading Communists,
however, such as Zakhariadis and Karagiorgis, immediately went into
hiding and found their way to the mountains. So did Partsalidis, who had
been arrested in July and put on trial at Corinth in September, but
escaped from the island of Ikaria in December. Tzimas also escaped from
Ikaria and arrived in the New Year at the Democratic Army's GHQ,
where Markos thus found himself uncomfortably surrounded by his
seniors in the party hierarchy.

Hitherto Markos had enjoyed a measure of independence in his conduct
of operations, largely because the KKE in Athens was doubtful how far
they could succeed. Among the last personal gestures in his period of undivided command were a communication to the United Nations on 5
September, calling for a cease-fire and a coalition government, and a
longer letter to *The Times* which was published in London on 10 September. The latter could be regarded as a counter-offer to the Government's amnesty, which had been announced a few days earlier; but it was
particularly directed at British public opinion, which Markos still believed
was more influential than American policy in Greece. He stated that the
Democratic Army had 'only democratic aims and aspirations', and would
willingly accept a cease-fire if a coalition government were formed of all
parties, including EAM. He declared the present frontiers to be inviolable,
and denied that his followers were 'stooges of the Slavs', or that they
wanted 'to take power by force'. Evidently his initiative had not been

---

* Ladas was later murdered by a man whom Zervas had arrested and his Liberal successor had
released. See pp. 232–3 below.

approved by the KKE. It must have been one of the examples Zakhariadis had in mind in 1950, when he accused Markos of pursuing an opportunist policy and running the Democratic Army as if it were his *chiflik* or feudal property.[35] Two days after his letter to *The Times* was published, the Third Plenum of the Central Committee met to consider very different lines of policy.

Only six out of twenty-five regular members of the Central Committee were present at the Third Plenum. There was no direct criticism of Markos on this occasion, though in retrospect he was accused of having misled the Plenum by his report on the state of the Democratic Army's reserves, which were later to prove its severest weakness.[36] He had in fact expressed anxiety about recruitment, but this did not prevent the Plenum from taking far-reaching decisions against his better judgment. It was resolved:

> to transfer the centre of gravity of the Party's activities to the mili-
> tary-political sector in order to make the Democratic Army the
> force which will bring about in the shortest possible time the
> establishment of a Free Greece, basically in all the areas of Northern
> Greece.[37]

It was further resolved 'to mobilise all the Party's forces for the un-qualified support, expansion and leadership of the Democratic Army's war effort'. In other words, the transition was to be made from guerrilla to conventional warfare, as well as from the towns to the mountains.

One of the results of the removal of the Communist leadership from Athens to the mountains was a continuing dispute about strategy. Zakhariadis had hitherto believed that the revolution would be won in the industrial centres. He had little respect for the potentialities of guerrilla warfare, in which he also had no experience. But once he took to the mountains, he began to study seriously the possibility that the revolution might be decided there instead. It has been said that he was much influenced in his reasoning by Mao Tse-Tung, and in particular by a speech Mao delivered to the Central Committee of the Chinese Communist Party on 25 December 1947; but the claim is not persuasive.[38] It is true that in 1948 Zakhariadis wrote a pamphlet analysing and endorsing the ten principles of guerrilla war which Mao had laid down. But on examination the ten principles appear to be little more than a description of the tactics which the Democratic Army had been pursuing for over a year, and from which Zakhariadis now intended to depart. What Mao did not say, and had not yet proved in practice, was that it was possible for a guerrilla army to take over the state unaided. Moreover Christmas Day 1947 – the date of Mao's speech – was the day on which the first blow was struck in the KKE's new strategy, which had been decided by the Politburo on 2 December. The KKE's policy was therefore determined independently of Mao's doctrine.

The new policy was to seize and hold an extensive area of 'Free Greece' containing a major town in which a governmental authority could be established. Konitsa was chosen for the purpose: it was the town nearest to Albania, and the terminus at that date of the road northwards from Ioannina towards Macedonia. Even before the Democratic Army launched its attack on Christmas Day, the Greeks were stunned to hear the announcement of a 'Provisional Democratic Government of Greece' on 24 December. It was actually announced a day earlier by Radio Belgrade.[39] Markos Vaphiadis himself was Prime Minister and Minister of War. Among his colleagues were Ioannidis, Petros Roussos and Porphyrogennis, all of whom were previously leaders of EAM; Bartzotas, Vlandas and Stringos, who were less well known; and Kokkalis, the doctor in whose clinic Siantos had died. Kokkalis, formerly a member of PEEA, was the only Minister not specifically labelled as a Communist. Partsalidis and Tzimas, who escaped from Ikaria only on Christmas Day, were too late to be included.

The programme of the Provisional Government included all the familiar objectives of the KKE, but on the crucial question of Macedonian autonomy it offered nothing more than 'recognition of the full equality of all minorities'. There was to be a 'special committee to advise the President on questions affecting national minorities'.[40] The other items in the ten-point programme were: the mobilisation of popular forces to liberate Greece; the establishment of popular justice; nationalisation of foreign assets, banks and heavy industries; agrarian reform; reconciliation among the Greek people; democratic reorganisation of the state; friendly relations with other democratic states within the framework of the UN; the creation of a democratic army, navy and air force to resist foreign aggression; and free elections as soon as conditions permitted. Zakhariadis was not a member of the Provisional Government, but he was certainly the moving spirit behind its policies.

The Provisional Government's first act of policy was the attack on Konitsa on 25 December. Despite the earlier attack in July, which had been the subject of an enquiry by the sub-committee of the UN Commission of Investigation, the National Army was taken by surprise. The high command was distracted partly by a diversionary operation against Salonika, which was also under shell-fire on Christmas Day, but more

seriously by its own miscalculations. After deciding at the Volos conference to initiate aggressive operations in the winter, it gave priority to the
Peloponnese, where the tightly-drawn network of roads seemed to favour
motorised troops, while the rebels were likely to be immobilised by snow
in the mountains. Operations were planned to begin there immediately
after Christmas, and in fact continued for two months, though with little
success. Meanwhile it was thought that the more inaccessible mountains
of the northern Pindus were less suitable for winter operations, and that
Konitsa in particular was likely to be judged by Markos too strong to be
attacked after his failure at Metsovo in October. A local reconnaissance
shortly before Christmas had convinced the Brigade Commander (who
was himself a native of Konitsa) that no movement on the part of the
Democratic Army was imminent. Consequently he allowed a number of
officers and men to go on leave for Christmas, leaving only 406 men in the
town. There was, however, a total of two battalions, with a unit of the
National Guard and another of gendarmes, available in and around Konitsa,
amounting to 1,300 men in all.[41]

Konitsa lies in a fold of the foothills of Mount Smolikas, barely five
miles from the Albanian frontier. It overlooks the confluence of the River
Aöos (in Albanian, Vijöse) with one of its tributaries, the Vikos. The
Aöos flows west and then north-west into Albania, where it joins the
Drin. Exactly on the frontier it is joined by the Sarandoporos (the river of
'forty fords'), which rises further north in Mount Grammos, only a mile
or two from the source of the Aliakmon, an even greater river which
flows in the opposite direction, eastwards to the Aegean. The valley of
Konitsa slopes westwards down to the Aöos. On the other three sides the
town is dominated by steep, rugged hills, in which the Democratic Army
was gathering its forces for the assault. From Ioannina, which lies due
south of Konitsa, the only motor-road runs at first north-westwards along
the slopes of Mount Mitsikeli. Just over half-way to Konitsa (the total
distance being forty miles), the road divides at Kalpaki: one route goes
due west into Albania, the other north and then east to Konitsa. In 1947
the latter route, after almost reaching the Albanian border, made a right-
angled turn at the last moment to cross the River Aöos by the Bourazani
bridge. A subsidiary route, scarcely passable to motor traffic, crossed the
Vikos higher up-stream by the Rombiki bridge and then crossed the Aöos
itself at the entrance to Konitsa. This subsidiary route, forming a hypo-
tenuse to the right angle of the route by way of the Bourazani bridge, has
since been converted into the main motor-road. It is both shorter and
more secure; but in December 1947 it was available only as an inadequate
ancillary to the main route.

For the purpose of isolating Konitsa, the Bourazani bridge was an essential target for the Democratic Army. Next in importance were the heights of Vigla and Mesovouni which overlook Kalpaki, where the motor-road divided, and the Rombiki bridge. If the Democratic Army held these key-points, no reinforcements could reach Konitsa by motor-transport; and the National Army's forces elsewhere – in Thessaly and Macedonia, for example – could not arrive in time by any other means. But the capture of these points was only subsidiary to the main assault on Konitsa. It was essential also to capture the surrounding heights to the north and east of the town, there being no practicable approach from due south, where the Aöos emerges from a precipitous gorge. For these tasks Markos had available two brigades from Macedonia, hidden in the hills north of Konitsa; three brigades already established in Epirus to the west of Kalpaki; one independent battalion close to the Albanian frontier; and two batteries of mountain artillery.* The total force comprised about ten infantry battalions, but by no means all of these were committed to the operation, because Markos anticipated an immediate counter-attack as soon as Konitsa fell. The maximum strength actually engaged, according to Communist sources, was two brigades and five or six guns.⁴²

The attack began at 09.15 on the morning of 25 December, with the speedy capture of the Bourazani bridge. From that moment the only access to Konitsa for supplies and reinforcements was by the subsidiary route across the Rombiki bridge five miles further south; and the heights overlooking the road, Vigla and Mesovouni were soon occupied by the rebels. At 10.00 on the same morning the Democratic Army began its assault on the heights above Konitsa. One of them (Tserniko) was quickly captured; two others (Vasi and Plaka) were severely threatened; but the most crucial of all, known like so many other peaks in Greece as Prophet Ilias, was unaccountably left alone. It was the same fatal mistake that the Democratic Army had made at Metsovo two months earlier. All through the first two days (25 and 26 December) the position remained unchanged. Then on the night of 26–27 December the defenders withdrew their small forces from the heights of Vasi and Plaka into the town, leaving the initiative with the enemy. Still the Democratic Army did not press home its advantage. Sporadic and ill-planned operations to the west of the town occupied the next four days. Meanwhile the defending forces had reacted energetically under the inspiration of the Army Commander, General Vendiris. Supplies were flown into Konitsa and dropped by Dakotas; reinforcements were brought to Epirus over the Katara pass above Met-

---

* Regimental numbers are omitted to avoid confusion, since both sides used closely similar numbers in their order of battle.

sovo, which was laboriously cleared of snow for the purpose; harassing operations were planned against the rebels holding the Bourazani bridge and the heights of Vigla and Mesovouni.

The Democratic Army was still in a strong position if its commanders had not wasted their opportunities. It was not until 29 December that they decided to take Prophet Ilias at all costs, and not until early on 31 December that the attack was mounted. Meanwhile Vendiris, taking personal command at Ioannina, had sent a brigade northwards to recapture the Bourazani bridge, and another to clear the heights overlooking Kalpaki and the Rombiki bridge. The two heights, Vigla and Mesovouni, were recovered by 30 December, and on the following day reinforcements, consisting of an infantry battalion and a battalion of gendarmes, were able to reach Konitsa by the shorter but less passable route from Kalpaki. Even at that date there was still a partial stalemate in the struggle: the National Army had not yet regained the Bourazani bridge, but the Democratic Army had failed to capture Prophet Ilias. It was already clear, however, that the attack had failed in its main object. The Democratic Army commanders were losing their nerve. They called off the attack on Prophet Ilias before nightfall on 31 December, and never renewed it. After three more days of deadlocked immobility, on the night of 3–4 January the National Army captured a height overlooking the Bourazani bridge from the north. During the course of 4 January the Democratic Army broke off the action and withdrew at all points.

The battle of Konitsa cost the National Army over 500 casualties, including 104 killed and 356 wounded. Democratic Army casualties were probably less severe in wounded, but over 250 were killed. Psychologically the result was even more decisive than militarily. The National Army had suddenly found a desperate will to victory, and recovered both its morale and the initiative. Symptomatic of the dramatic change was the appearance in Konitsa of Queen Frederika almost before the battle was over. In Athens too the spirit of determination was reinforced: among other measures, the KKE was belatedly outlawed, the members of Markos's government were deprived of Greek nationality, and a purge of the civil service was begun.

There were recriminations at first over the fact that the defence had initially been taken by surprise, and Vendiris felt it necessary to resign in protest. It could be pointed out in reply to criticism that Konitsa was only one of the towns which the Democratic Army might have tried to seize for its capital: others were Kastoria, Nestorion, Florina, Edessa; and it was impossible for the National Army to be effectively disposed equally to defend them all. But recriminations on the nationalist side were of minor significance compared to the consternation of the Communists at the consequences of their defeat. Impelled partly by the failure to take Konitsa, and partly by the warnings issued in strong terms by the American and British Governments and the United Nations Special Committee on the Balkans, the Communist governments of eastern Europe all refrained from recognising Markos's Provisional Government. A gloomy inquest was held by the KKE at Pyli on Lake Prespa, in the extreme north-west corner of Greece, beginning on 15 January 1948.

What takes place at a secret conference of Communists can never be more than a matter of conjecture. In the present case speculation has been reinforced by a worthless forgery purporting to be the text of a letter from Markos to Zakhariadis.[43] At most the document shows what a patriotic forger expected the Greek people to believe about the KKE: that the party had trusted too implicitly in Stalin and his allies, and had been let down by them. There is no evidence in fact to show either that this was the case or that the leaders of the KKE thought so. If they examined matters honestly, they must have concluded that the failure was entirely their own. They had no reason yet to doubt that their allies would continue to support them, and would even recognise their Provisional Government if they could redeem the defeat at Konitsa by a victory else-where. The recriminations were in fact personal between Markos and Zakhariadis. Markos believed that the lesson of Konitsa pointed to a re-version to guerrilla warfare without attempting to hold ground perma-nently. Since guerrilla warfare by itself could never achieve a final and decisive victory, the implication was that eventually the northern allies would have to intervene. Zakhariadis, on the other hand, persisted in believing that the Democratic Army as now organised could win the civil war by itself.

Although Zakhariadis later called this the first occasion of conflict between Markos and the Central Committee of the KKE, he also recalled some past disputes.[44] At the Third Plenum four months earlier, when Markos was not present, he had been criticised for seeking to defend un-successful commanders. He was also accused in December of misleading the Third Plenum over the state of the reserves, which had an important bearing on the battle of Konitsa. The total manpower available to the Democratic Army at this time was about 26,000, which was distributed as follows: Epirus 2,600; Western Macedonia 6,000; Central Macedonia 3,900; Eastern Macedonia and Thrace 4,700; Thessaly 2,600; Roumeli 2,600; the Peloponnese 3,000; the islands 600.[45] Probably this total was never exceeded, though a Russian source puts the maximum as high as thirty thousand.[46] The discrepancy may be accounted for by partly trained reserves in the neighbouring countries; but although the principal camps held up to ten thousand men and women, it is doubtful how many of them could be regarded as effectives. Bulkes is described as being by this time no more than a concentration-camp for undesirables.[47] It may have been precisely this that was held against Markos: as in the days of ELAS, the nominal rolls probably contained thousands of useless non-combatants.

Karagiorgis wrote a letter to Zakhariadis a few months later, on 18 March 1948, deploring the fact that the decision to hide arms after Varkiza was not accompanied by 'another decision that those who hid them should leave the country'.[48] The implication of the complaint is that a shortage of trained manpower was already being felt. Although forced recruiting had begun at the latest by the middle of 1947, it has also been suggested that a ceiling was deliberately imposed on the Democratic Army either because of difficulties of control or because the Communist powers would not supply a larger number.[49]

The rebels never had sufficient weapons to fill its tables of equipment, but there was no real shortage of infantry weapons in 1948. Probably no precise decision on the proper size of the Democratic Army was ever taken; clearly none was based on logistic calculation. But the development of conventional formations necessitated of itself a growth of ancillary services: hospitals, ordnance, commissariat, communications, training schools. These could only be provided at the expense of combat troops. The level of recruitment still exceeded the wastage, though by a diminishing figure. Markos could retort to Zakhariadis that the Democratic Army's problems were caused not by the shortage of reserves but by the unsuitable organisation and tactics imposed by the transition to conventional warfare.

He could not deny, however, that losses were heavy, and desertions were increasingly common. The morale and security procedures of the National Army were steadily improving, so that desertions on that side were relatively few. Two features of the conference at Pyli show the impact which the shifting balance of forces was having on the Democratic Army. First, each higher formation was to have a recruiting unit in order to conscript young men forcibly from the villages and towns; and the recruitment both of girls and of Slavo-Macedonians was expanded. Such measures naturally created problems of morale and reliability. To combat these a substantial improvement was needed in the service of information and propaganda, with a consequent expansion in the number of political commissars. At the end of 1947 they numbered only eighteen, but in 1948 the total rose to seven hundred. The second particular feature of the conference on 15 January was an address by Zakhariadis on the

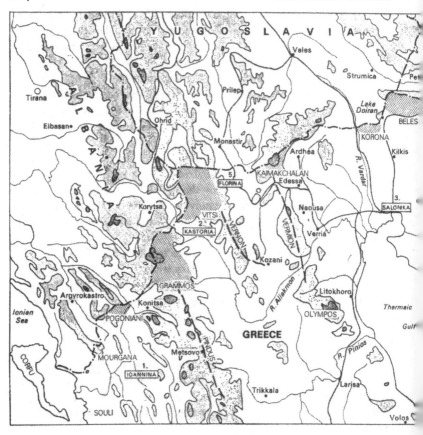

commissar's role: 'to enlighten, orientate and guide our soldiers, so as to
promote their popular-democratic ideological equipment, to keep their
morale high, and make them ever ready to fight and fulfil their mission to
the end'. Even their enemies admitted that the political commissars did
their duty with courage and dedication; but political education en-
croached more and more on military training.[50]

Supply was another problem that was aggravated as the Democratic
Army became a more complex structure. It has been estimated that each
guerrilla needed about five pounds of supplies a day (as compared with
thirty-seven pounds for a US soldier at the same date).[51] All rations were
drawn from the country; some clothing (including British battle-dress)
and some weapons and ammunition were obtained from the enemy. For
the rest, the rebels were dependent on supplies from abroad. The bulk of

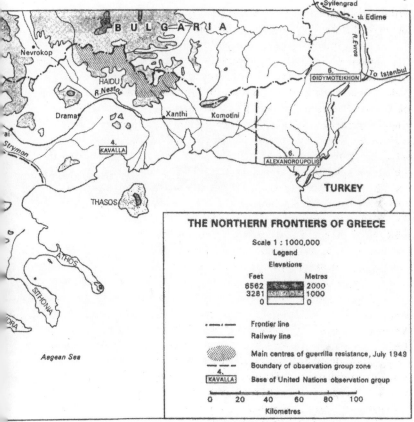

THE NORTHERN FRONTIERS OF GREECE

Scale 1 : 1,000,000
Legend
Elevations

Feet		Metres
6562		2000
3281		1000
0		0

Frontier line
Railway line
Main centres of guerrilla resistance, July 1949
Boundary of observation group zone
Base of United Nations observation group

0   20   40   60   80   100
Kilometres

them passed through Albania, but did not originate there. The main routes of supply seem to have been *via* Bucarest to Berkovitsa (north of Sofia); thence to forward depots at or near Tirana, Skopje, Monastir, Petrich and Plovdiv; thence into Greece at a score of points along the Albanian, Yugoslav and Bulgarian frontiers.[52]

Up to these points transport was mostly by motor-road. Further south, the rebels were supplied by large trains of mules: as many as fourteen hundred were in constant movement up and down the Pindus range. The extent of foreign support is difficult to estimate exactly. The neighbouring Communist governments had problems of their own, and could not afford to be lavish. Two things are certain, however: that the rebellion could not have continued without some foreign support; and that the KKE was disappointed with its scale. To Markos this was another argument for reducing military activity, but Zakhariadis, with the zeal of a convert, still believed that a quick victory was possible by means of a maximum effort.

Operational plans for 1948 were laid by the KKE at the conference of 15 January on the basis of a compromise between the rival views. The organisation of the Democratic Army was to be further developed as Zakhariadis wished: Divisions were to be superimposed on the existing Brigades and Battalions; appropriate services were to be attached to the higher formations; and GHQ, while retaining responsibility for Epirus and Western Macedonia, was to detach two échelons (*klimákia*), responsible respectively for Southern Greece (KGANE), from Thessaly to the Peloponnese inclusive, and for Central and Eastern Macedonia and Thrace (KGAKAMT). In this way the whole country would be covered by a uniform system of command, while Markos's supremacy would be diminished. But there was to be no further attempt to acquire a capital for the Provisional Government. The tactics were to be closer to the ideas of Markos: to disrupt the organisation and communications of the national forces; to attack outposts and troops on the move; to seize small towns only for long enough to carry off supplies and recruits; to improve training and efficiency; and to develop the rebellion in new areas, particularly the larger islands, where it could not be represented as merely an extension of Communist imperialism on the part of Greece's northern neighbours. On the last point considerable success was achieved, for the official history by the Greek General Staff recorded rebel activity at the end of 1947 in Evvia (Euboea), Cephallonia, Mytilini (Lesbos), Samos and western Crete.[53]

It was recognised on both sides at the turn of the year 1947–8 that the moral and psychological struggle for the hearts and minds of the Greek people had come to take first place. The following year was to be one of military stalemate while that struggle was grimly fought out. It was not a struggle between classes, for all classes were equally represented on both sides. Nor was it fundamentally a struggle between national enemies, for there was still no more than a handful of non-Greek combatants in the Democratic Army. To this extent the conflict was genuinely ideological, between two conceptions of society, one traditional and one revolutionary, but both Greek in character. It was perhaps all the more bitter for that reason. As the ideological lines became firmly drawn, polarisation and extremism were the inexorable consequences. To be found on the wrong side at the end of the civil war could be anticipated to be disastrous; and those who were most vulnerable were those who stood initially nearest to the line of demarcation while it was still ill-defined. Chief among them were those who had been associated with the Resistance during the German occupation.

Apart from Zervas's followers, the Resistance had special reason for bitterness as the civil war intensified. On the one hand, the courts had ruled that to have joined the Security Battalions was not a crime, since their sole purpose was to maintain order; and that was no doubt true of some who joined, because the Communists forced it upon them. On the other hand, to have been on the left-wing of the Resistance was in itself suspect. Many moderate and patriotic officers, like General Kalambalikis, were exiled; the Bishop of Kozani was deprived of his see for having supported EAM; Captain Koutsogiannopoulos, once a prisoner of the Germans under sentence of death as a British agent, was put on trial for treason. Even the politicians of the Centre had to tread warily. Papandreou, who had resisted the KKE in 1944, found it necessary to publish an article in November 1947 defining what he meant by the idea of 'Democratic Socialism', lest he be misunderstood.[54] With a self-styled 'Democratic Army' and 'Democratic Government' active in the mountains, the adjective itself (with its twin meaning of 'Republican') was almost as prejudicial as the noun 'Socialism'. Sophoulis himself was criticised for having once said that 'democratic citizens are being persecuted'; and General Vendiris was more than once under attack by right-wing politicians for being a Liberal.[55] The left-centre newspaper *Elevtheria*, despite or because of its fine record in the Resistance, had to tread warily with its daily slogan: 'Greece is Democratic.'

Under the stress of extreme peril, it was understandable that people's opinions, and consequently their loyalties, should become grossly oversimplified. The process was not confined to Greece, nor to one side only in the struggle: it was a general symptom of the Cold War. An English observer wrote in 1948 that the 'Greek sedition', as he called it, was 'not to be explained in terms of revolt against misrule, or indeed in any terms of cause and effect operating exclusively within the confines of Greece'; and he saw it, like Spain in the 1930s, as a 'testing-ground and laboratory' for the next war.[56] Papandreou even used 'The Third War' as the title of a collection of articles published in English in 1948. Events were to prove these phrases exaggerated, but those who used them had at least correctly divined that a much more important struggle, or rather two struggles, were now overlaid on the armed battle in the mountains. That battle swayed to and fro during 1948, to reach deadlock and stalemate. But it took second place to the psychological struggle in Greece; and it took third place to the international struggle in Washington and New York, Moscow and London, which began with the Truman Doctrine and had no foreseeable end.

9

Deadlock and Stalemate
January–December 1948

WHEN PORPHYROGENNIS addressed the Congress of the French Communist Party at Strasbourg in July 1947, he had declared that 'the political, military and international pre-conditions exist for the proclamation of a Free Democratic Government in Greece'. His words accorded with the conviction later expressed by Zakhariadis in speaking of the conditions for the rising in 1946, that the situation was favourable in every respect and 'the decision was indisputably right'.[1] Most Greeks would have agreed that the tide appeared to be flowing strongly for the KKE: politically, because their morale was high and the Government's prestige was crumbling; militarily, because the transition of the Democratic Army from guerrilla to conventional warfare was being successfully carried out; above all internationally, because the initiative seemed to lie with the Soviet bloc, and the American reaction seemed to be both clumsy and belated.

But the situation in the north, which was so disquieting to nationalist Greeks, was in fact already turning in their favour. Superficially, the Soviet bloc was consolidating, but the reality was very different. On 25 November 1947 Tito signed a treaty of friendship with Bulgaria in Sofia, and on 8 December with Hungary in Budapest; on 16 December Albania and Bulgaria signed a treaty of friendship; on 19 December Tito signed another with Rumania in Bucarest; and at the end of the month a Yugoslav mission went to Moscow. But Stalin resented Tito's initiatives, and disapproved of the creation of a Free Greek government. One of his purposes in summoning the Yugoslav mission to Moscow was to lay down Soviet policy with regard to Albania. He did so, according to Kardelj and Djilas, who were members of the mission, in a peremptory and sometimes unintelligible fashion.[2] Kardelj said that the 'direct cause' of the Soviet–Yugoslav dispute was Tito's decision to send two Yugoslav divisions and a unit of fighter aircraft into Albania to defend the country against possible attack by 'the Greek monarcho-fascists'. Djilas said that Stalin seemed at first inclined to take control of Albanian relations out of Tito's hands into his own, but then unexpectedly urged the Yugoslavs to 'swallow Albania'.

More serious from Stalin's point of view than the trend of Yugoslav–Albanian relations was that of Yugoslav–Bulgarian relations. The agreement signed between Tito and Dimitrov at Bled in August 1947 had been meant, according to Kardelj, only as a 'preliminary statement of intent'. The Soviet Government had been informed of it in advance, and had raised no objection.[3] But Dimitrov went further at the end of January 1948, when he spoke at a press conference in Bucarest of the eventual formation of a federation comprising Albania, Yugoslavia, Bulgaria, Rumania, Hungary, Poland, Czechoslovakia and even Greece. Stalin was almost as shocked by this suggestion as the Greek Government. On 29 January *Pravda* denounced Dimitrov's 'problematical and fantastic federations and confederations'. Dimitrov was summoned to Moscow, and the Yugoslav delegation was summoned back, to meet Stalin on 10 February.

Once again Stalin's definition of policy was dictatorial but confused. He ruled out any kind of union between Bulgaria and Rumania, but spoke favourably of three possible federations, all to be formed within the Soviet Union: Hungary, Rumania and the Ukraine; Byelorussia, Poland and Czechoslovakia; Albania, Yugoslavia and Bulgaria.[4] He wanted Yugoslavia and Bulgaria to unite 'tomorrow', and Albania to join them soon afterwards. But his only reference to Greece was to say that the rebellion should be 'rolled up' as soon as possible and brought to an end.[5] It had no prospect of success, he argued. Unlike Zachariadis, he saw no comparison between the Greek case and that of China. The Greek civil war merely annoyed the British and Americans, who would never allow their line of communications through the Mediterranean to be broken. 'Besides', he concluded, 'we have no navy.'

Kardelj, according to Dedijer's account, demurred at Stalin's advice. He said he was convinced that the Greek Democratic Army could still win, 'but only if foreign intervention in Greece does not increase and if the Greek Partisans do not make serious political and strategic mistakes'. In fact neither condition was to be fulfilled, but the Yugoslavs nevertheless continued their support for the Democratic Army in defiance of Stalin's wishes. Nothing further seems to have been said either then or later about Greece between the Soviet and Yugoslav Governments, nor is there any reference to the Greek civil war in the protracted correspondence which led up to their ultimate breach. For the time being the Yugoslavs had to give way to Stalin on most of the matters in dispute: Kardelj had to sign an agreement on 11 February to consult the Soviet Government on matters of foreign policy, and to accept Stalin's attitude towards Balkan federation. But by this time the instinct for national survival was strongly developed in Yugoslavia. Tito feared Stalin's intention of absorbing the countries of eastern Europe piecemeal into the Soviet empire, which was the fate of Czechoslovakia only a few weeks later. The Yugoslavs also genuinely feared the nationalist Greeks with their Western allies. They resolved not to yield on any matter which affected their national integrity; and the civil war in Greece was such a matter.

Firm evidence on the relations of the Yugoslav Government and the KKE is still lacking, and much is speculative. It is generally accepted that, in addition to their other disagreements, Markos Vaphiadis was inclined to support and rely on Tito, while Zakhariadis was a Stalinist. One account has it that after the setback at Konitsa, Markos went to Belgrade for consultations; according to another account, Zakhariadis was in Moscow at about the same time: both stories are consistent with the supposed alignments of the two men, but neither is definitely proved.[6] In any case Zakhariadis commanded no respect in Moscow, least of all with Stalin personally. One of the few stories which even connect their names has it that once a complete issue of the *Cominform Journal* had to be destroyed because Stalin disapproved of an article in it by Zakhariadis.[7]

Djilas's statement that 'the Soviet Government took no direct action over the uprising in Greece' is borne out by the virtual absence of any Soviet commanders to help direct it: only one (the Ukrainian General Kovpak) is named, and that doubtfully.[8] It has been said, however, that about May 1947 the direction of the Democratic Army was 'taken over by satellite personnel'.[9] If that were true, Yugoslavs would presumably have been prominent among them; but few names of Yugoslav generals are in fact directly linked with the Democratic Army. Dapčević and Nadj are named by Zapheiropoulos, the former being also confirmed by Djilas; and NOF is said to have supplied instructors, though it may be doubted whether they had much to offer.[10] It became apparent, on the other hand, that Tito was beginning to lose interest in the Democratic Army after its failures in 1947. Yet material help from Yugoslavia continued at a fairly high level through 1948, and the camp at Bulkes was allowed to function right up to the end.[11]

Probably the explanation of Tito's policy, like Stalin's, is that it was primarily determined by his country's national interests as he judged them. His judgment varied from time to time and, again like Stalin's, it could be mistaken. As the months passed in 1948, an element of obstinacy must also have crept into it. If Stalin wanted the Greek civil war to be liquidated, he did so for selfish reasons; and that may have become in Tito's mind a reason in itself for continuing the struggle. The correspondence between the two Communist Parties began in March 1948 – bitter from the first on the Soviet side, hurt and puzzled initially on the Yugoslav side — only a month after the last painful visit of the Yugoslav delegation to Moscow. Tito's attitude towards the KKE was bound to be affected by it, just as was the KKE's attitude towards him. It has reasonably been assumed that once the quarrel became generally known Markos wished to align the KKE with Tito and Zakhariadis wished to align it with Stalin. But their dispute had already been in existence for a long time, not over Titoism but over tactics.

Defeat at Konitsa had convinced Markos that the Democratic Army could not win the civil war on its own. Victory would become possible, he argued, only when circumstances favoured an outright intervention by the Soviet bloc.[12] Until then the scale and tempo of operations must be reduced; regular battles must be avoided; and his forces must revert to sub-conventional or guerrilla warfare. His reasoning seems to have been intuitive, based on his experience in ELAS. If he thought out the problem of reserves at all at this time, he could have argued that the rate of replacement was still narrowly favourable: about two thousand recruits a month against fifteen hundred casualties.[13] But the proportion of forced recruits was already high, and even the numerical balance was deteriorating. This was no doubt another argument in Zakhariadis's mind for forcing the issue to a quick decision rather than fighting a war of attrition. He could also reasonably argue against Markos that the probability of Soviet intervention, and even of a third world war, was by no means remote when the blockade of Berlin began on 1 July 1948. The correct strategy was repeatedly disputed between the two men: at the inquest on Konitsa on 15 January, in the Politburo on 12 February, at the Fourth Plenum on 28 June and at the Supreme War Council on 21 August. Others joined in the dispute: Karagiorgis and Khrysa Khatzivasiliou, for instance, on Markos's side; but Ioannidis, Bartzotas and most of the rest on the side of Zakhariadis.

The leaders of the KKE insulated their dispute among themselves, so that it remained unknown to the rank and file and had little effect on operations. When a new version of *Rizospastis* was first issued on 9 April, it contained a proclamation decrying defeatism, signed by all the principal leaders, including Markos and Zakhariadis. The actual conduct of operations bore the marks of compromise. A divisional structure was superimposed on the existing brigades and regiments by an order dated 28 August 1948. But no operations on a scale comparable with Konitsa were undertaken until the end of the year. Throughout 1948 the initiative generally lay with the National Army, which is not to say that it was generally successful. The tactics of Markos's forces were either defensive or diversionary: defensive to maintain their strongholds in the mountains of Grammos and Vitsi, where an independent state comprising some one hundred and fifty villages was coming into existence; diversionary to engage the National Army elsewhere. Two other purposes were also served by the latter type of operation. One was to promote the flow north-wards of recruits and supplies, both taken largely by force; the other was to persuade UN observers and public opinion throughout the world that the rebellion was countrywide and popularly supported. This became an increasingly urgent matter as the meeting of the General Assembly of the United Nations in September approached.

Despite Konitsa, the Democratic Army was becoming in many respects better equipped for the type of warfare which Markos favoured. It was a war on the civil population and on the economic and social foundations of the state rather than on the National Army.[14] The rebels' infrastructure, though modest and rudimentary, was efficient. Control of their base areas near the northern frontiers was complete and ruthless: some seventy per cent of their manpower was concentrated there, including a growing proportion of forced conscripts, women and Slavo-Macedonians. The 'state of Grammos', as it was sometimes called, had its own system of administration, education, justice and communications. Supply-routes from Albania, Yugoslavia and Bulgaria radiated across the frontiers and penetrated deep into southern Greece, including the Peloponnese and the islands. The scale and quality of military equipment improved, though it was always mixed, and short of ammunition and spares. In addition to rifles, automatics and grenades, the Democratic Army had available land-mines, flame-throwers and artillery, including anti-tank and anti-aircraft guns. The formal weapons-table of rebel units was never in fact completely filled, but there was enough to do great damage in ambushes and guerrilla attacks.

There were, however, notable failures, which were periodically admit-ted in frank discussion. One was the unsatisfactory level of voluntary recruitment; another, the lack of sufficient support from the northern neighbours; and even the counter-productive effect of looting and atroci-ties was bluntly assessed.[15] Most disturbing of all was the failure to achieve any success in the cities. The working class as such was indifferent to the struggle, and offered little resistance as the Government gradually brought the trade unions under control. Although the *Aftoámyna* was successful as a clandestine organisation, it had no prospect of developing an urban guerrilla warfare. According to an open letter from the Politburo dated 30 March 1948, its main tasks were to send men to the mountains – a reversal of Zakhariadis's earlier policy – and to organise an 'armed struggle in the towns'.[16] Of the latter there were few signs, apart from one or two acts of individual violence: Ladas, the Minister of Justice, was murdered in Athens at the beginning of May; George Polk, an American journalist, was abducted in Salonika and later found dead in the sea during June;[17] and incitements to assassinate leading Greek commanders, such as 'the butcher Tsakalotos', were issued from Markos's GHQ. Zakhariadis criticised the organisation of the KKE in the cities, starting with the treachery of Siantos. In October the entire Politburo of the organisation in Athens was dismissed. But in fact they failed because their task was impossible.

The rebels failed because the mass of the Greek people was against them. The year 1948 was the one in which, for all the disappointments that were to come, that psychological fact became indisputable. There were other factors at work: the growing scale of United States aid, the moral support of the British presence, the discord within the Communist alliance, the reports of the United Nations Special Committee on the Balkans (UNSCOB) and the consequent votes in the General Assembly. But none of these could have been decisive without a clear determination on the part of the Greek people. Undoubtedly they had real grievances which the KKE could exploit. It is inconceivable that the Democratic Army was entirely recruited and retained under arms by force. Zapheiropoulos fairly gives credit to the democratic character of its organisation, and estimates its non-Communist component as high as seventy per cent, while emphasising also the extreme brutality of the discipline imposed on them.[18] Greece was indeed genuinely, not artificially, divided. There was right and wrong on both sides. But when the Greek people had to choose, on balance, if without enthusiasm or euphoria, they deliberately chose the nation-state they knew rather than the Communist paradise they were offered.

The moment of awakening is generally identified with the shock of Konitsa. It was then that a total mobilisation of resources began. Men who had evaded military service were conscripted, and one -- the son of a wealthy businessman -- was shot for evasion. Communists abroad were deprived of their nationality and in some cases condemned to death *in absentia*. A determined drive against the *Aftoámyna* was launched, assisted in Athens by the fact that the murderer of Ladas was immediately caught and talked freely. Communists trying to escape abroad, including Manolis Glezos, were caught, tried and condemned to death. A wave of executions -- at least fifty in February alone -- led to protests from abroad, and consequently to a number of reprieves. Widespread arrests led to some notable successes, including the disruption of a group of Communist conspirators in the Navy during March. Vigorous action was also extended to the trade unions. The ninth Congress of the General Confederation of Trade Unions was held at the end of March without the participation of ERGAS; and despite the denunciation of its proceedings by the KKE and a dispute between rival anti-Communist leaders, the Government's nominee, Photis Makris, emerged as Secretary-General.[19] In these conditions it was hardly necessary to make strikes illegal: a General Strike over wages was in fact threatened in the middle of 1948, but called off at the last minute through the intervention of American labour advisers.[20] The Government was gradually reasserting its control over the principal instruments of state.

The mood of the year was a balance of hopes and fears. The hopeful signs were mostly the fruits of American aid. Traffic by road between Athens and Salonika was restored, though only in military convoys; the Corinth Canal was reopened; so were some stretches of the railway; and the equipment, training and morale of the armed forces visibly improved. In external relations there were a number of encouraging signs. The Dodecanese was transferred to Greece under the peace treaty with Italy; and the King hinted publicly at a similar claim to Cyprus on 27 July, though this was rebuffed by the British Government and disowned, under pressure, by his own Prime Minister. The value of the British connection came increasingly into question as that with the USA grew stronger, but few Greeks wished to see it lapse altogether. Although the British Army HQ withdrew in January from Athens to Salonika, and British officers took no part in anti-guerrilla operations, important links remained: British missions continued to train all three services, British officers served in the mixed General Staff group with their Greek and American counterparts, and British equipment, including Spitfires in the Air Force and rifles in the Army, continued to be used until the USA could gradually replace them.

Britain's moral support was more significant. Ernest Bevin's hostility to Communism was an asset to the Greek Government, which was otherwise unpopular with most of his party. At a time when his Australian colleague, Dr Evatt, was being notably lukewarm at the United Nations, Bevin took an opportunity at the Labour Party Conference on 19 May to defend the Greek Government before a critical audience. Privately, he went further. He sent the former commander of the British Mission to the Partisans, Fitzroy Maclean, on a secret visit to Tito, to persuade him of the unwisdom of his policy towards Greece. In dealing with Albania he was even more uncompromising, having never forgiven the Communist government for mining British destroyers in the Corfu Strait in 1946. Misled by inaccurate reports of the strength of potential resistance to Communism within the country, he gave tacit sanction to the formation of a 'Free Albanian' organisation abroad, which mounted a disastrously unsuccessful attempt to infiltrate anti-Communist agents into Albania in the hope of undermining the Government. The operation was betrayed in advance, but there was little reason to expect it to succeed in any case. The only result of these policies was to identify Bevin as fully committed to Greek anti-communism.

Greece was accustomed to the British, but the Americans were an uncertain quantity. They were apt to assume that history began when they first came on the scene. The Greeks found them naïve at first, as they knew little of the background of the civil war. It seemed ironic that the same people who had shown a benevolent neutrality towards EAM and ELAS during their conflict with the British in 1944 were now engaged in a conflict of their own with the same enemy. The Greeks also found them harder to deal with than the British: more inflexible, less adaptable, less willing to make allowances, more inclined to impose American methods regardless of national characteristics. On the other hand, they had great advantages. They came fresh to the job, without the staleness and disillusionment which characterised the British in the post-war years. They were vigorous, resourceful and immensely efficient. Both the officers of the American Mission for Aid to Greece (AMAG) and the civilians of the European Co-operation Administration (ECA) learned their jobs fast.

To begin with they underestimated the scale of their task. It was not at first sight obvious that Greece had suffered more severely than the rest of Europe under German occupation, and that since 1945 conditions in many areas had grown worse instead of better. Nor was it obvious how differently the economic suffering was distributed in comparison with the years of enemy occupation. Nature has divided Greece, both economically and strategically, into distinct geographical units. First, there is the division between the cities and the provinces – more absolute than elsewhere, for Athens, Piraeus and Salonika between them comprise a quarter of the population. The provinces in turn are divided between the mountains and the plains. The islands are another distinct world. Of the four components – cities, mountains, plains, islands – only the plains and some islands (notably Crete) were economically self-supporting. In normal times their population could not only feed and maintain themselves but also helped to support the mountains and the cities, though large quantities of food had also to be imported from abroad. Under the German occupation therefore the plains suffered least, except when they were the scene of military operations. They did not starve, as many people did both in the cities and in the mountains. Between 1941 and 1945 the greatest suffering was in Athens and other major towns.

After 1946, however, the balance of suffering was different. The mountains themselves were now the scene of ferocious warfare, which they had been only exceptionally under the German occupation. In the plains it was impossible either to maintain agricultural production or to restore and develop industries, since there too the rebels were constantly active. The cities suffered much less. Apart from occasional incidents, they were spared from the fighting. Being for the most part on or near the sea, they were accessible to supplies from abroad, which had been cut off during the Occupation. Athens, Salonika and other cities therefore suffered less than the provinces, though they had other problems: for instance, the accommodation of hundreds of thousands of refugees from the fighting areas, and the complete disruption of communications with the rest of Greece. Such problems demanded resources and administrative abilities which were lacking. The Greeks were tempted to meet them by demanding more aid from the USA, and by resigning the management of their affairs into American hands. The signs of demoralisation were disquieting, and led more than once to threats by senior American officials of abandoning Greece altogether. From the summer of 1948, when the Soviet blockade of Berlin started, the US Government had more important claims on its attention and resources. But from the Greek point of view it seemed evident that if a major war broke out, their country would become more and not less important than before.

It was the combination of complacency and defeatism which nearly reduced the Americans to despair. The commander of the American Military Mission, General Van Fleet, who took up his post on 7 February 1948, was a vigorous and fearless soldier who spoke his mind. He was quick to see which of the Greek commanders were competent and which owed their appointments to political intrigue. He saw to it that able men like Vendiris and Tsakalotos were brought back to the fore, but he was unable to relegate the failures entirely to the background, if they enjoyed political favour. The relative failure of operations in 1948 was due chiefly to poor commanders and low morale.[21] The wrangles over tactics between senior generals make pitiful reading.[22] It was largely to overcome the inadequacy in the high command that strong pressure developed, from as early as February 1948, to recall Papagos as Commander-in-Chief; but his terms were unacceptable at that time. Unfortunately there were more or less valid excuses available to the high command for their shortcomings. Changes in training from British to American methods, the introduction of new tactics, the belated delivery of weapons, and the ceiling imposed on the expansion of the armed forces, were all held to blame.

Of all the excuses offered, the least unjustifiable concerned military supplies. The Greeks did not realise how long shipments would take, but the Americans did not immediately realise what was needed. A post-war analysis concluded that AMAG did not achieve its full results until after hostilities were over.[23] Automatic rifles and machine-guns reached only two operational Divisions by the end of the civil war; rocket-launchers and recoil-less rifles were in service only in the closing weeks. The need for mules and mountain artillery was appreciated only late in 1948 – in the latter case, partly through a direct initiative by Queen Frederika to General Marshall.[24] The importance of the Navy and the Air Force was only slowly appreciated, no doubt because the rebels possessed neither (though ELAN was reactivated to operate a handful of *caiques*). Only six American patrol craft were added to the Navy, which was no stronger at the end of the war than at the beginning; and Helldivers entered service in the Air Force only in the last days. There was prolonged hesitation before controversial new weapons such as napalm were provided to the national forces. Some Communist apologists report napalm in use in 1948; Greek historians say that requests for napalm were refused; its use is only certain in the closing stages.[25] Allegations of the use of gas and defoliants seem less plausible, at any stage.[26]

The main burden of complaint against the Americans was that they would not raise the permitted level of the armed forces high enough. The manpower ceiling for the Army rose from 120,000 in 1947 to 132,000 early in 1948, and then to 147,000 in May, largely in order to allow suffi-cient time for training replacements. But losses were at their peak in 1948: the casualty rate for officers (killed, wounded and missing) was over 100 a month, and over 1,700 a month for other ranks.[27] Both figures were more than four times higher than in 1947, whereas the casualty rate of the Democratic Army had little more than doubled. The length of training in the National Army was progressively reduced from seventeen weeks to eight and later to six weeks.[28] To improve these un-satisfactory figures the Greek high command pressed for even further increases. In January 1948 the National Defence Corps (commonly known as the *Ethnophrourà*) was formed, to take over the local 'home guard' functions of the former MAY and MAD, with an initial establishment of 20,000 men which was soon increased to 50,000. Still it was not enough. By the end of the civil war the total of all services was 232,500 (including 13,500 in the Navy and 7,500 in the Air Force); but General Papagos was demanding 250,000 for the Army alone. In fact the rebels came near to forcing on the Government a concentration of resources on the military programme which would have led to the collapse of the national economy.

The order of battle in the spring of 1948 still consisted basically of three Army Corps, though each was stronger than in the previous year. Their main reinforcement came from the National Defence Corps (*Ethnophrourà*). The garrison of the Peloponnese consisted entirely of thirteen battalions of *Ethnophrourà*. North of the Isthmus of Corinth, with an area reaching up to a line from Preveza to Volos, I Corps consisted of three divisions and eighteen battalions of *Ethnophrourà*. North of I Corps, with an area bounded by the northern frontier and on the east by a line from Edessa to Mount Olympus, was II Corps comprising three divisions and thirty battalions of *Ethnophrourà*. East of II Corps, with responsibility for the whole north-eastern area, was III Corps comprising two divisions and thirty-three battalions of *Ethnophrourà*. The distribution of regular forces and National Defence Corps reflected the General Staff's estimate of the likely burden of operations. It was expected to fall most heavily on I and II Corps (in other words, in Roumeli, Thessaly and the north-west), which therefore had six regular divisions between them. Areas like the Peloponnese and the north-east, where no more than holding operations were expected, had to rely predominantly on the *Ethnophrourà*.[29]

It was not increased numbers that the Greek forces needed most in 1948; nor was it more equipment. What they needed was greater efficiency, more determination and new tactics. The early months of the year held the promise that all these would be forthcoming, but the promise faded by the autumn. In a sense the Americans were the victims of British failings. The training effort of the British missions had been half-hearted and misdirected. It was assumed that a long period of peaceful reorganisation lay ahead, while security could be left to the police. Even if it had been realised by the British missions that there would be years of bitter fighting in a style more familiar under the German occupation than on the European fronts of the Second World War, there were few officers available with the necessary experience. Criticism of British training methods by American officers was justified. Unit training was neglected; the formation of Commandos was an inappropriate expedient; and foreign interference in senior appointments was resented. But the improvements introduced by the Joint US Military Advisory and Planning Group (JUSMAPG) were not in the end decisive, because their fruits came too late. It was the Greek high command itself which eventually, at the eleventh hour, achieved its own regeneration; and the new tactics which came near to complete success in 1948 were devised by Greek initiative, with no more than moral support from JUSMAPG.

Although they came near to complete success, it was not quite near enough. An attempt to take the initiative before the end of the winter, by clearing the Mourgana salient in Epirus, failed twice in February and

March (Operations Pergamos and Falcon).[30] The campaigning season
proper began in mid-April with Operation Dawn, to clear Roumeli of the
rebels. Among the principal lessons learned from the previous season, two
of particular value were put into effect. First, no time-limit was imposed;
secondly, the tactics of sweeping up the valleys, without either destroying
the rebels or holding ground against their return, were replaced by hot
pursuit in successive waves. Both innovations implied that the National
Army was better off for manpower and equipment than in 1947, and even
better off than was willingly admitted to the Americans. There were still,
however, important lessons which had not been learned. One was that
winter handicapped the Democratic Army more than its opponents, since
their movements were more restricted by weather conditions and more
visible to aerial reconnaissance. Because the national forces neglected
their advantage, the rebels had succeeded during the winter months in
spreading back into Roumeli: the areas of Navpaktia, Lokris and Sper-
kheiada, the island of Evvoia, and even Mount Parnes overlooking Athens,
were now infested with units of the Democratic Army. The national
forces were also slow to learn the advantages of attack by night. Despite
the decisions taken at Volos in the previous autumn, night operations
were rarely ventured.

There had been, however, some improvement on the part of the
commanding generals. Tsakalotos took over I Corps at the end of February
1948, and issued an aggressive order of the day to which he consistently
adhered. His Corps HQ was established in Athens, but he moved it forward to Lamia and kept it mobile. Before launching operations on 15
April, he made his first target the *Aftoámyna*. Some 4,500 suspects were
arrested during March throughout Roumeli. No doubt many were harm-
less, but a sufficient number of subversive agents was caught to dislocate
the *Aftoámyna* and to demonstrate the improvement in the Government's
intelligence system. The disadvantage of the preliminary round-up was to
give the KKE early warning of the impending attack. But Tsakalotos had
other tactical surprises in store. On 13–14 April a diversionary raid into
the mountains of Agrapha by a Commando battalion neutralised an important rebel HQ at the village of Mastrogianni and established the initiative
in tactical aggression for the first time on the side of the National Army.[31]
Next, instead of a sweep from south to north, as in 1947, which had the
effect of driving the rebels back to their more secure bases, Operation
Dawn aimed to concentrate and crush them in central Roumeli. A series
of concentric drives from the Lamia–Karpenisi road in the north, from
Agrinion in the west, and from the mountains of Giona and Parnassus in
the east, caught the main forces of the Democratic Army in the valley of

the River Mornos, north of Lidoriki. To the south, their escape was
barred by the Gulf of Corinth, which was patrolled by the Navy.

By 15 May, when the operation ceased, the rebels had suffered a severe
but not decisive defeat. According to Tsakalotos's own estimate, they
suffered two thousand casualties and only some four hundred escaped.[32]
The official historians gave a less optimistic picture: the area of central
Roumeli was not completely cleared, and many rebels escaped to the
north from Agrapha and Orthrys.[33] The operations could only be called
successful on balance, because they relieved the forces preparing to
assault Grammos from the risk of attack from the south. The same was
true of the operations launched in May by the National Army's III Corps
in the north-east and II Corps in the north-west, to complete the isolation
of the Democratic Army in Grammos. These operations too had only
moderate success. Central and Eastern Macedonia and Thrace were largely
cleared of rebels between March and May by a series of operations in the
mountains stretching from Vermion eastward to the Turkish frontier; but
the rebels' unrestricted freedom of movement across the Yugoslav and
Bulgarian frontiers, which UNSCOB was already able to confirm, made
these successes of little value. In Epirus the Mourgana salient was finally
cleared in early September at the third attempt; but again the rebels were
able to retreat into Albania. Meanwhile the Democratic Army showed its
resilience by launching attacks in the Peloponnese – on Sparta and Kalavryta in April, and on Tripoli in August.

When the National Army launched Operation Summit to clear Grammos in the middle of June, there were already signs that it was premature
and inadequately planned. Initially the high command suffered from over-
confidence. For the first time there was strong air-cover by Spitfires; the
National Army's fire-power was much increased; and morale was high.
The order of battle even included a battalion drawn exclusively from the
reindoctrination camp on Makronisos. The operation was directed by II
Corps under General Kalogeropoulos, who had six divisions under his
command. Expert opinion was that this was too large a combination for
a single formation to control. The Corps HQ at first failed to keep in
sufficiently close touch with the divisional commanders, and later inter-
fered with them too much. Their difficulties were increased by the terrain. The only communication by road between the divisions in Epirus
and those in Macedonia was through Ioannina, Metsovo and Kalambaka,
a long and circuitous route. The location of the Corps HQ at Larisa was
remote from both sectors. The plan of operations was dismissed by Tsakalotos as 'childish', and Zapheiropoulos also criticised it for relying too
much on frontal attacks against strongly prepared positions.[34] The effec-

tiveness of the Democratic Army's artillery and mines came as a shock to the national forces. Some of the latter's commanders lost their nerve and had to be replaced in mid-battle, including the Corps Commander himself. Nevertheless it would be wrong to dismiss Operation Summit as a failure. Tactically, it was a victory for the National Army, though its strategic outcome was disappointing.[35]

Grammos is a complex of almost impassable mountains straddling the frontier between Greece and Albania. Its highest ridge is the watershed between two great rivers, rising within a mile or two of each other: the Sarandoporos, which flows south and then west to join the Aöos, and thence through Albania (where they become the River Drin) into the Adriatic; and the Aliakmon, which flows east to reach the Thermaic Gulf on the Aegean within a few miles of the Vardar, an even greater and more historic river. A motor-road has been constructed since the civil war through the Sarandoporos valley, to connect Konitsa in Epirus with Neapolis, which lies between Kastoria and Siatista in Western Macedonia. But in 1948 no road crossed the northern Pindus range anywhere north of the Metsovo pass. To the west, the Grammos range is bounded by the road across the Albanian frontier from Epirus to Korytsa. Almost the whole length of it lies in Albania, so it was available only to the Democratic Army and its Communist allies. To the north the range is bounded by a road from Korytsa to Florina, only part of which was usable by motor transport. The roads bounding the east flank of Grammos (Kastoria–Siatista–Grevena–Kalambaka) and the south flank (Kalambaka–Metsovo–Ioannina) were under the National Army's control; but even these were subject to ambush and sabotage. From a variety of points minor roads penetrated short distances into the mountains: as far as Konitsa from the south-west and Pendalophos from the east, for example; but all came to a sudden end in the foothills of Grammos. In the centre of the range lies Aëtomilitsa, where Markos had his GHQ and seat of government. The name appropriately combines a Greek with a Slavonic root.

His defences were arranged in a horse-shoe round Aëtomilitsa, the forward posts being some ten to fifteen miles from his command-post. The curve of the horse-shoe fronted east and south, the tips pointed north-west. Connecting the tips was the highest ridge of Grammos, over eight thousand feet, which formed the frontier with Albania. Only if the National Army could gain control of this ridge could they destroy the rebels without hope of escape; but the lightning assault necessary to cut off Markos's force from its base in Albania was beyond the capacity of the Greek high command. They chose instead to drive frontally on the target area from Konitsa, Metsovo, Neapolis and Nestorion, as though to squeeze, reduce and crush the perimeter of the horse-shoe. It was an un-imaginative plan, and the execution was indifferent. The official historians give a melancholy account of the operational conference at Kozani a few days after the attack had started.[36] Kalogeropoulos was already pessimistic; Giantzis overruled him, but issued conflicting orders; Van Fleet and the American and British officers who were present hesitated to intervene. For once, in Tsakalotos's opinion, criticism in the press of the Greek high command was justified.[37] The results were such as might have been expected.

Bitter fighting on Grammos lasted from 14 June to 22 August. The resistance was strengthened by a failure of intelligence on the part of the National Army. Although a deception plan had been prepared and deliber-ately leaked to the rebels, they knew that it was false and they also knew the details of the real plan.[38] In consequence they were able to beat off the two main assaults – on the heights of Smolikas, north-east of Konitsa, and Ammouda, north-west of Nestorion – throughout the latter part of June and the whole of July. It was not until the first week of August that the National Army broke through to capture the two key heights. Once they had fallen, there was little difficulty in capturing the remaining objectives and gaining complete control of Grammos. Only in the last stages of Operation Summit was the National Army able to push a force north-eastwards from the River Sarandoporos to seize the topmost ridge of Grammos which formed the frontier with Albania. A tiny chapel was built on the peak, and a thanksgiving was offered. Such was perhaps the intended symbolism of the code-name, Operation Summit. But it was al-ready too late, and final victory had once more eluded the National Army.

It had been assumed that if Grammos was cleared, the rebel state of which it formed the nucleus would cease to exist. But since they were free to retreat into Albania and re-emerge elsewhere, the assumption was baseless. The destruction of the KKE's organisation in the Grammos region perhaps actually helped Markos to revert to the type of guerrilla warfare in which he excelled. So it was a Pyrrhic victory which the National Army gained from Operation Summit. The state of Grammos was virtually eliminated, at an estimated cost of some 7,000 casualties to the National Army and nearly 10,000 to the Democratic Army (including more than 2,000 who were captured or surrendered voluntarily).[39] But Markos escaped with some 6,000 of his forces into Albania, and returned a few weeks later into Mount Vitsi, some distance further north. So far from losing heart, the Democratic Army actually undertook diversionary operations on a large scale during the summer, behind the lines of the National Army's advance. In June and July they attacked Asprangeloi,

Igoumenitsa and Arta in Epirus; Ptolemais, Vogiatsiko and Kozani in Macedonia; Amphilokhia, Karpenisi and Amphissa in Roumeli; and in August and September they attacked Kalambaka, Trikkala, Tyrnavos, Agyia and Larisa in Thessaly.[40] They also launched a campaign of forced recruitment in the Peloponnese during July.

Instead of raising morale, the end of Operation Summit had a depressing effect on the Greek high command. On 20 July, while the operation was still at its height, Kalogeropoulos was relieved of the command of II Corps, which was split into more manageable components. At the same time Tsakalotos, with the HQ of I Corps, was moved to Ioannina to take command of the Epirus sector, where he quickly cleared the area of Souli from rebel activity and brought the National Army's protracted attacks on the Mourgana salient to a successful conclusion by mid-September. But on the Macedonian sector much worse was to follow. The new Corps Commander, General Kitrilakis, had previously been Deputy Chief of the General Staff, and as such was partly responsible for the planning of Operation Summit. Tsakalotos, indeed, held him more to blame than Kalogeropoulos, and openly called him a defeatist and a political intriguer.[41] Kitrilakis seems to have had little confidence in Operation Summit, and he forecast on 9 August that the rebels would re-emerge in Vitsi because the numbers that had escaped into Albania were too numerous to be allowed to stay there.[42] The closing stages of Operation Summit were carried through by I Corps under Tsakalotos, who claimed that by 21 August he had taken not only all his own Corps' targets but most of those of II Corps as well. When the Democratic Army re-entered Greece and occupied Vitsi in September, several units of II Corps panicked and fled. For some days there was a serious risk that Kastoria would fall to the rebels, who made two determined efforts, on 20 September and 10 October, to clinch their victory. Kitrilakis resigned his command and was replaced by Papagiorgiou, who proved himself no more effective.

The confidence of the national forces was now at a low ebb. Sophoulis personally visited Kastoria in October to restore morale; but the National Army was incapable of any further major effort during 1948. The military authorities, looking back on the sorry episode, were emphatic in their verdict though differing about the reasons for it. One of the divisional commanders, General Petzopoulos — the same who had written the pessimistic appreciation in February 1947 — wrote that 'on Vitsi there was no lack of forces, but of direction and command'. Tsakalotos ominously concluded that 'the balance had begun to turn against the national forces'.[43] He laid the blame partly on the demoralisation of Papagiorgiou, who was replaced after only a few weeks in command of II Corps; and partly on the policy of putting veterans of the Albanian war of 1940 in the front line while young recruits, without family commitments, were left at the rear. Zapheiropoulos, who was not personally involved, gave a more circumstantial explanation.[44] He blamed the rout at Kastoria on inadequate commanders, on insufficient forces, on their weariness and the fall of their morale in face of the unexpected recovery of the Democratic Army, on delays due to successive changes in the Corps command, on the interventions of the allied missions and other causes, most of them remediable. But it was evident once more that victory was after all not yet in sight, and that it depended on factors which were for the most part not within the soldiers' control: on the raising of morale by the Government, on the appointment of capable commanders, on American support and supplies, on the backing of the United Nations, on disunity within the Communist alliance and above all within the KKE and the Democratic Army.

On the last count, the Government still had little ground for high hopes. With significant exceptions, the rebels' morale remained high throughout 1948. An illustration of it can be seen in the diary of a schoolmaster from Olympus serving in the Democratic Army.[45] He took part in the escort of a large column of over 1,000 men, including unarmed new recruits, which was sent from Thessaly to reinforce Grammos in March. The journey took over seven weeks on foot, under constant harassment from the National Army and Air Force. The men also suffered extremes of hunger and cold. In the first two days there were more than twenty cases of frost-bitten feet. Mules died of starvation. After three days of continuous fighting, the column had to take charge additionally of over 700 refugees from destroyed villages, these including sick and wounded, children and old people. During the next week 15 men had died of cold and exposure; a number of others deserted – presumably forced conscripts. A week later it was found 40 more men had vanished from the column, and 65 were suffering from frost-bite. The losses in action were less serious, but they amounted to at least 20. In the end, they failed to reach Grammos, and by the late summer the diarist was back in Olympus. His time was divided between teaching and fighting: losses were still heavy, and the cold was again severe as early as November; but his confidence was unshaken. Very different, however, but unknown to the rank and file, were the reactions of Zachariadis. After the battle of Grammos he ordered the execution of one of his senior officers for failing in his duty; and it was said that he tried to have Markos murdered during the retreat into Albania.[46]

Morale was even more a cause for concern at the top level on the

Government's side. The narrow escape from disaster at Kastoria shook the Government, and drove it first to desperate measures and then almost to collapse. On 29 October martial law was proclaimed throughout the country. During November, the Greek representative at the United Nations admitted some 1,500 executions in the past two years, but the Communists claimed that there had been 2,150 up to June alone.[47] On 4 November ten seamen were condemned to death in Athens, including the leading Communist Ambatielos, who had a British wife. The Greek Seamen's Union (OENO), which had powerful contacts abroad, was able to mobilise pressure at the United Nations on the condemned men's behalf; and even a number of Greek Liberal Deputies signed a telegram to the President of the UN General Assembly (who happened to be Dr Evatt, the Australian Labour Government's Minister for External Affairs) appealing for a suspension of execution. At the same time the debates in the General Assembly and its Political Committee on the reports of UNSCOB had unleashed furious attacks on Greece by the Communist delegates, and revealed some reluctance to defend the Greek Government on the part of western powers, particularly Australia and France. The Americans were hinting again at a withdrawal from Greece, which was openly demanded by Svolos and other fellow-travellers.[48]

Sophoulis conceded the suspension of the death sentences on Ambatielos and others, and accepted the resolution of the United Nations, passed on 11 November, that Greece and her northern neighbours should undertake negotiations to settle their differences through the good offices of Dr Evatt and the Secretary General of the UN, Trygve Lie. But he did so with a heavy heart, and repudiated any suggestion of compromise with the Greek rebels. Confidence in his capacity to lead the country to victory at an age well over eighty was waning, and his control of Parliament began to disintegrate with the decision of Venizelos and Papandreou (who were not Ministers) that they would no longer support him. Sophoulis offered his resignation on 12 November and advised the King to offer the mandate to Tsaldaris; but in the evenly divided parliament Tsaldaris was unable to form a government, and Sophoulis was recalled on 18 November to form a new coalition with Tsaldaris as Deputy Prime Minister. He won a vote of confidence on 21 November by the narrow margin of 169 to 167, and almost immediately afterwards became seriously ill. One of the more important changes in the new government was the replacement of the Populist Stratos by the Liberal Rendis as Minister of War. Although it made no substantial difference to the planning of operations, the change corroborated the impression that something was seriously wrong with the high command.

What was lacking was the impetus of aggressive and determined generals. Three changes in as many months in the command of II Corps were evidence of inadequacy. A temporary solution was found in the appointment on 27 October of Tsakalotos, the successful commander of I Corps, to command II Corps as well, although he had himself earlier argued that one of the causes of the failure in the summer had been the concentration of too many divisions on two separate sectors under a single commander. He was a sick man at the time, and his relations with the equally strong-minded American General, Van Fleet, were an uncertain factor. His demands for freedom of tactical manoeuvre from the Ionian Sea to Mount Vermion (the boundary with III Corps) together with control over the appointment of senior officers, caused some anxiety. To make matters worse, he had a narrow escape from death when his aircraft struck a mine while landing at Florina on 29 October. But his energy and confidence soon had a stimulating effect. He set up his Corps HQ at Kozani, with an advanced tactical HQ at Argos Orestikon a few miles south of Kastoria; he replaced most of the staff officers of II Corps; and he set about meeting as many officers and men as possible to brief them frankly and redress their grievances. In many respects he proved himself, perhaps consciously, a Greek Montgomery.

He had an early opportunity to justify his appointment when the Democratic Army captured the height of Bikovik, overlooking Kastoria, on the night of 10–11 November. A determined counter-attack re-took it three days later. To compare small things with greater, it may be called the National Army's El Alamein, redeeming the Tobruk which they had suffered in Vitsi. Tsakalotos rapidly made a few fresh dispositions, bringing the Ninth Division from Epirus to reinforce the defence of Kastoria. There were protests from Giantzis, and also from Van Fleet, on the grounds that the Ninth Division was destined for the Peloponnese. But Tsakalotos overbore them: 'When Kastoria falls,' he declared, 'there will be no Peloponnese.' Giantzis yielded, as did Van Fleet after a night's reflection. Tsakalotos proceeded at once to submit a devastating appreciation of the reasons for past failure, all directly deriving from the roots of morale.[49] There must, he argued, be more financial help for officers' families; more decorations for bravery; more privileges for the infantry; more liberal promotion. Evasion of military service must be suppressed; incompetent officers must be removed; arms must be distributed to civilians in the villages; the General Staff must be reorganised. He did not hesitate to criticise Kitrilakis, who was now again Deputy CGS, and the high command in general.

All this was true and well said; but Kitrilakis and the high command had another idea, which was shared by Sophoulis. They believed that only the appointment of Papagos as Commander-in-Chief could save the situation. He was the victor of Albania in 1940; his conduct under the German occupation was impeccable, if not glorious; he was senior to all other generals, none of whom sufficiently outranked the rest; and he enjoyed the confidence of the King. The suggestion was mooted several times during 1948. Kitrilakis had proposed the appointment of a Commander-in-Chief in February, though without specifically naming Papagos for the post.[50] Papagos received it coolly, especially after he witnessed Operation Dawn as an observer with Van Fleet. In June Sophoulis consulted his service Ministers on the possibility, but found them unreceptive. On 9 July, nevertheless, Sophoulis put the proposal to the King, who advised him not to press it against his colleagues' advice. With the change of Ministers in November, the subject was reopened. Papagos himself had laid down his conditions of acceptance in a letter to Sophoulis on 11 November: complete control of planning, order of battle, appointments and operations; no interference by the allied missions; martial law throughout the country, with strict censorship; and command over the Navy, Air Force and Gendarmerie as well as the Army.[51] These demands had not yet been agreed by the end of the year.

Papagos's demands had implications for Greece's international relations. On the one hand, he expressed doubts of the reliability of the United Nations as a defender of the country's integrity, and therefore required an army of at least 250,000 men to win the civil war. On the other hand, such a force would require American support on a still greater scale. But if the American Government could not secure the backing of the United Nations, in which the USA was by far the most powerful member, then the inclination to abandon the costly struggle might well prove decisive in Washington. The Americans were vigorous in mobilising support for the Greek Government at the United Nations, because there the enemy was the Soviet Union. But they were critical of the Greek Government's performance and loth to meet all its material demands. Despite this reluctance, a substantial increase of appropriations for military aid to Greece was agreed in February 1948 for the period to the end of June, and again in June for the following period. The allocation of civil aid under the Marshall Plan for 1948–9 was also generous. By the end of September economic aid to Greece from the USA since the beginning totalled 114 million dollars, military aid totalled 260 million dollars, and the strength of the armed forces had reached 168,500. The equipment supplied amounted to 140 aircraft, 3,890 guns and mortars, 97,000 rifles and 10,000 motor vehicles; and since some 26,000 rebels had been eliminated, they had cost ten thousand dollars a head.[52] But on 6 October the State Department made it known that the Greeks were demanding still further increases. Later in the same month General Marshall himself visited Athens to assess the situation.

Dissatisfaction was plain in statements made by a number of American authorities: for example, by President Truman himself in his quarterly reports to Congress on the Greek–Turkish aid programme; by Ambassador Griswold on behalf of AMAG on 11 March; and by Paul Hoffman on behalf of ECA on 20 April and 11 September. Truman's second report on 16 February spoke of 'ever-increasing pressure' and hinted that 'if the guerrilla menace should increase as a result of greater outside assistance, a new situation would be created which would have to be dealt with in the light of circumstances prevailing at the time'. On 6 December he blamed the 'military stalemate' partly on foreign aid to the rebels but also partly on the Greek Army's lack of determination. Griswold in March pointed gloomily to the fact that in spite of superior fire-power and 'magnificent fighting men', the National Army was doing no more than to contain the Communist forces. The reports of ECA were not, of course, confined to Greece. In the first year of the European Recovery Programme, from 1 April 1948, Greece was to rank tenth, receiving 146 million dollars, as against 600 million dollars for Italy and 500 million dollars for the Netherlands. The Greeks thought that the West did not realise how desperate was their predicament; they were not much more encouraged by the proceedings of the United Nations Special Committee on the Balkans during 1948.

Circumstances imposed differences on the reports of UNSCOB from those of its predecessor, the UN Commission of Investigation. Although its national composition was nominally the same, being drawn from the membership of the Security Council, the two Communist governments, Russian and Polish, never filled their places in UNSCOB; and the Communist states adjoining Greece refused to admit UNSCOB representatives, with one exception in Bulgaria. The observer teams of UNSCOB, five in number, were therefore limited to observation from the Greek side of the frontier, and their reports were denounced by left-wing critics as biased. Even the French and Australian members of UNSCOB more than once dissented from their colleagues. The successive reports of UNSCOB to the General Assembly — in June, September and October 1948, and again in 1949 and 1950 — were unavoidably one-sided. But few of their conclusions were open to serious doubt. Since their tasks included securing the co-operation of the four Balkan neighbours in establishing normal diplomatic relations, drafting frontier conventions and handling the problems of refugees, it is undeniable that they were frustrated by the total refusal of the Albanian, Yugoslav and Bulgarian Governments to cooperate. More controversial were their allegations about aid to the Democratic Army from across the frontiers, including the free movement of rebel troops and the abduction of Greek children.

Although they were bitterly argued, there is little doubt that they were substantially true. To the Slavo-Macedonians, who were increasingly numerous in the Democratic Army, the truth was itself an absurdity, since they did not recognise the frontier as anything but an offence. They scarcely troubled to conceal their movements across it. On many occasions the UNSCOB observers witnessed convoys of troops and supplies actually crossing the frontier; they observed supporting fire from points in Albanian territory during rebel attacks on the National Army; and they questioned prisoners and defectors from the Democratic Army who admitted that they had been trained and equipped outside Greece. Their general conclusion on each occasion was that the Greek guerrillas (whom they never called rebels) 'have received aid and assistance from Albania, Bulgaria and Yugoslavia'.[53] They identified a rebel camp at Moskhopolis, ten miles west of Korytsa; and they reported the capture of a *caique* loaded with arms and propaganda from Albania in a bay of the Peloponnese on 6 September. Their only direct contacts with the Communist powers came on 29 April, when they briefly entered Bulgaria to terminate a frontier clash for which they held the Greeks to blame; and on 6–8 September, when a clash between Greek and Yugoslav forces at Koutsoubei caused twenty deaths among the latter. A number of prisoners were taken on both sides, whose release was secured by UNSCOB.

Perhaps the Committee's most intractable problem was to arrive at the truth about the children whom the Communists were alleged to have abducted. That many Greek children had gone from their homes across the northern frontiers was not in doubt. UNSCOB recorded an admission by the Yugoslav Red Cross that a 'considerable number' of Greek children had passed through their hands. The rebel government made no secret of the fact, claiming that they had removed the children from the fighting zone in their own interests. A year later Dr Kokkalis, who was responsible for education in the Provisional Democratic Government, invited the International Red Cross to send a deputation to investigate the circumstances.[54] Although UNSCOB established that 23,696 children had been removed (a figure later raised to about 28,000), only 10,344 applications were made for repatriation after the civil war was over.[55] The problem facing UNSCOB was that, since they were not allowed to enter any of the Communist countries, they could not verify the facts. Some independent observers were more fortunate: a BBC correspondent, for example, visited a hostel for 170 Greek children between two and fifteen years old at Plovdiv in Bulgaria.[56] But second-hand information was not an adequate basis for UNSCOB's conclusions, which were consequently controversial.

The debates in the General Assembly on the UNSCOB reports invariably led to divisions on lines determined by the Cold War. Most of the facts were plain, though some judgments were questionable. The Australian representatives consistently maintained that it was beyond the competence of UNSCOB to pass judgments at all. The Greek Government criticised UNSCOB for failing to insist on entering the Communist countries, for taking the Bulgarian side in the disputed incident of 29 April and for the weakness of its recommendations.[57] The resolutions passed by the General Assembly on the basis of the first three Reports were half-hearted. On 27 November the vote was forty-eight to six in favour of a western resolution upholding UNSCOB's conclusions and calling on Greece's neighbours to cease intervention; forty-seven to six against a Soviet resolution calling for the withdrawal of foreign forces from Greece; and unanimous in favour of resolutions calling on Greece and her neighbours to settle their differences 'in a spirit of mutual comprehension', and to enter into direct negotiations with each other. The General Assembly instructed UNSCOB to continue its work, though without voting sufficient funds to enable it to do so. A significant new note was creeping into the UNSCOB reports, for the Yugoslavs were on the brink of a new policy.

Whereas the first two reports, covering the period to 10 September 1948, had criticised Greece's three northern neighbours in almost identical terms, the third report, dated 22 October, indicated a slight improvement in relations between Greece and Yugoslavia. There were still ugly incidents, such as that at Koutsoubei; there were frequent crossings of the Yugoslav frontier by the rebels; and there was still logistic and medical aid across that frontier. But the Yugoslavs were now less intransigent than the Albanians and Bulgarians. The reason was already well understood. All through the year relations had been deteriorating between the Soviet and Yugoslav CPs to the wonder of the western world, and even of Tito and his colleagues. The famous correspondence between the two Communist Parties began on 18 March with a letter from Belgrade to Moscow which has never been published. The rest of the correspondence is now common knowledge.[58] Essentially the fateful decision on a breach was taken by Stalin before the correspondence began, for the withdrawal of the Red Army mission from Yugoslavia was notified on the opening day. Behind the camouflage of doctrinal criticism, the Soviet intention was clearly to overthrow Tito and instal a more compliant leadership in the Yugoslav CP. The intention failed, but it was not until the end of June that Tito recognised the finality of the breach.

The first published letter, from Tito to Molotov on 20 March, complained of the withdrawal of Soviet military and civilian advisers, and denied that they had been refused information or treated inhospitably. It also warned the Soviet leadership not to be misled by false information 'from other people', which was neither objective nor well-intentioned. In an abrupt reply dated 27 March the Central Committee of the Communist Party of the Soviet Union rejected Tito's explanations as 'incorrect and therefore completely unsatisfactory'. The letter was signed by Stalin and Molotov personally, though this fact was concealed by both sides when it was first published.[59] It complained of Yugoslav criticisms of Soviet military advisers and of Djilas's insulting statement – a recurrent theme of complaint – comparing Soviet officers unfavourably with British officers. Soviet representatives, it said, were controlled and supervised in Yugoslavia just as in bourgeois states; the Yugoslavs had talked of 'great power chauvinism rampant in the USSR', just as the degenerate Trotsky had once done; and 'English spies' like Velebit were still employed in the Yugoslav Ministry of Foreign Affairs.* The Yugoslav CP was also said to be ideologically unsound, because the organs of the state were superior to the Party and 'the spirit of the policy of class struggle is not felt in the CPY'. A long and pained reply was sent by Tito and Kardelj, addressed to Stalin and Molotov, on 13 April, which contained the memorable statement that: 'No matter how much each of us loves the land of Socialism, the USSR, he can in no case love his country less, which also is developing socialism.'

The Yugoslav letter of 13 April clearly looked forward to personal explanations and reconciliation, and professed entire loyalty. But the reply, on 4 May, once again signed by Stalin and Molotov, was an absolute rebuff. All the former accusations were repeated, and more were added. Tito was rebuked for criticising Soviet policy over Trieste and for saying at Ljubljana in May 1945: 'We demand that everyone shall be master in his own house.' A long passage complained of the unworthy treatment of the Soviet Ambassador in Belgrade, and another repeated the complaint about Djilas's anti-Soviet remarks. Criticisms of the Yugoslav CP accused it of a 'complete contradiction of Marxism–Leninism' over the class struggle and of the 'cardinal error of the Mensheviks' over relations between a Communist Party and a Popular Front. The letter ended with an

---

* Vladko Velebit, a distinguished Partisan leader under the Occupation, served later as Ambassador in London.

ominous proposal that 'this question be discussed at the next session of
the Cominform'. A reply from Tito and Kardelj, on 17 May, briefly re-
butted the accusations, refused to attend the meeting of the Cominform,
and affirmed that 'we will resolutely construct socialism and remain loyal
to the Soviet Union'. A further reply from the Yugoslav CP on 20 May
has never been published. It was the subject, along with its predecessor,
of another tirade from the Central Committee of the CPSU on 22 May.

This was the last letter exchanged between the two sides. On 22 June
the Central Committee of the CPY wrote to the Cominform Conference,
which was due to be held on 26 June in Bucharest, explaining its reasons
for refusing to attend. On 28 June a communiqué was published by the
Cominform Conference, endorsing the line taken by the CPSU and announcing the expulsion of the Yugoslav CP. On 29 June the Central
Committee of the CPY issued a statement on the communiqué, once
more affirming its loyalty to the CPSU. Indeed, Tito was still not persuaded that the breach was irrevocable. His first reactions were cautious
and far from violent. A few Stalinists in the Yugoslav CP, notably Hebrang
and Žujović, were arrested, but their lives were not in danger. Some
others tried to escape abroad, one of whom, General Jovanović, was shot
dead on the Rumanian frontier. But there was no reign of terror.

The Yugoslav people, including non-Communists, on the whole rallied
to Tito as the champion of their national freedom. It became apparent for
the first time that it was possible to be a nationalist without ceasing to be
a Communist, and to be a Communist without accepting a blind subservience to Stalin's slightest whim. If there could have been any doubt
about the alternative, it was dispelled by Stalin's blunt statement in the
Cominform Journal on 5 December 1948, that 'the attitude towards the
Soviet Union is now the test of devotion to the cause of proletarian inter-
nationalism'. To Stalin it was inconceivable that any Communist could
challenge that dogma and survive; but Tito already appeared to be doing
so successfully. The lesson had far-reaching consequences for international
relations throughout the world, particularly in eastern Europe and above
all in Greece.

The effects of the convulsion spread quickly through the Balkans. The
Albanian Communist Party, which only six months earlier had been discussing incorporation into the Yugoslav Federation, immediately announced that it had 'always' been in conflict with the Yugoslav CP. It held
anti-Tito demonstrations without delay, and denounced all but one of its
pacts with Yugoslavia.[60] The Bulgarians, on the other hand, hesitated for
a short time. In April 1948 (according to Pijade, writing in Borba on 29
September 1949) Dimitrov advised Tito to 'stand firm'; on 25 May he

was the only Balkan leader who sent Tito a telegram on his birthday; and on 29 June the Bulgarian CP assured the Yugoslav CP that it was still friendly. But the mood did not last. In July the Bulgarians began expelling Yugoslav teachers from Pirin Macedonia because, as Dimitrov himself put it on 19 December, their cultural facilities were being used for purposes of propaganda. At the same time Dimitrov reaffirmed that all Communist Parties were still dependent on the Soviet Union.

The phase of the great purges had not yet reached Bulgaria, but it was soon to do so. Elsewhere it was already in full swing. Rajk was summoned from Budapest to Moscow in July, and demoted from the Ministry of Internal Affairs to that of Foreign Affairs. Gomulka, who had absented himself from the Cominform meeting which condemned Tito, made a secret speech to the Central Committee of the Polish CP on 3 June, defending Tito. He was called upon by the Politburo on 16 August to exercise self-criticism, and dismissed as Secretary-General of the Party on 31 August. But he resisted all pressures until the autumn, when he was denounced in *Pravda* on 9 September as a Titoist; and he was finally dismissed from all remaining offices in December. In Albania Xoxe was similarly denounced as a Titoist in September, and dismissed on 3 October. The trials for treason were to follow later.

But it was by no means certain how the Soviet–Yugoslav breach would affect the Greek rebellion. There was no mention of Greece in the Soviet–Yugoslav correspondence, nor was Macedonia expressly at issue. Vlandas has a story that at the end of June Tsaldaris, as Deputy Prime Minister, made a secret offer to negotiate terms with the rebels, which was rebuffed by Zakhariadis, Bartzotas and Markos without consulting their colleagues. The implication is that the Greek Government expected the breach to affect the rebellion at once, but Zakhariadis was confident it would not.[61] In fact, Yugoslav as well as Albanian and Bulgarian help to the Democratic Army continued with no apparent diminution. In July, at the Fifth Congress of the Yugoslav Communist Party, Tempo emphasised the close collaboration of the Macedonian and Greek Partisans. In the same month the Central Committee of the Yugoslav Macedonian CP denounced the Albanian and Bulgarian CPs, but not the KKE. Macedonians in Yugoslavia on the whole remained loyal to Tito, although they were themselves subject to some adverse discrimination.

On the other hand, in August the Slavo-Macedonian Communist organisation, NOF, which was co-operating with the Democratic Army, began a purge of its pro-Yugoslav elements; and by December it was reported to be reasserting its 'national claims', which meant an autonomous Macedonia. The leaders of the KKE were soon to find themselves compelled to reformulate their attitude to the Macedonian question, if only because it was impossible for them to avoid the choice between supporting the Yugoslavs and supporting the Bulgarians, the two rival claimants to Macedonia; and that meant taking sides between Tito and Stalin. A conflict on this question preoccupied the KKE throughout the summer and autumn of 1948. To make matters worse, the two protagonists, Markos and Zakhariadis, were already divided about tactics, and even on the question whether the civil war should be continued at all.

After the inquest on Konitsa, the two men remained on hostile terms. Of the other leading Communists, a majority probably supported Zakhariadis, but some of the most intelligent ranged themselves with Markos: among them Karagiorgis, who wrote a critical letter to Zakhariadis on 18 March (though his criticisms were aimed more directly at Siantos); and Tzimas, who reappeared at Markos's GHQ in April, to receive a frosty welcome from Zakhariadis and Bartzotas. For a time Markos seemed to prevail: it was noticed that the broadcasts by the rebel radio had a markedly nationalist rather than a Stalinist tone; and on 30 May a peace offer was broadcast which bore the stamp of Markos's thinking, but it was immediately rejected by the Greek Government. The conflict between the two leaders continued through the summer – at the Fourth Plenum on 28–29 July in particular, and again on 18 August at the village of Agios Zakharias in Grammos. But gradually Zakhariadis's will prevailed, as a number of indications showed. He expounded his theories of guerrilla warfare in a series of speeches, articles and pamphlets throughout 1948; and by claiming to be in accord with Mao Tse-Tung he overbore the doctrines of Markos.[62] In August, immediately after the battle of Grammos, he convened the Supreme War Council and insisted, against Markos's advice, that the Politburo should commit itself to continuing the struggle. Most important of all, he secured a secret resolution by the Fourth Plenum to back the Cominform against Tito. The ultimate logic of this decision was a renewal of past commitments to Macedonian autonomy, which Zakhariadis dared not yet reveal to his followers.

By July the political breach between Tito and Stalin overlaid the tactical dispute between Markos and Zakhariadis, which dispute continued through the autumn. Markos was still nominally in command, but it was put about that he was ill. In November he submitted a pessimistic appreciation of the Democratic Army's prospects to the Politburo, which became known as his 'platform' – a term commonly used in Communist parlance for a dissident view.[63] He drew attention to the problem of reserves, admitting that new recruits amounted to less than ten per cent of young Greeks and that 'since the middle of 1947, recruitment was achieved almost entirely by force'. He acknowledged the 'relative stabilisation' achieved by the 'monarcho-fascist régime' and the failure of the KKE in urban centres. He concluded once more that the Democratic Army could not win without external intervention, which was at present impossible. Therefore, he argued, the Democratic Army must revert to 'intensive, guerrilla-type activity, by small, mobile, lightly armed contingents, saboteurs and snipers, able to choose where and when to fight'. The object for the time being must be to cause 'a continuous military and economic haemorrhage'. There was no word of surrender in Markos's 'platform', but Zakhariadis denounced it as 'opportunist and defeatist'. On 15 November he secured a resolution of the Politburo declaring that it had no confidence in Markos, and had indeed distrusted him since the Third Plenum in September 1947.[64]

Effectively Markos no longer commanded the Democratic Army, though orders were still issued in his name. He was sent on sick leave to Albania, and thence to Yugoslavia. In his place, after the post had been refused by Markos's wartime colleague, Kikitsas, a little-known Communist called George Vrondisios (Goussias) was appointed Commander-in-Chief.* But the real power lay with Zakhariadis, who was still confident of victory. The morale of the Democratic Army had been successfully insulated from the internecine squabbles of the Balkan Communists, and it was still an effective fighting force. After the front had been stabilised in Vitsi, renewed attacks were launched elsewhere, as far afield as Voulgareli in Epirus, Serrai in Eastern Macedonia, Edessa and Naoussa in Western Macedonia, and many points in Thessaly, Roumeli and the Peloponnese. The extent of rebel control in the Peloponnese was shown by two dramatic kidnappings in the autumn of 1948. A BBC correspondent, Kenneth Matthews, was captured at Mycenae in October, and an American engineer, McShane, in November.[65] Both were held for about two weeks, to show them the extent of the rebels' power; but their impressions coincided in giving the rebel state little prospect of permanent success.

It emerges from Matthews's account that communications were still sufficiently good to enable the Democratic Army in the Peloponnese to be controlled from the southern échelon of GHQ (KGANE), located north of the Gulf of Corinth. The leading figure in the KGANE (Échelon of General Headquarters for Southern Greece) was Karagiorgis, the able journalist who now held the titular rank of Lieutenant-General. It was he who ordered the release of Matthews, and sent him a personal message of good will. It was he also who conducted the most important operation in

* He came from a village near Ioannina, like Tsakalotos, the principal commander against him: Tsakalotos, II, p. 212.

the closing months of the year. His target was Karditsa, a large county town in the plain of Thessaly, which had been the first to be taken from the Germans by ELAS during the Occupation. Karagiorgis was on familiar ground. But he knew that such an assault, in open country accessible by motor-road from many directions, was not a matter for guerrilla tactics. It required professional planning, executed by regular troops. Soldiers on the opposite side praised Karagiorgis for the diligent preparation of the attack, the accurate intelligence and the model operation orders – a more trustworthy tribute than Zakhariadis's later judgment that the failure of KGANE was due to the treason of Karagiorgis, whom 'documents prove to have been long an agent of the Intelligence Service and American espionage'.[66]

Karagiorgis had his HQ in the upland plain of Nevroupolis, the site of the first landing-ground constructed during the enemy occupation.* Under his command he had two divisions each consisting of two brigades (all below their nominal strength of 1,500 men), a cavalry brigade, a battery of three mountain guns and a section of the Democratic Army's Officers' School.[67] The total force at that time amounted to about 6,000, including women. Such a concentration of force clearly foreshadowed a decisive operation. The garrison of Karditsa consisted only of one battalion and one company, totalling 55 officers and 860 men; but there were two battalions at Trikkala and one each at Sophades and Larisa from which assistance could be summoned. Some twenty posts round the town, at a distance of five or six miles, were manned by small units of five to seven men. The rebels' plan of attack was to isolate and destroy, or by-pass, these posts and to approach the town from the north-west and south, where the foothills of Agrapha provided the nearest cover. The first phase was launched in the late evening of 11 December, and by early morning the rebels were in the outskirts of the town. Throughout 12 December they pinned the garrison down in a number of fortified buildings, while they collected supplies and seized recruits, which was the main object of the operation.

During the second night Karagiorgis decided to try to hold the town for another twenty-four hours instead of withdrawing on 13 December, as originally planned; but his orders reached only the brigade in the northern part of the town.[68] As a result, the southern brigade began to withdraw at dawn on 13 December, followed only later in the day by the northern force after another skirmish in the town. By the middle of the day reinforcements for the garrison were arriving from other parts of Thessaly, including armoured units from Larisa. Since Karagiorgis's force was

---

* Today it is covered by an artificial lake. See p. 53 above.

encumbered by looted supplies and forced recruits, it presented a vulnerable and slow-moving target, especially to air attack, but the hills of Agrapha were near. In the event Karagiorgis made good his escape with losses of about 600 men and women (the latter of whom were said to have shown the greater ferocity in action).

The losses of the garrison were about 200 people killed, wounded and missing. But most serious of all were the civilian casualties: 150 killed and wounded, and over 1,000 were abducted, of whom about thirty-five per cent were women.[69] The high proportion of women in the Democratic Army in its later stages has often been remarked: one historian put it between eighteen and thirty per cent; and later enquiries showed that many of them joined voluntarily, though rarely for ideological reasons.[70] But at Karditsa there can be no doubt of the compulsion exercised, especially as a number soon escaped and returned home. Brutal as the operation was, it was a notable success for Karagiorgis. Less clear were the future implications for the rebellion.

In a sense the operation embodied a compromise between the doctrines of Markos and those of Zakhariadis. It was a guerrilla operation under a divisional command: the order of battle was that of Zakhariadis, the tactics those of Markos. It showed that the Democratic Army was still capable of taking the initiative and launching well-planned assaults far from its base. It presaged a further attempt in the New Year, again commanded by Karagiorgis, to mount a repetition of the attack on Konitsa: not, this time, a hit-and-run raid in force, as at Karditsa, but a second attempt by a full-scale operation to seize and hold an isolated county town in the mountains. The high command of the National Army, foreseeing such a repetition, had much to preoccupy it during the winter of 1948–9.

The balance of forces had not greatly changed, to all appearance, from a year earlier. The strength of the Democratic Army, though past its peak, was probably still in the neighbourhood of 25,000 men and women. They were organised in nine divisions controlling 23 brigades, 42 battalions, 25 double companies and 18 independent companies.[71] This was not their final organisation, for during 1949 they increased the number of battalions to 70, though with no increase of manpower. Apart from infantry equipment they also had artillery on a fairly formidable scale: 60 field guns, 31 anti-aircraft guns, 41 anti-tank guns and 12 heavy mortars.[72]

No direct comparison between the two forces is possible, since each formation and unit in the National Army was about double the size of corresponding designations in the Democratic Army; and whereas the former had nothing corresponding to the *Aftoámyna*, the latter naturally had a much less elaborate administrative 'tail'. The National Army, though far stronger in manpower and equipment, had also still not achieved its final organisation. Its divisions were being converted from two types (field divisions of 10,500 men and mountain divisions of 8,500) to a standard type of 9,300; and their number was being increased from seven to eight, the Commandos being converted to divisional troops. The total strength of the Army and its armed auxiliaries was over 200,000, but by no means all its needs were met. In particular, air support remained seriously inadequate; and both in the air and on the ground equipment still consisted predominantly of British surplus stocks. Material comparisons, although to the advantage of the National Army, are therefore inconclusive. All depended on leadership and morale.

The Final Breakthrough
January–December 1949

BOTH SIDES were re-grouping and preparing themselves for the final struggle. The National Army's plan was to conduct a holding operation in the north while it cleared the Peloponnese and Roumeli once for all. After counter-attacks at Edessa, Naoussa and Ardea between 21 and 31 December, they left the Macedonian front quiescent. Tsakalotos, as the most successful Corps commander, was transferred to the Peloponnese on 10 December. Petzopoulos, who had been successful as a divisional commander in Macedonia, became the field commander under him. They quickly cleared the coastal areas of the north and west, and Tsakalotos then launched an assault on the *Aftoámyna* in the principal towns during the night of 27–28 December. In absolute secrecy, which was not breached even to General Giantzis, the CGS, or to the Government, he arrested 4,300 suspects, having first cut the telephone wires to Athens so that the news could not become known until they were on board ship on their way to Makronisos and Trikkeri.[1] Political uproar followed: Rendis, the Minister for War, who represented Corinth in Parliament, complained that many of his own supporters were arrested. Tsakalotos admitted some errors but remained unrepentant. On 29 December Rendis, Giantzis and Van Fleet visited his HQ in Corinth to study his operational plans, and in the end approved them. Operation Pigeon was ready to proceed.

Corinth was not, however, the main centre of activity in January 1949. The crucial events on the Government side were taking place in Athens, and they revolved round the personalities of Sophoulis and Papagos. Papagos had at last agreed to become Commander-in-Chief, and he was appointed on 19 January. All his demands had been accepted, including an additional one that the unwieldy Supreme Council of National Defence should be dissolved and replaced by a smaller War Council, of which he himself and the heads of the allied missions would be members. This new body met for the first time on 25 January. In the meantime, two other crises had supervened. First, Papagos had indicated that he had little confidence in the Government. His view was shared for different reasons by Venizelos and Papandreou, but they agreed to join a coalition under an ex-Governor of the Bank of Greece, Alexander Diomidis. Sophoulis offered his resignation on 15 January, but Diomidis was unable to command sufficient support. After the King had passionately urged the politicians to settle their differences, Sophoulis succeeded in forming a more broadly based government on 19 January (the day of Papagos's appointment), in which he was joined by all the principal leaders with the exception of Papandreou, who objected to Papagos's dissolution of the Supreme Council of National Defence, and of Zervas and Gonatas, who were not invited. But no sooner was the Government crisis settled than a military crisis arose on the same day, when a large force of the Democratic Army attacked Karpenisi. As at Karditsa a few weeks before, the attack was mounted by the southern HQ (KGANE) under Karagiorgis.

Karpenisi is the highest county town in Greece and one of the most isolated. In the heart of the southern Pindus range, it is surrounded by mountains, including the formidable Veloukhi (Tymphristos). A single motor-road approached it from Lamia on the eastern side, which was very vulnerable to ambush. The road continued a few miles beyond Karpenisi to the west — as far as Koryskhades, where EAM's national assembly had met in the spring of 1944 — but only in later years was it joined to the motor-road reaching north-eastwards from Agrinion. It was therefore comparatively easy for a determined force to isolate and capture Karpenisi. Karagiorgis planned his assault well. He had much the same order of battle as against Karditsa, but his units were depleted by casualties, and the forced recruits who replaced them had only two weeks' training.[2] The total strength of the rebels has been variously estimated between 2,900 and 6,000, but was probably nearer to the lower figure: a Communist source speaks of the 'assault units of two divisions'.[3] The garrison of the town amounted to two infantry battalions, a battalion of the National Defence Corps and a unit of gendarmerie, totalling less than two thousand in all.

The situation of Karpenisi made it harder to defend or to relieve than Karditsa. It was impossible, without a much larger force, to hold all the heights overlooking the town; and the most important of them, which lay to the north, were taken without difficulty during the night 19–20 January. Twenty-four hours later the rebels forced their way into the town itself, and held it for more than a week. On 22 January an American aircraft was shot down near Karpenisi, and the pilot's body was later found mutilated. He had probably the unenviable distinction of being the first American serviceman to be killed in action by Communist arms. The rebels took the incident as proof of direct American intervention in the fighting. Although the US authorities denied that the aircraft was armed, it was engaged in reconnaissance for the Greek national forces. Both on the ground and in the air, American support was becoming increasingly active, and the theoretical line between advice, intelligence and combat was a narrow one. American 'advisers' were often in the front line: Van Fleet himself was twice lost in enemy territory.[4] Officers of the recently formed Central Intelligence Agency also gave positive services to the Greek Government.[5] It was impossible to expect the rebels to regard the American service missions, like their British predecessors, as non-combatants; and the unlucky pilot at Karpenisi was the victim of an inexorable logic of insurgency.

It was not until 29 January that the National Army was able to mount counter-attacks on Karpenisi. They came from two directions, one force advancing north-eastwards from Agrinion, and one westwards from Lamia. The first counter-attack was beaten off: it was the only occasion in the civil war that the rebels held a major town against the National Army. Karagiorgis's men were not forced out of the town until 9 February, after which they conducted a fighting retreat throughout the month, dividing into three columns: one moving northwards into the mountains of Agrapha, and two moving separately westwards until they re-united and moved southwards into the mountains of Vardoussia. The final outcome must be judged indecisive. On the Government side, there had been failures of intelligence and planning, for which the commanding officer, General Ketseas, was relieved of his post and court-martialled. On the rebel side, the operation had been tactically successful but had not achieved its strategic object. It was the last major initiative that the Democratic Army proved capable of taking in central Greece.

Tsakalotos and Petzopoulos had not yet completely cleared the Peloponnese, though the back of the rebels' resistance there was broken. The National Army had, as usual, a great superiority in numbers: a division, a brigade and thirteen battalions of light infantry (nearly 20,000 men), against a force of 3,500 after the elimination of the *Aftodmyna*. One major battle at Agios Vasileios in Kynouria on 22 January destroyed the strongest brigade of the Democratic Army; and although the peninsula was not completely cleared for some weeks, on 29 January Tsakalotos felt justified in handing over his command. Petzopoulos, who succeeded him, finished clearing the peninsula with a ruthlessness which earned him the reputation of a 'second Ibrahim Pasha' among the rebel survivors.[6] In the seven weeks since Operation Pigeon began, the rebels had lost 679 killed, 1,601 prisoners and 628 voluntarily surrendered, in addition to the complete destruction of the *Aftodmyna*.[7] The Peloponnese was virtually free of rebels, and it was so for good. Next it was the turn of Roumeli, where Tsakalotos was transferred on 26 January.

The rebels were still able to mount formidable operations in many parts of Greece. On the night of 11–12 January they again attacked and captured Naoussa, and held it for five days. Between 12 and 15 January they launched another attack on Florina, which failed because the National Army had good intelligence in advance. At the end of February a small force of rebels entered Larisa, and was only dislodged the following day. During March they made an abortive attack on Arta, and in Central Macedonia and the Khalkidiki peninsula they remained active well into April. These were their last offensives outside their stronghold on the Albanian frontier, and their effect was not negligible.

The activity of the Democratic Army was conducted against a background of deep but secret dissension in the KKE. By the turn of the year Zakhariadis's will had prevailed. Of his principal antagonists, Markos and Tzimas had been relegated to Yugoslavia, ostensibly for reasons of health; Khrysa Khatzivasiliou was dying of leukaemia; and Karagiorgis, having been removed to Roumeli, was soon to be labelled a traitor for supporting Markos. With a handful of faithful Stalinists and the leaders of NOF, Zakhariadis was master of the KKE, both in policy and strategy. But he was also the political prisoner of NOF, which was increasingly the mouth-piece of the Bulgarian Communists.

The proportion of Slavo-Macedonians in the Democratic Army grew sharply as the southern areas of Greece were cleared. They numbered 11,000 out of 25,000 in 1948, but 14,000 out of less than 20,000 by mid-1949.[8] The area of Vitsi had been particularly affected by the Bulgarian occupation, many of the villages being predominantly Slavophone. The Bulgarian Communist Party was once more calling for a Balkan Federation, including an autonomous Macedonia. While Tito's Macedonian CP held its First Congress at Skopje in December 1948 to denounce Bulgarian propaganda, the Bulgarian CP held its Fifth Congress in Sofia to denounce Tito; and Zakhariadis, together with Vlandas, attended the latter. The results were seen a month later at the Fifth Plenum of the Central Committee of the KKE whose optimistic resolutions were described by a Communist historian as 'far removed from reality'.[9]

On 27 January the 'Free Greece' radio, which was situated safely outside the country (probably in Rumania) broadcast an offer to make peace on conditions which included the removal of foreign military missions, a general amnesty, the re-establishment of political freedom and free trade unions and negotiations on the formation of a new government 'acceptable to both sides'. The terms were scornfully rejected by the Greek Government: indeed, they must have helped to ensure it a decisive vote of confidence in Parliament by 245 votes to 50. The Greek Government had no reason at this time to weaken in its resolve, which was reflected in a firm but not boastful order of the day by Papagos on 2 February: 'I am unshakeably convinced that our existing resources are sufficient to achieve a decisive improvement of the situation and to capture the initiative from the bandits.'[10] He already knew that the problem of reserves had become an insuperable one for the Democratic Army, which was now losing 4,000 men a month and recruiting only 1,000 replacements.[11]

On 4 February the Free Greece radio announced the replacement of Markos Vaphiadis on grounds of ill-health and the formation of a new 'provisional government'. The decisions which had been taken by the Fifth Plenum between 29 and 31 January were extremely far-reaching. It adopted a six-point programme for 1949: to continue attacks on large inhabited areas throughout the country; to enlarge the free areas in northern Greece; to establish a free area in the central Pindus; to wear down the enemy in Thessaly and Roumeli; to create a new front in the Peloponnese and continue pressure on Salonika; and to create a third front by a mass rising in the cities and countryside.[12] The programme was ambitious and unrealistic. But it was not the most dramatic of the decisions taken at the Fifth Plenum. More important were the renewed adoption of the policy of an autonomous Macedonian state, and the appointment of a new 'provisional government' and Politburo of the KKE. The head of the new government was Ioannidis, though his proved to be only a temporary appointment; the head of the Politburo was Zakhariadis himself. Other decisions by the Fifth Plenum – to support the Cominform against Tito, to denounce Markos for defeatism and to admit Slavo-Macedonians into the 'provisional government' – were regarded as too explosive to be published immediately. There was no reference to them in the broadcasts of Free Greece Radio which immediately followed.[13]

Reactions in Yugoslavia to these events were not clear at the time, but Tempo's account two years later may be regarded as an official version. His references to 'the mysterious removal of Markos' show a genuine surprise.[14] Markos had been induced to issue a statement of his resignation on 8 February; and on 16 June Free Greece Radio published a letter from him to the Central Committee disowning an attempt, which had been made in an article by Djilas in *Borba* the previous day, to link him with Xoxe and Gomulka, and therefore by implication with Tito.[15] Tempo expressed suspicion of Zakhariadis's new policy of self-determination for Macedonia, quoting examples of the KKE's repudiation of such a policy in the past. The real object, he suggested, was to support the Soviet policy of detaching Yugoslav Macedonia from Tito.[16] His indictment of the KKE was twofold: on the one hand, he interpreted its

repeated offers of a compromise peace and a coalition government of
national unity as proof that it was guilty of 'social-democratic conceptions'; on the other hand, he accused it of serving the 'hegemonistic
policy of the Soviet Union', particularly against Yugoslavia.[17] According
to Tempo, Zakhariadis's contribution to this policy was to hold as much
ground as possible in the closing stages, using 'tactics of frontal defence in
mountain country by means of a system of built fortifications and strong-
points in the mountainside and in impassable ravines'.[18]

The confused sequence of events within the Balkan Communist Parties
in the next few weeks could only be reconstructed in retrospect. Stalin,
who had lost all interest in the Greek rebellion, was using the Macedonian
autonomist movement chiefly to subvert Tito. This was the sense of a
decision by the Second Plenum of the Central Committee of NOF on 3
February, that its second Congress in March would proclaim 'the union
of Macedonia into a complete, independent and equal Macedonian nation
within the Popular Democratic Federation of the Balkan Peoples'.[19] Tito
at once condemned the resolution, but the reactions of Greek Communists were mixed. Zakhariadis had attended the NOF Plenum, and the Free
Greece radio broadcast the resolution on 1 March. But a week later the
radio denied any commitment by the KKE beyond 'self-determination'
for Macedonia; and a statement by NOF on 9 March appeared to agree.[20]
Yet it was evident to patriots on the left which way the wind was blowing.
On 20 March Svolos's newspaper, *Makhi*, published a denunciation of the
KKE for its folly in 'committing hara-kiri on the door-step of the NOF'.
Meanwhile Zakhariadis met Karagiorgis in north-west Greece to discuss
the problem.[21] They agreed to form within the KKE a Communist Organisation of Aegean Macedonia (KOAM) which had little success but caused
great uneasiness among Greek Communists. Karagiorgis also addressed the
second Congress of NOF on 25 March, at which nothing more was said
about Macedonian autonomy. This was just as well, since the date was
Greece's national Independence Day. But Karagiorgis promised that
officers of NOF would be appointed to the GHQ of the Democratic Army.

Meanwhile Soviet intentions were becoming more obscure. There was
trouble within the Bulgarian CP: on 27 March Kostov was dismissed as
Secretary-General, and accused of nationalism and hostility to the Soviet
Union. Later the charges against him extended to Titoism and a fantastic
miscellany of other crimes, including a plot to cede Pirin Macedonia to a
Balkan Federation under Tito's leadership.[22] Kolarov, the Foreign Minister, who was to be Kostov's effective successor, declared on 18 March
that there was no truth in western reports that Bulgaria intended to form
a Balkan Federation. This appeared to be confirmed by a statement in

Pravda on 13 June emphasising the territorial integrity of Greece. But in April a number of events heightened the uncertainty. Dimitrov, once the dominant figure of Bulgarian Communism and the Comintern, was sent to Moscow for the sake of his health, never to return. Tito once more asserted his loyalty to Stalin, and at the Third Congress of the Yugoslav Popular Front on 10 April it was stated that policy towards Greece was unchanged.[23] But this was not strictly true, for the US Government had already begun to relax its restrictions on trade with Yugoslavia, probably in consequence of a Yugoslav decision to reduce its aid to the Greek rebels from the preceding November.[24]

Because the Balkan Communist Parties were in a state of disarray which precluded any coherent policy towards Greece, the KKE was left to solve its problems alone. Signs of internal dissension became increasingly apparent, over other matters besides Titoism and Macedonian autonomy. At times there was total inconsistency in the broadcasts of the Free Greece radio. On 14 April, for example, it announced a decree (Law twenty-two) granting an amnesty to all its opponents except eighteen named persons, including the King and Queen, Sophoulis, Tsaldaris, Papagos, Zervas, Kanellopoulos, Papandreou and Tsakalotos, among others.[25] A week later it broadcast a new offer of peace terms, which the KKE cannot have expected to be taken seriously in the light of 'Law twenty-two'. Clearly different attitudes co-existed uneasily among the Communist leaders. One attitude looked forward to victory and the establishment of a revolutionary state. The other was more cautious about ends, contemplating the possibility of an ultimate compromise short of victory, and concentrating its efforts pragmatically upon means, from which unforeseeable ends might emerge. It would be hard to say which was the real view of Zakhariadis: probably he veered from one to the other.

Sometimes he appeared to be still convinced that a decisive victory could be won in 1949. If the object was the total ruin of Greece, his belief was not baseless, for it was doubtful if the Greek people could endure such another year of setbacks as 1948. At a time when other countries of Europe were already recovering from the destruction of the Second World War, the Greek national economy continued its deterioration to still lower levels. Statistics can barely convey the full tragedy of the situation.[26] Whereas before the war Greece could cover about three-fifths of her imports with exports, since 1945 the figure had sunk below a quarter. Greek tobacco had lost its traditional markets for good; revenue from shipping and emigrants' remittances was disappointing; and the pipe-dream of tourism was a decade away. There was little confidence in the currency or willingness to subscribe to loans, especially since the interest on both foreign and internal debts was suspended. The cost of living had multiplied some twenty times since 1945. At least thirteen million sovereigns were in private hands, only reluctantly to be exchanged for paper money. The destruction of crops and forests, sheep and goats, would take years to make good. The development programme launched by the ECA in 1948, with its emphasis on improving agriculture, re-equipping industry, improving communications and extending electrification, had to be slowed down in the following year. Dependence on American aid was a matter not of rehabilitation but of survival.

What was worse, the people were almost demoralised. The number of refugees at its peak in 1949 was 684,300, including 200,000 in Macedonia alone. Perhaps two and a half million were partly or wholly dependent on state assistance, though the official figure of unemployed was only four per cent. On the other hand, many who were in a position to re-insure themselves against a Communist victory were unscrupulously doing so. The economist and former Minister, Professor Varvaressos, pointed bitterly to the contrast. There was, on the one hand, 'the world of the wage-earner, the pensioner and the peasant in which the price of goods produced by commerce and industry is almost prohibitive and for which the satisfaction of even the most elementary needs involves serious sacrifices'; and on the other hand, 'the world of easy profits, of unrestricted living, of hoarding, in which the current prices are the ordinary price a man gets for the product he sells and in which a man pays with ease for the goods he needs.'[27] It was the former that bore the brunt of the civil war, while the latter lived on the black market. But the gains of the latter, whether legal or illegal, were often used to secure the profiteers against Communist vengeance. Bankers, merchants, deputies, lawyers and other leading figures were believed to be secretly financing the KKE, while priests, journalists and civil servants showed faint enthusiasm for the Government's cause.[28] The King himself, whose own conduct was impeccable throughout, felt compelled to call on the upper classes for more willing sacrifices in a speech at Corinth on 11 January 1949.

Demoralisation took many forms, high and low. A cloud of despondency had descended on the cities: in Athens dancing in a public place was forbidden. The fear of defeat, or at best of an inescapable compromise with the rebels, prevailed in many quarters: a British observer found it still persistent as late as April 1949.[29] Economic misery led for the first time to two strikes by civil servants in April and May. The Americans were impatient over the repeated failures of the high command and the waste of valuable aid; the public, hardly less so, talked nostalgically of dictatorship. The King, it was said, was 'inundated with letters . . . especially from the villages', urging him to appoint a dictator.[30] The pressure was reinforced by officers belonging to IDEA, who talked 'unreservedly, even to American correspondents, about "traitors in the rear", about the need to "clear up the situation" and to impose a new regime, about the imposition of moral discipline, and so on.'[31] They demanded 'a Directory for the supposed salvation of the endangered country'. Although victory was eventually won without such extreme measures, it was nevertheless found expedient to suspend the sitting of Parliament for over four months from the beginning of February.

The rebels were in no better case, though the Communist leaders were more skilful at concealing it. Morale was affected by the high proportion of the rank and file of the Democratic Army who were either forced conscripts or Slavo-Macedonians. Those who had joined the rebellion initially inspired by a genuine sense of injustice and desire for reform were sickened by the perversion of its motives in practice. Vlandas, in a report made in October 1950, placed first among the causes of failure 'the policy of devastation of the countryside'; and an ex-Communist who defected much earlier attributed it to 'the extremely low moral level of the revolution'.[32] The results were visible in the early months of 1949. The rebels had lost their primacy in the field of intelligence with the destruction of the *Aftoámyna*, as was shown by the failure of their attack on Florina in February, when they lost seven hundred dead and four hundred prisoners in three days of abortive assaults. Their communications with southern Greece, both by land and sea, were disrupted. The captured diary of a rebel officer in Roumeli reveals the state of morale in an entry for 23 April 1949: 'No food for over forty-eight hours! Can't remember when we last had bread: perhaps a month! No rations: nothing to be had!'[33]

For the minority of Greek volunteers still with the Democratic Army, the physical hardships were less demoralising than the growing sense of moral corruption. An army in which the proportion of forced recruits probably exceeded fifty per cent could not have a high level of morale. More and more men and women were surrendering voluntarily. A British witness who spoke to such a group in 1948 found that only five out of twenty admitted to having joined the Democratic Army voluntarily.[34] He also found first-hand evidence of rape, robbery and sadistic brutality committed by individual rebels. Post-war interrogation of women prisoners by an American social scientist showed that typically they had been deceived into joining the Communists by promises of 'fine homes and machine-made dresses'.[35] There is a pathetic contrast between the high ideals with which the rebellion began in the minds of many patriotic

Greeks and the grim reality into which it degenerated. But although their levels of morale were probably in the end about equally low, that of the National Army was slowly rising while that of the Democratic Army was steeply declining.

Though seriously weakened, however, the KKE was still capable of causing dramatic shocks. On 5 April the Free Greece radio announced that the Provisional Government had been re-formed under Partsalidis, with Ioannidis as Deputy Prime Minister and a number of familiar names in office: Petros Roussos as Foreign Minister, Vlandas as Minister of War, Bartzotas as Minister of the Interior, Stringos as Minister of Finance, Kokkalis as Minister of Education, Porphyrogennis as Minister of Justice and Karagiorgis as Minister of War Supply. Most of these were men who had been associated with EAM, ELAS or PEEA. But the most startling news was the inclusion of two Slavo-Macedonians: Pascal Mitrovski as Minister of Food and Kraste Kotsev as Director for National Minorities in the Ministry of the Interior.* Another Slavo-Macedonian, V. Koitsev, was included in the Military Council. Nor was this the last shock that the rebels had for the Greek authorities. At the beginning of April it became known that the Democratic Army was moving back into Grammos, from which it had been evicted during the previous summer. The effect was to delay and almost to disrupt the carefully laid plans which Papagos had approved for the National Army's operations in the summer.

Planning operations for 1949 did not present much technical difficulty for the Greek high command. No strategic innovations followed the appointment of Papagos, since none was possible. Once the Peloponnese was cleared, there was no choice but to roll up the Democratic Army on the mainland from south to north, and to do it as fast as possible in order to forestall re-infiltration into the cleared areas. The alternative of trying to clear and hold a broad zone along the northern frontiers, leaving the rebellion to wither away for want of support from the Communist neighbours, would have required a greater force than the National Army could deploy. It was not seriously considered, the obvious and straightforward course being preferred. The only controversy was over the timing of the different phases of operation in Roumeli, Epirus, Thessaly and Macedonia. This matter proved very controversial, partly because the start of operations was delayed by unexpected circumstances, and partly because Papagos found himself in disagreement with some of his subordinates, particularly Tsakalotos.

The Peloponnese (Operation Pigeon) caused the first of the delays.

---

* Kotsev is not to be confused with Gotchev (Gotsis), the former leader of SNOF, who sided with the Yugoslavs.

Resistance there was not finally liquidated until mid-March. Meanwhile Tsakalotos was engaged in pursuing the remnants of Karagiorgis's force from Karpenisi. The pursuit westwards through Roumeli lasted through February and most of March, culminating in an abortive attack by the rebels on Arta, which Tsakalotos anticipated by good intelligence on 19 March. Although the rebels were then forced to retreat back south-eastwards into Agrapha, they were by no means a spent force. Elsewhere, the Democratic Army proved itself still capable of diversionary operations in May and June, between Florina and Amyntaion, to relieve the pressure on Vitsi. Its order of battle at the end of the winter of 1948–9 was still formidable: in the central Pindus about 3,500; in eastern Roumeli 500–600; in Epirus 600–700; in Thessaly and southern Macedonia 1,800–2,000; in central Macedonia 900–1,000; in eastern Macedonia 2,700–3,000; in Thrace 1,500; and in Grammos and Vitsi about 6,500, organised in four divisions and equipped with at least twenty guns.[36] Communist sources show that the strength of the Democratic Army was dwindling, but it was still between 18,000 and 19,000.[37] Against them, the National Army had an established force (excluding auxiliaries) of 168,500, but it was burdened with a weighty 'tail'.

The dispute between Papagos and Tsakalotos was in part personal, because Tsakalotos protested against the court-martial of General Ketseas, the unsuccessful commander in the battle of Karpenisi; but more seriously, it was also about the phasing of operations.[38] While Tsakalotos was repelling the rebels from Arta on 19 March, a large force of the Democratic Army from Vitsi had eluded II Corps to re-enter Grammos. Tsakalotos felt impelled to counter-attack at once against Grammos from the south. He launched an assault on Pyrgos, the southernmost spur of Grammos, and called upon Papagos for reinforcement with the Ninth Division, which Tsakalotos had had under him in the Peloponnese. Papagos refused the reinforcement, and ordered Tsakalotos to give priority to his own plan (Operation Hunter) to clear the central Pindus and Roumeli. Tsakalotos replied with a tart message justifying his need for reinforcements on the basis of his Corps' heavy losses. General Van Fleet intervened personally to warn Tsakalotos against antagonising Papagos, who himself retorted with a severe memorandum on 14 April, criticising Tsakalotos's tactical shortcomings. Again Van Fleet tried to be conciliatory. Tsakalotos warned him that the command of II Corps would 'fail the nation' again, and insisted that his own plan was correct. All he needed to take Grammos, he argued, was the Ninth Division for a short time; but Papagos's refusal continued to be absolute. Finally on 16 April, under protest, Tsakalotos gave way.

The disharmony between Papagos and Tsakalotos was rather like that between Eisenhower and Montgomery in the Second World War. Tsakalotos was a brilliant field-commander, egoistic and impetuous, always convinced that the crux of any strategic problem was where he happened to be in command. Papagos was a superlative staff officer, impeccable in logistic planning and exact calculation, a master of the politics and diplomacy of war, with little experience of high command in battle. He seldom even visited the front line. On one of his rare visits to the Macedonian front, his car (in which Tsakalotos accompanied him) was almost blown up by a mine, which killed an old woman on a mule alongside them.[39] During the final stages of the civil war Papagos was taken ill and unable to leave Athens.[40] Although everyone agreed that his appointment was a decisive contribution to the victory of the National Army, it has been rightly said that 'the Army was simply made to do what it was capable of doing', and even his predecessor, General Giantzis, had virtually won the war before he was unjustly removed.[41] Papagos's chief asset was his seniority: he could impose his own plans and wishes on both the Greek high command and the allied military missions, which had been for some months at loggerheads with each other.

His plans, however, were straightforward and not original; his wishes were merely that they should be carried out to the letter. The operations of 1949 were conceived as a totality, involving all three Army Corps in concerted action, under the general code-name Operation Rocket. The forces available were: I Corps in Roumeli, consisting of one division, one brigade and thirty-five battalions; II Corps covering Epirus and Macedonia, consisting of four divisions, two brigades and fifteen battalions; III Corps covering Eastern Macedonia and Thrace, consisting of two divisions, thirty-three battalions and some armoured units; in addition, at the beginning of the year, one division, one brigade and thirteen battalions in the Peloponnese.[42] Morale was reasonably good everywhere except among the units which had suffered defeat on Vitsi in the preceding autumn. All formations were supported by artillery, armoured cars and motor transport. Air power was also available both for reconnaissance and for close support, though Spitfires were still the only effective aircraft until the last days of the war. The National Army was a compact, well-balanced and well-equipped force. There were still some doubts about the high command, however. Papagos tried to resolve them by replacing the commander of II Corps yet again with General Manidakis, and recalling Vendiris once more as Army Commander over I and II Corps combined.

Operation Rocket was to proceed in four co-ordinated stages against the successive target areas: first the Peloponnese in January–February;

then Roumeli in February–March, simultaneously with Eastern and Central Macedonia; then Grammos and Vitsi from both Epirus and Western Macedonia in June–July. Each stage was somewhat delayed by circumstances. After the Peloponnese and Roumeli were cleared in March, the Democratic Army still succeeded in reinforcing some outlying areas from its stronghold in Vitsi. In the north-east, III Corps cleared the area of Kerdyllia and Khalkidiki, east of Salonika, in March, and the strip of Eastern Macedonia and Thrace fronting Bulgaria in early May. In Mount Kaimakchalan, adjoining the Yugoslav frontier between Florina and Edessa, and in Vermion, between Edessa and Kozani, the Democratic Army still held out till July. Having no confidence in the other Corps Commanders, Tsakalotos feared that final victory was once more going to elude the national forces. At one moment he believed that Vendiris had no confidence in himself, and tried to resign his command. After his narrow escape from death on a mine, he retired to Athens to recover, but resumed his command on 22 July in time for the final phase. He then established two forward HQ's at Konitsa and Argos Orestikon, directed against Grammos. Vendiris had his Army HQ at Kozani, where Tsakalotos met him and Papagos on 30 July for the last conference before the decisive attacks.

'All had been forgotten – both suspicions and fears of lack of confidence,' wrote Tsakalotos in retrospect.[43] Even the presence of Kitrilakis as Papagos's observer at his advanced HQ was tolerated. But he still had his doubts about the command of II Corps, whose target was Vitsi. The tactical plan was to make an initial feint at Grammos, in order to draw further reinforcements from the Democratic Army on Vitsi (Operation Torch A); then to deliver a decisive assault on Vitsi (Torch B); finally to destroy the Democratic Army on Grammos (Torch C). By early August all the preliminaries were complete. The Greek Government was able to announce on 10 July that Mount Kaimakchalan was cleared; by 19 July the same was true of Vermion; and in the first week of August Mount Beles, along the Bulgarian frontier, was also cleared. As before, the remnants of the Democratic Army in Western and Eastern Macedonia could retreat into Albania and Bulgaria respectively; but their reception was no longer enthusiastic, and the Yugoslav frontier itself was in process of being closed.[44] Since the same was true of the Yugoslav frontier with Albania, the rebels' source of supply was also drying up, for Albania could only serve as a channel for military resources drawn from elsewhere.

During the crucial months which settled the fate of the Communist rebellion, events elsewhere moved overwhelmingly against them. On 4 April the North Atlantic Treaty was signed by twelve countries, later expanded to fifteen (including Greece and Turkey). It was an event the force of which Stalin readily understood, and Soviet reactions were speedy. Three weeks later, on 26 April, two striking initiatives were taken. The *Tass* Agency announced the Soviet Government's willingness to end the blockade of Berlin, which in fact came about on 12 May. At the same time the Soviet delegate at the United Nations held talks on mediation in Greece with the American and British Under-Secretaries of State. Although these talks were soon adjourned and not renewed until September, the initiative showed that Stalin as well as Tito was ready to abandon the KKE. The KKE itself again offered peace terms on 3 May through Porphyrogennis in Prague. An appeal was also sent over the signature of Partsalidis to Dr Evatt, the Australian President of the General Assembly, for mediation by the United Nations.[45] It was couched in terms which characteristically combined defiance with conciliation. But although the rebels' offer was more far-reaching than ever before, the Greek Government, supported by the Americans and British, rejected any suggestion of mediation.

This was Sophoulis's last act of defiance, for he died on 24 June. It thus fell unexpectedly to his Deputy, the banker Diomidis, to preside over the final act; but it no longer mattered by this time who was Prime Minister. It was clear in Athens that the Communist states were in disarray, and all were ready in different degrees to reach a settlement. Discussions on the restoration of diplomatic relations between Greece and her northern neighbours actually began in May, though they soon broke down again, and only with the Yugoslavs did some understanding begin to emerge. Secret talks were also rumoured to have taken place between Tsaldaris and Tito; and Greek and Yugoslav staff officers were said to have met on the frontier. On 23 May UNSCOB reported a marked diminution of Yugoslav aid to the Democratic Army, though it had not yet altogether ceased. It was even alleged that the Yugoslavs had allowed the National Army to use their territory in its operations against Mount Kaimakchalan; but this was strenuously denied.[46] The Yugoslavs claimed to have been assisting the Democratic Army as late as November, and Belgrade Radio repudiated all accusations of treachery against Tito in December.[47] But there was an undeniable ambiguity in Tito's position in the latter part of 1949, which exposed him to bitter attacks by the Albanians and Bulgarians as well as the Greek Communists.

Albania and Bulgaria, however, had more to worry about than their relations with the Greeks. The Stalinist purges in consequence of the defection of Tito were now in full swing. In May Xoxe was put on trial in Tirana, and executed in June. In the latter month Kostov was expelled from the Bulgarian CP as a Titoist, and tried and executed in November. Dimitrov conveniently died in Moscow in July. Further afield, but for the same causes, Rajk was dismissed from the Hungarian Government and arrested in June: his trial and execution followed in the autumn. Gomulka had already fallen in Warsaw, though he survived to recover power in 1956. The purges in Rumania and Czechoslovakia were still to come, but the writing was on the wall. Former comrades-in-arms were also encouraged to denounce each other across national frontiers. Bulgarians were put on trial in Skopje for sabotage against Yugoslavia. Albanian and Bulgarian broadcasts accused Tito of collaborating with the Greek 'monarcho-fascists'. The Free Greece radio denounced Titoist agents such as the KKE's former ally, Gotchev, the wartime leader of SNOF. The Yugoslavs, on the other hand, denounced the KKE for having set up the Communist Organisation of Aegean Macedonia (KOAM) as an instrument of Macedonian autonomy. Tito, speaking at Skopje, openly criticised the KKE for the first time at the end of July. The Greek people's struggle, he declared, had been 'stifled and defeated' by their own leaders. On Ilinden day, 2 August, he boasted that the greater part of the Democratic Army was composed of Macedonians.

But he had already announced on 10 July the 'progressive closure' of the frontier with Greece. Belgrade Radio broadcast an offer of refuge in the Macedonian People's Republic for 'all Macedonians who lack a national home', which suggested rather the abandonment of any immediate hope of annexing Greek Macedonia.[48] On 21 July UNSCOB observers reported that the closure of the frontier had become effectively complete, and this was formally confirmed two days later by Kardelj, the Yugoslav Foreign Minister. A Greek Government memorandum to UNSCOB on 19 July gave fresh details of aid to the rebels from Albania and Bulgaria, but none from Yugoslavia. On 1 August the *Cominform Journal* published a bitter attack by Zakhariadis on the conduct of the Yugoslav CP during the Second World War and in December 1944; a similar article by Petros Roussos was published a week later.[49] Both the Albanian and Bulgarian Governments complained to the United Nations during August that the Greek National Army was infringing their frontiers in pursuit of the rebels. A sign of the changing times was that the Albanians ordered the internment of all Greek soldiers who crossed the frontier, without discrimination between the two sides. The Greek Government, however, still claimed that Albanians were to be found among the rebel prisoners taken, though these may in fact have been Albanian-speaking Chams, who were Greek nationals. The Free Greece radio accused the Yugoslavs of attacking the Democratic Army in the rear. In this topsy-turvy situation, yet another offer of peace terms by the rebels on 15 August was scarcely noticed.

Stalin had long since washed his hands of the Greek civil war: his one concern in the Balkans was to crush Tito. The omens were obvious even to people much less expert than the Communists at reading between the lines. On 13 June came *Pravda*'s acknowledgment of the territorial integrity of Greece. A week later the Soviet Government agreed in the Council of Foreign Ministers on terms for ending the blockade of Berlin. On 8 August Greece and Turkey were invited to join the Council of Europe. In fact, though the world did not yet know it, a polarisation of forces was taking place on both flanks of the Soviet Union, for 1949 was also the year of victory for the Chinese Communists. The emergence of Mao Tse-Tung had a strong appeal for Zakhariadis, and later seduced the Albanian Communists from their loyalty to Moscow. Mao was to prove a new Tito on a far greater scale, and he was recognised as such by the Yugoslavs themselves;[50] but that lay in the future. One Tito at a time was enough for Stalin, who still believed that he could be destroyed. On 17 August the Soviet journal *New Times* attacked him as an 'enemy of the Soviet Union'; and on 29 September the Soviet–Yugoslav Treaty of Friendship was denounced.

Evidence of the changed situation continued to accumulate under the eyes of the UNSCOB observers. In their report dated 2 August 1949, on the eve of the decisive battles, they again noted an improvement in relations between Greece and Yugoslavia, and reported 'less evidence of assistance by Yugoslavia to the Greek guerrillas'.[51] They also noted the continuing support of the rebels, both moral and material, by the neighbouring Communist powers. They were in no doubt about the use of Albanian and Bulgarian territory for supply and tactical movements, and for hospitals and training camps; and they had evidence that Greek children down to fourteen years of age were being trained as guerrillas in eastern Europe. They had also located the Free Greece radio on Rumanian territory – a significant move, since it had previously been in Yugoslavia. It was not yet the case, however, that the Yugoslavs had terminated all help to the rebels. Supplies were still entering Greece from Yugoslavia, and camps and hospitals were still in use, though all on a diminishing scale.[52] There was also some tactical use of Yugoslav territory, though chiefly in transit to other Balkan countries. The evidence was consistent with the view that Tito was gradually disengaging from his alliances, but had not yet reached the point of final breach.

First-hand evidence from a former political commissar in the Democratic Army confirms the interpretation given by UNSCOB.[53] Writing over twenty years later in a Yugoslav periodical, he gave a credible account of the evolution of Yugoslav policy as seen from the field, in the area of Kaimakchalan, where he served from 1947 to 1949. Support from north of the border for the Democratic Army was unqualified in 1947, and continued in the autumn of 1948 even while the breach between Tito and the Stalinist leadership of the KKE was growing. The official policy at that time was to disarm any Greek troops who crossed the frontier, whether belonging to the Democratic Army or to the Government forces. But in practice the Yugoslav frontier units still discriminated in favour of the rebels in many ways, including free passage into and out of Yugoslavia. Even as late as July 1949, the writer and his unit repeatedly crossed the frontier, though on one occasion they were temporarily held up from re-entering Greek territory. He was not in a position to verify the allegation by anti-Yugoslav propaganda that a meeting took place on 4 July 1949 between officers of the Greek National Army and the Yugoslavs, nor could he positively deny that Government forces were allowed to cross the border at any point during the final battle for Kaimakchalan. But he asserted that on the same date a friendly meeting took place between members of his own headquarters and a Yugoslav border-post, and that 'the attitude of our Yugoslav neighbours towards units of the Democratic Army near their borders remained favourable, despite the grave accusations of the Information Bureau' (the Cominform).

Yugoslav propaganda continued after the civil war to emphasise the scale of the help given to their Greek comrades. Refuting the accusation that they had deserted their allies and gone over to the imperialist camp overnight, Tempo asserted (in an ill-translated phrase) that 'only encrusted splitters could give credit to such fables'.[54] Yugoslavia, he said, had helped the people's revolutionary struggle in Greece 'far more than all the other countries led by the Soviet Union put together'.[55] He blamed the final catastrophe partly on the KKE's errors of policy, some of which 'could only be explained by the supremacy within the leadership of paid agents and by the influence of British imperialism'; and partly on the indifference of the Soviet Union, which 'had no interest whatever in a victory of the people's revolutionary movement in Greece'.[56] The first argument cannot be taken seriously, though it echoes Zakhariadis's own accusations against Siantos. It is especially absurd when set alongside Tempo's other allegation that the KKE had become 'an appendage of the foreign policy of the Soviet Government'. But his argument on Soviet indifference is likely to be correct; and the Albanians and Bulgarians had certainly become appendages of Soviet foreign policy.

In later analyses of the civil war, all Greek Communists placed the

Soviet–Yugoslav dispute high among the causes of defeat. Many put it first; some blamed Tito's defection alone. Greek and American military historians were more cautious. A detailed American examination identified three decisive factors: the appointment of Papagos, the defection of Tito and the Democratic Army's departure from guerrilla tactics.[57] To these factors, all of which he included, Zapheiropoulos added British and US aid, the morale of the Greek people, international understanding, the lack of popular support for the rebellion and the rebels' sheer weariness of the struggle.[58] Tsakalotos was disinclined to give credit to Papagos, and ascribed the National Army's victory to its success in gradually overcoming its own defects and the rebels' advantages, which he analysed in detail.[59] He pointed to a crucial factor when he argued that guerrilla operations are the natural resort of those 'who lack the means to confront superior and well-organised forces in open battle'. Here was a dilemma which Markos divined and Zakhariadis tried to override. Unless the rebels so confronted the enemy in the end, they could only win as a result of foreign intervention. But since there was going to be no such foreign intervention, the direct confrontation had to be risked; and once it was risked, defeat by the superior enemy was certain.

Such was the nature of the drama which reached its climax in August 1949. The other factors were incidental to the dilemma that logistically the Democratic Army must either surrender or be defeated. The appointment of Papagos was important, but any general could have given the necessary orders. The defection of Tito was also significant, though it left the Albanian frontier still open to the rebels. The superiority of the National Army's equipment was overwhelming, though the rebellion should have been defeated much earlier with much less. What was decisive was the fundamental logic of warfare, of which these were only symptoms. Pure guerrilla warfare can never win a final victory on its own. Either it must have the external support of conventional forces, or it must itself effect the transition from a guerrilla to a conventional war; and the timing of that transition is crucial, because if it is chosen wrongly there can be no going back. Markos was right in believing that the timing had been wrongly chosen in 1947–8, but Zakhariadis was right in maintaining that, once made, the choice was irreversible in 1948–9. He had no option but to stand by his tactical mistake, to dismiss Markos and to stand and fight in open battle on Vitsi and Grammos. For him to admit defeat was unthinkable. As late as 27 July he was still calling on soldiers of the National Army to desert, 'although at the time desertions were taking place in precisely the opposite direction'.[60] Even on 9 August, when Operation Torch A was already under way, he issued an order of the day declaring that: 'The defeat of the enemy on Vitsi will basically decide the battle of 1949 ... Our slogan is: not a step in retreat! ... Victory on Vitsi opens the way to victory throughout Greece!'[61]

If Zakhariadis believed his own words, he was deceiving himself as well as his followers. The Democratic Army could still be saved from destruction by retreat into Albania, but victory was no longer possible. At the beginning of August 1949, for the first time, a direct comparison of strength was possible because the Democratic Army, like its antagonists, was fully organised in divisions, brigades and lower formations. Apart from the disparity of equipment, the difference in sheer numbers was decisive.[62] On Grammos, the Democratic Army had two divisions, three brigades, one infantry battalion, one engineer battalion, sixteen field guns and a number of anti-tank and anti-aircraft guns and mortars. They faced two divisions, a brigade, three infantry battalions, two artillery regiments, and two squadrons and a troop of armoured vehicles. On Vitsi the rebels had two divisions, two brigades (one drawn from the Officers' School), forty-five mountain guns, twenty-seven anti-tank guns, fifteen anti-aircraft guns and supporting units of engineers and supply. Against them the National Army had five divisions, with one in reserve, a brigade and a regiment of light infantry, six battalions of the National Guard, four regiments of field artillery, three batteries of medium artillery, five batteries of mountain artillery, two regiments and a squadron of armoured vehicles and ample supporting services. Nor is a simple comparison of units conclusive, for in all cases the complement of those in the National Army was about double that of the Democratic Army. The contrast in numbers of battle-worthy troops was of the order of 4,700 against 25,000 on Grammos and 7,700 against more than 50,000 on Vitsi. These figures exclude the *Ethnophrourà* (National Guard), which could now be relegated to reserve and garrison duties.

Even more decisive was the support from other arms enjoyed by the National Army.[63] Having complete control of the sea, the Greek high command was able to supply the western sector through Preveza and the eastern sector through Salonika. Subject only to the risk of mines, the forward movement of supplies to road-heads at Konitsa, Kozani, Neapolis and Florina was relatively easy. Equally the national forces completely controlled the air, with advanced landing grounds at Kozani, Argos Orestikon and Florina. The operational units were three squadrons of Spitfires (totalling fifty-four aircraft), three reconnaissance flights of Harvards (twelve aircraft), one transport squadron of Dakotas (eleven aircraft), one flight assigned to artillery observation (ten aircraft) and an aerial photography flight. Most of the aircraft were operated from Kozani, which was equi-distant from both Vitsi and Grammos. The Air Force was reinforced on 22 August with forty-nine American Helldivers, which its Commander-in-Chief, Air Marshal Kelaidis, insisted, against US advice, on throwing immediately into the battle. Between 24 and 29 August the Air Force flew 826 sorties, and delivered 250 tons of bombs, rockets and napalm. An American observer commented that 'the return from the air effort immeasurably exceeded the return from any comparable effort on the ground'.[64] Hitherto, he wrote, 'the infantry-man paid the forfeit for past neglect of the close support problem'; but in the end air support was decisive.

For the first time, in other words, the Greek national forces were fully prepared for battle. Hitherto the need for air support had been neglected because each year's campaign was expected to be the last: in 1949 it was not neglected, and therefore the campaign was the last. Training too had never been taken so seriously as in the closing stages, when a special school was established at Drepanon, near Kozani, through which passed units of all the divisions due to be engaged in Operation Torch. An example of the meticulous planning was the training and equipment of a special unit of engineers to operate pontoons and collapsible boats, in order to cut off the expected line of retreat across the greater and lesser Lake Prespa. Another was the deception plan, which involved not only a feint against Grammos while the main attack was launched against Vitsi, but also the leakage of faked intelligence to the enemy. The only factors which could not be anticipated were chance and human failings. Both played some part in the final battles, but they did no more than delay the outcome by a few days. The basic plan of a feint at Grammos, an assault on Vitsi, followed by a final assault on Grammos, was in its general outline successful. For this the National Army had to thank not only the vast superiority furnished by the Americans, but also the improvement in its own high command, and the displacement of Markos by Zachariadis.

Operation Torch A, the feint at Grammos, began on 2 August under the command of Tsakalotos. The object was not merely to distract the rebels' attention from the main assault on Vitsi but also to gain positions which would facilitate the final assault on Grammos itself. The operation was limited by time rather than by objectives, since some of the units engaged had to be transferred to Vitsi not later than 9 August. Tsakalotos attacked with two brigades and two battalions from the north, based on Argos Orestikon, and with three brigades from the south, based on Konitsa. On the northern sector he captured a key height on the first day and two more on 5 August. The effect was to sever connection on Greek territory (though not, of course, the route through Albania) between

Grammos and Vitsi. Although all these positions were held by the National Army, no more progress was made on the northern sector before 9 August. On the southern sector one important height was taken, but otherwise the battle was inconclusive. The National Army's casualties were very heavy, and the advance less than had been hoped. Tsakalotos blamed one of his brigadiers for faltering at a crucial moment; and he was also unlucky with bad weather. But he was indignant when Vendiris, the Army Commander, withdrew his artillery on 8 August, although this was according to plan. The artillery was needed for Operation Torch B, the assault on Vitsi.

Vitsi is separated from Grammos by a broad valley running north-westwards at right-angles to the Albanian frontier. The valley was the boundary between I and II Corps, and it was now wholly under the control of the National Army up to the frontier. Several tributary streams flowed through it, to join the River Aliakmon immediately west of Kastoria. The Aliakmon itself divided Vitsi, with the motor-road from Kastoria to Florina running alongside it for much of its course. Several other tributaries of the Aliakmon also carved valleys through Vitsi, and these were to provide the National Army with its lines of attack. The plan provided for five main thrusts up the valleys.[65] The spearhead was the Third Commando Division, which was to drive its way up the Aliakmon and to reach the Prespa lakes as soon as possible in order to cut off the main line of retreat into Albania, which lay across a narrow neck (Laimos) between the greater and the lesser Prespa. Two divisions, the Tenth and Eleventh, were to follow up the Commandos on a converging course. The Second Division was to safeguard the flanks of the Eleventh Division by gaining control of the heights north of Florina, running parallel with the Yugoslav frontier. The Ninth Division, on the left flank, was to thrust northwards parallel to the Albanian frontier. If all these attacks succeeded, the Democratic Army would be driven back upon the Prespa lakes but prevented from escaping either into Yugoslavia or into Albania.

The execution was imperfect, but not disastrously so. After an initial bombardment from the air, beginning at 05.00 on 10 August, and from the artillery at 05.30, the attack was launched by a brigade of the Second Division on the northern sector. It met strong resistance, and only succeeded in capturing its main targets by the evening of 11 August. Consequently the right flank of the Third Commando Division, and the Eleventh Division in support of it, was left exposed. Fortunately for them, the Democratic Army failed to exploit its opportunity, but the commander of II Corps was shaken by the setback and his subsequent judgment was more than once at fault. Both the Commando Division and the Tenth and Eleventh Divisions gained their targets during 10 August, but were obliged to consolidate their positions on the following day against counter-attacks. Meanwhile the Corps Commander had wrongly deduced that the rebels were on the run, and ordered the Ninth Division to advance by day on 11 August northwards along the Albanian frontier to cut off their retreat. The advance took place over open ground within range of the enemy's artillery on the frontier-line (perhaps actually on Albanian territory), a dangerous exposure for which the Corps Commander was criticised by Papagos. Vendiris, the Army Commander, less justifiably removed the Divisional Commander from his post. But once more the Democratic Army failed to exploit its opportunity.

The third day of the operation, 12 August, was a day of deadlock, in which the National Army made no progress and suffered heavy losses. But by the following day the high command of the Democratic Army began to find the pressure too great. Constant attacks from the air, inferior equipment on the ground, exhaustion of their troops and depletion of their limited ammunition, had all exacted a heavy toll. It was simply impossible to continue the battle for more than a few days against an enemy to whom time was no object. On 14 August the rebels were beginning an orderly retreat along two routes into Albania: the northern route across the Laimos strip between the Prespa lakes, and a more southerly route through Kroustallopigi, along which in peace-time runs the only motor-road from Greek Macedonia into Albania. The Third Commando Division and the Ninth Division had both failed to reach their targets in time to cut off the retreat. Only on 15 August were the boating engineers able to carry out crossings of the lesser Lake Prespa, but by that time between 5,000 and 6,000 rebels had escaped into Albania, of whom between 2,000 and 2,500 were able to re-enter Grammos as organised units.[66] Their known losses were 1,182 killed and 637 captured; but Zakhariadis was able to claim that 'the main body of the Democratic Army is intact with its rifle at the ready'. The National Army lost 116 killed and 1,526 wounded. It was an undoubted victory, but at heavy cost, and it was not the final battle.

The main consequence of the battle of Vitsi, apart from the fact that it regained a crucial area of territory for the Greek Government, was the loss of equipment by the Democratic Army. Captured equipment included 39 field guns, 33 anti-tank guns, 16 anti-aircraft guns, 115 mortars and 436 machine-guns and light automatics. The rebels had no possibility of replacing them. Remnants of four brigades and the Officers' School re-entered Grammos from Albania in time for the final battle, but their equipment was inadequate and their morale low. They joined three divisions, comprising nine brigades, already entrenched on Grammos, making a total of about 7,000 to 8,000 men, with very poor supporting services. Against them Tsakalotos could now deploy five divisions (two of which, the Third and Ninth, had been transferred from Vitsi), totalling fifteen brigades, with four regiments of light infantry, five regiments of field artillery, three batteries of medium artillery, five batteries of mountain artillery and one of anti-tank guns, and a regiment and two squadrons of armoured vehicles. His overwhelming superiority was reinforced by the Air Force, to which the American Helldivers were added just in time. On 13 August Kitrilakis conveyed to Tsakalotos the final order from Papagos to carry out Operation Torch C.

Another ten days were to pass, however, before the attack was launched. The basic plan of operations was simple. Grammos was under pressure from the east and south, its northern and western flanks being protected by the Albanian frontier. Reading from north to south, Tsakalotos deployed against the eastern flank the Third Commando Division and the Ninth Division, both transferred from Vitsi to the nearest point on the foothills of Grammos; the First and Fifteenth Divisions; and the Seventy-seventh Brigade, operating independently. The southern arm of the semi-circle was completed by the Eighth Division, whose function was to block the rebels' retreat as they were driven southwards by the main thrust of the four northern divisions. But Tsakalotos was a perfectionist, and difficulties arose. Morale was not good, there were disagreements among the senior commanders, and the Americans were reluctant to commit the Helldivers with inexperienced pilots.[67] Tsakalotos did his best to overcome the first trouble by a series of personal visits, to talk to his officers and men. He left them with a watch-word alluding to the principal target on Grammos: 'Rendezvous at the chapel on point 2520'. The third trouble was overcome by the personal insistence of the Commander-in-Chief of the Royal Hellenic Air Force. But the tactical disagreements of the generals proved more intractable, and took some days to resolve.

The ultimate target was the highest ridge of Grammos, formed by a row of peaks running eastwards from the Albanian frontier: point 2520 (the summit) – Skyrtsa – Kiapha – Souphlikas. On either side of this ridge rose the two great rivers, the Aliakmon on the northern slope, and the Sarandoporos on the southern. Grammos was thus divided into two sectors, the northern and southern, not by a valley like Vitsi but by a formidable ridge, which Papagos himself called the backbone of the rebels' defensive position, 'because whoever holds it is master of the whole area'. The original plan approved by Vendiris provided for an immediate direct assault on Kiapha from the north. Tsakalotos's staff argued that such an assault was impossible. Moreover, even if Kiapha were taken, there were routes of escape into Albania both north and south of the ridge, the most important being by way of the village of Slimnitsa and the pass known as Porta Osman in the north-west corner of Grammos. Tsakalotos saw that the strongest point held by the Democratic Army was the ridge of Tsarno, to the north-east of the Kiapha ridge, and that this directly covered the passage through Porta Osman, which was a route of supply as well as escape.

Tsakalotos therefore proposed to Vendiris, at the conference in Kozani on 19 August, that Tsarno should be the first target, followed by Kiapha, with a feint further south to disguise the direction of attack. Other senior generals were hesitant, and Kitrilakis wanted to refer the change to Papagos, who was on his sick-bed in Athens. Tsakalotos angrily insisted, and Vendiris finally gave way. The attack on Tsarno was entrusted to the First Division, with the Third Commando Division to exploit it in the direction of the summit ridge, and the Fifteenth Division to carry out the diversionary operation to the south. The Ninth Division was to move west and then south along the Albanian frontier to cut off the rebels' route through Porta Osman – a manoeuvre similar to that which had been entrusted to the same division on Vitsi, but this time to be carried out by night and under a new commander. In the southern sector the Eighth Division and the Seventy-seventh Independent Brigade were to conduct a holding operation, preventing any escape southwards out of Grammos. By 20 August, when Tsakalotos held a final conference with his divisional commanders at Nestorion, all was settled. But he still had trouble with the commander of the Third Commando Division, who happened to be Papagos's brother-in-law, General Kallinski. Kallinski argued that his men needed more rest after their exertions on Vitsi. Tsakalotos retorted that they could not honourably be absent in the hour of victory.

The attack was to begin during the night of 24–25 August. So confident was the Greek high command of victory that King Paul was invited to the Corps HQ, where he arrived on 23 August. On the following day Tsakalotos conducted him, together with Van Fleet and other American and British senior officers, to his observation-post outside the village of Ammouda, west of Nestorion. The King spent the night of 24–25 August at the command-post, and gave the formal order for the attack to begin at 21.00 on the 24th. During the night the Ninth Division successfully captured its targets between the Albanian frontier and the upper waters of the Aliakmon. On the 25th the First Division, supported by an overwhelming barrage of artillery and the first sorties of the Helldivers, captured the height of Tsarno by midday against resolute opposition. With

characteristic flamboyance, Tsakalotos turned to the King at 12.15 and
said: 'Your Majesty, Grammos has fallen; you can start on your return
journey whenever you decide.' It was a pardonable exaggeration. In fact
the battle was to last another three days. The Fifteenth Division, faced by
rugged terrain and fierce resistance, failed to make any substantial advance
during the 25th; and Kallinski ignored his orders to launch the Third
Commando Division into action until the 27th. But as Tsakalotos later
wrote, 'after two or three heights fell, the enemy did not offer strong
resistance'.

The heroes of the battle for Grammos were the Ninth Division, who
had so nearly disgraced themselves on Vitsi. On 25–26 August they moved
rapidly parallel to the frontier to cut off Porta Osman. The commander of
the Fifteenth Division, finding himself checked on the southern ridge,
detached a brigade with Tsakalotos's consent to reinforce the success of
the Ninth Division in the north. After a severe battle, Porta Osman was
captured by 12.30 on 27 August, leaving the rebels with no escape into
Albania except south of the main ridge. On the same day the First Division
was able to continue its advance from Tsarno, and the Third Commando
Division moved at last from the north. The two divisions advanced in
parallel southwards upon the main ridge of Grammos, the First Division
making for Souphlikas and Kiapha, the Third for Skyrtsa. But it was the
Ninth Division that reached the summit of Grammos first, at point 2520.
All the heights of the great ridge fell on 28 August. On the following day
the Commandos and the Ninth Division pressed on southwards to close
the last of the passes in Grammos through which the rebels could escape.
By 30 August the battle was over. The National Army lost 245 dead, 1,452
wounded and 11 missing on Grammos. The Democratic Army lost 922
dead, 765 captured and 179 surrendered. Most of their heavy equipment
was captured or destroyed. In July they still had 16,400 names on their
nominal roll; at the end of August there were only 3,710.[68]

Operation Torch in its three phases effectively ended the civil war; but
this was not immediately obvious. The rebel leaders were taken by surprise at the overwhelming strength of the attack. They had expected a
victory as late as 20 August, the eve of battle, when a resolution of the
Politburo declared that:

On Grammos, in any event, we have all the capability needed for
dealing a mortal blow to the enemy. We have sufficient forces and
equipment. More favourable ground (than on Vitsi) . . . Here we can
and must bury monarcho-fascism. Our watch-word is: Grammos
will be the tomb of monarcho-fascism.'[69]

Karagiorgis was similarly reported to have said that 'Grammos will in future be the main seat of our defence,' and forecast using it as a base for new aggression.[70] Even after the battle the leadership of the KKE did not at once give up hope of recovery. Zakhariadis and his staff escaped into Albania, and made their way thence to Bulgaria. Probably 2,000 or 3,000 men escaped with their leaders, and another 1,000 had escaped from III Corps into Bulgaria. Others were still in Albanian or Bulgarian training-camps. On 2 September the Greek high command announced that 'not more than five thousand rebels' remained on Greek soil. But even that figure was exaggerated, for Communist records show their strength dwindling from 3,710 to 2,150 in September, 1,760 in October, 1,275 in November and only 815 at the end of the year.[71]

On 19 September 1949 UNSCOB submitted a supplementary report to the General Assembly, in which it stated that 'the Greek Armed Forces have eliminated guerrilla resistance along the northern borders of Greece and have resumed effective control of those areas', but added that 'a large proportion of the Greek guerrillas together with large numbers of other Greek nationals have sought refuge in or been forcibly taken into the territories of the northern neighbours of Greece, in particular Albania'.[72] Although it was reported that they had been disarmed and interned, UNSCOB thought fit to remind the Communist governments of their duty 'to prevent use of their territories in any way against the security of the Greek State' and 'to cease forthwith their aid to the Greek guerrillas'. The Yugoslav Government was exempted from these adjurations, in acknowledgment of its decision to close the frontier. But neither UNSCOB nor the Greek Government was inclined to rule out all possibility of renewed attack. To remind the international community that the Balkan problem was not solved, the Secretary-General of the United Nations added a note on the abducted Greek children, including a report by the International Red Cross on its abortive efforts to secure their repatriation from eastern Europe.[73]

No doubt Zakhariadis discussed with his Albanian and Bulgarian allies the prospect of resuming the fight. But the defection of Tito and the indifference of Stalin were sufficient reasons for rejecting the idea. In the same month, September 1949, the Yugoslav Government began openly to re-define its position as a neutral between East and West: on 4 September *Borba* actually warned the Yugoslav people of the risk of war, and hinted at the possibility of western aid. Elsewhere in eastern Europe the convulsions consequent on Tito's defection left little attention for the woes of the KKE. Compared to the trials of Rajk in September and Kostov in November, and the final disgrace of Gomulka in December, the fate of

Zakhariadis and his colleagues was of little moment. The remnants of the Democratic Army were received without friendliness in Albania and Bulgaria, and with vindictive hostility by their own high command, within which bitter recriminations had already broken out.[74]

On 9 October the Sixth Plenum finally accepted the inevitable. After passing a formal resolution denouncing Tito and once more modifying its Macedonian policy into the old formula based on 'the rights of minorities', it decided to 'discontinue the armed struggle for the time being, leaving only small guerrilla detachments as a means of exerting pressure'.[75] The announcement of this decision on 16 October was accompanied by the threat that 'the monarcho-fascists would be mistaken if they think that the struggle has ended and that the Democratic Army has ceased to exist'. Both UNSCOB and the Greek Government took the threat at its face value, though Dean Acheson in Washington declared on 19 October that the civil war was 'substantially over', and President Truman acclaimed the Greek Government's victory in his report to Congress on 28 November.

Zakhariadis admitted in his speech to the Sixth Plenum (which was published as a pamphlet under the title *New Situation, New Tasks*) that the Democratic Army gave up the struggle simply because it had been beaten, though at the same time he claimed that the Revolution had not really been defeated.[76] The one specific cause of failure which he identified on this occasion was the treachery of Tito. For the rest, he did indeed look to the future, with copious quotations from Lenin and Stalin. In particular, he saluted the proclamation of the Chinese People's Republic, which had taken place a week earlier, on 1 October. So far as Greece was concerned, he declared that the economic and political struggle would continue; that the King was planning to establish a military dictatorship; and that Anglo-American imperialism was doomed to fail. He referred only by implication to the revision of policy on Macedonia. It was on the whole a courageous and skilful performance from a man who had suffered a disastrous defeat for which the responsibility was mainly his own. Nor did he flag in the bitter years that followed. In 1950 he published another pamphlet called *The Communist as People's Champion*, and in 1952 another called *The Problems of Leadership of the KKE*. Both were extensively used for training new cadres, the latter in particular in a 'Fighters' Seminar' from June to September 1952. Clearly Zakhariadis meant what he said: a 'fourth round' was not to be excluded.

Meanwhile Greece was left to face the ruins, not without material aid but in a state of numbed shock. Various estimates have been made of the total damage, among which a reasonable average can be struck.[77] On the

Government side, the dead have been put at 70,000, including over 1,000 officers and over 14,000 other ranks. (Figures compiled by the General Staff are somewhat lower, but to them must be added the wounded and missing, many of whom would later have to be recorded as killed.) Rebel casualties were put by the General Staff at well over 38,000 killed: there were additionally over 40,000 captured or surrendered, who had somehow to be rehabilitated. Of those recorded as killed, well over 5,000 men were executed by one side or the other, the great majority by the Communists (whose tally included 165 priests). There were also about three-quarters of a million made homeless, and about 28,000 children taken abroad. Physical damage to property, livestock and communications is literally incalculable: suffice it to say that it was far greater than under the German occupation. It is not surprising that recovery was slow to begin. Not until Papagos became Prime Minister in 1952 did it gather real momentum. For at least the first two years after 1949 it was difficult for the Greeks to believe that their ordeal was really over. When even in 1950 they still lost 14 officers and 177 men from guerrilla action, their doubts are understandable. Despite the confidence of the Americans, others besides the Greeks also shared their doubts.

The Political Committee of the UN General Assembly voted on 4 November 1949 to continue the work of UNSCOB and to recommend an arms embargo against Albania and Bulgaria, which was confirmed by the General Assembly itself on 18 November. The difference between the Communist states was underlined by the decision of the US Government at the same time to relax restrictions on the export of strategic materials to Yugoslavia. UNSCOB in fact continued to operate for another two years. Two of its reports in 1950 blamed the Albanians and Bulgarians as before, and showed evidence of the continued existence of rebel units on a small scale. There were minor raids, sabotage, propaganda and contacts in the villages, mainly based on Bulgaria: 'external support of the remaining guerrilla activity within Greece has not ceased'.[78] As late as 30 August 1950 UNSCOB observers interrogated a rebel who had entered Greece only a few days before.[79] He had been trained in Poland and infiltrated by way of Albania, where he said there were still rebel camps near Elbasan and Boureli. About the same time three subversive agents were captured in Corfu, who confirmed the existence of the Albanian camps. By 1951 major networks of espionage were again at work in Athens. Many Communist declarations confirmed the intention to fight on. On 14 November 1949 the Politburo ordered the renewal of guerrilla tactics; and at the Seventh Plenum in June 1950 Vlandas claimed that 'the main forces of the

Democratic Army in Greece' were still in being. Recruits were still being received in Bulgaria and Albania in 1951 and later.[80]

Nevertheless the assumption that these threats were bluff persisted, and was to prove correct. In the last week of November 1949 the final withdrawal of British troops began, though the training missions remained for a time. A new law was passed suspending all capital sentences passed by court-martial, subject to review by the Supreme Court of Appeal, and martial law was lifted in Attica and the Peloponnese by the end of the year. Fresh attempts at reconciliation, first by the Australian delegation to the United Nations and then by the Soviet Union, proved abortive because the Greek Government no longer had any need to compromise. But they were not vindictive: in January they informed the United Nations that they were ready to settle their differences with Yugoslavia and to restore diplomatic relations with Albania and Bulgaria.

Still less were the Greek people in a mood of *mnisikakía* or 'remembrance of wrongs'. At the General Election in March 1950, there was a pronounced swing leftwards. Although, as usual, no single party won an overall majority, the Liberal groups emerged as the strongest, and first Venizelos and then Plastiras formed coalition governments. The latter was criticised from the right for favouring an early amnesty. More remarkable was the electoral success of a 'Democratic Group' which was commonly recognised to be a front for the KKE. It won 153,000 votes and twenty-two seats (including eighteen Communists). Among those elected were Saraphis and Mandakas, the two most senior survivors of ELAS, neither of whom had served in the Democratic Army.

Gradually the pretence that the KKE could renew the civil war faded into mythology. Other problems supervened: the Korean War in June 1950, the gradual emergence of a Yugoslav–Greek alliance, the intensification both of the Cold War and of the Stalinist purges in eastern Europe. The KKE faithfully reacted to every turn of the international screw by splitting again and again. At the Seventh Plenum in May 1950 Zakhariadis was under attack from Bartzotas; and Karagiorgis sharply criticised him in a letter to the Central Committee in the following month. At the Third Party Conference in October 1950, when Partsalidis also criticised Zakhariadis, the latter found it expedient to ally himself with Bartzotas in denouncing Partsalidis, Markos, Karagiorgis and (posthumously) Aris Veloukhiotis and Siantos. This was the beginning of a clean sweep of the old leadership, to which both Zakhariadis and Bartzotas eventually fell victims. At the Sixth Plenum of the new Central Committee in March 1956, both men were removed from office, while Markos was briefly rehabilitated. A new leadership emerged under Grozos, Partsalidis,

Koligiannis and Stringos. This transformation of the KKE was influenced by the Twentieth Congress of the Communist Party of the Soviet Union held a month earlier, at which Khrushchev delivered his famous denunciation of Stalin, followed by his partial reconciliation with Tito. But the changes were difficult to interpret correctly, and they proved ephemeral: Markos, for example, was disgraced again in 1957.

The Soviet–Yugoslav reconciliation had the effect of weakening the Yugoslav–Greek alliance, which had been formalised in 1954 in a three-power pact with Turkey. Simultaneously the Cypriot dispute, which had begun to emerge seriously in 1950, soured relations between Greece and Turkey. The KKE found itself with new opportunities to exploit, but doubtful whether it had the right leadership to exploit them. On the one hand, Greek nationalism was in the ascendant: to exploit this it was necessary to form a patriotic front, which the KKE duly did under the name of the United Democratic Left (EDA). EDA prospered in Parliament and gradually evolved a distinct policy of its own, by no means subservient to the exiled leaders of the KKE: in 1956 it openly supported Greece's membership of NATO, and in 1958 it became the second party in Parliament. On the other hand, it became desirable to shed the leaders who had so badly failed the party in the civil war, whether they were Titoists or Stalinists. By the end of the 1950s all the leaders of the KKE in the Resistance and the Civil War were either dead or expelled from the Party. So the KKE proceeded from schism to schism as events twisted and turned to their disadvantage. The Cyprus dispute, the Sino-Soviet quarrel, the military coup in April 1967, all aggravated the disintegration, until twenty years after the civil war it was possible to identify at least five distinct factions each claiming the mantle of the KKE.

It was characteristic of the KKE that a change in the party line necessitated a change in the leadership. In this respect once more it differed from all other Greek parties, which were loose alliances grouped around a personality rather than a policy. Precisely for this reason Greek Communism was vulnerable to the vagaries of Stalinism, which had little regard for any consideration other than the security of the Soviet Union. Soviet security dictated many changes of policy towards major powers which Stalin could not hope to dominate (Britain, France, Germany, the USA). Towards lesser powers in eastern Europe (Poland, Rumania, Hungary, Czechoslovakia) it dictated a consistent line of policy which culminated in domination. Towards the unsatisfied Balkan neighbours of Greece (Albania, Yugoslavia, Bulgaria) not even the dictates of Soviet security could be consistent; and policy towards Greece was simply the incoherent residuum of all these forces. This was a fact which patriotic Greeks could never appreciate, since they held it to be axiomatic that Greece was central to the foreign policy of every major power. But the Greek Communists, if they did not know the awful truth at the beginning of the first round, certainly learned it by the end of the third. The rank and file of the KKE, and in particular its leaders, were expendable. Without a trace of compunction, Stalin let them go to their doom.

Notes

CHAPTER I

1. Text in Lagdas, II, pp. 461–71.
2. Lagdas, II, p. 460.
3. Quoted in Pentzopoulos, p. 133.
4. Pre-war statistics in Barker, p. 12.
5. Pentzopoulos, pp. 97–8, 134–6.
6. Kofos, p. 5. For the cautious habit, see Dakin, p. 168.
7. Kofos, p. 44.
8. Barker, p. 11; Dakin, p. 25.
9. Kofos, p. 68.
10. Auty, p. 46; Palmer and King, pp. 23–4.
11. Palmer and King, pp. 32–5.
12. Burks, p. 78.
13. Burks, pp. 26, 42.
14. Pentzopoulos, pp. 188, 192.
15. Zakhariadis, p. 10.
16. Quoted in Christidès, p. 122.
17. See, especially, Kousoulas, pp. 127–38.
18. Texts in Papakonstantinou, pp. 146–9.
19. Papakonstantinou, p. 149.
20. Papandreou, p. 18.
21. Woodward, II. p. 222.
22. Khrysokhoou, I, p. 10; Papakonstantinou, pp. 151–2; facsimile of the German order in The Conspiracy Against Greece, p. 17.
23. Khrysokhoou, I, p. 55.

CHAPTER 2

1. G. Laskaris, quoted in Jecchinis, p. 62.
2. Kanellopoulos, p. 36.
3. Text in Istorikòn Arkheion, No. 1, p. 26. The version in Documents Regarding the Situation in Greece, January 1945 (Cmd 6592) is corrupt.
4. Tsouderos, pp. 46–8; Pipinelis, p. 130.
5. SOE Operations in Greece, App. III, p. 8.
6. Enepekidis, p. 35.
7. See, particularly, Iatrides, pp. 81–7, 118–22.
8. Pyromaglou, Kartalis, I, p. 156n.
9. Gatopoulos, pp. 224–8.
10. Neubacher, p. 102.
11. Gardner, p. 58; Khrysokhoou, pp. 20–5; Modis, pp. 178–87.
12. SOE Operations, App. III(A), p. 2. The date may be a mistake for 1942.
13. Khoutas, p. 84; Gatopoulos, p. 642.
14. Pyrsos (1967), No. 6, p. 23.
15. Zakhariadis, p. 4.
16. Khrysokhoou, I, p. 44.

17. Myers, p. 212.
18. Djilas, p. 33.
19. Vukmanović, p. 33.
20. Pyromaglou, pp. 65–6.
21. Khrysokhoou, I, pp. 39–40.
22. Stavridis, p. 531; Lagdas, I, pp. 391–2.
23. Text in Khoutas, pp. 62–3.
24. Kanellopoulos, p. 41.
25. Dalton, *The Fateful Years*, pp. 367, 382.
26. See Woodhouse in *Balkan Studies*, Vol. XII, No. 2, p. 354.
27. Saraphis, pp. 7–14.
28. Saraphis, p. 18; Kédros, p. 225.
29. Myers, p. 102.
30. Eudes, pp. 45–8; Kédros, pp. 176–9. Tzimas in *Pyrsos* (1967), No. 6, p. 22, records that on the same day he was married. The words quoted were addressed to myself.
31. For detailed evidence, see Woodhouse in *Balkan Studies*, Vol. XII, No. 2, pp. 347–55.
32. *SOE Records*, Cairo to Harling, No. 28, 21 December 1942.
33. *SOE Records*, Harling to Cairo, No. 37, 24 January 1943.
34. *SOE Records*, Cairo to Harling, No. 59 of 29 January 1943.
35. *SOE Records*, Harling to Cairo, No. 76 of 3 February 1943.
36. *SOE Records*, Harling to Cairo, No. 62 of 24 February 1943, drafted by myself.
37. *SOE Records*, Harling to Cairo, No. 44 of 24 January 1943.
38. *SOE Records*, Harling to Cairo, No. 50 of 21 February 1943.
39. Leeper, p. 4.
40. Iatrides, p. 21.
41. Pyromaglou, p. 53; Hamson, pp. 91, 100; Myers, p. 72.
42. Tzimas in *Pyrsos* (1967), No. 6, p. 20.
43. Pyromaglou, pp. 71–2; Myers, pp. 114–15.
44. Myers, pp. 148–9; Pyromaglou, p. 85, correcting Woodhouse, p. 70.
45. Myers, p. 130.
46. Khrysokhoou, pp. 33–6.
47. *Pyrsos* (1967), No. 2, p. 20.
48. Eudes, p. 77; Nepheloudis, p. 15.
49. Tsouderos, pp. 33–6.
50. Gatopoulos, pp. 224–31; Khrysokhoou, I, pp. 74–5.
51. Khoutas, pp. 152–3.
52. *SOE Records*, Harling to Cairo, No. 264, 9 March 1943. Zervas later wrote that his declaration was virtually extorted from him by myself (Kédros, p. 216n.). My recollection is that it went far beyond my expectations. Recalling it only from memory in 1947, I wrongly described it as two distinct telegrams, one to the King and one to the British Government (*Apple of Discord*, p. 74). This error has regrettably led astray some later writers, particularly Richter. He gives the English text correctly, but tries to dissect it into separate components (Richter, pp. 274–7, 595), which are imaginary.
53. Gould Lee, p. 206.
54. Pyromaglou, p. 79.
55. The fullest account of the diplomatic and political background will be found in Woodward, *British Foreign Policy in the Second World War*, III, pp. 383–95. Woodward points out (p. 390n.) that his account is based solely on Foreign Office records, not those of SOE.
56. Condit, pp. 101–3.
57. *SOE Operations in Greece*, p. 23.
58. Myers, p. 127; Hamson, p. 156.
59. *SOE Operations in Greece*, App. II(A). For details of the following exchanges, see Woodhouse in Auty and Clogg, pp. 136–8.
60. *SOE Operations in Greece*, App. II(A).
61. *SOE Operations in Greece*, App. II, p. 4.
62. *FO Documents*, 371/37202, RR5396, 21 June 1943.
63. *SOE Operations in Greece*, App. II(A).
64. Myers, pp. 189–90.
65. Estimates of EDES and ELAS based on *SOE Operations in Greece*, App. III(A).

66. Saraphis, pp. 50–1; Tzimas in *Pyrsos* (1967), No. 6, pp. 22–3.

67. Tzimas in *Pyrsos* (1967), No. 6, p. 20; Saraphis, p. 10.

68. Richter, p. 293.

69. Saraphis, p. 65; Myers, pp. 177, 194.

70. Myers, *Greek Entanglement* (London, 1955); Saraphis, *Greek Resistance Army* (English translation, London, 1951); Tzimas, two articles in *Pyrsòs* (Dresden, 1967), Nos. 1 and 6. See also Woodhouse in Auty and Clogg, pp. 124–30.

71. For example, the text of the first draft of the National Bands Agreement was published in Athens by an anti-Communist organisation in June 1943 (*Tò EAM apénanti toù éthnous*, pp. 23–4).

72. *Pyrsos* (1967), No. 1, p. 19.

73. Vukmanović, p. 34; Papandreou, pp. 20–1.

74. Djilas, p. 13.

75. Khoutas, pp. 198–9.

76. Sweet-Escott, *Baker Street Irregular*, p. 161.

77. Myers, pp. 222–3.

78. Saraphis, p. 28.

79. Sweet-Escott, *Greece*, p. 96, quoting *Bank of Greece Review*, December 1951.

80. Text of the message in *EAM White Book*, Document 34. See also Wilson, p. 166; Gatopoulos, p. 666.

81. *Pyrsos* (1967), No. 1, p. 21.

82. Eudes, p. 230; and see pp. 104, 137 below.

83. Pyromaglou, pp. 96, 171.

84. *EAM White Book*, Document 37.

85. Vlandas's MS., p. 44.

86. Zakhariadis, p. 9.

87. Vukmanović, pp. 31, 86.

88. Vukmanović, pp. 14–44.

89. Petsopoulos, pp. 94–100.

90. For details, see Woodhouse in Auty and Clogg, pp. 125–7.

91. Pyromaglou, pp. 89, 98–9.

92. Pyromaglou, p. 75; Khoutas, p. 187.

93. Pyromaglou, pp. 97–109.

94. Eudes, p. 67.

95. Papandreou, p. 40.

96. Palmer and King, pp. 97–9; Auty, p. 92.

97. *SOE Records*, Mobility to Cairo, No. S148, 1 July 1943. 'Mobility' was the code-name of Myers's HQ on the move.

98. Myers, p. 211.

99. Eudes, p. 66; Palmer and King, pp. 95–9.

100. Matthews, p. 79; Vukmanović, pp. 14–16.

101. Eudes, pp. 67–9. An order forecasting a Balkan GHQ was alleged to have been issued by ELAS GHQ over the signatures of Tzimas, Aris and Saraphis on 9 August 1943 (text in *The Conspiracy Against Greece*, p. 13); but Tzimas was certainly elsewhere on that date (Myers, p. 241), and the decision placing ELAS under the British GHQ, Middle East, was already in effective operation.

102. Palmer and King, pp. 103–6; Richter, p. 296n.

103. *SOE Records*, Mobility to Cairo, No. S148, 1 July 1943.

104. *SOE Records*, Cairo to Mobility, unnumbered, 9 July 1943. The warning was originated by myself: Myers, p. 230.

105. Wilson, p. 179.

106. Details in Pijade, pp. 6–23.

107. Condit, pp. 223–68; Gardner, pp. 128–61.

108. 400 H. C. Deb. 5 s. (24 May 1944), col. 778.

109. *SOE Records*, Harling to Cairo, No. 214, 1 March 1943; Enepekidis, pp. 111–12.

110. Kofos, p. 132.

111. Palmer and King, 82, 98, 118–19.

112. Greek text in Khoutas, p. 324; English translation in *The Conspiracy Against Greece*, pp. 11–12. See also Kofos, pp. 134–5, and Armstrong, p. 199.

113. Enepekidis, pp. 78–82.

114. Papandreou, pp. 13–25.

115. Pipinelis, p. 124.
116. Kanellopoulos, pp. 215–17; Pipinelis, pp. 125–6.
117. Tsouderos, p. 62.

CHAPTER 3

1. Myers, pp. 241–2; *SOE Records*, Lemon to Cairo, No. 294, 24 July 1943. Lemon was the code-name of the BMM HQ. For fuller details, see Woodhouse in Auty and Clogg, pp. 139–40.
2. First-hand accounts: Leeper, pp. 30–5; Myers, pp. 236–65; Pipinelis, pp. 153–6; Pyromaglou, pp. 146–65; Tsouderos, pp. 63–9; Wilson, pp. 166–8. Other accounts: Eudes, pp. 89–94; Kédros, pp. 300–6; Kousoulas, pp. 167–73; Woodward, III, pp. 392–5; Auty and Clogg, pp. 139–43.
3. Pyromaglou, pp. 149–50, 160; texts of documents in Pyromaglou, pp. 154–5.
4. Tsouderos, pp. 66–7; Pyromaglou, pp. 156–7; Churchill, V, pp. 473–4.
5. Woodward, III, p. 393.
6. Iatrides, pp. 38–40, 82–93.
7. Myers, pp. 249–50, 259–61.
8. Saraphis, p. 70.
9. Saraphis, pp. 96–9.
10. Text in Woodhouse, p. 301.
11. Gardner, p. 169.
12. ELD, *Théseis*, p. 12.
13. Woodhouse, pp. 78, 295; Khoutas, pp. 381–4, 398–9; Loverdo, pp. 226–7.
14. See pp. 91–2 below.
15. Khoutas, pp. 420–1.
16. Bartzotas, p. 49, quoted in Kousoulas, p. 189.
17. Enepekidis, pp. 180–5.
18. Woodward, III, pp. 395–8; Churchill, V, p. 475. The latter is somewhat ambiguous about the timing envisaged in his minute of 29 September 1943.
19. Gardner, p. 138; Saraphis, p. 130.
20. Pyromaglou, pp. 199–200.
21. Condit, p. 266 (map of destroyed villages).
22. Myers, p. 224.
23. Examples in Enepekidis, pp. 40, 69–77, 180–5, 205.
24. Enepekidis, pp. 69–72, 95, 153.
25. Enepekidis, pp. 100–2, 160–4.
26. Gardner, p. 156.
27. Examples in Enepekidis, pp. 121–6.
28. See, particularly, Campbell and Sherrard, ch. 10.
29. Examples in Voigt, pp. 144–6, 182–5.
30. Saraphis, p. 52. Examples of Aris's methods are reported in Hamson, p. 124; Myers, p. 73.
31. Djilas, pp. 81–2. Moundrikhas told me of his experiences in April 1969.
32. Tsouderos, pp. 78–80, 161; Iatrides, pp. 43, 46–7.
33. Text in Woodhouse, p. 304.
34. Richter, pp. 382–3; Nepheloudis, p. 42; Pyromaglou, p. 215. The most extensive account is given in Pyromaglou, *Kartalis*, I, pp. 233–78.
35. Kofos, pp. 117–18; Palmer and King, 105–7.
36. Text in Kofos, pp. 128–31; see also Khrysokhoou, p. 95.
37. Christidès, pp. 132–3.
38. Christidès, p. 127.
39. Khrysokhoou, pp. 55, 65–9.
40. Khrysokhoou, p. 99.
41. Iatrides, p. 318.
42. Maclean, p. 245.
43. Djilas, p. 17; Dedijer, p. 213.
44. Tsouderos, pp. 163–5.
45. Eden, II, pp. 409, 430.
46. Neubacher, pp. 203–4. He mis-dates the episode to the end of 1942.
47. Wilson, pp. 167, 180.
48. Tsouderos, pp. 72–6; Gould Lee, p. 167; Eden, II, pp. 430–1; Leeper, p. 34.

49. Wilson, p. 180.

50. Woodward, III, pp. 397–400; Churchill, V, pp. 475–6.

51. Eden, II, p. 430; Iatrides, pp. 95–7. When I was writing *Apple of Discord*, Eden asked me to omit Roosevelt's role, for the sake of his reputation.

52. For the details on which this paragraph is based, see: Tsouderos, pp. 78–115; Leeper, pp. 34–41; Woodward, III, pp. 402–8.

53. Pyromaglou, pp. 216–17.

54. Pyromaglou, p. 153.

55. Woodhouse in *Balkan Studies*, Vol. XIII, No. 2 (1973) p. 354.

56. Papandreou, pp. 30–7.

57. Pyromaglou, p. 222.

58. Saraphis, p. 276; Enepekidis, p. 152.

59. Stavrianos in *Journal of Modern History* (1952), p. 45.

60. Condit, pp. 213, 234–7; Enepekidis, p. 150.

61. Enepekidis, p. 151; *SOE Operations*, App. III(A), p. 5.

62. Phosteridis, pp. 255–67.

63. Kousoulas, p. 186; Tsatsos, p. 21.

64. Grigoriadis, V, p. 23; Eudes, p. 130.

65. Details in Tsouderos, pp. 84–5, 124–50. See also Kousoulas, pp. 182–5; Iatrides, pp. 47–54.

66. Papandreou, pp. 13–25, 37–45, 51–8.

67. Papandreou, p. 14.

68. Saraphis, p. 195.

69. Selected details of the trials in Nepheloudis, pp. 85–114.

70. Kousoulas, p. 189; Zakhariadis, p. 9.

71. Iatrides, pp. 58–63; Papandreou, pp. 132–3.

72. Iatrides, pp. 50, 236.

73. Iatrides, pp. 120–2.

74. Iatrides, pp. 56, 60; Leeper, p. xvii.

75. Iatrides, p. 59.

76. Iatrides, p. 54.

Chapter 4

1. Zakhariadis, pp. 9, 19.

2. Iatrides, pp. 78–80.

3. Details in Woodward, III, pp. 115–23, 150–3.

4. Zakhariadis, pp. 9–10.

5. Vlandas's MS., pp. 44–5.

6. Text of the official record in Tsakalotos, I, pp. 450–76.

7. Texts in Papandreou, pp. 73–81; Woodhouse, p. 305.

8. Iatrides, pp. 69–70; Papandreou, pp. 106–19.

9. Iatrides, pp. 296–303.

10. Iatrides, pp. 68, 100.

11. Papandreou, p. 117.

12. Papandreou, p. 51.

13. Jecchinis, p. 63; Condit, p. 268.

14. Zakhariadis, p. 26; *Cominform Journal*, 1 August 1949.

15. Papandreou, pp. 104, 137, 150, 179.

16. Papandreou, pp. 99, 153–4.

17. Saraphis, p. 257.

18. Woodhouse in *Vierteljahrshefte für Zeitgeschichte*, Vol. VI, No. 2 (1958), p. 149. Lanz was present when this paper was delivered in Munich on 13 November 1957.

19. Khoutas, pp. 587–90; *The Conspiracy Against Greece*, pp. 15–16.

20. Examples in Enepekidis, pp. 85–8.

21. Khrysokhoou, I, pp. 166–9; Khoutas, p. 589.

22. Gatopoulos, p. 694; Saraphis, pp. 262–3; Khrysokhoou, I, p. 156.

23. Hillgrüber, II, pp. 669–70, 674, 677–80; Kédros, pp. 346–9.

24. Hampe, pp. 47–8; Condit, pp. 162–4.

25. Neubacher, pp. 146–7; Enepekidis, pp. 93–8; Richter, pp. 356–71.

26. Neubacher, pp. 146–7.
27. *EAM White Book*, Document 37.
28. Kédros, p. 349, quoting Pyromaglou, pp. 176–81.
29. Gardner, pp. 178–80.
30. Saraphis, pp. 224–5.
31. Eudes, pp. 147–8.
32. Iatrides, p. 75n.; Papandreou, p. 120.
33. References in Iatrides, p. 78n.
34. Barker, pp. 99, 110, 136, 149; Christidès, p. 134.
35. Iatrides, pp. 112–14; text in Pyromaglou, *Kartalis*, I, pp. 373–5.
36. Iatrides, pp. 109–11.
37. Saraphis, pp. 244–5, 247–53; Vlandas's MS., p. 47; Iatrides, pp. 115–16.
38. Text in Woodhouse, pp. 306–7.
39. Papandreou, pp. 273–5, 299–301.
40. Tsouderos, pp. 181–5.
41. Kanellopoulos, pp. 98–9.
42. Papandreou, pp. 121–3, 132–3. I advised Churchill against denouncing EAM, on 15 July 1944 at Chequers.
43. Walter Hagen, quoted in Pyromaglou, *Kartalis*, I, p. 545.
44. Neubacher, pp. 203–4.
45. Grigoriadis, I, p. 21n.
46. Richter, pp. 488–91.
47. *SOE Operations in Greece*, p. 12.
48. *SOE Operations in Greece*, App. VI, p. 6.
49. Hampe, pp. 70–1.
50. Hampe, p. 99.
51. Spencer, pp. 71–2; Zevgos, p. 23; ELD, *Théseis*, p. 17.
52. Papandreou, p. 299.
53. Grigoriadis, *Tò dévtero antártiko*, I, p. 27; Iatrides, 143.
54. Eudes, p. 157, quoting Bartzotas, p. 48.
55. Saraphis, pp. 221–2.
56. Eudes, pp. 158–9.
57. Iatrides, pp. 103–4, 314–19.
58. Iatrides, pp. 148–9.
59. Zakhariadis, pp. 9–10; Vlandas's MS., p. 44.
60. Zakhariadis, pp. 19–28.
61. Papandreou, p. 178.
62. Zakhariadis, p. 9.
63. Zakhariadis, p. 10; Stavridis, p. 547.
64. Saraphis, p. 253.
65. Ehrman, VI, p. 61.
66. Pipinelis, pp. 164–5; Papandreou, pp. 104–5, 132–3, 136–7, 150–2, 155, 165, 179.
67. Tsakalotos, I, p. 578.
68. Spencer, p. 79.
69. Kousoulas, p. 197.
70. Jecchinis, pp. 63–4.
71. Iatrides, p. 132.
72. Papandreou, pp. 169–76, 185–98.
73. Zapheiropoulos, pp. 63–4.
74. Woodhouse in *Balkan Studies*, Vol. XII, No. 2 (1971), pp. 347–63.
75. Khrysokhoou, 37–9.
76. Tsakalotos, I, p. 435.
77. Pyromaglou, p. 17.
78. Khoutas, p. 19.
79. Condit, pp. 6, 196, 229. 'Woodhouse ... at times belittled the military value of Greek guerrilla activities' (Condit, p. 213). I am happy to be corrected.
80. Sweet-Escott, p. 96; *SOE Operations*, App. XII.
81. Condit, p. 7; *SOE Operations*, App. XI.
82. Compare Zevgos, p. 69, with Leeper, p. 144.

83. Eudes, p. 230.
84. Condit, p. 6.
85. Figures based on an unpublished history of SOE, by Professor W. J. M. Mackenzie.
86. Figures in this paragraph are based on Condit, pp. 6–8, and Enepekidis, p. 15.
87. Tsakalotos, II, p. 11.
88. Condit, pp. 229, 237–8, 262; Kédros, pp. 235–6.
89. Saraphis, pp. 273–9; Ehrman, *Grand Strategy*, VI, p. 45.
90. Figure from *Der Endkampf auf dem Balkan* (Heidelberg, 1955), by General Erich Schmidt-Richberg (formerly Chief of Staff in Greece), cited in Enepekidis, p. 28.
91. Woodhouse in *Zeitgeschichte* (Munich, April 1958), p. 149.
92. Woodward, III, p. 390n.; Auty and Clogg, p. 167.
93. Ehrman, VI, p. 45; Howard, IV, p. 486.
94. Churchill, V, p. 473.
95. Hubatsch (ed. Trevor-Roper), pp. 142–4, 194–5; Richter, p. 356; Neubacher, pp. 146–7.
96. Condit, p. 259; Gardner, pp. 156–61.
97. See p. 39 above.
98. See p. 44 above.
99. Pyromaglou, pp. 112–13.
100. Condit, p. 167.
101. Papandreou, p. 299.

CHAPTER 5

1. Macmillan, II, p. 593; Iatrides, pp. 221–3.
2. Iatrides, pp. 156–7.
3. Leeper, p. 85.
4. Arguments for this view are well summarised in Iatrides, pp. 152–60.
5. Leeper, p. 91.
6. Papandreou, p. 204.
7. Papandreou, pp. 202–3.
8. Leeper, p. 92; Iatrides, pp. 159–60.
9. Leeper, p. 92.
10. Churchill, VI, p. 250.
11. Papakonstantinou, p. 169.
12. Iatrides, p. 156.
13. Iatrides, p. 157.
14. Tsakalotos, I, p. 587.
15. Iatrides, pp. 157–8.
16. Saraphis, p. 288.
17. Saraphis, pp. 291–2; Leeper, p. 93.
18. Figures based on Ehrman, VI, p. 61.
19. Iatrides, p. 163.
20. Leeper, pp. 92–6.
21. Iatrides, pp. 161, 164–6.
22. Jecchinis, pp. 65–6.
23. Leeper, pp. 96–7, where the anniversary is mis-dated 26 November.
24. Leeper, p. 93; Saraphis, p. 292.
25. Papakonstantinou, p. 169.
26. Iatrides, pp. 169–70.
27. McNeill, p. 131; Iatrides, p. 169.
28. Kosta Karagiorgis, *Gýro apò tò Dekémvri* (Athens, 1945).
29. See, for example, Stavrianos, p. 128; Richter, p. 507.
30. *Levkí Vívlos toù EAM*, pp. 60–1.
31. Capell, p. 121.
32. Saraphis, *O ELAS*, p. 578. The syntax is defective in the original. See also the English edition: Saraphis, pp. 299–300.
33. Leeper, p. 95; Woodhouse, p. 215.
34. Ehrman, *Grand Strategy*, Vol. VI; Woodward, *British Foreign Policy*, Vol. III.

35. The archives in London and Athens have been examined for me by Mr Richard Clogg and Mrs Domna Dontas respectively.

36. *FO Documents*, R18580/745/19 of 15 November 1944.

37. PM Minute M1113/4 of 19 November, in same file.

38. *FO Documents*, R19341/745/19 of 26 November 1944.

39. Papandreou, pp. 107–8.

40. Saraphis, p. 253; Iatrides, p. 171.

41. A variety of views will be found in Kousoulas, pp. 198–200; Eudes, pp. 185–6; Papakonstantinou, p. 172; Iatrides, pp. 173–7.

42. Iatrides, p. 171; Saraphis, pp. 293–5.

43. Papandreou, p. 207.

44. Saraphis, pp. 299–300.

45. Papandreou, pp. 208–10; *EAM White Book*, Documents 31 and 33.

46. Iatrides, p. 173.

47. Papandreou, p. 211.

48. Eudes, pp. 185–6, based on Tzimas; Kousoulas, pp. 200–1, based on Orestis.

49. Palmer and King, pp. 120–3.

50. Iatrides, pp. 178–81.

51. Saraphis, pp. 301–3.

52. Iatrides, p. 180n.; Papakonstantinou, pp. 172, 173n., quoting A. Kalligas; Saraphis, p. 304.

53. Papandreou, pp. 211–12.

54. ELD, *Théseis*, p. 24.

55. Tsatsos, p. 87.

56. Macmillan, II, pp. 600–1; Leeper, p. 97.

57. Zevgos, pp. 35–52.

58. Saraphis, p. 301.

59. Saraphis, p. 301.

60. Saraphis, pp. 301–2.

61. Saraphis, p. 304.

62. Khoutas, p. 605; Grigoriadis, I, pp. 313–14 (describing the telegram as a forgery).

63. Saraphis, p. 304.

64. Saraphis, p. 307.

65. Kousoulas, pp. 207–8; Eudes, p. 196.

66. Zakhariadis, p. 10.

67. Saraphis, p. 304.

68. Papandreou, p. 216.

69. Iatrides, p. 188.

70. Giannaris, *Mikis Theodorakis*, p. 39.

71. Papandreou, p. 221; McNeill, p. 140.

72. Leeper, p. 101; Iatrides, pp. 190–1.

73. Grigoriadis, I, pp. 158–9.

74. McNeill, p. 140; Saraphis, p. 303.

75. Iatrides, pp. 198, 215–16.

76. Saraphis, p. 304.

77. Churchill, VI, p. 252.

78. Gardner, pp. 204–5; Tsakalotos, I, pp. 596–9.

79. Saraphis, p. 302; Grigoriadis, I, pp. 227–8, 234–5.

80. Saraphis, pp. 305–6.

81. Papandreou, pp. 228–34.

82. Iatrides, pp. 210–13; Capell, p. 129; Xydis, p. 63.

83. Saraphis, p. 306.

84. My diary records this order on 8 December.

85. Churchill, VI, p. 254.

86. Iatrides, pp. 226, 247.

87. Based on Eudes, pp. 195–6; Saraphis, p. 304; Capell, pp. 125–6; Ehrman, VI, p. 61; Woodward, III, p. 413.

88. Tsakalotos, I, p. 608.

89. Zakhariadis, p. 10.

90. Gardner, p. 206; Tsakalotos, I, p. 608.

91. Grigoriadis, III, p. 340; Aneurin Bevan in 406 H.C. Deb. 5s. (20 December 1944), col. 1880.
92. Macmillan, II, pp. 607–8; North, pp. 141–2; Leeper, pp. 114–15; Iatrides, pp. 227–8.
93. Tsakalotos, I, pp. 614–17; Gardner, p. 205.
94. Personal information from Leeper, some years after the event.
95. Wilson, p. 243; Iatrides, p. 213.
96. Tsakalotos, I, p. 621; Grigoriadis, I, p. 240.
97. Leeper, pp. 117–18.
98. Grigoriadis, I, pp. 283–91.
99. Leeper, p. 118.
100. Churchill, VI, p. 269.
101. Iatrides, pp. 218–40, and sources there quoted.
102. Details in Tsakalotos, I, pp. 640–57; *EAM White Book*, Document 80.
103. Iatrides, p. 241.
104. Hourmouzios, pp. 168–9; Pipinelis, pp. 172–7.
105. Saraphis, p. 320; Zevgos, pp. 12, 56–7; Grigoriadis, III, pp. 341–4; Matthews, pp. 93–6.
Fuller details in TUC Report, *What we Saw in Greece* (London, 1945); photographs in *Avtò eínai tò KKE–EAM–ELAS stin Ellàda* (Athens, 1945).
106. Saraphis, pp. 309–13, and Grigoriadis, I, pp. 292–320, give the ELAS version; Khoutas, pp. 605–17, and Pyromaglou in Richter, pp. 595–601, the EDES version.
107. Tsakalotos, I, p. 670n.
108. Text in Saraphis, pp. 316–18.
109. Leeper, p. 133.
110. Saraphis, p. 315.
111. *Documents Regarding the Situation in Greece, January 1945* (HMSO, Cmd. 6592).
112. See, particularly, Jecchinis, pp. 65–89.
113. Leeper, pp. 140–2.
114. Papakonstantinou, p. 181.
115. Eden, II, p. 500; Macmillan, II, p. 638; Leeper, p. 140.
116. Leeper, pp. 142–52; Macmillan, II, pp. 652–8.
117. Leeper, pp. 143–4.
118. Eudes, pp. 225–6.
119. Karagiorgis, pp. 79–81.
120. Macmillan, II, p. 622.
121. ELD, *Théseis*, pp. 26–9.
122. Text in Woodhouse, pp. 308–10; Greek original in *I symphonía tis Várkizas* (Athens, 1945).
123. Leeper, p. 144; Zevgos, p. 69.
124. Leeper, p. 150.
125. Tsakalotos, I, p. 678.
126. Tsakalotos, I, p. 679.
127. Text in Saraphis, p. 323.
128. Lagdas, II, pp. 481–3.

CHAPTER 6

1. ELD, *Théseis*, pp. 23–9, 43, 52.
2. Vlandas's MS., p. 52.
3. Chandler, p. 98.
4. Grigoriadis, II, pp. 357–9, 381–2.
5. Kousoulas, p. 225.
6. Chandler, p. 87.
7. Based on Zapheiropoulos, p. 60; Xydis, p. 467; Kofos, pp. 148–9.
8. Papakonstantinou, p. 183.
9. Based on Lagdas, II, pp. 494–502, and Grigoriadis, II, pp. 389–458.
10. Vukmanović, p. 98.
11. Zakhariadis, p. 15.
12. Vukmanović, p. 67.
13. Zakhariadis, p. 19.
14. Shoup, p. 157.
15. Vukmanović, pp. 45–9.

16. Zakhariadis, p. 12.
17. Zakhariadis, p. 26.
18. Eudes, p. 250; Papakonstantinou, p. 193; Zapheiropoulos, p. 47; O'Ballance, p. 142.
19. Xydis, p. 166.
20. Capell, p. 200.
21. Macmillan, II, p. 655.
22. Zevgos, p. 12.
23. Zevgos, p. 103.
24. Lagdas, II, p. 480.
25. Zakhariadis, p. 13.
26. *EAM White Book*, Document 119.
27. Text in Grigoriadis, II, pp. 503-6.
28. Grigoriadis, II, p. 630.
29. Chandler, pp. 72-3.
30. Tsakalotos, I, pp. 710-12; Macmillan, II, p. 665.
31. Chandler, pp. 49-50; Matthews, p. 112; Leeper, p. 159.
32. Chandler, pp. 70-3.
33. Examples in Matthews, pp. 93-6; Chandler, pp. 72-3; Capell, pp. 170-2.
34. Macmillan, II, pp. 640-2; Stavridis, p. 558.
35. Leeper, pp. 140, 168.
36. Macmillan, II, pp. 640, 663.
37. Chandler, p. 84.
38. Djilas, pp. 70, 164.
39. Zakhariadis, pp. 9, 26.
40. Winifred N. Hadsel in *Foreign Policy Reports* (New York, 1947), Vol. XXIII, No. 12, p. 146.
41. William Reitzel in *The Yale Review* (1947), pp. 637-88.
42. In conversation with myself in September 1945.
43. Voigt, p. 39.
44. Sweet-Escott, p. 56.
45. For this paragraph, see, particularly, Jecchinis, pp. 65-89.
46. Leeper, p. 182; Iatrides, p. 258.
47. Chandler, pp. 87, 97.
48. Vukmanović, pp. 61-2.
49. Vukmanović, pp. 67-8.
50. Details in Jecchinis, pp. 90-3.
51. Iatrides, p. 264; Xydis, pp. 106-7; Leeper, p. 179. Leeper put the arguments to Bevin, on a brief prepared by myself, during the Regent's visit to London in September.
52. Pipinelis, pp. 181-3; Hourmouzios, p. 171.
53. Pipinelis, pp. 186-7.
54. Kanellopoulos, p. 83.
55. Leeper, pp. 195-8.
56. Chandler, p. 124.
57. Kousoulas, p. 230.
58. O'Ballance, p. 121; Eudes, pp. 340-1.
59. Iatrides, p. 254.
60. Macmillan, II, p. 667.
61. Iatrides, pp. 271-2.
62. Iatrides, pp. 252-4.
63. For this paragraph, see particularly: Iatrides, pp. 268-73; Xydis, pp. 97-8, 112-18, 130-3, 143-4.
64. Dedijer, p. 267; Auty, p. 248; Djilas, pp. 90-4.
65. Armstrong, pp. 198, 214; Kofos, p. 142.
66. Armstrong, p. 74; *The Soviet-Yugoslav Dispute*, p. 38.
67. Kofos, p. 150.
68. Xydis, p. 116; Kofos, pp. 151-2.
69. Christidès, p. 113; *The Conspiracy Against Greece*, p. 46.
70. Zapheiropoulos, p. 43; Papakonstantinou, p. 188.
71. Barker, p. 117; Kofos, p. 152; Christidès, p. 114.
72. Eudes, p. 260.

73. Kousoulas, pp. 230–1.
74. Gatopoulos, p. 9.
75. Sweet-Escott, *Greece*, p. 93.
76. Leeper, pp. 177, 181.
77. Chandler, pp. 87, 109, 134. Sourlas was later, quite improperly, recognised as a leader of the nationalist Resistance, by the military government established in 1967.
78. Chandler, p. 93.
79. Tsoucalas, p. 94.
80. Leeper, p. 199.
81. *Elevtheria*, 29 December 1945, in an inconspicuous position on the back page.

Chapter 7

1. *BBC Monitoring Service*, 4 November and 6 December 1949; *Elevtheria*, 5 November and 7 December 1949, quoted in Papakonstantinou, p. 190. In the edition of the pamphlet published in Nicosia in 1950, the crucial passage is on p. 37.
2. Zakhariadis, p. 28.
3. Quoted in Kousoulas, p. 239.
4. Eudes, p. 262.
5. Spencer, p. 98.
6. Grigoriadis, III, pp. 668–9.
7. Anon., 'From Litokhoro to Grammos and Vitsi', in *Dimokratikos Stratos*, 1948.
8. Eudes, p. 265.
9. Grigoriadis, III, p. 666.
10. Zakhariadis, pp. 28–9.
11. Vlandas's MS., pp. 67–9.
12. Chandler, pp. 70–3.
13. Kousoulas, p. 233; Vlandas's MS., p. 64; Eudes, p. 261.
14. Eudes, p. 288; Zakhariadis, pp. 16–17.
15. *Kathimerini*, 5 March 1946.
16. *Kathimerini*, 26 March 1946.
17. Zapheiropoulos, p. 171; Tsakalotos, II, p. 313.
18. Vlandas's phrase quoted in Kousoulas, p. 239, should not be taken as implying the contrary.
19. Grigoriadis, III, pp. 666–8; Vukmanović, p. 65.
20. *Report of the Allied Mission to Observe the Greek Elections* (Cmd. 6812, HMSO, 1946). Apart from critics with left-wing sympathies, the figures have been described as 'wishful speculation' by John Campbell in *The International Regulation of Civil Wars* (ed. Evan Luard, London, 1972), p. 46.
21. Zakhariadis, p. 17.
22. Eudes, p. 265.
23. Vlandas's MS., p. 62.
24. Zakhariadis, p. 34; Eudes, p. 274.
25. Vukmanović, p. 65.
26. Details in Jecchinis, pp. 93–107.
27. Tsakalotos, II, p. 90.
28. Chandler, pp. 155–6.
29. Tsakalotos, II, p. 49; Zapheiropoulos, p. 183.
30. Papakonstantinou, p. 33; Xydis, p. 167.
31. First-hand evidence in *Pòs zísame stò Parapétasma*, pp. 26–30.
32. Wainhouse in *Military Review* (June 1957), p. 18.
33. Dedijer, pp. 281, 285.
34. Djilas, p. 119.
35. Vukmanović, pp. 3–6.
36. Vukmanović, p. 69.
37. Eudes, pp. 268–9.
38. Vlandas's MS., p. 73.
39. Vlandas's MS., p. 68; Zakhariadis, p. 30.
40. Vlandas's MS., p. 67.
41. Zapheiropoulos, p. 76.
42. Tsakalotos, II, p. 311.

43. Chandler, pp. 156–7; Eudes, pp. 365–6.
44. Chandler, pp. 156–7, 178.
45. Chandler, p. 169.
46. Xydis, pp. 254–5.
47. Tsakalotos, II, p. 313.
48. Murray in *Marine Corps Gazette*, May 1954, pp. 52–8.
49. Chandler, p. 157.
50. Eudes, p. 354; Tsakalotos, II, p. 15; Zapheiropoulos, pp. 60–1; Murray in *Marine Corps Gazette*, January 1954, pp. 18–19.
51. Tsakalotos, II, pp. 325–6.
52. Murray in *Marine Corps Gazette*, January 1954, p. 19.
53. Vlandas's MS., pp. 71–2.
54. Numerous examples in *The Conspiracy Against Greece*, pp. 48–62, all quoted from the Yugoslav and Bulgarian press.
55. See, particularly, the catalogue of incidents on the Albanian, Bulgarian and Yugoslav frontiers, from the beginning of January 1946 to the late summer of 1947, listed in *The Conspiracy Against Greece*, pp. 71–81. Although this is an unreliable publication, not all the incidents can have been fabricated.
56. Grigoriadis, III, p. 785.
57. Christidès, pp. 114–15; Kofos, p. 168; *Rizospastis*, 18 June 1946.
58. Details of the Greek claims in Dragoumis, p. 13.
59. Xydis, pp. 270–84, 293–9, 317–35, 366–94.
60. Matthews, pp. 141–3; Eudes, pp. 251–2, 288–90.
61. Grigoriadis, III, p. 805.
62. Zakhariadis, pp. 6, 17, 34–5.
63. Zakhariadis, p. 29.
64. Jones, p. 130.
65. Xydis, pp. 243, 257, 262, 317, 395, 406, 433.
66. Matthews, pp. 141–3.
67. *The Conspiracy Against Greece*, pp. 90–138.
68. Accounts of the Commission's travels will be found in *Le Monde*, 20 and 21 September 1947, quoted in Eudes, pp. 282–3; and in Matthews, pp. 143–4. For the interview with Markos, see Eudes, pp. 284–8.
69. Pipinelis, pp. 198–9.
70. Tsakalotos, II, pp. 52–5.
71. *Economic Survey for 1947* (Cmd. 7046).
72. Text in Oikonomou-Gouras, pp. 123–5.
73. Examples in Oikonomou-Gouras, pp. 68–77; Xydis, pp. 487–94.
74. Acheson, pp. 219, 223–4.
75. Jones, pp. 151, 191, 195.
76. Jones, p. 223. Texts of the principal speeches by Truman, Acheson and Marshall, in Jones, pp. 269–84.

Chapter 8

1. Details in Xydis, p. 500.
2. Texts of both speeches in Jones, pp. 274–84.
3. *Report by the Commission of Investigation Concerning Greek Frontier Incidents to the Security Council* (S/360 of 23 May 1947).
4. Tsakalotos, II, pp. 59–60.
5. Details in this paragraph based on Murray in *Marine Corps Gazette*, April 1954, pp. 55–6; Tsakalotos, II, p. 47; Zapheiropoulos, pp. 94–5.
6. Zapheiropoulos, pp. 107–23.
7. O'Ballance, p. 143.
8. Grigoriadis, III, p. 903; IV, p. 1359.
9. Murray in *Marine Corps Gazette*, January 1954, p. 19.
10. Grigoriadis, III, pp. 914–15.
11. Tsakalotos, II, p. 311.
12. Tsakalotos, II, pp. 58–60.

13. Grigoriadis, III, p. 913.
14. Zapheiropoulos, p. 246.
15. Quoted in Sweet-Escott, p. 93.
16. Sweet-Escott, p. 131.
17. Sweet-Escott, p. 71.
18. Zapheiropoulos, pp. 195, 664.
19. For a list of all senior commanders throughout the civil war, see Zapheiropoulos, p. 679.
20. Tsakalotos, II, p. 314; Zapheiropoulos, p. 266.
21. Zapheiropoulos, pp. 50, 299. Two captured guns of Yugoslav origin are still on display as trophies of war in Florina.
22. Zapheiropoulos, p. 262.
23. Quoted in Vukmanović, pp. 72–7.
24. Grigoriadis, III, p. 492; IV, p. 1001.
25. Zapheiropoulos, p. 313.
26. Murray in *Marine Corps Gazette*, February 1954, pp. 53–4.
27. Tsakalotos, II, pp. 92, 199; Chandler, p. 192; Zakhariadis, p. 37; Matthews, p. 194.
28. Sweet-Escott, p. 105.
29. Text in UNSCOB Report of 30 June 1948 (General Assembly, Official Records, A/574).
30. Voigt, p. 22.
31. Hourmouzios, p. 215.
32. *Deuxième livre bleu*, pp. 56–60; Grigoriadis, IV, pp. 963–92; Sweet-Escott, p. 75.
33. *Pòs zísame stò parapétasma*, pp. 7, 15.
34. Zapheiropoulos, pp. 29–31.
35. Zakhariadis, pp. 34–5.
36. Zakhariadis, p. 31.
37. Kousoulas, p. 247.
38. Papakonstantinou, pp. 110–15; Zapheiropoulos, pp. 62–3.
39. Zapheiropoulos, p. 323.
40. Grigoriadis, III, p. 932.
41. Tsakalotos, II, p. 69; Zapheiropoulos, p. 306. The following account relies chiefly on Zapheiropoulos, pp. 301–18.
42. Grigoriadis, III, p. 941.
43. English text in Voigt, pp. 254–8.
44. Zakhariadis, pp. 31–2.
45. Zapheiropoulos, pp. 340–2.
46. S. E. Belikov, quoted in Burks, p. 101n.; cp. Murray in *Marine Corps Gazette*, January 1954, p. 18.
47. Eudes, pp. 288–90; Burks, p. 32; Matthews, pp. 132, 141–3.
48. Tsakalotos, I, p. 678.
49. Murray in *Marine Corps Gazette*, January 1954, p. 18; and February 1954, pp. 55–6.
50. Zapheiropoulos, pp. 29–31; Murray in *Marine Corps Gazette*, March 1954, p. 53.
51. Murray in *Marine Corps Gazette*, April 1954, p. 58.
52. Based on map in Zapheiropoulos, p. 150, and Official History (1948), Map I.
53. Official History (1948), p. 2 and Map II.
54. English text in Papandreou, *The Third War*, pp. 63–8.
55. Tsakalotos, II, pp. 41, 74.
56. Voigt, pp. 39, 87.

CHAPTER 9

1. Zakhariadis, p. 30.
2. Djilas, pp. 121–9, 155–6; Dedijer, pp. 318–20.
3. Djilas, pp. 158–63.
4. Djilas, p. 160.
5. Djilas, p. 164; Dedijer, p. 331.
6. O'Ballance, p. 162; Voigt, p. 210. Neither quotes a source.
7. Dedijer, p. 308.
8. Zapheiropoulos, p. 72, quoting C. L. Sulzberger.
9. Murray in *Marine Corps Gazette*, March 1954, p. 51.

10. Zapheiropoulos, p. 72; Djilas, p. 177; Palmer and King, p. 129.
11. Grigoriadis, IV, p. 1340.
12. Kousoulas, p. 252.
13. Murray in *Marine Corps Gazette*, January 1954, p. 20.
14. Murray in *Marine Corps Gazette*, January 1954, p. 17; February 1954, p. 52.
15. Examples in Papakonstantinou, p. 238n.
16. Zapheiropoulos, p. 20.
17. Although a court convicted two Communists *in absentia* of Polk's murder, some of his colleagues believed that it was not the work of the KKE (Matthews, pp. 184–92). The rebel government strenuously denied responsibility (*Livre bleu*, p. 33; *Deuxième livre bleu*, pp. 54–6).
18. Zapheiropoulos, pp. 34, 369, 392, 416.
19. Details in Jecchinis, pp. 115–19.
20. Jecchinis, pp. 126–7.
21. Zapheiropoulos, pp. 330, 458; Official History (1948), p. 13.
22. Examples in Tsakalotos, II, pp. 121, 130, 154, 161, 170, 209, 215.
23. Murray in *Marine Corps Gazette*, February 1954, p. 58.
24. Hourmouzios, pp. 190–2.
25. Eudes, pp. 411, 448; Zapheiropoulos, p. 375; Murray in *Marine Corps Gazette*, May 1954, p. 54.
26. *Deuxième livre bleu*, p. 120; Eudes, p. 310.
27. Zapheiropoulos, p. 670.
28. Murray in *Marine Corps Gazette*, March 1954, p. 54.
29. Based on Official History (1948), Map IV.
30. Official History (1948), pp. 24–5, 33–8.
31. Zacharakis in *Revue Militaire Générale* (July 1960), pp. 194–8.
32. Tsakalotos, II, p. 120.
33. Official History (1948), pp. 91–2.
34. Tsakalotos, II, p. 123; Zapheiropoulos, p. 429.
35. A full account is contained in the Official History (1948), pp. 93–336.
36. Official History (1948), pp. 154–60.
37. Tsakalotos, II, p. 125.
38. Official History (1948), p. 105.
39. Zapheiropoulos, p. 430; but the figures may be exaggerated, since Communist sources estimate their strength in Grammos before the operation at only 7,030 (*Deuxième livre bleu*, pp. 100–9).
40. Map in Zapheiropoulos, p. 433.
41. Tsakalotos, II, pp. 130, 163.
42. Official History (1948), p. 394.
43. Tsakalotos, II, pp. 165–9.
44. Zapheiropoulos, pp. 330, 455–61.
45. Grigoriadis, IV, pp. 1005–8, 1213–18.
46. Grigoriadis, IV, p. 1171; Eudes, pp. 330–2.
47. Joannidis, p. 109.
48. Tsakalotos, II, p. 171.
49. Tsakalotos, II, pp. 179–88.
50. Official History (1948), pp. 343–56.
51. Hourmouzios, pp. 202–3.
52. Matthews, p. 259.
53. UNSCOB Report, General Assembly A/574 (New York, 1948), para 188; confirmed in A/644 (Paris, 1948), para 63; and A/692 (Paris, 1948), para 56.
54. *Deuxième livre bleu*, pp. 137–48.
55. Sweet-Escott, p. 71.
56. Matthews, p. 181.
57. UNSCOB Report, A/644 (Paris, 1948), pp. 13–15.
58. Texts in *The Soviet–Yugoslav Dispute* (Royal Institute of International Affairs, London, 1948).
59. Maclean, p. 371.
60. Skendi, pp. 24, 348–9.
61. Vlandas's MS., pp. 76–7.
62. Papakonstantinou, pp. 109–14; Zapheiropoulos, pp. 29–30.
63. Kousoulas, pp. 252–3. The text, originally published in *Neos Kosmos* (Bucarest, August 1950),

Vol. 8, pp. 476–83, is reproduced in Grigoriadis, IV, pp. 1191–1200, and extensively quoted in Eudes, pp. 335–8.
64. Text in Grigoriadis, IV, pp. 1200–2.
65. Matthews, pp. 217–58; Voigt, pp. 202–3.
66. Zapheiropoulos, p. 548; Zakhariadis, pp. 6, 36.
67. Zapheiropoulos, p. 544.
68. Grigoriadis, IV, p. 1211.
69. Zapheiropoulos, p. 547.
70. Zapheiropoulos, p. 33; Burks, pp. 67–70.
71. Zapheiropoulos, p. 59; Murray in *Marine Corps Gazette*, February 1954, p. 53, gives only eight divisions.
72. Zapheiropoulos, p. 51; Tsakalotos, II, p. 15.

CHAPTER 10

1. Tsakalotos, II, pp. 202–3.
2. Zapheiropoulos, p. 551; Tsakalotos, II, p. 223; Murray in *Marine Corps Gazette*, March 1954, p. 50.
3. Grigoriadis, IV, p. 1255.
4. Tsakalotos, II, p. 92.
5. An outstanding example in the Peloponnese is cited by Tsakalotos, II, p. 199.
6. Grigoriadis, IV, pp. 1248–53.
7. Tsakalotos, II, p. 210; Zapheiropoulos, p. 523.
8. Burks, p. 102; Zapheiropoulos, p. 61; Murray in *Marine Corps Gazette*, January 1954, p. 18.
9. Grigoriadis, IV, p. 1265.
10. Zapheiropoulos, p. 537; full text in Official History (1949), pp. 10–11.
11. Murray in *Marine Corps Gazette*, January 1954, p. 20.
12. Text of the communiqué in Christidès, pp. 129–30.
13. BBC Monitoring Service, 4, 7, 8, 11 February 1949.
14. Vukmanović, pp. 56, 90.
15. BBC Monitoring Service, 8 February and 16 June 1949.
16. Vukmanović, pp. 50–4.
17. Vukmanović, pp. 6, 68, 91.
18. Vukmanović, p. 77.
19. Barker, pp. 108, 120–2; Christidès, pp. 130–1.
20. Kofos, pp. 182–3.
21. Armstrong, p. 201; Shoup, pp. 160–1.
22. Details in Dellin, *Bulgaria*, p. 127.
23. Armstrong, p. 106; Kofos, p. 184.
24. Armstrong, pp. 134–5, 202.
25. Text in Tsakalotos, II, p. 33.
26. See, especially, Sweet-Escott, pp. 105–56.
27. Varvaressos, *Ekthesis*, pp. 84–5, quoted by Sweet-Escott, p. 133.
28. Zapheiropoulos, pp. 145–6.
29. Voigt, p. 8.
30. Voigt, p. 10.
31. Zapheiropoulos, p. 334.
32. Zapheiropoulos, p. 660; Papakonstantinou, p. 238.
33. Zapheiropoulos, p. 568.
34. Gould Lee, pp. 259–61.
35. Burks, pp. 67–70.
36. Based on Zapheiropoulos, pp. 584–5.
37. Grigoriadis, IV, p. 1341.
38. Detailed account in Tsakalotos, II, pp. 229–45.
39. Tsakalotos, II, p. 254.
40. Zapheiropoulos, p. 538.
41. Murray in *Marine Corps Gazette*, March 1954, p. 57; Tsakalotos, II, p. 214.
42. Based on Zapheiropoulos, pp. 522–3.
43. Tsakalotos, II, p. 260.

44. Grigoriadis, IV, p. 1341.
45. Text in Partsalidis, pp. 2–10; *Deuxième livre bleu*, pp. 11–15.
46. *Deuxième livre bleu*, pp. 172–5; Grigoriadis, IV, p. 1341.
47. *Borba*, 5 November 1949, quoted in Papakonstantinou, pp. 215–16n.; BBC Monitoring Service, 7 December 1949.
48. Armstrong, p. 202.
49. Vukmanović, pp. 80–5.
50. Vukmanović, pp. 28–9, linked Tito and Mao Tse-Tung as the two great partisan leaders. In 1953, Dedijer, pp. 448–9, reported a forecast by Tito of a Sino-Soviet conflict, despite the fact that Mao was then supporting the CPSU against him.
51. UNSCOB Report A/935 (New York, 1949), para 52.
52. Grigoriadis, IV, p. 1341.
53. Papapanaghiotis in *Glasnik*, No. 7 (1971), translated in *Kommounistiki Epitheórisi*, No. 4 (Rome, April 1972), Appendix.
54. Vukmanović, p. 95.
55. Vukmanović, p. 92.
56. Vukmanović, pp. 3, 89–91.
57. Murray in *Marine Corps Gazette*, May 1954, p. 58.
58. Zapheiropoulos, pp. 547–60.
59. Tsakalotos, II, pp. 321–9.
60. Grigoriadis, IV, pp. 1338–9.
61. Quoted in Papakonstantinou, p. 227n.
62. Figures based on Official History (1949), pp. 21–3, and Zapheiropoulos, pp. 600–3.
63. Based on Zapheiropoulos, pp. 598, 603, 609.
64. Murray in *Marine Corps Gazette*, May 1954, pp. 53–4.
65. Zapheiropoulos, pp. 602–22; Tsakalotos, II, pp. 264–5.
66. Zapheiropoulos, p. 624.
67. Tsakalotos, II, pp. 266–72.
68. Grigoriadis, IV, p. 1341.
69. Papakonstantinou, p. 227n.
70. Tsakalotos, II, p. 281.
71. Grigoriadis, IV, p. 1341.
72. UNSCOB Supplementary Report, A/981 (New York, 1949), p. 1.
73. Document A/1014, 20 October 1949.
74. Papapanaghiotis in *Kommounistiki Epitheorisi*, No. 4 (Rome, 1972), Appendix, pp. XVIII–XX; Kousoulas, pp. 274–5.
75. Kousoulas, p. 272.
76. BBC Monitoring Service, 3–8 December 1949.
77. Figures in this paragraph are based on: Zapheiropoulos, p. 670; Tsakalotos, II, p. 311; Kofos, p. 186; Hourmouzios, p. 213. Much higher, and no doubt exaggerated, figures were given in *Elevtheria*, 18 March 1952.
78. UNSCOB Report A/1307 (New York, 1950), para 62.
79. UN General Assembly, Fifth Session, debate on 'Threats to the political independence and territorial integrity of Greece', 1 December 1950.
80. *Pòs zísame stò parapétasma*, pp. 15–16, 19–23.

Bibliography

THIS LIST is not intended as a complete bibliography, particularly not of the Occupation and Resistance. I have included only works which I have regularly consulted, and often cited in the text.

References to books are usually given simply by the author's name or an abbreviation of the title. In cases where two or more books are listed by the same author, the one cited by his name alone is indicated by an asterisk. References to articles are given more fully, to avoid confusion.

A few books not directly related to the period and subject of this work are cited incidentally in the text. In these cases full references are given in the notes, and the books are not included in the list below.

Some books in Greek and German have not been available to me, but are cited in other works. References to these are given as 'quoted in' such and such a work.

A. BOOKS

Acheson, Dean: *Present at the Creation* (London, 1970)

Armstrong, Hamilton F.: *Tito and Goliath* (London, 1951)

Auty, Phyllis: *Tito — A Biography* (London, 1970)

Auty, Phyllis, and Clogg, Richard: *British Policy towards Wartime Resistance in Yugoslavia and Greece* (London, 1975)

Averoff-Tossizza, Evangelos: *Le Feu et la hache — Grèce 1946–1949* (Paris, 1973)

Avon, Earl of: *The Eden Memoirs*, Vol. II — *The Reckoning* (London, 1965)†

Barker, Elisabeth: *Macedonia — Its Place in Balkan Power Politics* (London, 1950)

Bartzotas, V.: *I politikì stelekhòn toù KKE stà televtaía déka khrónia* (KKE, 1950)

Brown, J. F.: *Bulgaria under Communist Rule* (London, 1970)

Burks, R. V.: *The Dynamics of Communism in Eastern Europe* (Princeton, 1961)

† Published as the third and last volume, but second in chronological order; cited as Eden, II.

308   BIBLIOGRAPHY

Campbell, John, and Sherrard, Philip: *Modern Greece* (London, 1968)
Capell, Richard: *Simiomata* (London, 1946)
Cervi, Mario: *Storia della guerra di Grecia* (Milan, 1965)
Chandler, Geoffrey: *The Divided Land* (London, 1959)
Christidès, Ch.: *Le Camouflage macédonien à la lumière des faits et des chiffres* (Athens, 1949)
Churchill, Winston S.: *The Second World War*, Vol. V (London, 1952)
Churchill, Winston S.: *The Second World War*, Vol. VI (London, 1954)
Clissold, Stephen (editor): *A Short History of Yugoslavia* (Cambridge, 1966)
Condit, D. M.: *Case Study in Guerrilla War – Greece during World War II* (Washington, 1961)
Dakin, Douglas: *The Greek Struggle in Macedonia, 1897–1913* (Thessaloniki, 1966)
Dalton, Hugh: *The Fateful Years* (London, 1957)
Daphnis, Grigorios: *I Ellàs metaxỳ duò polémon 1923–1940* (Athens, 1955)
Deakin, F. W.: *The Embattled Mountain* (London, 1972)
Dedijer, Vladimir: *Tito Speaks* (London, 1953)
Dellin, L. A. D.: *Bulgaria* (New York, 1956)
Dimitriou-Nikiphoros, D. N.: *Andártes stà vounà tìs Roúmelis* (3 vols., Athens, 1965)
*Djilas, Milovan: *Conversations with Stalin* (London, 1962)
Djilas, Milovan: *Memoir of a Revolutionary* (London, 1973)
Dragoumis, Ph.: *Prosokhì stì voreían Elláda* (Thessaloniki, 1949)
*Dragoumis, Ph.: *Tà Ellinikà díkaia stì diáskepsi tìs Eirínis* (Thessaloniki, 1949)
Dzélépy, E. E.: *Le drame de la Résistance grecque* (Paris, 1946)
Ehrman, John: *Grand Strategy*, Vols. V and VI (London, 1956)
Enepekidis, P. K.: *I Ellinikì Antístasis, 1941–1944* (Athens, 1964)
Eudes, Dominique: *The Kapetanios* (London, 1972)
Fontaine, André: *Histoire de la Guerre Froide*, Vol. I (Paris, 1965); Vol. II (Paris, 1967)
Gardner, Hugh H.: *Guerrilla and Counterguerrilla Warfare in Greece, 1941–1945* (Washington, 1962)
Gatopoulos, D.: *Istoría tìs Katokhìs* (Athens, n.d.)
Glynos, D.: *Tì eínai kaì tì thélei nà eínai tò EAM* (Athens, 1942)
Gonatas, Stylianos: *Apomnimonévmata* (Athens, 1958)
Grigoriadis, Ph.: *Oi andártes* (5 vols., Athens, 1964)
*Grigoriadis, Ph.: *Istoría toù emphylíou polémou, 1945–49–Tò dévtero andártiko* (4 vols., Athens, n.d.)
Hagen, Walter: *Die geheime Front* (Linz–Wien, 1950)
Hamson, Denys: *We Fell Among Greeks* (London, 1946)

Heiber, Helmut: *Hitlers Lagebesprechungen – die Protokollfragmente seiner militärischen Konferenzen, 1942–1945* (Stuttgart, 1962)

Heilbrunn, Otto: *Partisan Warfare* (London, 1962)

Hillgruber, A.: *Südost-Europa im zweiten Weltkrieg* (Frankfurt, 1962)

*Hillgruber, A.: *Kriegstagebuch des Oberkommandos der Wehrmacht* (4 vols., Frankfurt, 1963)

Hourmouzios, Stelio: *No Ordinary Crown* (London, 1972)

Howard, Michael: *Grand Strategy*, Vol. IV (London, 1972)

Hubatsch, Walter: *Hitlers Weisungen für die Kriegsführung, 1939–45* (Frankfurt, 1962)

*Hubatsch, Walter: *Hitler's War Directives* (ed. H. R. Trevor-Roper, London, 1964)

Iatrides, John O.: *Revolt in Athens* (Princeton, 1972)

Jecchinis, Christos: *Trade Unionism in Greece* (Chicago, 1967)

Joannidis, E.: *Bloody but Unbowed* (London, 1949)

Jones, Joseph M.: *The Fifteen Weeks* (New York, 1955)

Kaimaras, G.: *Istoría tìs ethnikìs antistáseos toù 5/42 syntágmatos Evzónon Psaroú, 1941–1944* (Athens, 1953)

Kalligas, A.: *Phlegoméni politeía – i mákhi tìs Athínas* (Athens, 1946)

Kanellopoulos, P.: *Tà khrónia toù megálou polémou, 1939–1944* (2nd edition, Athens, 1964)

Karagiannis, G.: *1940–1952: Tò dráma tìs Elládos* (Athens, 1964)

Karagiorgis, Kosta: *Gýro apò tò Dekémvri* (Athens, 1945)

Kédros, A.: *La Résistance grecque, 1940–1944* (Paris, 1966)

Khoutas, Stylianos: *I ethnikì antístasis tòn Ellínon, 1941–1945* (Athens, 1961)

Khrysokhoou, A. I.: *I katokhì en Makedoníai*, Vol. I: *I drásis toù KKE* (Thessaloniki, 1949)

Kofos, Evangelos: *Nationalism and Communism in Macedonia* (Thessaloniki, 1964)

Kordatos, G.: *Oi epemváseis tòn Anglon stìn Elláda* (Athens, 1946)

Kousoulas, D. G.: *The Price of Freedom – Greece in World Affairs, 1939–1953* (Syracuse, 1953)

*Kousoulas, D. G.: *Revolution and Defeat – The Story of the Greek Communist Party* (London, 1965)

Kyriakidis, G. D.: *Grazhdanskaya Voina v Gretsii, 1946–1949* (Moscow, 1972)

Kyrou, A.: *I néa epíthesis katà tìs Elládos* (Athens, 1949)

Lagdas, Panos: *Aris Veloukhiótis* (two vols. in one, Athens, 1964)

Laskaris, G.: *Dimokratikòs kaì kommounistikòs syndikalismòs* (Athens, 1958)

Lee, Arthur S. Gould: *The Royal House of Greece* (London, 1948)

Leeper, Sir Reginald: *When Greek Meets Greek* (London, 1951)

Logothetopoulos, K.: *Idoù i alítheia* (Athens, 1948)

Loverdo, Costa de: *Les Maquis rouges des Balkans* (Paris, 1967)

Maclean, Fitzroy: *Disputed Barricade* (London, 1957)

McNeill, W. H.: *The Greek Dilemma – War and Aftermath* (London, 1947)

Macmillan, Harold: *Memoirs*, Vol. II: *The Blast of War* (London, 1967)

Matthews, Kenneth: *Memories of a Mountain War – Greece 1944–49* (London, 1972)

Mavroidis, L.: *Capture and Kill* (Sofia, 1948)

Meynaud, Jean: *Les Forces politiques en Grèce* (Montreal, 1965)

Mikhailidis, K. I.: *Grazhdanskaya Voina v Gretsii 1946–1949* (Moscow, 1963)

Modis, G.: *Khorià-phroúria tìs Makedonías* (Athens, 1956)

Mpirka, K.: *Giatì polemísame – i alítheia kaì tò psévdos già tìn ethnikì antístasi* (Athens, 1956)

Myers, E. C. W.: *Greek Entanglement* (London, 1955)

Naltsas, Kh.: *Tò makedonikòn zítima kaì i sovietikì politikì* (Thessaloniki, 1954)

Natsina, A.: *Andartopólemos* (Athens, 1950)

Neal, Fred W.: *Titoism in Action* (Berkeley, 1958)

Nepheloudis, V.: *Ellines polemistaì stì mési anatolì* (Athens, 1945)

Neubacher, Hermann: *Sonderauftrag Südost 1940–1945* (Göttingen, 1957)

North, John: *The Alexander Memoirs, 1939–1945* (London, 1962)

O'Ballance, Edgar: *The Greek Civil War* (London, 1966)

Oikonomou-Gouras, P.: *Tò dógma Truman* (Athens, 1957)

Palmer, Stephen E., and King, Robert R.: *Yugoslav Communism and the Macedonian Question* (Hamden, Conn., 1971)

Panaiotov, Ivan: *Greeks and Bulgarians* (Sofia, 1946)

Papagos, Alexander: *The Battle of Greece, 1940–1941* (Athens, 1949)

Papakonstantinou, Th.: *Anatomía tìs epanastáseos* (Athens, 1952)

Papandreou, George: *The Third War* (Athens, 1948)

*Papandreou, George: *I apelevthérosis tìs Elládos* (3rd edition, Athens, 1949)

Pejov, Naum: *Makedontsite: Graganskata vojna vo Grtsija* (Skopje, 1968)

Pentzopoulos, D.: *The Balkan Exchange of Minorities and its Impact upon Greece* (Paris, 1962)

Petsopoulos, G.: *Tà ethnikà zitímata kaì oi Ellines Kommounistaì* (Athens, 1946)

*Petsopoulos, G.: *Tà pragmatikà aítia tìs diagraphís mou apò tò KKE* (Athens, 1946)

Petsopoulos, Thomas: *Tragikì poreía* (Athens, 1953)

Phosteridis, Antonios: *Ethnikì antístasis katà tìs Voulgarikìs katokhìs* (Thessaloniki, 1959)

Pipinelis, Panaghiotis: *Geórgios Ḃ'* (Athens, 1951)

Piyade, Mosha (Moša Pijade): *About the Legend that the Yugoslav Uprising owed its Existence to Soviet Assistance* (London, 1950)

Pyromaglou, K.: *I ethnikì antístasis* (Athens, 1947)

*Pyromaglou, K.: *O doúreios íppos* (Athens, 1958)

Pyromaglou, K.: *O Geórgios Kartális* (Vol. I, Athens, 1965)

Richter, Heinz: *Griechenland zwischen Revolution und Konterrevolution, 1936–1946* (Frankfurt, 1973)

Roberts, Walter R.: *Tito, Mihailović and the Allies 1941–1945* (New Brunswick, N.J., 1973)

Sarafis, Stefanos: *Greek Resistance Army* (London, 1951)

Saraphis, Stephanos: *O ELAS* (new edition, Athens, 1958)

Schmidt-Richberg, Erich: *Der Endkampf auf dem Balkan* (Heidelberg, 1955)

Seton-Watson, G. H. N.: *The East European Revolution* (London, 1950)

Shepherd, A. W.: *Britain in Greece* (London, 1947)

Shoup, Paul: *Communism and the Yugoslav National Question* (New York, 1968)

Smothers, Frank, and McNeill, W. H. and Elizabeth D.: *Report on the Greeks* (New York, 1948)

Spencer, Floyd A.: *War and Postwar Greece* (Washington, 1952)

*Stavrianos, L. S.: *Greece — American Dilemma and Opportunity* (Chicago, 1952)

Stavrianos, L. S.: *The Balkans, 1815–1914* (New York, 1963)

Stavridis, E. E.: *Tà paraskínia toù KKE* (Athens, 1953)

Svolos, A.: *Istoría miàs prospatheías* (Athens, 1945)

*Sweet-Escott, Bickham: *Greece — A Political and Economic Survey, 1939–1953* (London, 1954)

Sweet-Escott, Bickham: *Baker Street Irregular* (London, 1965)

Tsakalotos, Th.: *40 khrónia stratiótis tìs Elládos* (2 vols., Athens, 1960)

Tsatsos, D.: *O Dekémvrios 1944* (Athens, 1945)

Tsatsos, Th.: *Ai paramonaì tìs apelevtheróseos, 1944* (2nd edition, Athens, 1973)

Tsoucalas, Constantine: *The Greek Tragedy* (London, 1969)

Tsouderos, Emmanuel: *Ellinikès anomalíes stì Mési Anatolì* (Athens, 1945)

Ulam, Adam B.: *Titoism and the Cominform* (Harvard, 1952)

Vlandas, D.: *Exártisis kaì antidimokratikótis* (unpublished, n.d.)

Voigt, F. A.: *The Greek Sedition* (London, 1949)

Vukmanović, Svetozar: *How and Why the People's Liberation Struggle of Greece met with Defeat* (London, 1950)

White, R., and Hawes, S.: *The Resistance Movement in Europe* (London, 1974)
Wilson, Field-Marshal Lord: *Eight Years Overseas* (London, 1948)
Wolff, Robert L.: *The Balkans in Our Time* (Cambridge, Mass., 1956)
Woodhouse, C. M.: *Apple of Discord* (London, 1948)
Woodward, Sir Llewellyn: *British Foreign Policy in the Second World War*, Vol. II (1971); Vol. III (London, 1972)
Xydis, Stephen G.: *Greece and the Great Powers, 1944–1947* (Thessaloniki, 1963)
Zakhariadis, Nikos: *Théseis già tìn istoría toù KKE* (Athens, 1945)
*Zakhariadis, Nikos: *Déka khrónia pális* (Nicosia, 1950)
Zakhariadis, Nikos: *Kainoúrgia katástasi, kainoúrgia kathíkonta* (Nicosia, 1950)
Zapheiropoulos, D.: *Tò KKE kaì i Makedonía* (Athens, 1948)
*Zapheiropoulos, D.: *O antisymmoriakòs agón, 1945–1949* (Athens, 1956)
Zepos, Dimitrios: *Laikì dikaiosýni eis tàs elevthéras periokhàs tìs ypò katokhìn Elládos* (Athens, 1945)
Zevgos, G.: *I laikì antístasis toù Dekémvri kaì tò neoellinikò próvlima* (Athens, 1945)
Zotiadis, George B.: *The Macedonian Controversy* (Thessaloniki, 1961)

B. ARTICLES

Anon.: Apò tò Litókhoro os tò Grámmo kaì tò Vítsi (in *Dimokratikos Stratos*, 1948)
Bartzotas, V.: I megáli mákhi toù Grámmou (in *Dimokratikos Stratos*, 1948)
Campbell, John: The Greek Civil War (in *The International Regulation of Civil Wars*, ed. Evan Luard, London, 1972)
Chandler, G.: The Unnecessary War (in *History Today*, Vol. VIII, No. 10, October 1958)
Hadsel, Winifred N.: American Policy towards Greece (in *Foreign Policy Reports*, Vol. XXIII, No. 12, September 1947)
McNeill, William H.: The Outbreak of Fighting in Athens, December 1944 (in *American Slavic and East European Review*, Vol. VIII, 1949)
Murray, Colonel J. C.: The Anti-Bandit War (in *U.S. Marine Corps Gazette*, January–May 1954)
Natsina, A.: Pòs propareskevásthi o trítos gýros (in *Stratiotika Nea*, June 1951)
Papapanaghiotis, A.: I alítheia già tò 'pisóplato khtýpima' (in *Kommounistiki Epitheorisi*, April 1972)

Porphyrogenis, M.: I prosorinì dimokratikì kyvérnisi (in *Dimokratikos Stratos*, 1949)

Stavrianos, L. S.: The Immediate Origins of the Battle of Athens (in *American Slavic and East European Review*, Vol. VIII, 1949)

Stavrianos, L. S.: The Greek National Liberation Front (EAM) – A Study in Resistance Organisations and Administration (in *Journal of Modern History*, March–December 1952)

Tzimas, A.: Pòs kaì póte o Stéphanos Saráphis proskhórise stòn ELAS (in *Pyrsos*, Dresden 1967, Nos. 1 and 6)

Vainas, P.: O DSE kaì oi Slavomakedónes (in *Dimokratikos Stratos*, 1948)

W.: Provlímata toù emphylíou polémou (in *Kommounistiki Epitheorisi*, May 1947)

Wainhouse, Lieutenant-Colonel Edward R.: Guerrilla War in Greece, 1946–49 – A Case Study (in *Military Review*, Fort Leavenworth, Kansas, June 1957)

Woodhouse, C. M.: Resistance in Griechenland (in *Vierteljahrshefte für Zeitgeschichte*, 6 Jahrgang, No. 2, 1958)

Woodhouse, C. M.: Early British Contacts with the Greek Resistance in 1942 (in *Balkan Studies*, Vol. XII, No. 2, 1971)

Xydis, Stephen G.: The Secret Anglo-Soviet Agreement on the Balkans of October 9, 1944 (in *Journal of Central European Affairs*, Vol. XV, October 1955)

Zacharakis, Lieutenant-Colonel E. E.: Lessons learned from the Anti-Guerrilla War in Greece, 1946–49 (in *Revue Militaire Générale*, No. 7, July 1960)

Zakhariadis, N.: I Ellàs stò drómo pròs tì níki (in *Dimokratikos Stratos*, February 1949)

Zevgos, I.: I ethnikès meionótites stòn koinò agóna (in *Kommounistiki Epitheorisi*, July 1944)

C. DOCUMENTS

1. GREEK GOVERNMENT AND NATIONALIST PUBLICATIONS

Ai mákhai toù Vítsi kaì toù Grámmou 1949 (General Staff of the Army Athens, 1951)*

Ai thysíai tìs khorophylakìs (Athens, 1971)

Avtò eínai tò KKE–EAM–ELAS stìn Elláda (Athens, 1945)

Istorikòn arkheíon ethnikìs antistáseos (Athens, 1958 seq.)

I symphonía tìs Várkizas (Ministry of Foreign Affairs, Athens, 1945)

---

* Cited as Official History, 1949.

O Ellinikòs stratòs katà tòn antisymmoriakòn agóna (1946–1949): i ekkathárisis tìs Roúmelis kaì i próti mákhi toù Grámmou (Directorate of Military History, Athens, 1970)*
Oi nekroí mas, 1946–1949 (Royal Gendarmerie, Athens, 1948)
Pòs zísame stò parapétasma (Society of Repatriates from the Iron Curtain, Athens, 1962)
The Conspiracy Against Greece (Ministry of Foreign Affairs, Athens, 1947)
Tò EAM apénanti toù éthnous (Athens, 1943)

2. COMMUNIST AND EAM PUBLICATIONS

Actes agressifs du gouvernement monarcho-fasciste grec contre l'Albanie (Tirana, 1947)
EAM White Book, May 1944–March 1945 (New York, 1945): see also *Levkì vívlos toù EAM*
ELD: Théseis già tà Dekemvrianà (Athens, 1945)
La vérité sur la Grèce monarcho-fasciste (Belgrade, 1947)
Levkì vívlos toù EAM (Trikkala, 1945)
Levkì vívlos: Dimokratikòs neofasismós July–October 1945 (Athens, 1945)
Livre bleu: la vérité sur la Grèce (Gouvernement democratique provisoire de Grèce, 1948)
Livre bleu, deuxième (Gouvernement democratique provisoire de Grèce, 1949)
Saránta khrónia toù KKE 1918–1958 (Athens, 1964)
Voithímata già tìn istoría toù KKE (KKE, 1952)

3. BRITISH PUBLICATIONS

BBC Monitoring Service: Free Greece Radio, 1948–1950
Documents Regarding the Situation in Greece, January 1945 (Cmd 6592, HMSO, London, 1945)
European Resistance Movements, 1939–45: First International Conference on the History of the Resistance Movements (Oxford–London, 1960)
Proceedings of a Conference on Britain and European Resistance at St. Antony's College (Oxford, 1962)
Report of the Allied Mission to Observe the Greek Elections (Cmd 6812, HMSO, London, 1946)
Report of the British Legal Mission to Greece (Cmd 6838, HMSO, London, 1946)
Report of the British Parliamentary Delegation to Greece, August 1946 (HMSO, London, 1947)

* Cited as Official History, 1948.

Report of the Supreme Allied Commander Mediterranean to the Combined Chiefs of Staff on Greece, 12th December 1944 to 9th May 1945 (London, 1949)

SOE Operations in Greece and the Aegean Sea (unpublished, 1945)

SOE Records: telegrams and other documents dated between September 1942 and December 1943 (private collection)

The Soviet–Yugoslav Dispute (Royal Institute of International Affairs, London, 1948)

What We Saw in Greece: Report of the TUC Delegation, February 1945 (London, 1945)

4. UNITED STATES PUBLICATIONS

Foreign Relations of the United States: Diplomatic Papers, 1939–1947 (Department of State, Washington, 1956–72)

Foreign Relations of the United States: The Conferences at Cairo and Teheran 1943 (Washington, 1961)

Foreign Relations of the United States: The Conferences at Malta and Yalta, 1945 (Washington, 1955)

Publications of the Department of State, No. 2909: Near Eastern Series, No. 9 (Washington, 1947)

The Story of the American Marshall Plan in Greece (ECA, Washington, 1952)

The Strategy and Tactics of World Communism, supplement IV: Five Hundred Leading Communists in the Eastern Hemisphere (US House Committee on Foreign Affairs, Washington, 1948)

5. SOVIET PUBLICATIONS

Correspondence between the Chairman of the Council of Ministers of the USSR and the Presidents of the USA and the Prime Ministers of Great Britain during the Great Patriotic War of 1941–1945 (New York, 1965)

The Tehran, Yalta and Potsdam Conferences – Documents (Moscow, 1969)

6. UNITED NATIONS PUBLICATIONS

Labour Problems in Greece: Report of the ILO Mission to Greece, October–November 1947 (Geneva, 1949)

Report by the Commission of Investigation Concerning Greek Frontier Incidents to the Security Council, S/360 (Paris, 1947)

Report of the United Nations Special Committee on the Balkans (UNSCOB), A/574 (New York, 1948)

Supplementary Report of UNSCOB, A/644 (Paris, 1948)

Third Interim Report of UNSCOB, 11 September to 22 October 1948, A/692 (Paris, 1948)

Report of the United Nations Special Committee on the Balkans (UNSCOB), A/935 (New York, 1949)

Supplementary Report of UNSCOB, A/981 (New York, 1949)

Report of the United Nations Special Committee on the Balkans (UNSCOB), A/1307 (New York, 1950)

Report of the United Nations Special Committee on the Balkans (UNSCOB), A/1857 (New York, 1951)

Index